Lewis Carroll

CHARLIE LOVETT

Lewis Carroll

FORMED BY FAITH

UNIVERSITY OF VIRGINIA PRESS

Charlottesville and London

University of Virginia Press
© 2022 by the Rector and Visitors of the University of Virginia
All rights reserved
Printed in the United States of America on acid-free paper

First published 2022

ISBN 978-0-8139-4739-6 (hardcover)
ISBN 978-0-8139-4740-2 (ebook)

1 3 5 7 9 8 6 4 2·

Library of Congress Cataloging-in-Publication Data
is available for this title.

Publication made possible with support from the
Lewis Carroll Society of North America.

Permission to use C. L. Dodgson copyrighted material has been granted
by the C. L. Dodgson Estate.

Frontispiece: Charles Lutwidge Dodgson, assisted self-portrait, 1875.
(Lovett Collection)

Cover image: Lewis Carroll, self-portrait, albumen print, 2 June 1857.
(© National Portrait Gallery, London, NPG P39)

For Stephanie

What I want to do is work for others, and work for which, somehow, I seem specially meant.

    —Charles Lutwidge Dodgson, *Supplement to "Twelve Months in a Curatorship,"* 1884

Contents

Illustration gallery follows page 140

Foreword

There are few figures more deserving of the label "polymath" than Lewis Carroll. He was a published mathematician, a pioneering photographer, a celebrated writer of nonsense verse, and a beloved children's author, but we seldom pause to think about an issue that was absolutely fundamental to him, his religion. Yet it is here, in reflecting on his Christian faith, that we gain the greatest insights into what formed him, how he thought, and how he conducted his life. Anyone who has spent time with Dodgson's letters and diaries will know the extent to which his faith is not some kind of side interest or hobby. It goes to the core of his being. The rhythms of the liturgy, the richness of his prayer life, his knowledge of the Bible and Christian classics all provided the context for his daily reflections and ongoing thinking. If we do not attempt to understand Dodgson's faith, we do not understand his life.

The resistance to taking Dodgson's faith seriously results in large part from the fact that contemporary readers struggle to enter a world in which Jesus, the church, and daily, practiced religion can be at the heart of someone's life. We live in a secularized society in which any expression of faith is regarded as something that should be private. But Charles Dodgson lived in a different era, when public life was at least ostensibly religious, and when ritual, prayer, and church attendance were means of demonstrating virtue.

Dodgson's letters and diaries show that he treasured two virtues above all others: resolution and reverence. His thoughts and prayers are dominated by repeated confessions, expressions of inadequacy, statements of repentance, and resolutions to do better. He was in this respect participating in the typical conventions of Victorian piety, but his humble confessions and earnest resolutions are nonetheless sincere, and no reader of his diaries will have any doubts about the heartfelt nature of his admissions of fault and his desperate desire to improve himself.

Perhaps the keynote of his religious thought, though, is his overwhelming conviction of the importance of reverence. Those who enjoy Dodgson's joyous wit and delightful imagination might be shocked to see how staid he could be in his approach to religious topics. He did not appreciate humor in sermons, and levity over religious issues was a matter of grave concern to him. Clergymen should not be mocked, and religious topics should never be associated with levity. To be truly religious was to be pious, austere, and reverent.

If modern readers at first find such attitudes surprising, this book confirms that the topic should be central to the study of Dodgson's life. *Lewis Carroll: Formed by Faith* is a different kind of biography. By looking at his life from the perspective of Dodgson's faith, Charlie Lovett is able to tell us more about Dodgson's family, his upbringing, his career, his relationships, and his thinking than we could ever have imagined. On page after page, Lovett's meticulous research is presented in a calm, authoritative, and eminently readable format that bristles with new insights and fresh perspectives. It is in one sense a narrative of Dodgson's religious life, the influence of his father, the role played by his schooling, his ordination as deacon, his failure to go on to priests' orders, his first sermons, and so on, but it is also an analysis of his religious thinking, charting his steady journey from his father's high church stance to his own more broad church perspective, alongside a theology that was often rather conservative, even old-fashioned, but that could be quite radical, most clearly in his challenge to the doctrine of eternal punishment.

What this delightful study demonstrates is that to tell the story of Dodgson's religion is to tell the story of Dodgson's life. But this is also a story about Victorian England, about how Christianity remained at the heart of the lives of those with whom Dodgson came into contact, in Daresbury, in Croft, at school in Richmond and then Rugby, and of course in Oxford and elsewhere, and all this in spite of the growing forces of secularism in a country that was undergoing dramatic changes.

The difficulty, of course, is that while we can all walk with Alice through Wonderland without having to do any prep, understanding Dodgson's religion takes a little more effort. It is not just that Dodgson's frequent references to the Christian Bible will make little sense to a biblically illiterate culture; it is that so much of his religious life is intelligible only to those immersed in the Church of England politics of the Victorian era, alongside the politics of Christ Church, Oxford, and other aspects of an academic life that now appears very old-fashioned. Readers need not have any concern.

At each point, Lovett patiently explains terminology, backgrounds, and contexts, and brings alive a religious and academic culture that goes from being foreign to familiar. And if anyone is in any doubt about the relevance of studying Dodgson's journey, it is worth remembering that at the very time when he was preaching his first sermons, and considering whether or not he should take up priests' orders, he was getting to know Alice Liddell and writing about her adventures in Wonderland.

Mark Goodacre
Frances Hill Fox Professor of Religious Studies,
Duke University

Lewis Carroll

· ONE ·

This Child Is Regenerate

On 11 July 1832, within the stone walls of All Saints Church, Daresbury, in rural Cheshire, twenty-seven-year-old Rev. George Heron held six-month-old Charles Lutwidge Dodgson, who would write the most famous children's book of his century. Accompanied by members of the Dodgson family, Heron faced the old stone font near the west end of the church. The boy's maternal aunt, Lucy Lutwidge, had, as godmother,[1] taken the vows of baptism in the child's name, along with the child's two godfathers. Following the rubric in the Book of Common Prayer, Heron dipped the child in the font's sanctified water, "discreetly and warily," saying, "Charles Lutwidge, I baptize thee in the Name of the Father, and of the Son, and of the Holy Ghost." The child who would become Lewis Carroll had begun his life in the Christian church.

Charles Lutwidge Dodgson's father was another Charles Dodgson, a thirty-two-year-old who had been an ordained priest for seven years and had served as perpetual curate in the isolated chapelry of Daresbury for five years. He would become an important voice in the Church of England and would exert a strong influence over the faith journey of his firstborn son. To follow the journey of the son, one must first journey with the father.

Charles Dodgson was born on 2 November 1800 in Hamilton, in what is now South Lanarkshire, Scotland. His father, Charles, a soldier, died in the line of duty when his elder son was three and his only other child, Hassard Hume Dodgson, was unborn. Charles's paternal grandfather had been an Anglican bishop in Ireland.

On 14 January 1811, Charles entered Westminster School, within the precincts of Westminster Abbey in London. In 1813, his brother Hassard joined him. Charles became a King's Scholar (one of forty foundation scholars) in 1814, eventually captaining this group. The King's Scholars produced an annual play in Latin, presented in the school dormitory, and attended by alumni and local dignitaries. Charles never acted in the play, but as captain of the King's Scholars he would have composed the prologue in 1817, had the play not been canceled owing to the death of Princess Charlotte. In 1820, Dodgson's brother Hassard acted in the play; Hassard's son Francis performed in the play in 1852.[2] The play's prologue often paid tribute to Westminster alumni who had died the previous year, including Rev. Charles Dodgson following his death in 1868. Each year a former scholar of Westminster contributed a comic epilogue on events of the day (in Latin verse). In 1865, Charles Dodgson wrote the epilogue for the *Trinummus* of Plautus.[3]

In May 1812, Dodgson's mother, Lucy Hume Dodgson, widowed for nine years, married Rev. George Marwood, canon of Chichester Cathedral. At sixty-seven, he was thirty years her senior. The couple had one child, Dodgson's half sister, Mary Anne Marwood.

From 25 to 28 April 1818, Westminster School held its annual election. Boys who had completed four years of study were examined by a body including representatives of the school; Westminster Abbey; Christ Church, Oxford; and Trinity College, Cambridge. The examination concluded with the election of three boys to each university. Charles Dodgson was elected to Christ Church, Oxford, the same college his stepfather's son George had attended from 1799 to 1803. On the final day of the election process, boys in the two upper divisions of the school traditionally delivered a number of Latin epigrams, written for the occasion, at a dinner given by the Dean and Chapter of Westminster. These epigrams were often written by former boys of the school, and Dodgson himself would contribute more than a dozen between 1849 and 1865.[4] From his continued connection to the school through the writing of these epigrams and the epilogue for the Latin play, it appears Dodgson thought fondly of his days at Westminster.

On 5 May 1818, Dodgson matriculated at Christ Church, Oxford. Just a few months later, on 18 September 1818, his mother died at the home of her father, James Hume, in Wandsworth, South London. She was forty-three. Dodgson may have been with her, for her death fell during the Long Vacation, and he likely attended her funeral service at Chichester Cathedral with his teenage brother, stepfather, and five-year-old half sister. Thirty-three years later, Charles Lutwidge Dodgson would also lose his mother just after beginning Oxford.

In December 1821, Charles Dodgson gained the rare academic distinction of a double first in mathematics and classics.[5] After receiving his bachelor's (1822) and master's (1824) degrees, he was appointed a Student of Christ Church (similar to what other colleges called a Fellow). As was required of all men resident in the college, he was ordained into the Church of England, taking deacon's orders at All Souls Chapel on 21 December 1823 and being ordained priest by the bishop of Oxford, Edward Legge, on 5 June 1825 in Christ Church Cathedral.[6]

At Oxford, Dodgson met many men who would become leaders in the English church. Charles Thomas Longley, six years his senior and a fellow Student of Christ Church, had also attended Westminster School. The two men's tenures at Westminster had overlapped by a year. When he became bishop of Ripon in 1836, Longley would be a powerful patron of Dodgson. One of Dodgson's exact contemporaries at Christ Church, Edward Bouverie Pusey, would be another ecclesiastical ally. Pusey became a friend, and affectionately inscribed a copy of his prize Latin poem to Dodgson.[7] Pusey became one of the leading members of the high church Oxford Movement beginning in the early 1830s, and his association with Dodgson would bring the latter into the circle of influence of that religious revival. The two other major leaders of the Oxford Movement were John Keble and John Henry Newman. When Dodgson took his examination for his bachelor's degree in 1822, one of his examiners was Keble, then a Fellow at Oriel College. Whether Dodgson became acquainted with Newman, a scholar at Trinity College and then a Fellow at Oriel College during Dodgson's Oxford years, is not known. But when, a few years later, the Oxford Movement took flight, Dodgson certainly knew Newman's name.

Richard Durnford, later bishop of Chichester, was a sometime visitor at the Dodgson family home in Daresbury. Dodgson had "formed a close friendship" (*Life* 14) with Durnford—a friendship that likely began at Oxford, where Durnford matriculated in 1820. Durnford became rector of Middleton, in the same diocese as Daresbury some thirty miles away. Dodgson's association with Durnford introduces the possibility that the former's high church sympathies may have predated the beginning of the Oxford Movement in the 1830s. Durnford's biographer described him as a "High Churchman who had formed his opinions before the 'Oxford' or 'Tractarian movement.' . . . He belonged to the old school of High Churchmen who derived their principles from a careful study of the Bible and Book of Common Prayer, together with the early fathers and the best divines of the reformed

Church of England."[8] Dodgson's later work and writings show a strong connection to this school of moderate high churchmanship.

Dodgson settled into a life of lecturing and tutoring mathematics at Christ Church, but because of a rule stating only bachelors could retain Studentships, when he married his first cousin Frances Jane Lutwidge on 5 April 1827, he forfeited his position at the college.

In anticipation of his change in status, the Dean and Chapter of Christ Church presented Dodgson with the perpetual curacy of Daresbury, a small country chapelry[9] in the Diocese of Cheshire, in February 1827.[10] Christ Church held the living of Daresbury (that is, the income of the church); for a modest stipend, Rev. Charles Dodgson undertook all the clerical duties. In September 1827, he arrived with his new bride in this remote district, where the parsonage stood more than a mile from the church.[11] In December 1827, he heard of the death, at age eighty-two, of his stepfather, George Marwood. Three months later, the next generation of Dodgsons began with the birth of Charles's daughter Frances Jane, the first of eleven children.

Dodgson threw himself into his work with energy and enthusiasm ("indefatigable" was one word used to describe his service).[12] An address given by the church warden at Dodgson's departure attributed to him

> the establishment and the successful maintenance of a Sunday School, now most numerously and regularly attended . . . no less than three Lectures each week, so held, that each portion of the parish may benefit in their turns. By your open-handed charities and personal efforts, the sick, the poor, and the afflicted, have been constantly relieved, instructed, and comforted. And by the blessing of the Almighty, through the instrumentality of his word, we have witnessed the cheering sight of a steadily increasing attendance in his house, at his holy altar. . . .
>
> During these sixteen years have we seen, that your labours of Christian love and active benevolence, have been shared by the excellent and amiable Ladies of your family. (*Diaries,* vol. 1, 15)

Since the eldest Dodgson daughter was only sixteen when the family departed Daresbury, the reference to ladies of the family must refer primarily to Mrs. Dodgson and her sister, Lucy Lutwidge. Lucy was listed as a resident of Daresbury parsonage on census night, 6 June 1841. While she may not have resided there permanently (correspondence survives between her and Mrs. Dodgson that indicates the two did not always live together), Lucy, who would take over as matriarch of the family following her sister's death in 1851, spent much of her time with the Dodgson family. In a letter of 6 February 1873, Charles Lutwidge Dodgson refers to her as "my Aunt, Miss Lucy Lutwidge, who has lived with us all our lives" (*Letters* 184).

The parish registers give insight into life in Daresbury and environs. The baptismal register records the occupations of those whom the Dodgsons met in the village, the surrounding countryside, and at church and Sunday School. The vast majority were laborers or farmers, with more skilled trades including brick-setter, tailor, millwright, wheelwright, sawyer, mason, butcher, joiner, blacksmith, and shoemaker. There were porters, ostlers, and publicans, a smattering of servants, and the occasional clerk, shopkeeper, soldier, and schoolmaster. The Bridgewater Canal brought boatmen and navigators, while the construction of a nearby railway line brought additional laborers, clerks, and an "over looker." Only rarely does the register mention "gentlemen" or an "agent to the trustees of the Duke of Bridgewater." The overwhelming majority of Dodgson's parishioners were rural working poor. The marriage register shows that about half were completely illiterate, unable to sign their own names. From the burial register comes the sobering fact that one-third of the people buried in the parish during Dodgson's sixteen years were children under age twelve.

Dodgson had occasional help from other nearby clergymen: Richard Janion, who had taken many of the Daresbury duties in the months between the death of the previous incumbent, Robert Fletcher, and the arrival of the Dodgsons and who was the incumbent at nearby Stretton until killed by a falling branch in 1831; Richard Greenall, who took over Janion's post in Stretton in 1831; Charles Thomas Quirk, a curate at Stretton; and George Heron, about whom more later. But his two most frequent assistants were Samuel Bagnall and Thomas Vere Bayne.

Bagnall had local connections, his father having possession of Hatton, in the chapelry of Daresbury. He attended Brasnose College, Oxford, in 1821, but moved to Downing College at the more evangelical Cambridge. In 1824 he was appointed to the curacy of Aston-by-Sutton, three miles from Daresbury, and in 1826 became perpetual curate there, a post he held until 1844. Bagnall assisted throughout Dodgson's tenure, performing about 5 percent of the burials and 7 percent of the marriages, but his greatest contribution came in baptisms. Dodgson favored public baptisms at regular Sunday services; Bagnall seemed to have no objections to weekday private baptisms— the baptismal registers of Aston make frequent note of private baptisms.

Bagnall performed 105 baptisms at Daresbury during Dodgson's tenure—93 on weekdays and 23 out of sequence in the registers (an out-of-sequence baptism was likely performed away from the church and entered into the register later). By comparison, of Dodgson's 608 baptisms, 115 were performed on weekdays and only 19 entered out of sequence. It appears Bagnall performed about half the private baptisms at Daresbury from 1827 to 1843.

Thomas Vere Bayne had been at Jesus College, Oxford, when Dodgson was at Christ Church. In 1828 he became headmaster of Boteler's Free Grammar School in Warrington, eight miles from Daresbury. His years at Warrington coincided closely with Dodgson's at Daresbury; in 1842 he became incumbent of St. John's, High Broughton. Vere Bayne did not preach high church *or* evangelical dogma from his pulpit. "He well knew," wrote a parishioner, "the baleful effects of a controversial spirit, and the unhappy influence it too frequently exercises on the Christian character." But, like Charles Dodgson, Vere Bayne believed in showing greater reverence for the sacraments and for saints' days and feasts. At Broughton he established more frequent services, including communion twice a month and "morning prayer on Wednesdays and Fridays and on all festivals and their vigils. On Saints' days he preached a short sermon, explanatory of the festival."[13]

According to Collingwood, Vere Bayne "used to occasionally assist in services at Daresbury" (*Life* 14), but the parish registers give a more detailed and mysterious view of his work. While he performed a smattering of marriages, and about 4 percent of the Daresbury burials during Dodgson's tenure, his chief contribution came in baptizing children. Unlike Bagnall, however, almost all of Vere Bayne's Daresbury baptisms (116 out of 120) came on Sundays. This means he either assisted Dodgson at regular Sunday services or took full responsibility for some of those services. Following 1836, other ministers often performed baptisms and burials when Dodgson traveled to Ripon to do his work as examining chaplain. But from 1829 to 1832 Thomas Vere Bayne performed 95 baptisms, while Charles Dodgson performed only 91. No evidence exists to explain this fact, but clearly Thomas Vere Bayne was a frequent presence in Daresbury during these years, and though he performed services much less often after 1832, he must still have been a presence both at the church and in the Dodgson household. His son, also Thomas Vere Bayne, became a playmate of Charles Lutwidge Dodgson, and the two would be close friends throughout their lives. Like the younger Dodgson, the younger Vere Bayne would become a Student of Christ Church, Oxford, and live his life in the college precincts. Rev. Charles

Dodgson may have traveled from Croft-on-Tees to Broughton, near Manchester, to attend the funeral of Thomas Vere Bayne in 1849. A newspaper account of the funeral lists among those attending "Mr. Dodgshon."[14]

The Bridgewater Canal passed through the Daresbury Chapelry, and Dodgson saw the canal men as an important part of his cure. In July 1839 he signed a public letter to the carriers on the Trent and Mersey Canals lobbying for the "cessation of traffic" on Sunday to eliminate the "sad desecration of the Sabbath."[15] In the Chapelry of Daresbury, most boatmen were itinerant, and Dodgson wanted to minister to this population: "Once, when walking with Lord Francis Egerton, who was a large landowner in the district, he spoke of his desire to provide some sort of religious privileges for them. 'If I only had £100,' he said, 'I would turn one of those barges into a chapel,' and, at his companion's request, he described exactly how he would have the chapel constructed and furnished. A few weeks later he received a letter from Lord Francis telling him that his wish was fulfilled, and that the chapel was ready" (*Life* 9–10).

Egerton matriculated at Christ Church just seven months before Dodgson and was a member of Parliament, writer, and patron of the arts. The floating chapel established by his munificence was situated at Preston Brook, an important station on the Bridgewater Canal. It opened in late 1840, and Dodgson held Sunday-evening services and Thursday lectures there for the next three years. It is described in different sources as seating either 120 or 200, and the services and lectures were heavily attended. As a means of ministering to the itinerant bargemen, the chapel was only partly successful. Egerton later paraphrased a letter from Dodgson: "Unfortunately, however, that Part of the Parish, which is an extensive one, is so totally destitute of any regular Accommodation for public Worship that this Floating Chapel is attended to a large Extent by many who have no Connexion with the Water, and so far I believe that sometimes not above Thirty or Forty of the Boatmen are able to get into it."[16]

Not long after arriving in Daresbury, Dodgson began to preach outside his own parish. On 8 June 1829, he preached to an annual gathering of thousands of schoolchildren (together with clergy and other adults) in the Collegiate Church, Manchester (now Manchester Cathedral).[17] On 7 October that year, he preached in Chester Cathedral, at the invitation of Bishop John Sumner.[18] Sumner, later archbishop of Canterbury from 1848 to 1862, was an evangelical—so while Dodgson felt the high church influence of his Oxford colleagues Pusey and Longley, the evangelical viewpoint was not unknown to him.[19]

On 14 July 1833, in Oxford, John Keble, responding to a proposal to dissolve the ten Anglican bishoprics in Roman Catholic Ireland, preached a sermon on "National Apostasy" at the University Church of St. Mary's and launched what would become known as the Oxford Movement. In Oxford, this high church movement was led by Keble; John Henry Newman, then vicar of St. Mary's; and Dodgson's friend E. B. Pusey, then Regius Professor of Hebrew. The movement was conducted partially through a series of *Tracts for the Times* written by Pusey, Keble, Newman, and others, and adherents to the Oxford Movement became known as Tractarians.

At the core of the movement was a desire to see the Church of England as a branch of the one true catholic church. Because some Tractarians believed long-neglected rituals should be returned to the church, they also became associated with ritualism. They sought to find forms of worship and interpretations of doctrine based on the earliest practices of the church, and so an understanding of the English reformers and a careful reading of the writings of the early church fathers became important to the movement. As Dodgson himself said: "The venerable structure of the English church had become so overlaid with modern innovations that we scarcely could know it for the same again. We know that the great object . . . of the reformers, was first to demolish these innovations; but . . . their fundamental object was the restoration of that which these innovations deformed. We became Protestants because it was necessary—and only so far as it was necessary—to enable us to re-assert the primitive doctrines of the first, apostolic, universal church."[20]

The Oxford Movement often stood in direct opposition to the evangelical party, and some claimed the Tractarians wanted to push the Church of England closer to (or even completely back to) the Roman Catholic Church. Many who participated in the Oxford Movement, including John Henry Newman, ultimately became Roman Catholic. Charles Dodgson found himself in sympathy with much, but not all, that the movement stood for.

In 1836, the Church of England created its first new diocese since the Reformation, carving the Diocese of Ripon out of the Dioceses of York and Chester. The first bishop of this new diocese was Charles Thomas Longley, consecrated at York Minster on 6 November 1836. He immediately looked to his old friend Charles Dodgson for assistance. On 3 December 1836, the *Leeds Intelligencer* reported that Longley had appointed Dodgson as his examining chaplain,[21] the official in charge of examining candidates for ordination, and Dodgson began an association with the Diocese of Ripon that would last the rest of his life.

Dodgson made the one-hundred-mile journey to Ripon frequently during the next seven years. On 15 January 1837, just over a month after his appointment, Dodgson preached at Longley's first ordination in a Ripon Cathedral "crowded to excess."[22] He preached to the candidates he had examined, and, according to the *Leeds Mercury,* the examination was "most strict and severe."[23] Dodgson took as his text St. Matthew's parable of the talents as a means of discussing the duties of the Christian minister. It became his first published sermon, and it contains themes that would recur throughout his career, especially that of finding the good that one can do and doing it: "To each individual is assigned his own peculiar sphere of action, within which he has to pursue an independent course, and to sustain an individual responsibility."[24]

The idea of finding one's "peculiar sphere of action" and contributing to the common good is one Charles Lutwidge Dodgson would ponder often.[25] Doubtless, when considering his own possible future in the Christian ministry, he also recalled these words of his father: "To no situation is there attached a higher degree of individual responsibility" (8).

As examining chaplain, Dodgson's primary responsibility was to see that candidates for ordination were properly prepared and fit for the task that lay ahead. The seriousness with which he took this job can be seen in this item from the *Newcastle Journal* of 5 July 1845: "Rev. Joshua Wood . . . has been elected Head Master of Kirby Hill Free Grammar School [in the Diocese of Ripon]. . . . On the day previous the candidate underwent a severe and searching examination (occupying six hours) by the Rev. Charles Dodgson."[26]

But if Dodgson could spend hours examining a possible headmaster, he could spend days examining prospective clergymen, and the Tractarian bent of his examinations came under fire in an anonymous pamphlet of 1838 entitled *The Lord Bishop of Ripon's Cobwebs to Catch Calvinists: Being a Few Remarks on His Lordship's Questions to Candidates at His Late Ordination at Ripon.* Dodgson wrote, in a rebuttal to this pamphlet, that he was the "true author" of the questions.[27] The "clergyman of the diocese" who penned the attack wrote, "We are truly astonished . . . at the rapid advance which is being made to conformity with the doctrines of the Church of Rome."[28] The writer complained that Dodgson's views on baptism, universal redemption, prayer, and predestination were inconsistent with both scripture and the English reformers.

The writer took particular issue with the question: "Show from expressions in the Catechism and in the Baptismal Service, that our Church holds that all infants duly baptized are—1. Justified. 2. Sanctified. But that this change of state does not imply that they will be necessarily saved in the end" (4). The writer argued against these doctrines, saying, "We do not find it stated [in scripture] that he that is not baptized shall be damned, but that he that believeth not" (7).

The writer also argued against the doctrine of universal redemption (i.e., that Christ came to save all men), which he accused Dodgson of putting forth, and then went on to address the subject of prayer: "Another question of the Bishop's deprives [God] of fore-knowledge or fore-appointment, and the plea that prayer would be useless were it so. So then prayer is to alter and change God's mind continually. Really the God that such profess is a perfect changeling" (17).

Finally, the writer challenged Dodgson on the subject of predestination, arguing that there is ample evidence that the English reformers supported the Calvinistic view of predestination, "that nothing takes place in time, but what was determined from all eternity" (18). Dodgson, the writer claimed, is more influenced by the free-will stance of the Arminian[29] viewpoint: "that God intended to create men free, and to deal with them according to the use that they should make of their liberty" (18). Charles Lutwidge Dodgson would believe strongly in free will.

A review of *Cobwebs to Catch Calvinists* in the *Christian Observer* (June 1838) heaped further criticism on the examination questions. The *Observer* was an evangelical periodical critical of the Oxford Movement and edited by Samuel Charles Wilks. While continuing to question their doctrinal soundness, particularly with respect to baptismal regeneration, the reviewer also condemned the way the questions were constructed: "They are abstruse, knotty, and . . . so constructed that the candidate must be of a particular school in order to answer them in a satisfactory manner."[30]

Dodgson found himself in the middle of a religious controversy. Though not named as author of the questions, he had been called a Pharisee and accused of reducing God to a weathercock; he had been called unjust, and both the style and content of his examinations called into question. He responded with a letter printed in the *Christian Observer* in August 1838. The editors of the *Observer* commented on his response and defended their own stance in long and detailed footnotes to Dodgson's letter.

Dodgson did little to defend himself against the doctrinal attacks leveled at him: "I have no intention of entering into any argument on points of doctrine. . . . Nor do I wish to offer any *defence* of the particular course adopted in the examination" ("Dodgson on the Ripon Ordination Questions" 486). He went on to explain that the questions "did not form above a sixth part of even the examination on paper" (500), that "an important, and in many cases the most important, part of [the examination] is conducted in private" (488), and that these private interviews included "much interesting and . . . not unprofitable conversation" (500). The first exercise in the examination, Dodgson explained, was "the composition of a sermon" on one of a set of biblical texts, which, he wrote, do not "savour of a Popish or sectarian spirit" (500). In attempting to counteract what he saw as the faulty assumptions of the *Observer,* he wrote:

> What if the questions were framed and proposed without any party views and intentions whatever? What if this was distinctly explained at the time to the candidates, and proved to their entire conviction? What if several among them did answer many of the questions in direct contradiction to the views of the examiner? What if those very candidates, after the private examinations and conversations, to which their answers gave rise, were among the first to express their personal sense of the anxiety shown (and, God knows, *felt*) to treat them with kindness and impartiality? What if *not one* of them was excluded? What if, at the close of the business, an unanimous expression of thanks from the whole body was conveyed, in strong and feeling terms, both to the Bishop and the examiner, for the examination itself, and the spirit in which it had been throughout conducted? (492–93)

Nonetheless, the *Observer* took Dodgson to task for evading the thrust of their previous argument. Pages of notes discussed the notion of baptismal regeneration which Dodgson supported and which, the editors claimed, contradicted the doctrine of justification by faith alone. The footnotes tied Dodgson to the Oxford tract writers, especially Pusey; and, indeed, one need look no further than Pusey's three tracts on baptism in the *Tracts for the Times* to discover where Dodgson may have gotten his views on baptismal regeneration.

At the core of this view was an idea that would cause controversy in the Church of England for years to come. Pusey believed that sacraments, and especially the sacrament of baptism, could confer grace and justification; others argued that this flew in the face of the doctrine of justification by faith alone. Dodgson's view of baptism, and that of the Tractarians, was that all infants, being in a state of innocence (as to enacted, not original, sin) and unconsciousness are receivers of grace and regeneration because of the act of baptism, though that grace may be lost through later sin; the evangelicals held that only those infants who were predestined to be elect received such grace. Pusey's *Tracts for the Times* (numbers 67–69), titled *Scriptural Views of Holy Baptism,* argue that universal baptismal regeneration is based directly on scriptural evidence.[31]

The debate over baptismal regeneration would explode in the late 1840s with the Gorham controversy—a case that commanded headlines and pitted the high church party against the evangelicals. In 1847, Henry Philpotts, the high church bishop of Exeter, refused to institute Rev. G. C. Gorham into a parish in his diocese on the grounds that Gorham held unsound views on baptism. Gorham did not believe regeneration took place at infant baptism. The Arches Court of Canterbury, the highest church court in the land, upheld the decision of the bishop, but Gorham appealed to the judicial committee of the Privy Council. The committee issued its judgment on 8 March 1850 and sided with Gorham, writing that the Thirty-Nine Articles (the official statement of the beliefs of the Church of England) intentionally allow for latitude of interpretation.

Dodgson responded to the Gorham judgment almost immediately. First he "placed the resignation of [his] office [of examining chaplain] in the Bishop's hands, to be accepted by him in the event of his thinking that any change ought to be made in the course [they] had invariably adopted in the examinations of the subject of Baptisms."[32] Finding that the bishop did not wish any such changes, Dodgson then issued the longest printed work of his career, the 102-page book *The Controversy of Faith—Advice to Candidates for Holy Orders on the Case of Gorham v. the Bishop of Exeter.* Dodgson's book was advertised as "Now Ready" in the *Morning Chronicle* on 29 May 1850, less than three months after the Privy Council's decision.

The book is not only a long defense of baptismal regeneration but also Dodgson's plea for thoughtful, learned, and logical disputation instead of what he saw as frequently uninformed bickering and "the anonymous dogmatism of the periodical press. . . . Men there unhappily are who prefer the excitement of a quarrel to the dull task of sober disputation,"[33] he wrote, words that would be echoed by his son years later when he wrote of the necessity of stating both sides of a religious argument clearly.

Dodgson warned candidates that the Gorham case had no bearing on their own situation: Gorham had already been ordained and was looking to be instituted into a living to which he had been appointed, a different legal situation from a young man hoping to be ordained. In the latter circumstance, the bishop had the power to reject a candidate for any reason. Dodgson went on to analyze the judgment itself—pointing out that the very factors that a clergyman must carefully consider (scripture, the teachings of the early church, and theological opinion) were excluded by the judicial committee. Dodgson then launched into a long argument showing that baptismal regeneration was supported by scripture, by the catechism and the Thirty-Nine Articles, by the baptism service, and by the early Christian writers and teachings of the primitive church. Dodgson's arguments are highly logical, reading almost like geometrical proofs as they proceed step by step from the presumed axiomatic evidence of his various sources.

After making his case, Dodgson provided the potential future clergyman with a series of arguments to defeat the many objections to that case raised by its opponents, writing that a clergyman "must acquaint himself also with the objections, with which [his view] will be met by others, and must prepare himself to answer them" (33).[34] He logically deconstructed the various arguments *against* baptismal regeneration: that it involves a work of man, that it "tends to diminish the sense of moral responsibility" (34), that it obliges the church to "call even profligate and openly irreligious men 'regenerate'" (40), and so on.

Having dispensed with the arguments against his own view, Dodgson made his argument against the views of others, again proceeding along logical lines to dismantle various (as he pointed out mutually inconsistent) evangelical views of baptism. In particular, Dodgson argued against the writing of William Goode in his book on the effects of infant baptism.[35] Dodgson took particular issue with Goode's argument that, since the English reformers were influenced by Calvinism, the Formularies of the Church of England (i.e., the catechism, Articles, and services) must be interpreted in a Calvinistic light. "I must still always maintain," wrote Dodgson, "the principle that where the authorized Formularies of a branch of the Catholic Church, in their most simple and natural sense,[36] affirm any primitive Catholic doctrine, no one has a right to look out of these to the opinion of any modern 'school of theology' for a mode of interpreting them in a manner inconsistent with that doctrine" (83).

Finally, Dodgson exhorted the new clergy to eschew the practice of private baptism, common in the eighteenth century, and to baptize children publicly before a congregation. This, and the incorporation of frequent allusions to baptism in sermons, would help clarify the issue in the minds of parishioners. From the newly ordained should come into the church, "a continual fresh stream of sound, vigorous, and healthy doctrine" (94).

This is what Dodgson saw as his task as examining chaplain—to infuse into the church a "continual fresh stream of sound, vigorous, and healthy doctrine." This entire controversy shows both Dodgson's developing Tractarianism and the seriousness with which he approached his job as examining chaplain. An examination under Rev. Charles Dodgson was no mere recitation of the catechism but a series of carefully constructed written assignments, including the composition of a sermon, and a long and attentive personal conversation, sometimes lasting for days, and designed not merely to evaluate the fitness of the candidate for Holy Orders but also to serve as a discussion for points of confusion or doubt. Dodgson, at times, served as much as counselor as he did examiner. Of his position he wrote, in *The Controversy of Faith,* that it allowed him to become "acquainted with the various doubts and perplexities, to which young men of thoughtful minds are liable on points of theological doctrine, and of tracing them to their true sources. On such occasions, I have frequently been able, by correcting some mistake as to facts, by removing some misapprehension, by offering some suggestion, or by setting before them some argument, with which my own reading and reflection during a long period of pastoral experience has furnished me, to give to a younger brother a clearer view and a steadier hold of some important point in the system of Ministerial Teaching" (6).

The candidates Dodgson examined, advised, and counseled had a deep appreciation for his work. In the autumn of 1852, a group of 185 clergymen, all of whom had been examined by him before their ordinations, presented a testimonial in his honor to the Diocese of Ripon in the form of a memorial stained-glass window in the private chapel at the Bishop's Palace. The clergymen wrote: "Having felt the value of your service . . . and highly estimating the learning and piety by which your important office has been sustained, as well as the great kindness of manner with which you have adorned it: we desire to record our sense of your merits."[37]

Bishop Longley, grateful to the clergymen for this moving tribute, concurred publicly with this view, noting Dodgson's "learning and ability with which he has conducted the Examinations; his diligence and faithfulness in the discharge of the delicate and important office which I entrusted to him; his constant readiness to convey instruction to the Candidates, and his desire to make the Examinations available, not only as a test of their present knowledge, but as suggestive likewise of future improvement by hints for their course of reading in future years."[38]

In a letter dated 28 September 1852, Dodgson replied to the testimonial: "I have earnestly wished to make the office . . . a means of good. I have felt painfully all its importance and responsibility; and it has been my constant desire that, however imperfectly filled in other respects, it should at least be discharged with honesty, with impartiality, and with a single regard to those plain principles of duty, which a consideration of its character and objects could not fail to dictate."[39]

But even as this testimonial was published, both as a pamphlet and in the Leeds newspaper, Dodgson had already plunged anew into the baptismal controversy—and this next difficulty revealed that Bishop Longley was an integral part of the examination process, and that the theological and personal affinity between the two men was substantial.

In *The Controversy of Faith,* Dodgson warned that the Gorham decision did not preclude a bishop from denying Holy Orders to a candidate who rejected the doctrine of baptismal regeneration. On 19 September 1852, Longley did exactly that, refusing to ordain George Hayward to the priesthood. Hayward had been ordained a deacon by the bishop of Ely, and had been offered, by Rev. Joseph Birch, the curacy of Brighouse, in the Diocese of Ripon. In order to accept the position, Hayward needed to be ordained a priest by Bishop Longley and thus examined by Rev. Charles Dodgson. Here, Birch takes up the story: "The Rev. C. Dodgson was not satisfied with [Mr. Hayward's] opinions on that difficult doctrine [of baptism]. . . . Mr. Dodgson then put the annexed questions [four handwritten questions] to [Mr. Hayward] . . . as tests of orthodoxy. Mr. Hayward retired with these four propositions into the Bishop's waiting-room, pondering the subject as well as he could under the circumstances of the case, in a spirit of prayer. The result was his inability to assent to the whole of them . . . and his consequent rejection by the revered prelate presiding over the diocese" (*Rev. C. Dodgson's New Tests* 8).

All this Birch wrote in his pamphlet *The Rev. C. Dodgson's New Tests of Orthodoxy,* the second edition of which included a lengthy correspondence between Dodgson and Birch. Dodgson began his correspondence by pointing out that the first edition of the pamphlet appeared to be an attack on Bishop Longley "under cover of one against his Chaplain only" (28), for Dodgson had previously informed Birch that "all which took place on the occasion passed in the presence of the Bishop, and his view of the case exactly coincided with my own" (27).

In a later letter, Dodgson, responding to the accusation that he was shift-ing the onus of his responsibility as examining chaplain to the bishop, wrote, "If the office is to be exercised beneficially for the Church, it is absolutely essential that the views, the acts, and the decisions of the Chaplain should be in the most exact accordance with those of the Bishop" (33).

The correspondence reached no very definite conclusion, but there was one more exchange that illuminates further the close relationship between Dodgson and Longley. Having been told by Birch that a leading article about the Hayward controversy had appeared in the *Record*,[40] Dodgson wrote:

Nothing, I think, can be more unworthy of a clergyman than to be moved by either the praise or blame of the Editors of what are called the religious newspapers. . . . I was delighted to witness this morning a practical evidence of the concurrence of our Bishop in such sentiments. I was with him, when the post came in, at breakfast. Some one had sent the number of the *Record,* containing the article which you told me of, and which was pointed out to him. Glancing at it for a moment or two, he returned it with a smile, and quietly continued the conversation which it had interrupted. He will, I am satisfied, never think of it again. (51–52)

It is important to understand that these debates were not mere intellec-tual exercises, nor even merely arguments about the future direction of the Church of England; at stake, in the minds of the debaters on all sides of the question, was the eternal salvation of immortal souls.

The Dodgson and Longley families became close over the years. When Charles Lutwidge Dodgson took up photography, the Longleys, including the bishop, were frequent sitters. Even when Bishop Longley was elevated to archbishop of Canterbury, the son of his late examining chaplain main-tained a friendship with the primate and his family.

Rev. George Heron had just dipped the child in the waters of baptism. After reciting the prayer of reception, Reverend Heron said, "Seeing now, dearly beloved brethren, that this Child is regenerate, and grafted into the body of Christ's Church, let us give thanks to Almighty God for these benefits; and with one accord make our prayers unto him, that this Child may lead the rest of his life according to his beginning."[41]

There is much about Charles Lutwidge Dodgson's baptism we do not know: His Aunt Lucy stood as godmother, but the rubric in the Book of

Common Prayer requires, for male children, one godmother and two god-fathers. Who were his godfathers? Why was he baptized on a Wednesday and not a Sunday? Rev. Charles Dodgson's own later feelings about baptism were rooted in the rubric in the Book of Common Prayer: "It is most convenient that Baptism should not be administered but upon Sundays, and other Holy-days, when the most number of people come together." Dodgson later supported public baptism in the presence of a congregation, writing in 1850 that such a baptism "serves to impress the minds of parents, of sponsors, and of entire congregations, with a due sense of its importance, and becoming reverence for its sanctity" (*Controversy* 96–97).

Yet 11 July 1832 was neither a Sunday nor a holy day, and likely no large congregation was present. That C. L. Dodgson was baptized in the stone font in Daresbury Church is only a matter of local tradition, unsupported by documentary evidence. Though it is the most likely site of the baptism, the weekday, almost certainly private, service could have taken place anywhere.

The baptismal register of Daresbury is revealing in what it shows about Rev. Charles Dodgson and the baptisms of his own children. None of his first five children (from Frances Jane in February 1828 to Mary Charlotte in March 1835) was baptized on a Sunday. Only two were baptized by Dodgson himself (Elizabeth and Caroline Hume were baptized by Thomas Vere Bayne). Beginning with Skeffington Hume in December 1836, the remaining five Dodgson children baptized at Daresbury were all baptized on Sundays, and only Henrietta Harrington in July 1843 was not baptized by her father (she was the last of the children baptized at Daresbury, at a time when the family was moving to Croft). So, Dodgson's position that children should be baptized on a Sunday as part of regular worship services, apparent in the fact that the vast majority of the baptisms he conducted were on Sundays, did not apply to his own family until 1836. What happened to change his mind?

Two things: he read E. B. Pusey's tracts on baptism, and he became examining chaplain to the bishop of Ripon. How could he tell future priests that they must baptize on a Sunday whenever possible, if he did not enforce such a rule in his own household? So, beginning in 1836, the Dodgson children were baptized on Sundays, and, when possible, by their own father.

The baptism of his eldest son came four years before this enlightenment, so what did Rev. Charles Dodgson, in 1832, believe actually happened at that stone font? The Oxford Movement was as yet unborn; Pusey's writings on baptism were still years away. Yet Dodgson may have been exposed to high church sympathies through his friend Richard Durnford. Did Dodgson give a passing thought to the meaning of that word "regenerate" in the baptismal service? Or was baptism, to him at that time, simply the welcoming of his firstborn son into the church?

Dodgson later expressed disapproval of what he saw as the lax eighteenth-century approach to baptism. In his 1850 book *Controversy of Faith,* he wrote with disdain of a hypothetical baptism of the previous century: "The infant son of a wealthy country gentleman was baptized. . . . The ceremony was performed by the Curate in the drawing-room of the family mansion; and was immediately followed by a sumptuous entertainment, and an evening of revelry not soon forgotten in the neighbourhood. . . . Much license and excess took place, which, *as it was on the occasion of a christening,* was good-naturedly pronounced to be quite excusable" (88–89).

The Rev. George Heron, who baptized Charles Lutwidge Dodgson, came from a local family, owners of the Manor of Daresbury, and among the few members of the educated classes residing near the Dodgsons. Heron lived at Moore Hall, about a mile and a half north of Daresbury. He had attended Brasenose College, Oxford, and, though he was five years younger than Charles Dodgson, their time at Oxford overlapped for four years. Heron became perpetual curate of Carrington, near Manchester, in 1831. The Heron family were good friends of the Dodgsons—so close that when the youngest Dodgson child was born in 1846, three years after the family left Cheshire, he was named Edwin Heron Dodgson. On rare occasions George Heron assisted with services at Daresbury. The registers show that, during the sixteen years Charles Dodgson held that curacy, Heron performed eight baptisms, nine burials, and four marriages (at least one of which involved a member of his own family). Most of these were before he was appointed perpetual curate at Carrington, twenty miles away; his final Daresbury baptism was that of Charles Lutwidge Dodgson.

Whatever the views of Rev. Charles Dodgson on the baptism of his son, whatever the reasons for a midweek christening, whatever the makeup of the congregation or the identity of the godfathers, one thing is certain: in the waters of baptism, on 11 July 1832, six-month-old Charles Lutwidge Dodgson began his journey of faith.

Did the adult Charles Lutwidge Dodgson share any of his father's views on baptism? He left few writings on baptism, but, like his father, he considered it a sacred subject worthy of reverence. When, at the age of sixty-two on

6 April 1894, he attended a performance of *The Little Squire* to see his child-friends Isa and Empsie Bowman on the stage of the Lyric Theatre, he wrote in his diary that he was pained by "some almost comic allusions to serious things, e.g. baptism, and the soul, which [he] thought most objectionable." The play had been adapted from the children's novel by Elizabeth Lydia Rochelle De la Pasture, by theatrical manager Horace Sedger and Mrs. William Greet. It was intended primarily for children, and it may have been partly for this reason, for he cared deeply about protecting children from evil and inculcating in them a reverence for things holy, that Lewis Carroll, using the influence of that nom de plume, wrote to Mrs. Greet to object to the treatment of baptism in her play.

> You will admit that the large majority of your audience believe in a life after death, in the immortality of the soul, and in a judgment to come, and recognise (in their better moments) the infinite seriousness and importance of such subjects, and that they are not things to be played with, and treated as themes for laughter.
>
> Then, most certainly, a large number of your audience believe that He, who died for our sins, left us the Sacrament of Baptism: and that this, also, is no fit subject for jesting on. . . .
>
> It gave *great* pain to hear such flippant talk, about baptism and the soul, put into the mouths of those two dear children. (*Letters* 1012)

Mrs. Greet evidently replied, for in a second letter, dated six days after the first, Carroll wrote:

> May I try, once more, to say in a few words why it is I still hope you may be induced to erase those few sentences, in your play.
>
> They put, in a comic light, things that should always be regarded *seriously*, by all who understand what reverence and irreverence really *are*.
>
> They give pain to good and reverent people (and the *more* reverent the people the *greater* the pain), at hearing holy things profaned.
>
> They give pleasure, a harmful, often a sinful, pleasure, to those who love to "make a mock at sin," and to turn sacred things into ridicule. (*Letters* 1018)

There is no evidence Greet made any changes to the script following this correspondence. The power of the stage for good or evil was something

C. L. Dodgson took seriously, but this is the only surviving document in which he specifically defends baptism as deserving of such reverence.

Charles Lutwidge Dodgson was ordained a deacon in the Church of England in 1861, and as such he had the right to perform baptisms in case of necessity. On 18 February 1863, he performed his first baptism when he took the evening service at Cowley, just outside Oxford. He performed two baptisms at his father's church in Croft, while home from Oxford for Long Vacations. On 2 August 1863, Dodgson baptized Margaret Elizabeth Hutchinson, the daughter of a laborer from Dalton. He recorded the details of the baptism in the register in his meticulous handwriting, and wrote in his diary, "Took the afternoon service with churching[42] and baptism." His second baptism he does not record in his diary;[43] however, it took place on 11 September 1864, when he baptized Annie Gibbon, daughter of a laborer from Croft.

Other than these few baptisms performed fairly early in his adult life, Dodgson's closest connection with the sacrament of baptism was through his godchildren. As a godfather to seven children,[44] he took upon himself their baptismal vows. Most often he did this *in absentia,* attending only two of his godchildren's baptisms—those of Clement Francis Rogers in 1866 and Edith Alice Dodgson in 1872. But he took the baptismal ceremony, and the taking on of vows for the baptized, seriously, writing to his sister Mary in 1870 when he agreed to be her son Stuart's godfather: "I cannot be present in person, but I hope you will give me due notice of the day of baptism, that I may at least be with you before the Throne of Grace, to pray for all present and future blessings for your boy" (*Letters* 147).

Three of his seven godchildren do not seem to have had any sort of special relationship with Dodgson. Two sons of his Oxford colleagues do not enter into his diaries or surviving letters at all, and his nephew Louis Henry "Hal" Dodgson is mentioned only vaguely in the context of family gatherings.

The story of his first godchild, his cousin Charles "Charlie" Hassard Wilcox, is a sad one. Dodgson saw the boy on occasion at family gatherings but only spent significant time with him in the Long Vacation of 1874, when twenty-two-year-old Charlie was ill with lung problems and staying at the Dodgson family home in Guildford. As Dodgson wrote: "I went home to help his sisters to nurse him, and stayed there 6 weeks, and afterwards went down with them to the Isle of Wight" (*Letters* 216).

On 11 November, about a month after he returned to Christ Church, Dodgson received the news that his "dear cousin and godson" had died. What Dodgson discussed with his godson during those long summer weeks of

1874 is unknown, but Charlie's illness and death are indelibly linked to one of Dodgson's literary masterpieces. On the morning of 18 July 1874, Dodgson sat up with his godson from 3:00 to 6:00 a.m. He had only three hours of sleep, and while walking in the Surrey hills the next day, as he later said, "there came into my head one line of verse—one solitary line 'For the Snark was Boojum, you see.' I knew not what it meant then; I know not what it means now, but I wrote it down."[45] It became the final line in his 1876 epic nonsense poem *The Hunting of the Snark,* in which death plays a prominent role.

Dodgson had a slightly closer relationship with his godson and first cousin once removed William "Willie" Melville Wilcox. Beginning in 1877, following the death of her husband, William, in 1876, Dodgson contributed £30 per annum to the education of Fanny Wilcox's children, making it clear that Willie need not be the only recipient of that largesse. Dodgson sent at least two letters to Willie at school at Canterbury, writing on 23 November 1880, "I hope you are thriving, in body and mind, at school, and that you are not quite so idle as *I* used to be at school" (*Letters* 393). Willie visited Dodgson for a few days at Christ Church when the boy was twenty-one. In September 1885, Dodgson sent William a long letter in response to a request for advice about higher education. William anticipated the possibility of entering Holy Orders, and Dodgson sent him a narrative of his own experience with taking Holy Orders (see p. 132 in this volume). Dodgson signed this letter, "Always your affectionate Cousin ('godfather' is a terminable relationship)" (*Letters* 603), acknowledging that he felt a special relationship on account of having *been* William's godfather, yet also that his official duties of godparent (to take on the boy's baptismal vows) ended when William was confirmed and took those vows on himself.

Dodgson traveled to Shropshire to attend the christening of his only goddaughter, Edith Alice Dodgson (daughter of his brother Wilfred), on 20 October 1872. He would see Edith on occasion throughout her childhood, but in 1890, their relationship became closer, as Edith came to study at Lady Margaret Hall, Oxford. "I am very sure you can't employ the next few years better than in improving to the utmost whatever powers God has given you," wrote Dodgson to his goddaughter. "You may be sure He has got *some* work for you to do" (*Letters* 810). Dodgson saw Edith often during her time in Oxford, but this only lasted a single term as she failed to pass her requisite examinations. Shortly after leaving Oxford, while struggling to find her purpose in life, Edith received a long letter from Dodgson helping her to see her situation in distinctly religious terms, and encouraging her to make the best of life. "And *I don't* mean, by 'the best of life,'" wrote Dodgson, "the best for *yourself,* but the best for *others.* That is a truth that is becoming more and more clear to me as life passes away—that God's purpose, in this wonderful complex life of ours, is mutual interaction, all round" (*Letters* 827).

Edith ultimately took her godfather's words about doing things for others to heart—in 1909 she became an Anglican nun, a member of the Community of Saint Mary the Virgin in Lincolnshire, an order founded as part of the religious revival that accompanied the Oxford Movement. For ten years, Sister Mary Edith lived and worked at St. Mary's Diocesan Home in Ketton, Lincolnshire, and at the Lincoln Diocesan Penitentiary in Boston—both homes for the rehabilitation and training of fallen women. There were many such homes in England at the end of the nineteenth century, and Charles Lutwidge Dodgson was a supporter of their work. From 1883 until the end of his life, he made an annual donation to the London Female Guardian Society, which had the same aim as the houses where his goddaughter worked. Edith remained a nun, working at schools and a home for drug addicts, until her death in 1950. That she felt a continuing connection to her godfather is perhaps illustrated by the fact that in 1997 Keys Fine Art Auctioneers offered for sale a tea cosy made by Edith and decorated with characters from *Alice in Wonderland.*

Of all his godchildren, Dodgson was closest to Stuart Dodgson Collingwood, son of his sister Mary. Though he was unable to attend Stuart's baptism in Southwick, County Durham, on 10 February 1870, he contributed significantly to the education of Stuart and his brother Bertram. The two boys were frequent residents at the Chestnuts, the Dodgson family home in Guildford, and the boys came, with various family parties, to join their uncle at the seaside for a week or two at least nine times in Stuart's first fifteen years. Though they are most often referred to in Dodgson's diaries as a pair, Dodgson does single out his godson on occasion. On the boy's eleventh birthday (10 January 1881), he took Stuart for a walk in Guildford, and during two seaside visits Dodgson records that he "took Stuart to church" in the morning. As Stuart grew, so did the reasons for a close relationship with his uncle. In May 1888, Stuart matriculated at Oxford University and came to study at Dodgson's college, Christ Church. For the next three years he saw his uncle frequently, and Dodgson invited Stuart for a meal when family visitors came to Oxford. He took Stuart to London on occasion and even introduced him to the theater.

On 29 December 1891, a few months after Stuart received his B.A., Dodgson wrote his godson a long letter of advice.

I think you *cannot* spend your time better than in trying to set down clearly, in that essay-form, your ideas on any subject that chances to interest you: and *specially* any theological subject that strikes you in the course of your reading for Holy Orders. . . .

The best advice that could be given to you, when you begin to compose sermons, would be what an old friend once gave to a young man, who was going out to be an Indian Judge . . . "Give your *decisions* boldly and clearly: they will probably be *right*. But do *not* give your *reasons: they* will probably be *wrong*." If your lot in life is to be in a *country* parish, it will perhaps not matter *much*, whether the reasons, given in your sermons, do or do not *prove* your conclusions. But even there you *might* meet, and in a town congregation you would be *sure* to meet, clever skeptics, who know well how to argue, who will detect your fallacies and point them out to those who are *not* yet troubled with doubts, and thus undermine *all* their confidence in your teaching. (*Letters* 879-79)

The issue of winning arguments with skeptics is one that had troubled Dodgson, and to which he believed the principles of logic must be applied. Dodgson preferred offering religious advice to his nephew (and others) via letters, which he could carefully construct, rather than through direct conversation. In 1894, he wrote to his sister Elizabeth: "No, I haven't had *any* talks, either with Stuart or Bertram, on religious difficulties. I have considerable dread of *argument,* with either of them—their powers in that direction being rather unusually developed" (*Letters* 1042).

In spite of the advice and guidance of his godfather, by 1896, Stuart seems to have given up the idea of Holy Orders and was trying to become a writer, with some assistance from his godfather. In a letter of 17 March 1896, Dodgson wrote to his godson: "I return your MSS, with 2 letters (which you need not return) from the Editor of 'Vanity Fair.' . . . I think this *professional* opinion is reliable. It does not, I fear, give any encouragement to your giving much time to such work."[46]

Stuart's father, C. S. Collingwood, had written several books, and Stuart's chance to break into authorship came in 1898 with the death of his godfather. The Dodgson family chose Stuart (but before his death Charles L. Dodgson would certainly have made his wishes known) to write the first biography of Lewis Carroll. "Intimately as I thought I knew Mr. Dodgson during his life," wrote Stuart in his preface, "I seem since his death to have become still better acquainted with him" (*Life* x). The biography was published in 1898, and in 1899 Stuart edited a volume of his uncle's obscure and unpublished writings under the title *The Lewis Carroll Picture Book.*

In 1901, Stuart lived in Guildford, a few blocks away from the family home at the Chestnuts, and worked as a private tutor. He served, for a time, as subeditor on the London staff of the *Manchester Guardian,*[47] but by 1911, he had undergone a major change in his life—a change during which he must certainly have given thought to the religious counsel of his godfather. Sometime before 1911, Stuart Dodgson Collingwood became a Roman Catholic. He worked in Ware, north of London, as a schoolmaster at St. Edmund's College and Seminary, a Roman Catholic school where he served under Father Bernard Ward. In 1926 Stuart took up a position as a master at St. Gerard's School, Bray, County Wicklow, Ireland, and he worked there for the remainder of his life, serving from 1934 to 1937 as headmaster.

Never a fan of "Romanism," Charles Lutwidge Dodgson might have been disturbed by his godson's decision to convert to Roman Catholicism; however, such a decision clearly indicated that Stuart thought deeply about religion, something that would have pleased his uncle. From his short-lived career as a writer, to his careful consideration of his religious life, Stuart Dodgson Collingwood certainly showed the influence of his godfather.

Charles Lutwidge Dodgson left behind no writings in which he confessed his feelings about being a godfather. Would he have nursed his cousin Charlie so assiduously had he not also been a godson? Would he have offered such thoughtful and often religious-based advice to Willie, Edith, and Stuart if they had been merely members of his extended family and not his godchildren? We cannot know, but surely the lives of all these were touched by the kindness, generosity, and thoughtful guidance of their godfather.

Charles had not held such a young child in his arms since his brother Edwin had been a baby in 1846. Now Edwin was nearly seventeen years old and studying at Rugby, and Charles was taking a service at the new church in Cowley, just outside of Oxford. The child in Charles's arms squirmed as he leaned over and dipped the head into the water of the font, speaking, for the first time, and in a slow steady voice, "I baptize thee in the Name of the Father, and of the Son, and of the Holy Ghost."

· TWO ·

An Instruction to Be Learned

The figures may have been enough to give a small boy a rich fantasy life: bizarre heavy-breasted sirens; a strange one-legged man; a gryphon; broad-winged angels with floating heads, odd haircuts, and no bodies. Sitting on a hard wooden pew in the chilly confines of All Saints Church, Daresbury, eight-year-old Charles Lutwidge Dodgson could not help but notice the carvings that adorned the Jacobean pulpit; and in that pulpit, as he was most Sundays for the boy's first eleven years, stood his father, Rev. Charles Dodgson, today preaching on the subject of the Sabbath:

"Whatever, therefore, those employments be, which tend the most to bring the soul into a close and holy communion with God, to assist its growth in Christian grace and Christian knowledge, and thus fit it the more, as it approaches the more nearly to it, for the eternal and perfect communion which is the portion of the Saints in heaven, such, we may be assured, are the most proper employments of the Sabbath."[1]

This was nothing new to young Charles Lutwidge Dodgson. His father's sermon on "The Sabbath a Delight" only repeated what he had heard many times before: that Sundays were a delight to the Christian when his "worldly labour is to be wholly laid aside" so that he might enjoy the twin contemplations of creation and salvation (240); that Divine Service, reading scriptures, and private prayer should be part of his everyday activity, but on Sunday should be uninterrupted by other concerns; that he should be thankful he was allowed one whole day out of seven to focus his mind on that one object, "which holds in the heart a place so much higher than the rest" (244). In his *Plain Catechism* (see pp. 89–91 in this volume), Rev. Charles Dodgson wrote of Sabbath observance, "We ought to leave off as much as possible our common employments and amusements, and to give up the day to the worship of God, to the reading of the Scriptures and other good Books, and to Religious meditation."[2]

But how did Charles Lutwidge Dodgson feel about the family's Sabbath observation, so central to his childhood religious education—walking a mile and a half to attend church in the morning and afternoon; Sunday School; and the rest of the day spent in Bible study, religious reading, and family prayer? Meals were cold, so servants need not work, and games and other amusements forbidden. Did the eight-year-old boy agree that all this was "a delight"?

Late in life, in his novel *Sylvie and Bruno,* Lewis Carroll wrote of two characters discussing the Sabbath:

> "You see I'm watering my flowers, though it *is* the Sabbath-Day. . . . Even on the Sabbath-Day works of mercy are allowed. But this *isn't* the Sabbath-Day. The Sabbath-Day has ceased to exist."
>
> "I know it's not *Saturday,*" Lady Muriel replied; "but isn't Sunday often called 'the Christian Sabbath'?"
>
> "It is so called, I think, in recognition of the *spirit* of the Jewish institution, that one day in seven should be a day of *rest.* But I hold that Christians are freed from the *literal* observance of the Fourth Commandment."
>
> "Then where is our *authority* for Sunday observance?"
>
> "We have, first, the fact that the seventh day was 'sanctified', when God rested from the work of Creation. That is binding on us as *Theists.* Secondly, we have the fact that 'the Lord's Day' is a *Christian* institution. That is binding on us as *Christians.*"
>
> "And your practical rules would be—?"
>
> "First, as Theists, to keep it *holy* in some special way, and to make it, so far as is reasonably possible, a day of *rest.* Secondly, as *Christians,* to attend public worship."
>
> "And what of *amusements?*"
>
> "I would say of them, as of all kinds of *work,* whatever is innocent on a week-day, is innocent on Sunday, provided it does not interfere with the duties of the day."
>
> "Then you would allow children to *play* on Sunday?"
>
> "Certainly I should. Why make the day irksome to their restless natures?"

Arthur goes on to relate a conversation he had years ago with a little girl:

"It was really touching to hear the melancholy tone in which she said 'On Sunday I mustn't play with my doll! On Sunday I mustn't run on the sands! On Sunday I mustn't dig in the garden!' Poor child! She had indeed abundant cause for hating Sunday!"

Muriel then reads a letter from another child bemoaning Sunday observances:

> It was no day of rest, but a day of texts, of catechisms (Watts'), of tracts about converted swearers, godly charwomen, and edifying deaths of sinners saved.
>
> "Up with the lark, hymns and portions of Scripture had to be learned by heart till 8 o'clock, when there were family-prayers, then breakfast, which I was never able to enjoy, partly from the fast already undergone, and partly from the outlook I dreaded.
>
> "At 9 came Sunday-School; and it made me indignant to be put into the class with the village-children, as well as alarmed lest, by some mistake of mine, I should be put below them.
>
> "The Church-Service was a veritable Wilderness of Zin. I wandered in it, pitching the tabernacle of my thoughts on the lining of the square family-pew, the fidgets of my small brothers, and the horror of knowing that, on the Monday, I should have to write out, from memory, jottings of the rambling disconnected extempore sermon, which might have had any text but its own, and to stand or fall by the result.
>
> "This was followed by a cold dinner at 1 (servants to have no work), Sunday-School again from 2 to 4, and Evening-Service at 6. The intervals were perhaps the greatest trial of all, from the efforts I had to make, to be less than usually sinful, by reading books and sermons as barren as the Dead Sea." . . .
>
> "Such teaching was well meant, no doubt," said Arthur; "but it must have driven many of its victims into deserting the Church-Services altogether."[3]

In his preface to *Sylvie and Bruno*, Dodgson states "The descriptions . . . of Sunday as spent by children of the last generation, are quoted *verbatim* from a speech made to me by a child friend and a letter written to me by a lady friend."[4] If he had not felt some sympathy with these remarks, would he have gone to the trouble to first record them and then include them in his novel? Certainly, Charles Lutwidge Dodgson's observance of Sunday as an adult finds him of a mind with Arthur. Barring any impediment, he attended service twice on Sundays. And he did write, in an 1891 letter to Mrs. Henry George Liddell, "years before that, I refused all *Sunday* invitations, on principle (though of course allowing to others the same liberty, which I claimed for myself, of judging that question)" (*Letters* 870). Yet, especially as a younger man, he clearly felt "whatever is innocent on a week-day, is innocent on Sunday," and in his diaries we read of Sundays being filled with social visits.

He did not arrive at this view of Sunday observation lightly. Charles Lutwidge Dodgson owned several books that included discussions of Sunday observations. Most pertinent was *Sunday, Its Origin, History and Present Obligation* by James A. Hessey. Writing in 1860, Hessey examined the history of the Lord's Day from the beginnings of Christianity, and fully extricated the "Lord's Day" of Christianity from the ancient Jewish Sabbath (a distinction Rev. Charles Dodgson did not make in his sermon). Hessey wrote that the Lord's Day was historically "the setting apart a day as a religious day simply—nothing being said about rest."[5] While he did argue that men should rest from their callings, he saw no reason to forbid reasonable amusements. One can see how Hessey, who used scholarship to advocate a *via media* between "the over-strictness of those who would look at [Sunday] solely on its Divine side [and the] laxity of those who look on it solely on its human side," would appeal to Charles Lutwidge Dodgson, who treasured both his Sunday worship and his Sunday amusements.[6]

Sabbath observance was an essential part of Charles Lutwidge Dodgson's early education, an education rooted in religious training and in which his father played a great part. To understand Charles's earliest religious learning, one must examine the place education held for his father.

If Rev. Charles Dodgson had a passion beyond faith, religion, and the church, it was education—but his work in education was merely an extension of his work in the church. In 1828, Dodgson, a struggling rural curate with a small income, made the substantial donation of ten pounds to help establish King's College in London, an Anglican institution founded in response to the creation in 1826 of the secular University College London. The advertisement for the college fund reflected Dodgson's beliefs about education: "Every system of general education for the youth of a Christian community ought to comprise instruction in the Christian religion as an indispensable part."[7]

In his later years, Dodgson's son Charles agreed that education and religion should be inextricably linked. In 1870, as the universities of England underwent reform, C. L. Dodgson signed his name to a letter of protest in which protestors "earnestly deprecate any legislative enactments which shall tend to separate Education from Religion, or fail to secure a Christian education for the youth of this country, in the Universities of Oxford and Cambridge."[8]

Although there were both a coeducational day school and a girls' boarding school in Daresbury,[9] Rev. Charles Dodgson educated his own children at home and took in students to earn extra income. The census of 1841 shows three boys of fifteen living at the Dodgson home as "private pupils." In 1828, Dodgson began the Sunday School at Daresbury at which, by 1833, "40 males and 60 females received gratuitous instruction."[10] He also took an interest in education on a broader scale. In January 1839, he and his friend Rev. Thomas Vere Bayne, then headmaster of a grammar school in Warrington, attended the "great diocesan meeting at Warrington, on the important and interesting subject of national education in connection with the Established Church."[11] This meeting had been called by the bishop of Chester, John Sumner, to form a "Diocesan Board of Education in mission with the National Society."[12]

The "National Society" was the National Society for the Promotion of the Education of the Poor in the Principles of the Established Church, founded in 1811 by Joshua Watson and three high church friends with the stated goal of building a school in every parish. In forty years, the society helped build twelve thousand "National Schools." Rev. Charles Dodgson would establish the Croft National School after his family moved to Yorkshire. The objective of the society was the same as Dodgson's own when it came to education: "That the national religion should be made the foundation of national education, and should be the first and chief thing taught to the poor, according to the excellent liturgy and catechism provided for that purpose."[13]

Dodgson was involved in the Chester Diocesan Board of Education from its inception. On 29 November 1841, he attended the second annual meeting as one of eight members of the board.[14] Following the delivery of the report, which noted the ongoing building of a training school for teachers in Chester, Dodgson spoke. His lengthy address reveals much about his views on education and on the church:

The people are ineffectually educated; to improve their education you must improve their schools; to improve their schools you must improve the masters of those schools; the qualifications of those masters depend on the system in which they themselves have been trained; that system on the superintendence under which it is placed. Thus we trace our way up to the first practical step which we have adopted—the establishment of a training school for masters. . . .

The establishment of model schools, which have been alluded to in the report, and, above all, the establishment of an efficient system of personal inspection of our schools, by a responsible and confidential officer,—these are the steps which we should expect next ought to be taken. . . .

The work in which we are engaged must be regarded, not as a single and insulated work, but as one which forms a part of a great general movement that has been going on for many years in this country, the great object of which seems to be to increase the efficiency of the church system. . . .

Church education is not to be regarded as something extrinsic to the church, as something in support of the church; but it is an essential part and parcel of the church system itself. . . .

[As to the question of] whether we shall, in the system of education which we are now endeavouring to raise, make any concessions with regard to the omission, under any circumstances, of . . . the church catechism. . . . The clergy have no option or discretion in the matter at all.—(Loud applause.)[15]

The work of creating and managing training schools for teachers and of asserting church principles and the church catechism in the education system would occupy Dodgson for much of the remainder of his life. To Dodgson, this work was part and parcel of the religious revival of the nineteenth century, what he called in his address "a sort of awakening to the fact that the church was not so efficient as it ought to be." In his 1850 book *Controversy of Faith,* Dodgson wrote a long description of a hypothetical churchman of a hundred years previous. On the subject of the young man's education, Dodgson wrote: "His education had commenced: and having, by dint of great toil, succeeded in committing to memory much that was incomprehensible to him, he was pronounced 'quite perfect in his catechism.' . . . Occasionally he would wonder what it all could mean; but he never asked, and he was never told."[16]

At a meeting of the Ripon Diocesan Board of Education (held immediately after the meeting of the Ripon Diocesan Church Building Society) on 9 March 1843, Dodgson, who had just been granted the living of Croft-on-Tees in that diocese, accepted the post of general secretary of those twin organizations, which he held for the next fourteen years. He seems to have been more involved with the Church Building Society, for he personally read the reports of the committee to the annual meetings of this organization from 1844 to 1850. But Dodgson was also active in the work of the Board of Education, serving as one of the inspectors of the diocesan training school for teachers. In December 1860, when the foundation stone for a new training institution for female teachers was laid at Ripon, Dodgson spoke of what he saw as the great principles of education:

> That education was not education unless it was based upon the true principle of education, the training of the immortal soul for eternity. No one valued intellectual qualifications, intellectual attainments, and learning of all kinds, or took a deeper interest in the progress of those attainments and that learning than himself, but still they must never forget that in educating an immortal soul the first principle was to train it for something higher and better than any intellectual attainments or worldly knowledge could possibly convey to it. . . .
>
> [T]he parish priest had a mission for everyone in the parish . . . to the child as well as to the adult . . . [his] duty it was to train the children of his parish for the teaching which, in their more mature years, they should receive from his lips by the public preaching in the church and by private ministrations in their own homes.[17]

While still at Daresbury, in 1839, Dodgson, through his work with the Society for the Relief of the Widows and Orphans of the Clergy of the Archdeaconry of Chester, was involved in the founding of a school for the female orphans of deceased clergymen. At a sermon preached in the Collegiate Church of Manchester on 18 July 1839, he took a more practical view of education, in part, no doubt, because those being educated were females with little or no prospect in life: "The Education, which we bestow, will enable those who enjoy it to learn by their own independent exertions, far more even of pecuniary support than the amount of expenditure which that Education required."[18]

Dodgson's most hands-on experience with education came in founding the Croft National School in 1844, examined more closely in the next chapter. The Croft National School remained dear to Rev. Charles Dodgson's heart for the rest of his life, and he and his family were closely involved in the school, which stood a short distance from the rectory.

Dodgson expressed his passion for education at every level: teaching his own children and providing education for the children of his parish;

serving on the Boards of Education for the two dioceses in which he was employed; overseeing the founding of schools and training institutions; and being closely involved, through his work as examining chaplain, with the education of clergymen. He even served as theological examiner at Durham University in 1849 and 1851.[19]

What Dodgson thought appropriate for one level of education, he may have shied away from at other levels. While, for instance, he was adamant in his high church stance on baptism when dealing with candidates for Holy Orders, we see no indication that he took such doctrinal stances with either schoolchildren or parishioners.

In his 1841 speech to the Chester Diocesan Board of Education, Dodgson—who had been involved in a baptismal controversy; who was in the process of translating the works of the early church father Tertullian for *A Library of Fathers,* edited by Pusey and published by the leaders of the Oxford Movement; who in this same speech alluded to Oxford Movement touchstones such as reasserting "the primitive doctrines of the first, apostolic, universal church" and "increasing veneration for the ordinances of the church, for the sacrament of baptism, [and] . . . the revival of the recollection of our fasts and festivals"—nonetheless spoke out at one point not just in favor of moderating differences among churchmen, but of ignoring them altogether:

> I deplore, as much as any man can deplore, the undeniable fact that so many members of the same church are arrayed the one against the other, in a spirit of mistrust, suspicion, and discord; . . . there is a vast body in the church, and, I would hope, a vast majority, who would rather hear nothing and know nothing of these divisions—(applause)—who claim the right to think and to speak, without the slightest reference to them . . . who refuse to be trammeled by dogmas, or enrolled under the nickname of party—(applause;) who are content with the simple title of English churchman, thankful to God for the privilege of being such; and who will not consent to exchange the broad, round basis of the Bible and Prayer-book, for any of the narrow and minuter systems included in pamphlets, tracts, magazines, or reviews, on one side or the other.—(Loud applause.)[20]

Here, in one speech, is the confluence of two Charles Dodgsons: one, the high churchman, friend to the leaders of the Oxford Movement, hard-line examining chaplain who refuses to compromise on matters of doctrine; the other, a village preacher, whose flock "would rather hear nothing and know nothing of these divisions." As he grew older, Dodgson came to believe that both the high church movement and the evangelical revival contributed to bringing the church out of "the alarming state of degeneracy and decay" into which it had fallen in the eighteenth century.[21] Speaking of these twin revivals, Dodgson, in an 1849 speech, used a rather remarkable scientific metaphor:

> It is a law in physical science that, if a body be acted upon by various forces in various directions, it will not, for of course it cannot, move in all those directions, but in some one distinct from all, determined by an impulse . . . called in technical language the resultant force. In such a case, particles loosely attached to the surface of the body may be severed from it, and carried away in the direction of some one of those forces: but this does not affect the motion of the entire body, which will continue to advance . . . in the direction of the resultant force. So has it been with the Church. . . . Some indeed of her loosely attached members have been carried away by one or the other of these particular movements to the verge, and beyond the verge of separatism . . . but the Church, as a body, has been meanwhile steadily advanced in the direction of good: her real character and constitution has been more generally and more closely investigated; and the more investigated, the better understood; and the better understood the more venerated and loved.[22]

It seems likely the first children Dodgson educated, in a room of the Daresbury parsonage, saw more often the less dogmatic priest, but a man who nonetheless cared passionately about investigating, with his pupils and his parishioners, the "real character and constitution" of the church. While there is no doubt that the adult Charles Lutwidge Dodgson knew of his father's Tractarian sympathies, it is possible, even likely, that such sympathies played little part in either the daily studies the young boy undertook with his father at the parsonage or in the sermons he heard preached throughout his childhood from the pulpit of All Saints.

Charles Lutwidge Dodgson's earliest education included religious instruction. Even before he was old enough for school lessons, he undoubtedly heard stories from scripture, and on Sundays, in addition to attending church and the Sunday School founded by his father, he probably reviewed the set of devotional cards that had been written out for the Dodgson children.

These cards, which survive in the family collection, offer an outline of what would remain, throughout his life, the bedrock of Charles's faith. Their simplicity is such that Charles probably studied and learned the twenty-eight "subjects" as a very young boy (the cards appear to date from the late 1830s or early 1840s). They were, for Charles, the predecessors to the catechism in the Book of Common Prayer (to be learned before his confirmation, usually at the age of fifteen) and the Thirty-Nine Articles, a more lengthy and complex statement of the faith of the Church of England, to which Charles would subscribe when he matriculated at Oxford University.

The first card offers a statement and scripture citations on the Sabbath; then follows a list of twelve biblical prophecies with citations for the prophecy and its fulfillment. But the meat of the cards is what follows: fourteen cards headed on each side with a "subject," most of them statements of faith, with each subject supported by one or more scripture citations. The "subjects" are:

1. God is the Creator and Governor of all things.
2. God created man perfectly good—free from pain, sickness, and fear of death.
3. The wicked spirit of the devil tempted man to sin.
4. Man disobeyed God's commands, and brought misery and death into the world.
5. God's great love towards us, in sending His Son Jesus Christ into the world to die for us.
6. Jesus Christ died for *all* mankind.
7. All mankind are sinners, and cannot therefore save themselves.
8. There is no way of salvation except through Jesus Christ.
9. All men are invited to come to Jesus Christ for salvation.
10. Forgiveness is offered to man thro' Jesus Christ.
11. Repentance is necessary in order to be saved through Jesus Christ.
12. Faith in Christ is necessary in order to be saved through Jesus Christ.
13. True faith will be followed by good works.
14. If our repentance is sincere, we shall confess, and forsake all sin, and wickedness.
15. Man is commanded and encouraged to resist the temptations of the devil.
16. Christ an example of holiness.
17. Man is not able to forsake sin without the help of God.

18. Men are commanded and encouraged to pray to God.
19. God will hear our prayers if they are offered up thro' the merits of Jesus Christ.
20. God will give his Holy Spirit to those who desire and pray for his help.
21. The Holy Ghost will guide us in the way to Heaven and strengthen us against sin.
22. God's great mercy and goodness towards mankind.
23. The Holy Scriptures are given to us by God for our instruction and guidance.
24. Man is commanded and encouraged to read the word of God.
25. God sees and knows all things.
26. Man must show his love to Christ by constantly endeavouring to obey His commandments.
27. True Christians will show love and kindness towards their fellow creatures.
28. Christ will come again at the Last Day to judge all mankind.[23]

These twenty-eight subjects not only pervaded Charles's early education but also remained with him throughout his life. Doubtless both his father and his mother did all in their power to see their son did not merely repeat these words and occasionally "wonder what it all could mean." Later in life, Charles Lutwidge Dodgson often referred to the ideas expressed on these cards, and while the bulk of the subjects are simple statements of the tenets of Christian faith, several bear closer inspection—whether because of their wording or because of the topic they present.

Taken together, number six, "Jesus Christ died for *all* mankind," and number nine, "All men are invited to come to Jesus Christ for salvation," present a distinctly different view from the Calvinistic concept of predestination—that only some are among the elect chosen from the beginning of time for salvation. Charles L. Dodgson would, as an adult, believe firmly that salvation is available for *all*.[24]

Numbers fourteen, "If our repentance is sincere, we shall confess, and forsake all sin, and wickedness"; fifteen, "Man is commanded and encouraged to resist the temptations of the devil"; and eighteen, "Men are commanded and encouraged to pray to God," can be seen as forming the basis for Charles L. Dodgson's prayer life (see chapter 11).

Perhaps the two subjects easiest for a child to understand would have been numbers twenty-five, "God sees and knows all things," and twenty-seven,

"True Christians will show love and kindness towards their fellow creatures."
The belief in a God who knows and sees all pervaded not just Dodgson's faith but affected almost everything he did.[25] Virtually all contemporary sources agree that Charles L. Dodgson was kind, and that kindness was inextricably linked to his faith. Even as a child he tried to perform acts of charity, if naïve and misguided. Collingwood wrote: "he used to peel rushes with the idea that the pith would afterwards 'be given to the poor,' though what possible use they could put it to he never attempted to explain" (*Life* 12).

Referring to Charles Dodgson the elder, Collingwood wrote, "Mr. Dodgson from the first used to take an active part in his son's education" (*Life* 12), and it was not just on Sundays, but every day, when Dodgson was not traveling to Ripon or elsewhere, that the young boy would have learned from his father in the parsonage at Daresbury. Rev. Charles Dodgson wrote that the education of his children was "that most sacred portion of a Parent's charge."[26]

Charles's father published five sermons during his years at Daresbury, including the sermon on the Sabbath already examined, and while all but one were certainly preached elsewhere, we may guess that some, at least, of the ideas they contained made it into the parsonage school room and wove themselves into sermons preached at All Saints Church in Daresbury. He preached his first three published sermons at ordination services in Ripon, presenting ideas that may have resonated with his son Charles.

Chief among these was one in his first published sermon, preached on 15 January 1837—that God gives each of us some talent and that we have a choice of whether to squander it or to use it for good. "No talent however small, is unregarded by [God],"[27] wrote Dodgson, and while his son's talents would prove to be anything but small, C. L. Dodgson often felt he ought to use those talents for good, striving to exhibit what his father called "a zealous and constant desire to improve the one talent, which he has received."[28] In the case of his writings, for instance, we see Charles taking greatest pleasure not in his own success or fame but in donating his books to sick or infirm children.[29]

The following summer, in another ordination sermon, Rev. Charles Dodgson preached about the error "of those who, in their zeal to maintain the all sufficiency of God's Word and Spirit to instruct and guide mankind, think it right to disparage all the aids of human learning, as something altogether distinct from, and independent of the teaching of God. . . . No one of the counsels of God has been more clearly stamped on the face of his general dispensations, than a design that man should feel his need of the aid of his fellow man, and that the various members of the great social body should be knit together by the bond of mutual dependence."[30]

Here in one paragraph are two ideas that certainly impressed young Charles. First, that the word of God was not separate from other types of learning and could be enhanced by other studies. Charles Lutwidge Dodgson would spend his entire adult life at an institution of learning; he would amass a significant library of religious and theological writings. From his earliest years, he learned that the pursuit of learning was the pursuit of God, that a fuller understanding of the world could lead to a fuller understanding of the Word. Further, he believed that studying and writing about nonreligious topics could still constitute work for God. Second was the idea, building on the 1837 sermon's notion of using one's God-given talents, that people are meant to depend on one another, "each contributing to the common stock the advantages with which Providence has peculiarly blest him."[31] This idea would resonate with Charles L. Dodgson throughout his life as he strove to find ways in which he could "contribute to the common stock." He saw his work not as work for himself but for others, and in some cases work that only *he* could do—his unique opportunity to contribute. Of his unfinished three-volume work on symbolic logic, he wrote, "there is no living man who could . . . arrange, and finish, and publish, the 2nd Part of the Logic" (*Letters* 1100). And he saw this work as not just contributing to the common good, but even as having a religious element. As he wrote in the introduction to the first volume: "Once master the machinery of Symbolic Logic, and you have . . . the power to detect fallacies, and to tear to pieces the flimsy illogical arguments, which you will so continually encounter in books, in newspapers, in speeches, and even in sermons."[32] And in a letter of 24 November 1894, he wrote to his sister Elizabeth, "*One* great use of the study of Logic . . . would be to help people who have *religious* difficulties to deal with, by making them see the absolute necessity of having clear *definitions,* so that, before entering on the discussion of any of these puzzling matters, they may have a clear idea *what it is they are talking about*" (*Letters* 1041).

In 1839, Rev. Charles Dodgson delivered the sermon "Preach the Gospel" at another Ripon ordination. He argued that while preaching should come from the word of God and not the opinions of man, contradictions can sometimes appear to be *in* that Word or contrary arguments made *from* that Word. "Nothing is presumed," wrote Dodgson, "except that the Word of God was rightly interpreted in the age of the Apostles."[33] It is the job of those who preach the Gospel, then, to trace tradition back as far as possible in order to eliminate heresies and determine the correct interpretation of God's Word: "By the application of the test of Tradition, the question, whether our Church has rightly interpreted the Gospel, is changed, from a mere conflict of individual opinions, into the definite and practicable inquiry, whether her doctrines are primitive and Catholic doctrines."[34]

This notion of drawing doctrine from the Apostolic Church, or as early a Christian church as possible, was promoted by the leaders of the Oxford Movement, particularly E. B. Pusey. Dodgson essentially said that no one can claim to understand the scriptures who has read *only* the scriptures— building on the same idea he presented in his sermon of the previous year. So young Charles would have learned from his father the importance of many types of learning as part of the "training of the immortal soul."

Later in 1839, Rev. Charles Dodgson preached a sermon in Manchester Collegiate Church (now Manchester Cathedral) on "The Providence of God Manifested in the Temporal Condition of the Poorer Clergy." He echoed a theme his son encountered in his childhood reading—a defense of the class system. Everyone has a place in God's scheme, went the argument, and one ought not to rise up against one's lot in life. Dodgson gave several reasons why God had been provident in depriving many of the English clergy of temporal comforts—not the least being that a poor but well-educated clergyman can minister to both his poor and his well-educated parishioners. Dodgson offered an interesting definition of poverty: "Poverty and affluence are relative terms. The views, which one man takes of the comforts and necessities of life, do not fairly measure those of another. The circumstances of birth and education, the position in society, which the individual occupies, and the habits and associations belonging to it, all these must be taken into account, before we can rightly estimate the proportion which his means bear to his wants, in other words the degree of his wealth or poverty."[35]

A poor man who has only known poverty can, in this worldview, be considered richer than a middle-class man who once knew great wealth. Charles Lutwidge Dodgson always remained keenly conscious of the difference between the classes and of what was widely considered appropriate and inappropriate intercourse among them. But the elder Dodgson was not wholly without sympathy in this sermon, and his message of caring for one's fellow man sprang directly from that subject that his children had studied on their devotional cards: "True Christians will show love and kindness towards their fellow creatures." "He who has disciplined himself to look unmoved on one species of misery," wrote Dodgson, "will find that he has, by the effort, lowered the tone of his sympathy for every other."[36] The notion that one can deaden one's sympathies by looking "unmoved on one species of misery" is reflected in Charles Lutwidge Dodgson's writings on the morality of vivisection, in which he argued that the greatest sin was not the cruelty to the animals, but the deadening of sympathy in the heart of the operator.[37]

If Rev. Charles Dodgson brought the ideas of his published sermons to the ears of his son, young Charles heard the repetition of three key points about Christian life: that education was essential to a true understanding of God's Word, that every man must discover his God-given talents and use them for the common good, and that we are put on Earth by God to help others.

In the summer of 1836, E. B. Pusey conceived an idea that he would pursue for the remainder of his life: the publication of a series of English translations of the works of the early church fathers, who, the Tractarians believed, provided a direct link to a time when Christianity was unified and followed closely its original teachers. In his prospectus for the proposed "Library of Fathers," Pusey wrote that "the knowledge of Christian antiquity is necessary in order to understand and maintain [the Anglican Church's] doctrines, and especially her Creeds and her Liturgy."[38] Pusey also saw the writings of the church fathers as a way to point out errors of both Roman Catholics and dissenters.

The first volume in the series (*The Confessions of Augustine*) was published in 1838; the forty-eighth and final volume appeared in 1885, three years after Pusey's death. For the translation of the tenth volume of the series, the works of the Carthaginian writer Tertullian, Pusey turned to his Christ Church friend Rev. Charles Dodgson. Between his Daresbury parochial duties, his teaching, and his travels to Ripon, Dodgson found time to translate hundreds of pages of ancient Latin religious writing for this Tractarian project.

Dodgson signed on for the project at least as early as 1838, when the advertisement of volumes "Preparing for Publication" listed him as the translator of Tertullian. Originally Dodgson and Pusey contemplated Dodgson's translating the entire body of Tertullian's works. In 1842, shortly before the Dodgson family left Daresbury, Dodgson's volume was published. It contained the Apologetic and Practical Treatises and was styled as "vol. 1" of the Tertullian.

In 1847, advertisements in volume 22 made clear that Dodgson was "preparing for publication" additional Tertullian material. However, that and several subsequent volumes contained a note, explaining that the collator working in Rome had discovered papers leading to what Dodgson hoped would be a more genuine text, and this discovery had delayed the translation. As late as 1850 the "works" of Tertullian continued to be listed as "in preparation" by Dodgson, but by 1854 Tertullian was listed among "other works originally contemplated." No second volume of Tertullian by Dodgson or any other translator was included in the series.

We cannot assume that, just because Dodgson was tapped to translate Tertullian, the teachings of that church father held any special place for him. He approached the project as a scholar, not an evangelist. We can, however, assume that he, like the Tractarians, placed an importance on the teachings of the church fathers as having come before the introduction of various heresies and corruptions. Neither he nor the other translators saw the writings of the church fathers as scripture; they felt only that, in the words of Pusey, "knowledge of Christian antiquity is necessary in order to understand and maintain [the church's] doctrines, and especially her Creeds and her Liturgy."[39]

Particular attention has been paid by some scholars to Dodgson's translation of *De spectaculis* (rendered by Dodgson as "Of Public Shows") as supporting the notion that he strongly opposed attendance at the theater. However, the argument is difficult to stand by in light of the fact that Tertullian was condemning the Roman theater and Rev. Charles Dodgson's one documented involvement in the theater was writing a prologue for a Roman play—the *Trinummus* of Plautus, written four hundred years before Tertullian. The primary conclusion to be drawn from Dodgson's translation is not that he either agreed with or taught to his children the writings of Tertullian, but that he was a talented scholar, well enough versed in Latin to translate hundreds of pages of ancient text.

How did Charles Lutwidge Dodgson feel about the early church fathers? While required to study some of their writings in preparation for ordination, he does not seem to have been a lifelong student of the fathers. No volumes from *A Library of Fathers* (or any other translations of the same writers) are listed in any of the extant records of his library, and while this does not mean that he owned none, it certainly does not point to a man for whom the teachings of the church fathers were central to his own faith. He does not mention Tertullian in his adult diaries or in any of his published letters. If his father did share the teachings of that Carthaginian with his young son, they did not make a particularly lasting impression.

For young Charles Lutwidge Dodgson, days began kneeling by his bedside, reciting this morning prayer:

Almighty and everlasting God, who hast mercifully preserved me in health, peace, and safety, to the beginning of another day, I thank Thee for this, and all Thy other mercies.

I acknowledge and bewail my unworthiness of the least of the many blessings I enjoy—my constant wanderings into sin, and forgetfulness of Thee—but, oh! gracious Father, deal not with me according to my sins, but according to Thine infinite love and mercy vouchsafed unto us, thro' the merits and mediation of Christ Jesus, Thy dear Son, our Saviour—For His sake, I beseech Thee to pardon all my sins, and grant me the constant guidance and help of Thy Holy Spirit, that each day of my life, I may become more and more truly religious—more able to resist temptation, and more devoted to Thy service.

Give me grace, to remember at all times, that Thou art about my path and seest all my ways, that I may ever live as in Thy sight, and endeavour, by the help of Thy Holy Spirit, to keep Thy commandments, in thought, word, and deed.

Bless all my relations and friends, I beseech Thee, especially my dear Parents, and all my Brothers and Sisters—preserve us all in health, and safety, thro' this day, and mercifully continue unto us the numberless blessings, and comforts, by which we are surrounded.

Grant us grace, that we may ever shew our love and gratitude to Thee, not only with our lips, but by our lives—by our constant endeavour to serve Thee more faithfully, and to promote the happiness, temporal and eternal, of our fellow creatures.[40]

This prayer survives in a small handwritten family prayer book, apparently written out by either Charles's mother or his maternal aunt, Lucy Lutwidge. Though undated, it appears to be from the Daresbury period. When the Rev. Charles Dodgson was at home, the family probably gathered to hear him read the services of Morning and Evening Prayer from the Book of Common Prayer each day. The family prayer book includes this prayer for morning and another, nearly identical, for evening, each with an addendum for Sundays. Probably written by Rev. Charles Dodgson, the prayers borrow language from the Book of Common Prayer, especially from the Confession and the General Thanksgiving. The prayers give us an important insight into the prayer life of the Dodgson family, and into Rev. Charles Dodgson's beliefs about how Christians should pray. They proceed through six steps:

Thankfulness for blessings
Acknowledgement of sinfulness
Asking forgiveness through Christ
Request for guidance
Request for blessings
Request for help in serving God and man

At the same time the prayers emphasize some of those twenty-eight subjects from the family devotional cards—sinfulness of man, forgiveness offered through Christ; and the two subjects already mentioned as having special power for a young child, the all-seeing God and the importance of showing love and kindness to all.

In these family prayers—combining the basic tenets of Christianity, some of the more powerful of the devotional subjects studied by Charles, the language and sentiments of the Book of Common Prayer, and the almost certain authorship of his father—lies the genesis of C. L. Dodgson's life in prayer.

While Charles's father was both teacher in the schoolroom of the Daresbury parsonage and preacher in the pulpit of Daresbury church, Charles's mother, née Frances Jane Lutwidge, also took part in the boy's education. Collingwood quotes an acquaintance as describing Mrs. Dodgson as, "One of the sweetest and gentlest women that ever lived, whom to know was to love. The earnestness of her simple faith and love shone forth in all she did and said; she seemed to live always in the conscious presence of God" (*Life* 8).

A log of Charles's reading from 1839 to 1842 comprises three categories and shows the influence of his mother on his religious education: "Religious Reading Private," "Religious Reading with Mamma," and "Daily Reading Useful Private."[41] His religious reading included *Pilgrim's Progress* (completed at age seven) and a variety of Bible stories and commentary in books such as *The Picture Testament, Stories from the Scriptures, Bible Illustrations,* and *Frank and His Father, or, Conversations on the First Three Chapters of Genesis.*

Rev. Charles Dodgson believed that God's word could only be fully understood by a thorough study of other sources. In an 1838 sermon, he said: "The word of God comes to us . . . intermixed with the records of national history . . . and associated with a multitude of those allusions to times and circumstances long since past [*sic*] away."[42]

As early as age ten, Charles was beginning to understand such allusions through his reading of books such as Bourne Hall Draper's *Bible*

Illustrations; or, A Description of Manners and Customs Peculiar to the East, Especially Explanatory of the Holy Scriptures, which teaches about daily life in biblical times, covering everything from houses to cooking, clothing, agriculture, books, climate, and more.

One work of fiction included in Charles's religious reading is a classic representation of early nineteenth-century didactic literature for children: *The Fairchild Family,* by Mary Martha Sherwood. Published in 1818, *The Fairchild Family* (subtitled *A Collection of Stories Calculated to Shew the Importance and Effects of a Religious Education*) consists of anecdotes about three young children and their religious education, primarily at the hands of their parents. Daily life for the Fairchilds would have been familiar to Charles, being a typical existence outside a small village—from daily chores and lessons to a Sunday routine much like his own. The children frequently get into trouble, often bringing dreadful punishments on themselves, and always a moral lesson from one or the other of the parents. Each chapter includes long digressions on religious matters, and the children regularly recite lengthy passages from scripture. Each chapter ends with a prayer and a hymn.

The general impression given of children is that, in the absence of adult Christian supervision, their natural state is one of sin and evil—left to their own devices the children do awful (in the moral worldview of the story) things. This is an allegorical representation of the relationship between man and Christ—our natural state is one of sin (subject card number seven: "All mankind are sinners, and cannot therefore save themselves"), redeemable only through Him. But to a child the message may have been simpler: children are evil and need saving by grownups. It is a philosophy that the grown Charles Lutwidge Dodgson would utterly reject. He saw children as the least evil of humans, coming "fresh from God's hands."[43] He saw them as vessels of innocence and a conduit to the Almighty.

C. L. Dodgson's own works for children rebel against the moralistic tales of his youth. They are consciously written without morals; his Alice behaves in a way that would have been soundly condemned and punished in the world of *The Fairchild Family;* yet, she ultimately faces no punishment or consequences. He even pokes fun directly at didactic children's stories both in the incessant moralizing of the Duchess and in this passage from chapter 1 of *Wonderland:* "She had read several nice little stories about children who had got burnt, and eaten up by wild beasts, and other unpleasant things, all because they *would* not remember the simple rules their friends had taught them: such as, that a red hot poker will burn you if you hold it too long; and that, if you cut your finger *very* deeply with a knife, it usually bleeds; and she had never forgotten that, if you drink much from a bottle marked 'poison', it is almost certain to disagree with you, sooner or later."[44]

In the world of *The Fairchild Family,* such rules were underpinned by Christian morals. Children who were "not brought up in the fear of God" exhibited bad behavior. One of these, the haughty daughter of a local nobleman, may have inspired C. L. Dodgson to write about holding onto red-hot pokers. Her governess warned her of the danger of touching the fire, but "Miss Augusta did not heed what her governess said this time any more than the last, but went on raking the fire, till at length Miss Beaumont, fearing some mischief, forced the poker out of her hand."[45]

A few chapters later, Augusta dies horribly when she is burned to death after taking a forbidden candle to an empty room. The reader infers that Augusta is not saved, will therefore spend eternity in the fires of hell, and that responsibility for this sits squarely on the shoulders of her parents, who taught her to "mock at religion and pious people" (159).

The moral lessons of *The Fairchild Family* are the same that young Charles would encounter elsewhere in his reading: parents must be obeyed ("I expect to be obeyed," says Mr. Fairchild to Henry. "I stand in the place of God to you whilst you are a child" [267]); people should know and be content with their place in society; the natural state of the human heart is filled with wickedness; God sees all (and especially all sin); sin will be punished. Whether or not Rev. Charles Dodgson felt he "stood in the place of God" for his children, young Charles was expected to look for moral guidance and authority first to scripture, and next to his father.

Also among Charles's religious reading were the *Cheap Repository Tracts,* a series of about 120 tracts, chiefly moral and religious, published in the late eighteenth century, more than half of which were written by Hannah More. Dodgson's reading log does not record which of these tracts he read, but typical of the series was More's *The Shepherd of Salisbury Plain.*[46] In this story, the shepherd, his crippled wife, and five children are happy in a life of poverty. His cheerfulness with his appointed lot in life is eventually rewarded with a job as parish clerk, a position he uses to start a Sunday School. Rev. Charles Dodgson touched on the close relationship between religion and accepting one's position in society in an 1839 sermon. Speaking of the low pay of the parochial clergy, he said: "Shall they . . . complain, if . . . they too are called upon to 'approve themselves as the Ministers of God in much patience, in afflictions, in necessities, in distresses?' . . . Men will ever receive with coldness and suspicion lessons of unworldliness from one, who is loaded with the good things of the world."[47]

C. L. Dodgson's earliest literary effort, a family magazine written around 1845 and called *Useful and Instructive Poetry,* shows the strong influence of the moralistic writings of Hannah More and Mary Martha Sherwood. Dodgson's youthful poems in this magazine are all of an instructive tone and many have morals such as "Don't Get Drunk" and "Behave." However, Charles was already, at age thirteen, rebelling against the didactic readings of his youth—while some of the poems in this collection might be changed for passages in *The Fairchild Family,* others cross over into parody. Consider for instance, this poem quoted by Mr. Fairchild in *The Fairchild Family,* when his children are caught quarreling:

> Let dogs delight to bark and bite,
>   For God has made them so;
> Let bears and lions growl and fight,
>   For 'tis their nature too:
> But children, you should never let
>   Such angry passions rise:
> Your little hands were never made
>   To tear each other's eyes.[48]

Compare this to Dodgson's parody on the many rules of the early Victorian household, "My Fairy," written in the same meter:

> I have a fairy by my side
>   Which says I must not sleep,
> When once in pain I loudly cried
>   It said "You must not weep."
> If, full of mirth, I smile and grin,
>   It says "You must not laugh,"
> When once I wished to drink some gin,
>   It said "You must not quaff."
> When once a meal I wished to taste
>   It said "You must not bite,"
> When to the wars I went in haste,

It said "You must not fight."
"What may I do?" At length I cried,
    Tired of the painful task,
The fairy quietly replied,
    And said "You must not ask."
        Moral: "You mustn't."[49]

While the adult Charles Lutwidge Dodgson did not question the content of his religious education, he certainly questioned the delivery system. He would become a man of deep faith, but he would have little patience for didactic stories or, when preached to children, boring sermons. One parishioner who, as a child, sat behind the Dodgson family pew, remembered Charles for his "buoyant spirits,"[50] hardly a phrase to describe one listening in rapt attention to his father's preaching. In the last piece C. L. Dodgson ever wrote for publication, an introduction to *The Lost Plum-Cake,* a children's story by his cousin E. G. Wilcox, the sixty-five-year-old looked back, perhaps, on the religious education of his childhood, and the enforced attention paid to his father's sermons. Of children in church, he wrote:

There is no doubt that so long a period of enforced quietude is a severe tax on their patience. The hymns, perhaps, tax it least. . . . The lessons and the prayers, are not wholly beyond them. . . . But the sermons! It goes to one's heart to see, as I so often do, little darlings of five or six years old, forced to sit still through a weary half-hour, with nothing to do and not one word of sermon that they can understand. . . . Would it be so *very* irreverent to let your child have a story-book to read during the sermon, to while away that tedious half-hour, and to make church-going a bright and happy memory?[51]

Among the books on young Charles's reading log headed "Daily Reading Useful—Private" was one that may have introduced him to comparative world religions, though in a highly xenophobic way. *Peter Parley's Tales about Europe, Asia, Africa, and America* is largely concerned with a perfunctory description of the peoples, sights, history, and customs of various countries. On the subject of world religions, here is just some of what the author has to say:

The people of Turkey . . . are not Christian, but followers of the false prophet Mahomet. . . . They are very bigoted, and hate all Christians.[52]

The Chinese are an ignorant and superstitious people, and their religion is a system contrived by cunning priests to obtain influence over them. (174)

The religion of the Hindoos teaches . . . if they will practice certain ceremonies, drown their children in the rivers, allow themselves to be buried alive in the earth, tear their bodies with hooks, cut their flesh with knives, and other things like these, that their gods will then look upon them with favour. (233–34)

The Jews, who were once a great nation, have now lost their power. . . . They still carry with them their peculiar religion, their singular customs, and their strange opinions and feelings. (265)

C. L. Dodgson certainly believed, as Peter Parley did, that Christianity was the one "true religion" (191); however, as an adult, he had an interest in and even an acceptance of the religions of other cultures that went far beyond the name-calling of Peter Parley.

Also on his "Daily Reading—Useful" list were the four volumes of Maria Edgeworth's *Early Lessons*. While less overtly religious than *The Fairchild Family,* Edgeworth's books are still highly moralistic. Children are rough stones to be hewn by all-knowing parents and even the most mundane daily occupations provide teaching moments. *Early Lessons* includes stories about children close to Charles's age when he read the books (eight), who constantly learn moral lessons, as just a few lines of parental dialogue illustrates.[53]

"Justice satisfies every body." (vol. 1, 188)

"Flattering . . . is praising you more than you deserve to be praised." (vol. 1, 198–99)

"Sensible people do not imitate every thing which they see others do; they imitate only what is useful or agreeable." (vol. 1, 209)

"It is a good thing to keep one's promise." (vol. 1, 238)

When Charles Lutwidge Dodgson set out to tell stories to Alice Liddell and her sisters in the 1860s, he adopted Edgeworth's frank style of narration and the child hero filled with curiosity, but rejected the child's bowing to adult authority, the religious overtones, and the overt moralizing.

Like the *Alice* books, the stories in *Early Lessons* are episodic, with no particular overarching narrative. But some of those episodes include the sort of action later parodied in *Wonderland*. When Harry and Lucy discuss numbers with their parents, and mathematical learning is woven into the dialogue (vol. 2, 262–67), they are anticipating Alice's failed attempts to recite her times tables in chapter 2 of *Wonderland.*

Perhaps the greatest thing the *Alice* books take from Dodgson's moralistic childhood reading is the pastoral nature of the stories. Both *The Fairchild Family* and *Early Lessons* are about life in the English countryside, and the final passage in *Alice's Adventures in Wonderland* could almost have been lifted from one of these predecessors. In *Early Lessons* we see the typical English love for gardens so apparent in *Wonderland,* and the children encounter many of the same creatures that Alice does, from a caterpillar to a rabbit.

One passage in *Early Lessons* must surely have stayed with Dodgson— the story of Rivuletta (vol. 2, 85). The narrator dreams of being able to see a fairy and hear the voice of the "fairy deity." The combination of dreaming and interacting with fairies is so close to the central premise of Dodgson's novel *Sylvie and Bruno* that it seems impossible he did not remember, if only subconsciously, this story from his childhood reading.

The one surviving family anecdote about Charles Lutwidge Dodgson's Daresbury education reads like an episode from *Early Lessons:* "One day, when Charles was a very small boy, he came up to his father and showed him a book of logarithms, with the request, 'Please explain.' Mr. Dodgson told him that he was much too young to understand anything about such a difficult subject. The child listened to what his father said, and appeared to think it irrelevant, for he still insisted, 'But, please, explain!'" [54] (*Life* 13).

Charles read many more books than those listed in the reading log, which covers at most three years. In addition to religious and moralistic texts, the log contains books about the world—just the sort of books that the children in *Early Lessons* read. But he would remember the didactic, moralizing tales of his childhood throughout his life: in his library at the time of his death, Carroll had not only a collection of books by Maria Edgeworth but also the complete works of Hannah More.

In 1843, when Charles Lutwidge Dodgson was eleven, the family's fortunes underwent an enormous change. For Charles, the world would never be the same, and, much as he may have disliked listening to sermons or reading moralistic storybooks, he would, nonetheless, look with nostalgic eyes on his Daresbury days.

Michaelmas Term 1859 had nearly ended, and Charles would soon board the train for the North, to return to his family for Christmas. As he stared into the dying fire, pen in hand, he considered the poem he hoped to submit to Mr. Dickens's periodical. He called the poem "Faces in the Fire." Why not, he thought, include a verse about his nostalgia for his childhood days in Daresbury? He dipped his pen into the inkwell, put it to the paper, and wrote, as the dim light flickered over the page:

> An island-farm 'mid seas of corn,
> Swayed by the wandering breath of morn,
> The happy spot where I was born.[55]

THREE

For the Good Education

Charles Lutwidge Dodgson concentrated on the numbers in front of him.[1] Despite the cold in the dim stone room and the smoke from the open fire at the other end, the thirteen-year-old boy had no trouble in making sense of "Reduction of Decimals." His mathematical master, Rev. Thomas Kenworthy Browne, would be proud of his answers. In a few minutes it would be time to close his book and return, through the gravestones of St. Mary's Churchyard, to Dr. Tate's house, for Charles lodged just a short distance away at the home of the headmaster of Richmond Grammar School and his family. He was happy that his father cared enough about education to send him to the tutelage of the kindly Dr. Tate.

As soon as he became examining chaplain for the Diocese of Ripon, Rev. Charles Dodgson and his bishop, Charles Longley, began to look for a parish for Dodgson to serve in that diocese. In February 1837 he was a candidate for the vacant Vicarage of Leeds, a post that ultimately went to Walter Farquhar Hook.[2] Three years later, when the Crown living of Catterick, near Richmond, fell open, Bishop Longley wrote to the prime minister, Lord Melbourne, asking him to appoint Dodgson to the post. While Melbourne acknowledged Dodgson's fitness, he awarded the living to John Croft, who had been a Fellow of Christ's College, Cambridge, for twenty-three years.

On 18 September 1841, Longley wrote to the new prime minister, Robert Peel, about "being compelled year after year to call on his Chaplain to discharge the laborious and responsible Duties of that office, without any prospect of being able to reward him." Longley further pointed out the dearth of livings in his own hands, as bishop of the new see of Ripon: "The first Bishop of Ripon therefore finds himself destitute of the means . . . of rewarding merit."[3] Longley noticed that the living of Croft-on-Tees, a rich appointment about thirty miles from Ripon, was then held by Rev. James Dalton, who was seventy-five and ailing. Croft was a Crown living, meaning the prime minister would be responsible for filling it, and Longley asked Peel to promise that he would appoint Dodgson as incumbent on Dalton's death. Peel replied, "I must observe that I have resolved with respect to every appointment . . . not to give any assurances calculated to raise expectations until the appointment be actually vacant."[4]

Rev. James Dalton died at Croft on 2 January 1843, and four days later Longley wrote again to Peel to put forward the case for Charles Dodgson, calling him "a Clergyman of high Professional Character, of first rate ability, and of much Theological attainment—one indeed who would adorn the very first Stations in the Church."[5]

Longley prevailed on a number of influential men to write letters on Dodgson's behalf, including Lord Francis Egerton, who wrote of "the care which [Dodgson] has extended to that very generally neglected but not ungrateful class, that of canal navigators";[6] and Dodgson's local member of Parliament, John Wilson Patten, who wrote, "he would receive the unanimous recommendation of a very extensive district in which [his] character is known and highly appreciated."[7]

Peel, though favoring Dodgson, was annoyed by the influx of recommendations, writing to Longley a week later: "I have determined, purely on the grounds of his very high character and attainments, and professional Services within the Diocese of Ripon, to prefer Rev'd Charles Dodgson to the numberless Competitors with him for the Living of Croft in the North Riding of Yorkshire. Excuse me for saying that I wish I had been left at liberty to make my selection of Mr Dodgson (which I was perfectly prepared to do) on the single grounds of his merits and claims—without the intervention of various Colleagues of mine and Members of Parliament."[8]

To Dodgson, Peel wrote, "exclusively upon the grounds of your professional services and claims, I have resolved to appoint you to the Living of Croft in the North Riding of Yorkshire."[9] The prime minister wrote that the appointment was made with the understanding that Dodgson would live at Croft and carry out the duties of the parish personally. It was a provision Dodgson did not strictly keep as the years went by. The appointment meant the family would go from living in near poverty and being forced to take in students to make ends meet to living in a large home with an income of more than £1,000 per annum. He wrote to Peel, "I beg to assure you that I shall be anxious to commence my residence at Croft with as little delay as circumstances will admit of."[10]

Apparently, circumstances did not immediately admit this commencement, for the move was delayed for at least six months. One reason may have been that Mrs. Dodgson was pregnant with their tenth child. Henrietta Harington Dodgson was born on 3 June 1843. Less than two weeks later, on 18 June, Charles Dodgson performed his last baptism in Daresbury. Henrietta was baptized there on 23 July by Rev. T. L. Claughton. By this time her father may have been spending some of his time in Croft. He was certainly in Daresbury on 6 July 1843, when he was presented with a testimonial of a handsomely bound Polyglot Bible from the congregation of his floating chapel. Again on 10 August, Rev. Charles Dodgson was in Daresbury to receive another testimonial when "the parishioners of Daresbury, presented the Rev. Charles Dodgson with a testimonial of esteem . . . consisting of a massive . . . Candlelabra [sic], with branches for four lights, with two pairs of candlesticks corresponding—also snuffers and tray—together with a handsome knotted oak case for containing the whole; at a cost of something more than £140. . . . A very appropriate address was read by Mr. Okell, church warden of the past year, which was replied to by the talented and reverend gentleman, in a feeling and grateful manner, with his usual impressive eloquence."[11]

By late summer the family had moved to Croft, and Dodgson's first appearance in the Croft parish registers came on 15 September 1843, when he performed a baptism. Dodgson's work at Croft was much different from what it had been at Daresbury. The parish served a substantially smaller population—at Daresbury the average total of baptisms, weddings, and burials each year had been 119; in Croft it was only 28. Even with the lighter workload of parish duties, as Dodgson took on other diocesan responsibilities, he was less involved in the day-to-day services at St. Peter's, Croft.

He already held the post of examining chaplain, a job in which he continued until 1856, when Bishop Longley was translated to the Diocese of Durham. On 18 March 1843, well before arriving in Croft, Dodgson became one of the general secretaries of both the Ripon Diocesan Church Building Society and the Ripon Diocesan Board of Education, posts he held until March 1857. He also served as inspector of the diocesan training school for teachers in 1851.

Shortly after settling in Croft, he began to preach and give speeches occasionally outside his parish, first on 6 December 1843 for the consecration of Trinity Church, Darlington. In August 1847, Bishop Longley appointed him rural dean for the Deanery of Richmond East, a post he held until at least 1852. As rural dean, Dodgson oversaw a group of about seventeen clergymen, likely holding regular meetings with them to discover any issues that needed to be brought to the attention of the bishop.

In 1850, under his direction, the Rural Deanery of Richmond made two official addresses to Longley. The first illustrates how, even within a relatively small Rural Deanery, Dodgson dealt with sectarian disagreement between high and low churchmen. The address responded to a pastoral letter by Bishop Longley on the subject of baptismal regeneration, and in it the undersigned thanked Longley for "reminding us that we are 'bound to pronounce each individual child who we baptize, regenerate.' . . . We rejoice to find our own convictions thus confirmed by the judgment of our Bishop."[12] The address was signed by Dodgson and twelve other clergymen, about four-fifths of the total members of the Rural Deanery. The following week, a rebuttal to this address, signed "An Incumbent of the Diocese of Ripon," appeared in the paper claiming the "the address, by implication, impeaches the character and impugns the teaching of many clergymen in this diocese."[13]

The second address from Dodgson's Rural Deanery was issued in November 1850, to object to the reestablishment by the Roman Catholic Church of its hierarchy within Britain: "We maintain that it was the fundamental principle of the English Reformation that the Church of England is a true National Branch of the Church Catholic."[14] This time, Dodgson mustered greater support within his Rural Deanery; sixteen of seventeen clergy signed the address.

To add to his extensive diocesan responsibilities, on 18 December 1852, Charles Dodgson was installed as a canon of Ripon Cathedral. He was required to be in residence at Ripon the first three months of each year and was a part of the cathedral chapter—the clergy who governed the cathedral. Following the death of John Headlam on 4 May 1854, Dodgson was made archdeacon of Richmond and installed in that post on 7 June 1854. At the same time, he assumed the office of chancellor of the diocese. Dodgson would continue in these two positions for the rest of his life.

As archdeacon he was the bishop's representative and deputy and delivered an annual charge to the clergy and churchwardens of his archdeaconry.[15] Dodgson published nine of these charges, delivered between 1855 and 1868, mostly to do with the national church, various threats to its work, and its place in society and government.

With his installation as canon, Dodgson, despite his assurances to Prime Minister Peel that he would personally carry out the work of his parish, began to look for a curate to assist him. From 1853 until his death in 1868, he generally had at least one curate to help perform parish duties.

A. R. Webster arrived in July 1853 and served until June or July 1855. He was followed by James Baker, who served from December 1855 until October 1858. Gordon Salmon came to Croft in March 1859 and served until March or April 1865. Edward Wright Whitaker came in March 1865 but stayed only a few months until November or December. Like both Charles Dodgsons, Whitaker was educated at Christ Church, Oxford, receiving his B.A. in 1863 and his M.A. in 1865. Charles Lutwidge Dodgson, a mathematical lecturer at Christ Church at the time, knew Whitaker. On 24 December 1864, the younger Dodgson recorded in his diary: "Wrote to Whitaker by my father's desire, inviting him to Ripon on the 16th. I am very hopeful that it will end in his being engaged as curate in place of Mr. Salmon." Mr. Dodgson was able to hire his own son, Skeffington Hume Dodgson, as curate in March 1866. A second curate, R. Fowler, arrived in April or May 1866. Both Fowler and Skeffington Dodgson served until after Rev. Charles Dodgson's death in 1868.

In the decade prior to the arrival of his first curate in 1853, Charles Dodgson performed 85 percent of the baptisms, weddings, and burials at Croft. In the fifteen years that followed, that number dropped to 12 percent. This certainly caused some discontent in his parish, foreshadowed by a letter to the editor that appeared in the *York Herald* when Dodgson was appointed canon of Ripon Cathedral in 1852, before he hired his first curate:

> The Rev. Charles Dodgson, rector of Croft, in the North-Riding of this county, a parish, having only a limited population, being altogether rural, and in consequence the *duties* are so *laborious* in proportion to the trifling salary received, (house, garden, hot-houses, glebe land, and tithes, amounting on the whole to about £1,200 per annum) that his patron and friend, the Bishop of Ripon, has actually been *obliged* to give him a salary of £300 per annum, as Canon of Ripon Cathedral, to leave his parish for three months in the year, and reside at Ripon to do still less than he does in the parish of Croft, which he ought not, and has no right, to leave.
>
> The only good part of the story is, that the Rev. C. D. is so highly beloved by the greater part of his parishioners, that, if agreeable to himself, they would not object to change his three months' absence into a permanent one.[16]

But if Dodgson was less busy with parish duties than at Daresbury, it did not mean he did nothing for his flock. Within a few months of the family's arrival in Croft, he decided that the size of his glebe lands and his income would enable him to establish a National School for boys and girls.

> Early in the year 1844, [he] resolved to grant a portion of his Glebe Land . . . as a site for a National School for the benefit of the Parishioners of Croft for ever; the object and purpose of such School being—
> 1st.—To train up the Children in Christian Knowledge, according to the doctrines and principles of the Established Church of England, and under the direction and superintendence of the Clergyman of the Parish.
> 2nd.—To provide instruction for them in other useful things, such as Reading, Writing, Arithmetic, and, for the Girls, needlework.[17]

Mr. Dodgson not only contributed more than £120 of his own money toward the building of the schools (more than a quarter of the total expenses), but he also convinced his father-in-law, Charles Lutwidge, to contribute £35 and his brother Hassard Hume Dodgson to add another £7 10. Additional funding came from the National Society (£75), the Privy Council Committee on Education (£100), and other private donors.

In October 1844, Bishop Longley came to Croft for the laying of the foundation stone, preaching in the church on Sunday, 20 October, and holding a confirmation there on Monday for more than one hundred confirmands. Young Charles Lutwidge Dodgson may have heard his father preach a sermon in Richmond in 1844 inspired by his establishment of the Croft National School—*The Position and Duties of the Clergy with Respect to the Religious Education of the People.*[18]

The Croft school opened almost a year later, on 7 October 1845: "The building is divided into two Schools, one for Boys and the other for Girls, each capable of containing about 60 scholars, and each measuring 21 ft. by 19 ft. . . . The School Rooms are separated from each other, each having a separate Play Ground attached to it. The two Play Grounds together contain about 1500 square yards."[19]

As rector, Rev. Charles Dodgson guaranteed funding for the school and generously donated to its operation (£30 in 1845). He also hired the schoolmaster and mistress. Mr. Henry Hobson and his wife, Sarah Gordon (who received £60 and £27 respectively), came from the Training Institute in York.[20] As the *Yorkshire Gazette* noted, "the vicar and his family will undertake the religious part of the instruction to be given."[21] "I do not hesitate to say," Dodgson wrote in 1850, "that no apportionment of a clergyman's time is more truly valuable to his Parish and to himself, than that of a daily hour to the superintendence of his parish schools."[22] For the rest of his life, Dodgson and his children, including his oldest son, Charles, assisted at the Croft National School.

Charles Lutwidge Dodgson's first involvement in the pursuit to which his father attached such great importance, the education of children, came at the Croft National School. On 5 July 1855, home from Oxford for the Long Vacation, the twenty-three-year-old wrote in his diary, "I went to the Boy's School to hear my Father teach, as I want to begin trying myself soon." Three days later he wrote, after teaching two classes of boys part of the life of St. John, "I liked my first attempt at teaching very much." Carroll's diaries give some additional peeks into the Croft schoolrooms. On 3 April 1856, he wrote: "Heard the singing lesson in the school, about 50 are learning, and there are many good voices among them: one piece they sang in full harmony. They are also learning a choral service, which Mr. Baker [Dodgson's curate] hopes to introduce in church on week days."

Later that year, he wrote of the end-of-year celebrations at the school and the following day of his own presentation of a magic lantern show.[23]

Dec: 31. (W). First exhibition of the Magic Lantern, the largest audience I ever had, about 80 children, and a large miscellaneous party besides of friends, servants, etc.

I expected the whole thing to last about an hour and a half. . . . As it turned out, it did not begin till two . . . and lasted till nearly half past four. I divided it into two parts, of 24 and 23 pictures, with a rest of about half an hour between. I introduced 13 songs in the course of the performance, six for myself, and seven for the children; and employed seven different voices.

Here, six years before he told the story that became *Alice's Adventures in Wonderland,* Charles Lutwidge Dodgson's telling of stories to children was nurtured and developed as a direct result of his father's passion for religious education.

During the family's first year at Croft, young Charles continued his education at home, but in August 1844, the twelve-year-old left home to be educated at the Richmond Grammar School, about eleven miles away.

Why did Rev. Charles Dodgson choose to educate his son at Richmond? Classical grammar schools, such as Richmond, added Greek and Latin to the curriculum that would have been available at a National School, preparing students not just for the Christian life, but for admission to university. Rev. Charles Dodgson foresaw for his son a path similar to his own, which meant preparing the boy for Oxford. Richmond also had the advantage of proximity and a stellar reputation. James Tate I had been headmaster of the school from 1796 until 1833, when he became a canon of St. Paul's Cathedral, London. Known as the "scholar of the North," Tate raised the reputation of Richmond Grammar School to great heights, and many of his former pupils achieved success at the universities and in the wider world.

William Edward Dickson, who attended Richmond School a few years before Dodgson, remembered the school thus: "The old School-house was a long, low building. . . . Within, about two-thirds of the building on the right hand or east side of the door were occupied by the main School-room the space on the left being covered by a much smaller room. . . . The throne or rostrum of the Headmaster was at the eastern extremity. . . . The boys did not sit on benches at desks . . . but within enclosures resembling pews, ranged along the walls on each side as in the chancels of churches, with a sloping book-board and a narrow shelf beneath it."[24]

When Charles Lutwidge Dodgson arrived at Richmond, the headmaster was James Tate II, son of the "scholar of the North." Tate had attended Richmond School under his father's tutelage before continuing on to Charterhouse and Trinity College, Cambridge. In 1832 Tate became second master at Richmond, working side by side with his father for a year before he took over the headmastership. Referring to James Tate I, the *Times* wrote on his death:

> His mode of communicating religious instruction from the pulpit was characterised by that mild and simple, yet eloquent and effectual style of persuasion, which he had found so useful in communicating secular instruction to the young persons whom he had trained with almost parental care to learning and virtue. . . . He had the strongest aversion to corporal punishments. . . . [T]he principle of fear was one which he seriously banished from his plan of education. Early in life he . . . had decided that the schoolhouse ought to be, not a house of bondage and of terror, but a house of play and of pleasure.[25]

While the historian of Richmond School claims that "as a schoolmaster and as a man, [James Tate II] bears no comparison with his illustrious father" (Wenham 82), nonetheless it is likely that the younger Tate tried to use his father's style of gentle encouragement when teaching Charles

Lutwidge Dodgson. The school history states that James Tate I maintained an influence over his son "long after death." Of the younger Tate, one townsperson wrote: "Was he not one of the kindest-hearted and most genial men that ever trod the streets of the town? A man who never made a foe. . . . Who always had a cheery word and look for those whom he addressed, whatever their circumstances" (82). William Edward Dickson remembered James Tate II in the early days of the latter's headmastership: "His health was delicate; this may have accounted for . . . a quiet tone of voice, and a gentleness of manner" (168).

Into the home of this kindhearted man arrived, in August 1844, Charles Lutwidge Dodgson. During his year and a half at Richmond, Charles would lodge with the burgeoning Tate family, and he seemed happy in a home which must have reminded him of his own (the Tates had six children ranging in age from eleven to two when Dodgson arrived; the family he left behind in Croft had, at the time, ten children from seventeen-year-old Frances Jane to one-year-old Henrietta). William Edward Dickson described the house as "large enough to accommodate about sixteen boarders besides Mr James Tate's young family, without any overcrowding. In the pleasant garden behind it were out-buildings containing three little rooms called 'studies' which were allotted to boys according to seniority, two or three in each study" (170).

Dodgson received both religious and moral guidance from James Tate II—in the schoolroom, in his lodgings at Swale House, and from the pulpit of St. Mary's Church on those occasions when Tate preached. Though he left no published sermons, a notebook containing notes by Tate from the late 1840s and early 1850s gives a sense of the sort of lessons he taught. Though a student who attended Richmond a few years before Dodgson, but still under Tate's headmastership, claimed that "in church teaching we were destitute of instruction," that same student also admitted having little personal contact with Tate (181). Dodgson, however, living in Tate's house, had daily contact with the headmaster, and even if the notes in the notebook were intended for sermons delivered outside the school, the ideas contained therein might well have passed from Tate to his boarders. While some of the entries appear to be drafts or outlines of sermons for a general congregation,[26] some were clearly intended for his students. He recorded notes on baptism, the Lord's Prayer, and several on particular scripture passages. Others have titles like "Expansive Power of Mind" and "Grace of God." In many of the entries, Tate wrote out only headings for what was likely a sermon or lesson—a habit Charles Lutwidge Dodgson would adopt in writing his own sermons.

On the topic of reading, Tate singled out Thackeray's *Vanity Fair* as particularly unsuited for young Christian minds. Tate wrote in 1848, just after the publication of Thackeray's novel and shortly after Dodgson's departure from Richmond, but his message to young Charles was likely similar. Tate objected to the moral darkness of characters, whom Robert Bell called "as vicious and odious as a clever condensation of the vilest qualities can make them."[27] "Let me follow this rule in reading," wrote Tate, "[accept] those books professing to inculcate religion; reject at once those, the tone of which is obviously . . . as that of this above work."

Tate taught the art of thinking, self-reflection, and abstraction. Another section of his notes reads in part:

1. Learn to think. Strive to form habits of distinct conception: Practice abstraction.

2. Avoid all books which are of the character noticed on p. preceding [*Vanity Fair*].

3. And, if you fall into conversation with persons whose views are erroneous and whose remarks have an irreligious tendency, do yourself justice and honour God and his Christ by modestly opposing and correcting what seems to you wrong.

4. In—with 2 & 3—be not dazzled by talent merely. Without Christ it is worthless.

To section 3, Tate added in pencil "See Bickersteth X Student," a reference to Edward Bickersteth's 1829 work *The Christian Student*. Bickersteth's work, addressed to students below the university level, discusses how to study scripture and theological writings in a spirit of holiness: "Holy tempers, and a holy conduct, are essential to our attaining the wise and great end, the happy experience, and the true enjoyment of divine knowledge."[28] The section titled "The Study of Controversial Works" applies directly to James Tate's advice to his students about opposing those whose "remarks have an irreligious tendency": "Vehement contention for truth may be a duty, and should be given with meekness and fear; meekness towards him who opposes, and fear towards God, lest we should dishonor his cause."[29] He also warns, "If called to actual controversy, let us not engage in it without study or prayer."[30]

Tates's advice about the careful choice of reading material may have made an impression on young Charles Lutwidge Dodgson.[31] In his early years of journal keeping (his surviving diaries begin in 1855), Dodgson occasionally reviewed his reading, often in Christian terms. "I finished reading *Shadows of the Clouds* by [James Anthony] Froude," he wrote on 14 May 1855, "which I have lately had bound, after cutting out the objectionable parts of the book." On 7 January 1856, he wrote, "Finished *Alton Locke*. . . . Kingsley's arguments in favour of miracles are much inferior to Paley's." He went on to write a long digression on his desire to do some social good, concluding, "I would thankfully spend and be spent so long as I were sure of really effecting something by the sacrifice, and not merely lying down under the wheels of some irresistible Juggernaut." He added: "What talents I have, I desire to devote to His service, and may he purify me, and take away my pride and selfishness. Oh that I might hear 'Well done, good and faithful servant'!"

A year later, on 7 January 1857, Dodgson wrote: "Finished *Hypatia* [by Charles Kingsley]: it is . . . outrageous to taste in some parts, which is a new fault (to me). I mean especially the sneers at Christianity which he puts into the mouths of some of the heathen characters."

Tate spent several pages in his notebook on the topic of self-examination. The longest piece, dated 20 December 1848, seems aimed at a young audience. In it, Tate again speaks of the need for his charges to "learn to think" before going on to what must surely have been a regular theme for boys passing through puberty—the battle between the spirit and the flesh.

> I would most strongly recommend you to cultivate a habit of abstracting your thoughts from objects around you and those of an ordinary nature and endeavouring to fix them upon the great facts of your condition as a man and as a Christian. Pass in review your original nature, your habitual feelings, your general conduct. Endeavour in your own instance to verify what you have read of man's inherent depravity as exhibited in excessive and regular longings after objects which your conscience condemns. Become experimentally convinced of the certainty and momentous[ness] of the warfare between the flesh and spirit. Regard yourself as the prize of the [battle]; your immortal spirit as risked on the result: and remember that until a "Champion" from Heaven be induced to aid you, you are struggling, if indeed you struggle at all, against fearful odds, and are sure to be overcome.

Nowhere in his extant writings did Charles Lutwidge Dodgson record his sexual feelings as he went through puberty and young adulthood. However, a slim volume in Dodgson's library gives a sense of the level of guilt a young man in the 1840s must have felt when experiencing what are now considered normal urges. Although William Pratt's *A Physician's Sermon to Young Men* was published in 1872, it reflects the general teaching about sex and sexual feelings that pervaded Victorian England. On the subject of masturbation, Pratt wrote it was "a vice which cannot be practiced without eventually injuring the body most severely. . . . [A]nd while injuring the body, this vice has an equally baneful influence over the mind. The imagination becomes polluted, the conception becomes defiled, the will is weakened, the dreams are rendered impure, the whole intellectual and moral life becomes unclean. In the course of a short time the subject of this wretched habit is unwell in his body, and unwell in his mind, without ambition, without energy, and without courage, thoroughly demoralized, fit for nothing."[32]

Pratt linked masturbation directly to religion: "This fornication with self, . . . this adultery with self, is a sin as grave as any of the more direct violations of the Seventh Commandment."[33] The struggle between the spirit and the flesh, of which James Tate II spoke to his students, was directly linked to feelings not just of baseness but of religious guilt.

One other surviving document gives some insight into Dodgson's religious education under James Tate II. Tate's book *First Classical Maps* is a collection of four maps of the Grecian and Roman worlds, simplified for schoolboys. Dodgson owned a copy of the first edition of 1845, acquired at Richmond. In the second edition of 1847, Tate added a "Sacred Chronology," attributing specific dates to major events in the scriptures, starting with the creation (4004 BC) and extending to the destruction to the Temple in Jerusalem (AD 70). From Tate, Charles Lutwidge Dodgson learned what he had almost certainly learned at home—the world was not yet six thousand years old. This belief had recently been challenged by the geologist Charles Lyell and would, in just a few years, be further refuted by the writings of Charles Darwin and others. But, to a schoolboy of 1845, it was as simple and accepted a fact as that two plus two equals four.

On Sunday, 4 August 1844, Charles L. Dodgson attended church for the first time away from his family. He went with the Tate family and wrote that at the morning service he could not hear "one sentence of the sermon" (*Letters* 6). In the afternoon the boys did not go to church, but "Mr. Tate read a discourse on the 5th Commandment." That evening, however, Charles returned to St. Mary's with the Tates and heard the farewell sermon of Rev. J. B. Birt-whistle, incumbent of Trinity Chapel, Richmond. "Papa wished me to tell him the texts I heard preached upon," wrote Charles (*Letters* 6), dutifully recording the evening text as 1 Corinthians 1:23, "We preach Christ crucified."

Birtwhistle used "great plainness of speech" in speaking of the impor-tance of preaching Christ as the only remedy for the universal spiritual sickness of sin.[34] Preaching Christ was "to set forth Christ as he is made known in scripture, as the only foundation of a sinner's hope" (7). Birtwhis-tle enjoined his flock to "be much in private prayer and meditation on God's word—to be diligent in your attendance at the house of God and the table of the Lord" (13). A passage toward the end of the sermon may have held spe-cial power for young Charles Dodgson; Birtwhistle addressed it directly to those "to whom it was my privilege to give instruction previous to the time of confirmation." He reminded these youngsters, only a few years older than Charles, of the solemn vows they had made of their own free will at their confirmation. "Do none hear me who have forgotten their vows and their promises?," he asked (14–15). "Once more I call you to repentance. Go to the footstool of your forgotten God, your despised Saviour, and with broken and contrite hearts confess your sin, and seek his face . . . else your broken vows will rise up in judgement against you and condemn you" (16).

This plainly spoken sermon about the most basic tenet of the Christian faith—that only through Christ can people be saved from their natural state of sin—welcomed Charles L. Dodgson to Richmond.

The statutes and ordinances of Richmond School required that the schoolmaster

diligently Instruct and Inform his Scholars in the Grounds of the Christian Religion, for which purpose We will that upon Saturdays from Tenn a clock in the Forenoons, till the time of leaving School, he shall teach and examine his Scholars in the principles of the Christian Religion, and shall, as much as in him lyes, cause such of them whose parents profess the Religion of the Church of England, to repair to the Church every Sunday, and thereto Attend During all the times of Divine Service, and shall carefully overlook their Carriage and behaviour there, and their Attention to the Instructions Delivered by the Preacher. (Wenham 149)

William Edward Dickson confirmed in his reminiscence about his days at Richmond just before Dodgson's arrival that, "On Sundays we went twice to Church, but not in a body or any kind of procession" (Wenham 172). Dodgson would have often heard the preaching of the rector of St. Mary's, Rev. Scott Surtees. As the schoolhouse stood within St. Mary's churchyard, Tate certainly knew Surtees. Rev. C. Dodgson, Surtees, and James Tate II served on the board of the Ripon Diocesan Church Building Society together at least as early as October 1844. Although the grammar school was not, like the nearby National Schools, under the direct superintendence of the rector, Surtees's ideas about Christian education may reflect, to some extent, what happened in the schoolhouse.

Surtees set out these ideas in his pamphlet *Education for the People:*

> Teach [children] what the bible evidently contains, tell them of a heavenly Father that loves them, of a kind and gentle Saviour who died to save them, of a Holy Spirit given them to put into their hearts good desires and enable them to bring the same to good effect, bring before them the moral precepts of the gospel, and enforce them by the solemn appeal "that they must one day stand before the judgment seat of Christ." Let them learn "that God is about their path and about their bed and spieth out all their secret ways," that their duty as Christians is "to love the Lord their God with all their heart, and their neighbours as themselves." . . . Well for us, if even this foundation is firmly laid, but it cannot be done effectually, without the bible be regularly read and taught by the accustomed master of the School. . . . Religious education ought not to be confined to times and seasons, but the children should have impressed upon them, that there is no time, in School or out of School, on Sundays or on week-days, when they ought not to be guided by its rules, and regulate their conduct by its precepts and directions.[35]

Shortly after Dodgson arrived at Richmond, Surtees preached a series of sermons, begun as instruction for candidates for confirmation, later published as *Sermons for the People.* They were characterized, as one reviewer wrote, by "simplicity and [their] teaching of the grand doctrines of our holy religion."[36] Internal evidence from Sermons I–V indicates they were preached from 22 September to 20 October 1844. Sermon VI follows directly on Sermon V in subject and was likely preached a week later. Later sermons are more difficult to date. It is likely that Charles L. Dodgson heard the first six of these sermons; he may have heard *some* of Sermons VII–XII; many, if not all, of the rest, were preached when he was home for vacation and perhaps even after his departure from Richmond. A look at sermons

I–VI and at some of the topics of the sermons VII–XII serves as a useful window into Dodgson's religious education from the pulpit of St. Mary's.

The first twelve of Surtees's sermons were aimed at candidates for confirmation. They explored the definition of confirmation itself; the baptismal covenant taken on by the confirmand; the sinful nature of man; and the Apostles' Creed, Lord's Prayer, and Ten Commandments. These sermons contain a repeated theme aimed at young people. While man is inherently evil, youngsters have not yet traveled too far down the path of darkness. Satan is particularly interested in seducing young people, and the decisions they make at this point in their lives might determine which of two paths— that of worldliness and sin or that of Christ—they find themselves on in years to come.

"O dedicate yourselves to him now; now whilst the day of life is dawning; now whilst all your faculties are bright and fresh and young," he said in Sermon I. "Wander not from the pasture your good Shepherd has prepared for you! Starvation to your soul, days of misery and nights of sorrow, will be yours ere you are brought back again."[37]

In Sermon II, he warned his young listeners, "The God you have rejected in your youth, may, probably will, reject you in your old age" (21). In Sermon III he painted a picture of two groups of people, one a "knot of young and thoughtless men thinking lightly of religion" who fall into a wide variety of sinful living; the other the "young 'growing in grace as [they] grow in years,'" who go through life "respected by all, and beloved, by the good and pious" (49). And he returned to the theme in Sermon V: "My younger brethren . . . it is you that [Satan] wishes to seduce from your Saviour's ranks, and to enlist . . . in his own;—it is you that need above all, the help of God's Spirit to enable you to resist his wiles" (61).

At the end of Sermon IV, he addressed the "younger brethren" with the "best advice I can give . . . whether in health, or sickness, in youth, or age, in joy, or sorrow, when you stand, or when you fall, in life, and in death,—*look to Jesus!*" (51). Another constant theme in these sermons was that the young listeners were incapable of choosing and keeping to the right path themselves; they could only do so through Christ and the Holy Ghost.

Sermons IV–VII carefully examined the Apostles' Creed. In Sermon IV, Surtees began with a precept he reiterated many times: that the great truths of Christianity "may all be proved from scripture" (38). Echoing Rev. Charles Dodgson, who complained of candidates for confirmation repeating the Creed and catechism by rote without full understanding, Surtees said, "it is not the being able to repeat the words of your belief . . . it is the receiving the truths in *your heart,* and bringing forth the fruits of them in your heart" (39).

Sermon VI was Surtees's one step into what might be considered controversy, for here, in speaking of the "one holy catholic church," he took a veiled swipe at the Oxford Movement, criticizing those who would leave the Church of England for the Roman Church. Surtees defended the separation of the Church of England from Rome with a long list of examples of how Roman Catholics teach things *not* found in the Bible.

James Tate's first report on Charles Lutwidge Dodgson showed a boy doing his best to live the Christian precepts he had been taught almost since birth. "I do not hesitate to express my opinion," wrote Tate, "that he possesses, along with other and excellent natural endowments, a very uncommon share of genius. Gentle and cheerful in his intercourse with others, playful and ready in conversation, he is capable of acquirements and knowledge far beyond his years, while his reason is so clear and so jealous of error, that he will not rest satisfied without a most exact solution of whatever appears to him obscure" (*Life* 25).

Charles excelled in mathematics, though he was sometimes careless in his classical studies. When he left Richmond School on 26 November 1845, Tate wrote again: "Be assured that I shall always feel a peculiar interest in the gentle, intelligent, and well-conducted boy who is now leaving us" (*Life* 26).

C. L. Dodgson was fond of Tate as well. As an adult, he kept in touch with Tate and his family. In August 1855 he walked to Richmond from Croft for a visit, and his diary entry makes clear he had last been in the Tate home two years earlier. Subsequent visits followed over the years, both in Croft and Richmond, and on 23 February 1863, Dodgson wrote in his diary "Heard of the death of my kind old schoolmaster, Mr. Tate of Richmond."

Charles burst through the door of the Croft Rectory into a bevy of sisters welcoming him home. He had enjoyed his time at school with Mr. Tate, but he had missed his family, and he submitted to various kisses and signs of affection with pleasure. Yet, having been gone for the past few months, he felt that something had changed. He was still a part of this loving, Christian family, but he was also somehow now separate from it. He had begun his life away from the bosom of home, the life that would lead him, by the grace of God, to adulthood.

· FOUR ·

Brought Up to Godliness

Charles sat before the fire in his tiny Rugby study, a six-foot-square sanctuary where he read through that day's lesson in Virgil and gloried in his
short time of privacy—no teasing, no fighting, no bowing and scraping to
the Sixth Formers, in short none of the noise and cruelty that too often pervaded the dormitory.[1] He set his Virgil down when he reached the end of
the assigned passage, pulled out a sheet of paper, and dipped his pen in the
inkwell. He had not written home in some time, and his sister had sent him
a long letter of news about life back in Croft. "Dear Elizabeth," he began.

In February 1846, Charles Lutwidge Dodgson began a new stage of his
education, arriving at the highly respected Rugby School in the English
Midlands, nearly two hundred miles from home.[2] For the bulk of the next
four years, he would be far removed from the comforts, protection, and love
of his family. This move was almost certainly the most difficult transition in
his life, but here he would enter the next phase of his religious education;
here he would be exposed to a much wider spectrum of religious thought;
here he would encounter, for the first time in a close and personal way, the
vagaries of an uncertain world, the ever-present threat of death, and the reality of evil. Here, too, Charles Lutwidge Dodgson would, in the eyes of the
church and of the world, become a man.

At the time, Rugby was under the headmastership of Archibald Campbell
Tait, later bishop of London and archbishop of Canterbury. But, to every
educated mind in England, one name was indelibly associated with Rugby
School—Thomas Arnold. "No other schoolmaster has ever occupied so large
a place as Arnold in the attention of England,"[3] wrote Tait's biographer.

Arnold became headmaster of Rugby in 1828, at a time when, as he said,
good men could declare that "public schools are the seats and nurseries of

vice."[4] The system which allowed substantial freedoms for older boys to police and exploit younger boys was widely abused, and, as Arnold's biographer Arthur Penrhyn Stanley wrote, schools suffered from a narrowness of curriculum and "the more undoubted evil of the absence of systematic attempts to give a more directly Christian character to what constituted the education of the sons of the whole English aristocracy."[5]

Into this world stepped the larger-than-life personality of Arnold, who believed "the business of a schoolmaster, no less than that of a parish minister, is the cure of souls" and who made it his chief object to make the school "a place of really Christian education." Arnold believed "every act of a Christian's life was at once secular as done on this earth, and religious as done in the presence of God; and every act was of importance, as affecting the great struggle everywhere and at all times going on between good and evil."[6] This viewpoint would remain at Rugby, and impress itself upon Charles Lutwidge Dodgson, long after Arnold's death.

Arnold ruled over Rugby for fourteen years, a tenure immortalized by one of his students, Thomas Hughes, whose novel *Tom Brown's School Days* is set at Arnold's Rugby. To his job of molding young Christian men he brought a distinctly broad church view,[7] and he strongly opposed the high church movement. Arnold taught his students to think for themselves; rather than imprinting them with his own opinions or doctrine, he helped them to consider evidence carefully and reach their own conclusions. These liberal ideas, in both theology and scholarship, would remain at Rugby during Dodgson's day, carried on by masters who had come to Rugby under Arnold. Arnold introduced the teaching of mathematics, modern history, and modern languages, and most famously used the oldest boys in the school (the Sixth Form, or Praepostors), with whom he had hourly contact, to exert a positive moral authority over the rest.

When Arnold died in 1842, his mythically large shoes were filled by Archibald Campbell Tait, who would be not only headmaster to the teenage Charles Lutwidge Dodgson but also his housemaster—Charles would live, from February 1846 until December 1849, in School House, home to Tait, his family, and some seventy boys ranging in age from nine to seventeen.

Tait was an Oxford man with little sympathy for the Oxford Movement. Born in Scotland in 1811 to Presbyterian parents, he matriculated at Oxford in 1830 and was ordained priest in the Church of England in 1838. A Fellow at Balliol, he was an influential figure at Oxford, but tension arose between him and his many friends who supported the Tractarians. In 1841, that tension erupted with the publication of what proved to be the final number in the *Tracts for the Times* series. In *Tract XC*, John Henry Newman's *Remarks on Certain Passages in the Thirty-Nine Articles*, Newman attempted to show that nothing in the English Articles was inconsistent with Roman Catholicism. Tait published a "Letter to the Editor of the *Tracts for the Times*" condemning the tract and signed by himself and three other Oxford tutors. This letter "lay a match to the tinder which had long been preparing,"[8] and the controversy over *Tract XC* ultimately ended in the bishop of Oxford, Richard Bagot, asking Newman to discontinue the *Tracts*, which he did, and *Tract XC* being censured by the university. Though Tait took no part in the public debate after the issuing of his letter, he was known as one of the four tutors who had brought the *Tracts* to an end.

The following year Tait came to Rugby. In 1843 he wrote to his fiancée, Catharine Spooner, words reminiscent of Arnold's: "Many people think that a schoolmaster's is not a proper profession for a clergyman. My opinion, on the contrary, is that there is no situation of so directly pastoral a nature as mine. How very few clergy have parishioners who are so willing to be led as my boys."[9]

Ironically, his fiancée strongly supported the high church party. Before she met Tait, she had heard that one of the four tutors who had helped bring an end to the *Tracts for the Times* was a candidate for the Rugby headmastership, and she "earnestly hoped he would not be successful."[10] Even after marrying Tait, she remained an outspoken high churchwoman. Thus C. L. Dodgson entered, in 1846, a house in which he would encounter both sympathy for his father's positions in Mrs. Tait, and a broader theology in Dr. Tait.

Tait's biographer collected many reminiscences about Tait's work at Rugby, including one by Arthur Gray Butler. Butler was the same age as Charles Lutwidge Dodgson, though he arrived at Rugby a year and a half earlier. He was at Rugby for the entire four years that Dodgson was there, though consistently in a higher form than Dodgson. For his last five terms he was a Praepostor. Like Dodgson, Butler resided in School House. Like Dodgson, he was the son of a clergyman, and like Dodgson he went on from Rugby to Oxford,[11] where he and C. L. Dodgson knew each other into the 1890s.

Since Dodgson left few memories about Dr. Tait, Butler's are a good guide to what it was like to live and learn in the presence of the headmaster.

The general impression of Dr. Tait made on boys was, in the first place, that of a most dignified and courteous gentleman, with a grave manner, an impressive voice, and an occasional sparkle of deep feeling or quiet humour, which we felt lying in the background, ready either to flash out upon our faults or make allowance for our shortcomings. Everything about him was dignified, kind, and trustful. He left us very much to ourselves, rarely interfering in any house affairs, taking little apparent interest in our sports or pleasures, but yet observant and well acquainted with what was going on, and, when the occasion came, striking in with a master-hand. Yet he rarely punished. It was a favourite joke with us to say that his admonitions, beginning most seriously, ended with a twinkle of the eye and a "Don't let it occur again."[12] . . . He knew exactly where to overlook and where to interfere. . . . No one can have read Arnold's Life without being struck by his deep, perhaps excessive, feeling of the evil incident to school life, and by the part which the Praepostors were called upon to play in the moral government of the School. This . . . was not, however, without its dangers. It produced strained and often hostile relations between the Sixth and the rest of the School, and it reacted in many cases injuriously on the character of these boy-masters, making them self-important and unnatural. This condition of things Tait did much to alter. . . . He regulated the authority of the Sixth, fixing limits to their power of inflicting punishment, and giving right of appeal to any lower boy who felt himself aggrieved.[13]

. . . Again I think he had something of the same object before him both in his pulpit teaching and in school lessons. More than once he protested in his sermons against introducing boys prematurely to political and religious controversies; and in School, whenever questions of a speculative character forced themselves upon his notice, he would endeavour to lead us to more practical considerations by throwing the burden of proof on impugners of received opinions. . . .

His teachings, sermons, [and] government, [were] all good and sensible, but somewhat cold and repressive; of a kind rather to create respect and confidence than affection and admiration. . . . In ordinary times there was little in [his sermons] either to arouse or stimulate. But on touching occasions, such as the death of a boy or master, he gave rein to his feelings, and moved us as deeply as he was himself moved.[14]

Why did Rev. Charles Dodgson choose to send his oldest son to Rugby? The simplest reason was geography—of the nine ancient boarding schools for boys opened to all willing to pay the fees, Rugby was closest. While it wasn't absolutely essential to attend one of these schools to gain entrance to Oxford, they represented the most promising road to university. Dodgson's friend and patron Bishop Charles Thomas Longley had sent his son Henry to Rugby the previous term.[15] It is not unlikely that Rev. C. Dodgson would have looked to Longley for advice on his son's education, especially as Longley had served as headmaster of Harrow School from 1829 to 1836.

Probably the chief factor in deciding on Rugby was the reputation with which Arnold had endowed the school, and chief among the improvements Arnold had made, in the mind of Dodgson, must have been his emphasis on forming Christian men and providing a solid religious education. Other schools had, by 1846, followed Rugby's lead, but nonetheless Rugby, as the first, had the greatest reputation in this area. As for Rev. C. Dodgson's own school, Westminster, it had been in a steady decline since the early part of the century. While Rugby had grown from four hundred students at the time of Arnold's death to five hundred by the mid-1840s, Westminster's enrollment had reached a low of just ninety at the same time.

Rugby had two terms (known as "half-years") each year, one beginning in February and lasting until mid- to late June, the other beginning in late August and ending in mid-December. Dodgson arrived in February 1846 into a world different from any he had ever known. From the villages of Daresbury and Croft and the small market town of Richmond he now arrived in a bustling town recently connected to London by railway. From a house of 16 boys and a school of 120, he now moved into a house of 70 boys and a school of 500.

His father sent Charles to Rugby to be shaped into a Christian man. But, especially as a new boy in the first half of 1846, Charles was often distracted from this goal by the frequent hazing of younger students. Rugby pranks were less lighthearted than those at Richmond, and, in the cruelty visited on younger boys by older, Dodgson got, perhaps, his first glimpses of what he considered true evil. Dodgson reflected briefly on the bullying he experienced at Rugby in his diary on 18 March 1857, after a visit to the boys' school Radley College in Oxfordshire:

The dormitory is the most unique feature of the whole, in two long rooms, by a very trifling expense in wood-work, every boy has a snug little bedroom secured to himself, where he is free from interruption and annoyance. This to the little boys must be a very great addition to their happiness, as being a kind of counterbalance to any bullying they may suffer during the day. From my own experience of school life at Rugby I can say that if I could have been thus secure from annoyance at night, the hardships of the daily life would have been comparative trifles to bear.

Though Dodgson never gave any specifics about the "interruption and annoyance" he suffered at night in the Rugby dormitories, it clearly tainted his memory of school life. After the comparative innocence of life at Daresbury, Croft, and Richmond, he was now witness to the evil he had so often read about in moral tales and religious writings. Dr. Arnold himself had bemoaned, "the evil of boy-nature."[16] One example of nocturnal bullying is given in a diary written by one of Charles's contemporaries at Rugby, John Lang Bickersteth, who entered the school just six months after Dodgson and was in the same form. On 31 August 1846, Bickersteth wrote: "Several boys came in, and made me show my colours and principles, for which I was well teased. After prayers, went to bed, and shortly after, some boys came in and put a dog upon me, which I pushed off: they repeated this several times, teasing and questioning me; but at last they went. Oh God! Have mercy upon me; confound their machinations, and turn their hearts."[17]

Collingwood writes of freezing nights in the Rugby dormitories for "small boys, whose beds in winter were denuded of blankets that the bigger ones might not feel cold" (*Life* 30). That Charles Dodgson, like John Bickersteth, turned to prayer when afflicted by such cruelties seems likely. Later in life, writing to the mother of a boy, Dodgson said, "The habit of prayer will be the best of all safe-guards for him as he gets into the world and comes to know the sin around him" (*Letters* 448).

And what of those "hardships of daily life?" *The Three Friends,* a book of reminiscences of Rugby thinly veiled as fiction, by Arthur Butler, contains an example of such difficulties as Dodgson, who at times suffered from a hesitation of speech, may have endured. While the master has his nose buried in a book, one of the boys takes a stuffed bird off a shelf and begins to pass it round the class.

> Then, in an evil moment, some one giggled, and the crime was out. The crow was in the hands of one Stammers. "Three hundred lines, Stammers,"[18] said the master. . . .
> "Please, sir, I started it," said Fleming. . . .
> "Then you do the lines! Or, stay. Why did you (to Stammers) not return the bird to the place it came from?"

"Pl-pl-pl-ea-ea-ea, please, sir," said the unfortunate Stammers, blushing horribly. "I-I-I only p-p-p-assed it on."

"That will do, Stammers! Any one can see that you had a hand in it. You do the lines also!"[19]

Stammers becomes a member of the Eleven (the highest-ranking cricket team in the school), and Dodgson was never a cricketer; however, the character could easily have been an amalgam of Rugby boys, including Dodgson. Clearly such a boy would have made an easy target for teasing.

In his later years at school Dodgson was not afraid to stand up against the "evil of boy-nature." "He was famous as a champion of the weak and small, while every bully had good reason to fear him. . . . [He] knew well how to use his fists in defense of a righteous cause" (*Life* 23).

In thus standing up in the face of evil, Dodgson heeded the call of his headmaster, who said, in a sermon in August 1848: "Many are come here to-day for the first time. You will remember how it is the duty of each of you who have experience to endeavour to assist these to what is right; certainly giving them no encouragement to what is wrong; nay, not even looking on in silence if you see them in danger of being misled."[20]

And, as Arthur Butler noted, when Tait "heard of any boy or boys contending against school evils, he would take occasion to thank them earnestly and kindly."[21] At Rugby, Charles was, probably for the first time, exposed to a wide variety of evils and misfortunes, from petty theft and burglary to injury, illness, and death. In December 1847, one of the servants of assistant master Bonamy Price was arrested for overseeing "an extensive system of robbery" that resulted in losses for many students.[22] This was one of several such burglaries during Dodgson's tenure. His second term at Rugby was delayed by two weeks due to outbreaks of cholera and typhus, and serious illness affected both Charles and Headmaster Tait during the former's Rugby years. In October 1847, a wall that was part of the new library construction collapsed, seriously injuring one of the workers. And events in the wider world, from the revolutions of 1848 to famine in Ireland and Scotland, were fodder for sermons and lectures at Rugby. Dodgson's religious growth at Rugby must be seen against the backdrop not just of the evil he witnessed in the dormitories but also in the context of his beginning to experience the dangers and uncertainties of the wider world.

John Lang Bickersteth provides an account of daily life at Rugby in the year of Dodgson's arrival:

On Monday morning, the servant comes into the room, and rouses us with the cry of "A quarter-past six!" and then we are expected to get up. At ten minutes to seven, the servant rings the house bell, which tells us it is time to go down to the Great School; and at the same time the bell of the Great School begins to summon us, and continues till the clock strikes seven, and then immediately the door is shut, and no one allowed to come in; then the master whose turn it is, reads prayers, whilst Dr. Tait acts as clerk, and says "Amen" at the end of each. . . . The boys then walk up and down in the cloisters, learning their lessons, until their several masters go into their respective rooms; for each form is heard in a separate room, by one particular master. The lesson usually lasts till eight, a.m., when we are numbered, and then go home for breakfast. We then learn second lesson, which is usually some construing lesson—either Virgil, Cicero, or Homer. At a quarter-past ten we go down to second lesson, and generally finish by half-past eleven; at a quarter to twelve we generally write, and at half past one have dinner. From that time till four we have to learn the third lesson, which is also generally a construing lesson. . . . We generally finish our third lesson by five; and at half-past five we go into the fourth lesson, which is generally a continuation of the third, and only lasts till six, from which time we are at liberty till half-past seven.[23]

Dodgson's academic progress through Rugby is detailed in the school lists, published at the end of each half-term and listing all the boys in the school, ranked in their class divisions according to their achievements—the number of "Marks" they received each half-year. In a letter to her sister (dated 25 June [1847]) Dodgson's mother wrote, "they have marks for *every*thing they do in their daily work and at the end of the Half they are added up."[24] Dodgson entered the school in the Lower Fifth Form, which, in the first half-year of 1846, was split into two divisions "of equal rank in the school."[25] In this first term, Dodgson ranked forty-second out of fifty students in his division. His form master for his first half-year was Rev. Charles Mayor, a young man who had studied at Rugby under Thomas Arnold and had come to the school as an assistant master under Arnold in 1840. In addition to the master in charge of their particular form, each Rugby boy was assigned a tutor, who remained in that position throughout the boy's time at the school. Dodgson's tutor was Rev. George Edward Lynch Cotton. Cotton, who had come to Rugby under Dr. Arnold in 1837, may also have taught Dodgson mathematics—he awarded Dodgson the Lower Mathematics Prize in December 1848 and June 1849.

His second half-year showed a marked improvement in Dodgson's class rank. Under form masters Rev. Charles Thomas Arnold (no relation to the former headmaster) and Rev. Richard Congreve, Dodgson finished forty-fifth out of 103 in a combined Lower Fifth Form. Arnold was another master who had been both a Rugby student and an assistant master under Thomas Arnold. Richard Congreve, who had also been at Rugby as a student under Dr. Arnold, arrived at Rugby as a master in 1844, after Tait had become headmaster. Congreve may also have taught mathematics, as he awarded Dodgson the Lower Mathematics Prize in December 1847 and June 1848. In the first half-year of 1847, Dodgson, now again in a split Lower Fifth and studying again under Charles Thomas Arnold, finished second out of fifty-three students in his division.

In August 1847, Dodgson entered the Middle Fifth Form, Lower Division, and studied under Rev. Henry James Buckoll, who had come to Rugby as a student in 1818 and as an assistant master in 1826, before the arrival of Dr. Arnold two years later. Dodgson ranked seventeenth out of fifty-seven in his form that term, and was one of the winners of the Lower Mathematics Prize, presented by Richard Congreve.

The year 1848 saw Dodgson's promotion to the Upper Division of the Middle Fifth Form, where he would study for two terms under Charles Alleyne Anstey, a member of the Rugby old guard. Anstey had entered Rugby as a student in 1811 and arrived as an assistant master in 1819, serving under Dr. Arnold for his entire headmastership. Dodgson's first term under Anstey saw him finish at the bottom of the class list due to absences (probably due to illness). Nonetheless he again received the Lower Mathematics Prize from Congreve. The following half-year, ending in December 1848, Dodgson had rebounded to the top spot among the forty-one students in the Upper Division of the Middle Fifth. This term, George Edward Lynch Cotton awarded Dodgson the Lower Mathematics Prize. Cotton would be Dodgson's form master for the first half of 1849, when Dodgson finished twenty-first out of thirty-eight in the Fifth Form and again received the Lower Mathematics Prize from Cotton.

In his final half-year, Dodgson was a member of "The Twenty," the division of the school directly below the Praepostors. His form master was Bonamy Price, who would go on to be a professor of political economy at Oxford and whom Dodgson would occasionally see socially in later years. Price had come to Rugby as an assistant master under Dr. Arnold in 1830. Dodgson finished the half-year thirteenth of twenty and was awarded the

Divinity Prize by Cotton. Dodgson's academic performance, then, was solid. While not consistently at the top of his class, he performed reasonably well, distinguished himself in mathematics, and showed an aptitude for divinity.

While his headmaster, who preached most Sundays in the chapel, and George Edward Lynch Cotton, examined in the next chapter, were the masters who most strongly influenced Dodgson's religious development at Rugby, one cannot ignore the influence of the form masters under whom Dodgson studied. These men had two important things in common. All were ordained clergymen in the Church of England, and all had come under the influence of Dr. Thomas Arnold.

Not all of Dodgson's instruction came from his form masters. Rugby also had masters who specialized in particular areas. Of these, only one who was not also his form master can we confirm as having instructed Dodgson— Rev. Robert Bickersteth Mayor, who arrived in Rugby as a mathematical master in 1844. Dodgson wrote, in a letter home to his sister Elizabeth, that few men were as clever at mathematics as Mayor, "Papa excepted" (*Life* 28). In 1848, Mayor wrote to Charles's father, "I have not had a more promising boy at his age since I came to Rugby" (*Life* 29).

Rugby boys said prayers twice daily, usually together with the members of the school or of their house. Arnold introduced the practice of nightly prayers and scripture reading at School House, a tradition Tait may have continued.

This rhythm of daily prayer, which Charles had learned in his Daresbury days, was at least partly codified in a book which remained in Dodgson's possession at the time of his death: *Short Prayers and Other Helps to Devotion, for the Use of the Scholars of Rugby School* by Rugby master George Edward Lynch Cotton. Given the "annoyances" of the Rugby dormitories, Charles must have felt a certain irony in offering up the "Prayer for Morning," which began, "Lord and heavenly Father, by whose great mercy I have spent this night in peace."[26] In addition to prayers for morning and evening, the book includes a selection of scripture verses as "Helps to Self-Recollection, and to the Application of the Scriptures to Daily Life," and prayers for two dozen specific occasions, from holy days like Christmas and Easter to events in the life of a schoolboy, such as holidays and examinations. There is a prayer for times of sickness and another "to be used during a slight illness." There are prayers for before and after "self-examination" and Communion. There are prayers that Charles might have turned to regularly, such as a "Prayer before Daily Work," and others which he may have spoken rarely, including "Prayer after the Occurrence of a Death in the School" and "Prayer after Some Particular and Grievous Sin."

The centrality not just of religion but of the Church of England to life at Rugby is illustrated by an event that occurred in December 1848, when three Rugby boys were caught attending mass at a Roman Catholic chapel in town. Tait had prohibited such attendance, and the boys were punished, but in spite of their promise not to return to the chapel, two of the boys did so and were immediately dismissed from the school. In writing to the press about the incident, a Rugby parent said: "The public may safely repose the utmost confidence in the zeal, discretion, and Christian earnestness of the present head master. The admirable scripture training of the boys is one of the distinguishing features of the school; and the high Protestant character of the Institution is in no danger of suffering in his hands."[27]

The Rugby boys received lessons on scripture, but perhaps the most powerful lessons came from the pulpit of the school chapel, where Dr. Tait or one of the other masters preached each Sunday. Tait often tied his sermons to some event that had taken place at the school or in the wider world, further linking the religious development of Charles to those dark parts of life he experienced, often for the first time, at Rugby.

In the first sermon Dodgson heard at Rugby, on 8 February 1846, Tait welcomed the new students with these words:

> There is almost no place in the world where a consistent Christian life, a determined resolution to walk always as knowing that God has his eye upon us may do more real good than here. Those of you who hold any higher station . . . may be the means of leading many away from sin. . . .
>
> There is no boy in any place in the School who chooses thus to live in prayer with the thought of Christ's continual presence who however he may be scoffed at for a time . . . will not soon gain an influence even over those who scoff at him.[28]

Dodgson may have learned his sometime practice of self-examination at the beginning and end of a term (seen in his diary prayers) while at Rugby, for at the beginning and end of each half-year Tait often made encouragements on this topic. On 22 August 1847, speaking at the beginning of the second half-year, he said, "True that the beginning of a half-year is the time for hope—all past failures may be supposed to be forgotten: we come with new resolutions, with God's blessing we will endeavour to do our best. . . .

But this very circumstance ought thus to bring our responsibilities at this time more distinctly before us, thus make us feel them more."[29]

In addition to his sermons, Tait gave Sunday-evening addresses in School Hall (whether these were for the entire student body or just for the members of School House is not clear. Dodgson would have heard them in either case). These addresses Tait often repeated, and in some cases Dodgson heard the same address two or three times. In a standard address for the end of term, which Dodgson heard three times, Tait again dwelled on self-examination.

"It is well for you now to be looking back at the many weeks which have elapsed since you last left home. And each one of you will do well to ask himself whether he is better or worse than he was then. . . . Your bodies have been changing and with the change of your bodies your minds have been changing also. . . . And besides the change of feeling which is incident to your time of life, you have changed also in your position relative to others in our Society. . . . Have you used the new influence which larger circumstance here amongst us gives you for advancing by your example what is right?"[30]

Tait also often returned to the theme of evil. "It was the great object of Christ's coming with the word," he said in a sermon of 15 March 1846, "to drive the evil Spirits forth."[31] And on 21 February 1847, he said: "The Devil is no metaphor. . . . He is busy here in the midst of us. He helps to close the heart, to make the conscience hard; and often leads some to do wicked acts."[32] Tait exhorted his boys in a sermon of 15 February 1846 to seek God's help in "resisting the beginnings of evil lest that which seems at first sight of no consequence or but an allowable . . . indulgence, . . . before he is aware of it hurry him to destruction."[33] And in an address in School Hall repeated twice during Dodgson's Rugby years, Tait echoed the words of Rev. Scott Surtees in Richmond: "There is no lesson more necessary to learn than this, that we must resist the beginnings of evil. Every man . . . [looks] back on his past years . . . when his further fate seemed hanging in the balance and the inclination to the one side of the other was to decide whether he should live and die an upright servant of Christ or a sensualist."[34]

On 31 August 1846, the day after the beginning of the new term which had been delayed by outbreaks of typhus and cholera, the school community was shaken by the death of one of the masters, Charles Mayor, at the age of thirty-one. Charles Mayor had been Dodgson's form master the previous year, so the death must have come as a shocking blow. Before the day had ended, the Rugby boys knew the details of Mayor's death: "A little before his death, his father came into the room, upon which Mr. [Mayor], in his delirium, called out, 'Christ is the Rock!' which, though uttered in delirium, showed that his mind must have previously been fixed on Christ."[35]

Although his father had presided over hundreds of burials at Daresbury, the Dodgson household had been spared the specter of death; Charles had probably never been in such personal proximity to death before, and the tragedy must surely have affected him deeply, as it did all of the closely knit community. A funeral service was held in the school chapel on Thursday, 3 September, and the following Sunday, Dr. Tait rose to the pulpit to address his shaken student body. He was "at times too much overcome with emotion to speak."[36] "The consolatory proof," he said, "when death comes, of our being of the number of those blessed who have died in the Lord and entered into their rest, must be found in our having laboured, by the Spirit's help, as Christ's servants while life and strength lasted" (Tait, *Lessons* 197).

While Tait did not state that good works in and of themselves paved the way to salvation, he did emphasize the importance of having done good works as a sign to oneself that one is saved. In encouraging his students to prepare for a death that may come at any time and to be ready to face that death without fear, he said:

> We ought to pray that we may fully know how terrible a power death is, though we pray to know also how much more powerful is our Saviour. . . .
> If we have, each ourselves to pass alone through a very awful struggle, in which no human friend can aid us, and in which all our past life and all the prospects that lie before us will be seen by the dying eye at last in their true colours, it is well that we should accustom ourselves to realize the thought of this solemn moment in our quiet solitary musings long before. . . . Let us pray that we may have so lived as to feel safe in the arms of the Lord our Saviour. (197–202)

Finally, Tait spoke of Mayor's own Christian life, especially at Rugby: "There are some here present who must remember, not without emotion, how he knelt by their beds to pray for them in the hour of danger" (206). When Charles Lutwidge Dodgson's death ultimately came, he would face it in a way consistent with Dr. Tait's words on that sad day in 1846.

Nor was this the only time death visited Rugby in that autumn of 1846, when Charles was fourteen years old. Just a week after Tait's sermon on the death of Mayor, John Lang Bickersteth wrote, "Dr. Tait preached a sermon, in which he alluded to a school-boy who had just died at home, and gave him a high Christian character."[37] On 17 November, Charles Donald Napier, a student just a year older than Charles, died at school.

The following January, before he could return to school from the Christmas holidays, Dodgson's contemporary John Lang Bickersteth died, and then, on 11 September 1847, as a new school term was beginning, came the death of the thirty-six-year-old composition master for the Sixth Form, George John Kennedy. Kennedy died on a Saturday, and the next day Tait stood in the pulpit before the student body for another solemn lesson on death and, after only three sentences, spoke words that are stunning in the direct link they provide between C. L. Dodgson's teenage faith and his later literary works.

"What is life?" said Tait. "Is it all a dream?" (*Lessons* [209]). In his congregation sat a fifteen-year-old boy who would grow up to write the two most famous dream narratives in English literature. He would close his acrostic poem at the end of *Through the Looking-Glass* with the line "Life, what is it but a dream?" His novel *Sylvie and Bruno*, while not strictly a dream narrative, would explore states of being similar to dreaming and their relationship to waking life. In his 1876 *Easter Greeting*, he would compare the passage from earthly life to life everlasting to waking from a dream.

In his sermon, Tait explored the question of whether life was as evanescent and as meaningless as a dream when compared to the reality of death. "Does the one moment of death make utter havoc of a whole life's attainments?," asked Tait. And he went on to enumerate what is lost at death—all wealth and possessions, the abilities of the body from "the tuneful voice" to the "robust and active frame" (210). But what of "the admired qualities of the mind?" Can "exquisite taste" or "stores of knowledge" or "wit or humour" outlive the moment of death? "In one view the answer is obvious. These things cannot survive of themselves. . . . What shall we say then of all the time and pains which have been spent in seeking them? Surely man walketh in a vain shadow; and disquieteth himself in vain.[38] Not so. . . . all qualities, whether of mind or body . . . may be . . . used to God's glory. . . . they may furnish also the appointed sphere of usefulness in which it is our duty, i.e. in which it is God's will, that we should move" (210–12).

Here Tait echoes Rev. C. Dodgson's first published sermon, in which he encouraged his listeners to contribute to the common good with their talents. But Tait adds another layer to the exhortation. In using one's ability for the glory of God, one is moving those talents from the realm of the worldly to the realm of the spiritual, from the realm of the mortal to the realm of the immortal. "We know," said Tait, "that if by God's grace a soul has become devout—earnest—humble—simple-minded—full of sympathy with goodness: it can never lose the qualities to all eternity" (216).

Here C. L. Dodgson was given a set of instructions for cheating the death that seemed to surround him at Rugby. And they were instructions that resonated with the boy and his incipient talents. "It is a mistake to suppose that nothing has a religious or spiritual effect upon the mind but such occupations as are in themselves directly spiritual. There is no quality which God has given, however earthly it may seem, which may not thus have been used in his service" (212–13).

So Dodgson would discover—if he had a talent for telling nonsense stories, and those stories brought smiles to the face of children, God had been glorified; if he had a talent for photography, and his pictures communicated to others the beauty of creation, God had been glorified. If he could teach others to think logically and that logic helped them to a better understanding of theological arguments, God had certainly been glorified.

Our concern, said Tait, is "to ascertain, simply, whether we are employed as God wills" (215). Dodgson would question at several times during his life whether he was "employed as God wills." This would happen especially as he considered the question of whether to be ordained into the priesthood in the 1860s. Tait had given Charles much to ponder, but as he left the chapel that day, mourning the loss of a second schoolmaster in just over a year, Tait's words spoken at the beginning of the sermon must have stayed with him: "What is life? Is it all a dream?"[39]

It was not just local tragedy that now began to impinge itself upon Charles's life. At Rugby he also became acutely aware of national and even international tragedies and tribulations and of how these events connected to his religious life.

On Wednesday, 24 March 1847, Queen Victoria declared a national day of fasting and humiliation due to the famines then raging in Scotland and Ireland.[40] The proclamation by the queen shows the close link in her mind between tragedy and religion, punishment and sin—a link that suffused English society at the time. "Providentialism," one scholar has noted, "was all but universal."[41] The fast was held, wrote Victoria, "so that both we and our people may humble ourselves before Almighty God, in order to obtain pardon of our sins, and may, in the most devout and solemn manner, send up our prayers and supplication to the Divine Majesty, for the removal of those heavy judgments which our manifold sins and provocations have most justly deserved."[42]

The fast was observed at Rugby and prefaced by a sermon by Tait the preceding Sunday in which he expounded on the idea of sin as introduced into the national discourse by the monarch. Taking as his text Cain's words, "Am I my brother's keeper," Tait argued that all sin is connected to others: "How much evil might be saved among us here, if each one remembered that he cannot sin alone: that in one sense, whether we wish it or no, we are each of us our brother's keeper" (*Lessons* 122–23).

Charles Dodgson had grown up in Daresbury as a member of a family and an extended household. In Richmond he had become a member of a larger, yet still intimate community. Now, a member of the five-hundred-person student body of Rugby, he began to understand he was a member, too, of a larger society—a society in which sin pervaded, and in which, he was taught, the sins of all were intertwined with the fates of all. Personal sin was not just a harm to Charles L. Dodgson, the sinner, but to others known and unknown. In *Sylvie and Bruno Concluded* (1893), the narrator says: "The sufferings of horses . . . are chiefly caused by Man's cruelty. So that is merely one of the many instances of Sin causing suffering to others than the Sinner himself" (297). In the same book Arthur Forester echoes the providentialism Dodgson encountered at Rugby: "Still, medicine, disease, pain, sorrow, sin—I fear they're all linked together. Banish sin, and you banish them all!" (257).

The best preparation against sin, argued Tait, was self-knowledge, so he set aside the day of the fast at Rugby as a time for a "faithful examination into the causes of our own weaknesses." And in sending his boys on their way to such self-examination, Tait echoed the words of his monarch, saying "the sins of nations are, of course, but the accumulation of the sins of individuals" (*Lessons* 127).

This same spirit of providentialism and need for repentance returned when Tait preached to his boys on 28 September 1849, a day appointed by the bishop of Worcester as a "day of prayer and humiliation" in light of the ongoing epidemic of cholera. "Every malady," said Tait, "speaks of the necessity for humiliation and repentance: for all suffering we believe to have been, in its first origin, the consequence and penalty of sin. . . . We do well, then, to take this day as a time for humiliation, for serious examination of our lives" (*Lessons* 163–65).

Tait also spoke, on this occasion, of the reasons to be thankful for suffering—that it turns the mind to serious religious thought and strengthens faith. "A storm at sea exalts the heart to trust in God, while it teaches that there are a thousand dangers in which man cannot help us" (168).

One line of Tait's sermon may have particularly resounded for young Charles, for it is directly connected to one of the key issues he addressed in his adult religious life. "None but fools, or the very wicked" said Tait, "can make a jest of death" (164). In later life, Dodgson would frequently speak out against the dangers of jesting on serious subjects.

While cholera did not strike Rugby in 1849, illness was very much a part of Charles's experience there. The start of the second half-year in August 1846 was delayed by two weeks "in consequence of the cholera and typhus fever prevailing in the place."[43] In a sermon on Christ as a physical and spiritual healer delivered when school began on 30 August, Headmaster Tait said: "Sickness prevailing throughout a country generally, from which it is vain to fly from place to place, reminds us very forcibly that we are in God's hands." He went on to exhort his charges, in purely Christian terms, to hygienic habits in "matters of bodily health"; to prayer, both public and private, for the relief of others; and to "remember still more the spiritual than the corporeal part of Christ's power as our physician" (*Lessons* 190–92).

In another sermon on illness at the end of the first half-year of 1848 (25 June), Tait spoke of what message the boys should take from nearby outbreaks of disease: "God has spoken to us in a low calm voice of warning during the whole half-year. The question which we ought to ask ourselves tonight is whether we have listened to His voice. And now that you may answer this question consider of what it is God wanted to warn you."[44]

At Rugby Charles suffered from both whooping cough and mumps, though the dates of both illnesses are uncertain. In a letter dated 11 November (no year), his mother, Frances Jane, wrote to her sister Lucy: "With regard to dearest Charlie I *hoped* to have heard from him again today, but I have not. In his letter received on Tuesday he says the mumps had gone but that they had left him very much more deaf than usual." And, in a letter to her sister dated 24 March (no year): "*You* will I am sure be as much surprised as *we* are to hear that dearest Charlie *really has* got the Hooping cough, after having been so proof against the complaint during the whole of his last summer holiday, constantly nursing and playing with the little ones who had it so *decidedly*."

The illness seems to have substantially interfered with Charles's routine, as his mother wrote on 5 July: "I think I may say now that dearest Charlie's Hooping cough has quite gone. He rarely coughs and never hoops, so that he began last Sunday to go to church as usual."[45] Likely this illness took place in the spring and early summer of 1848, as in that term Dodgson, now in the Upper Division of the Middle Fifth Form, finished last in his class with the notation in the school list that he had been absent.

So, it is quite possible that for three months, Charles attended neither the chapel at Rugby nor the church at Croft. What sort of divine ministry did he receive during his times of illness? During any time he was confined to the sickroom at Rugby, that ministry was undertaken by the headmaster's wife, Catharine Tait. "The boys in the sick-room were her especial care," wrote her husband.[46]

Catharine was "worshipped by the boys, the chivalrous, romantic admiration of her youth and beauty being joined to their grateful sense of her kindliness, and her manifold acts of sympathy and affection, rendered to them when they were in sickness, or in any way needed her watchful care. . . . I can see her now, her hand full of instructive or amusing books, wherewith to beguile the lonely hours of the boys in the infirmary. She constantly visited them, read and prayed with them" (228–31).

Into Charles L. Dodgson's sickroom came the ray of sunlight that was Catharine Tait, and in her he may well have found a sympathetic ally, for, unlike her husband and the masters who had worked under Arnold, Catharine Tait was very much aligned with Charles's father when it came to church matters. Might the two have discussed the Tractarians or the high church movement, which the woman so strongly supported?

Prayer was absolutely central to Catharine's life; it was her "continual habit" (230), that she shared with the boys in the infirmary. If Dodgson spent any length of time there, Catharine might well have influenced his prayer life. Her husband, writing of recovery from his own illness, wrote that Catharine was "ready to pray with me and to repeat helpful texts and hymns" (26).

"She knew almost every Psalm by heart; her mind was stored with the old hymns she had learned in childhood, and passages of Cowper which had been her father's delight; she knew every part of 'The Christian Year,' and loved to repeat it, and choice passages from Wordsworth, Trench, and Tennyson, she always had ready, to give us food for thought" (24).

Visits with Catharine Tait in the infirmary undoubtedly formed a part of Charles Dodgson's religious development at Rugby. In his library he had many of the same thought-provoking authors that she quoted, particularly Tennyson, Wordsworth, and John Keble's book of verse *The Christian Year*. He took comfort in hearing the words of "old hymns" when in great illness—and on his deathbed he requested exactly that. Whether these comforts and intellectual stimuli had their genesis in visits from Mrs. Tait in the Rugby infirmary is not known; certainly if illness kept him from corporate worship, it did not keep him from prayer, scripture, and the private ministry of one who showed love and tenderness to all the boys in her husband's charge.

Illness was nothing unusual at Rugby, but in February 1848 came a shock to the entire community, as their young headmaster (he was then thirty-six) was struck down by rheumatic fever and lay on his deathbed. On Ash Wednesday, 8 March, the students were told that death could come at any moment. The headmaster dictated a farewell letter to the Sixth Form as well as a letter to the boys of School House. "He begged us," wrote Arthur Gray Butler, "as a dying man to think seriously of the great issues of our school life, and never to go to bed at night without reading some portion of our Bibles. . . . Not only then, but for a long time after, there was an unwonted silence after evening prayers in the long schoolhouse passages as singly, or by twos or threes, we read our Bibles."[47]

Against all odds, Tait turned back from death's door, and by Easter was enough recovered to receive "the Holy Communion amid the bright band of youthful worshippers in the dear Rugby chapel" (Benham, *Catherine and Crauford Tait* 26).

Tait did not resume his full duties as headmaster until the following half-year, when in August 1848, on the first Sunday of the half-year, he stood once more in the pulpit of Rugby chapel, to deliver the first sermon since his recovery. While it was, in some ways, a typical "beginning of term" sermon, it was more somber than most. "The very fact that so many months have passed since I last spoke to you from this place," said Tait, "and the cause of this long silence, may remind us how uncertain life is" (Tait, *Lessons* 230).

Tait preached on how Christ was knocking at the door of each boy's heart and of the importance of answering that call, of not putting off "the business of to-day till to-morrow, [lest they] find that there is no morrow remaining" (234). In Tait's words we find foreshadowing of many of C. L. Dodgson's private prayers, recorded in his diaries, in which, especially on occasions such as the end of a year or the beginning of a term, he bewailed his past sinfulness and hoped for a newer, holier life.

"Now we begin a new course," said Tait, "and a new course must be begun, with new resolutions. There ought not to be one of you . . . who does not come here to-day with a deep sense that in all his past time there is much to deplore: countless opportunities of good wasted which will never return. And if we are thus to think of sins past, it is that we may resolve better for the future: and how can resolutions be sustained unless we are full of hope?" (226–27).

"Certainly, judging by usual experience," he said, "if this half-year is to be like others which have gone before it, it must have sickness, and even death, in store for some of us who are now rejoicing in vigour" (231). To Charles and others who had lived through the deaths of masters and schoolmates, and the near-deadly illness of Tait himself, the warning to open the door to Christ sooner rather than later was backed with the weight of experience.

Charles Lutwidge Dodgson may not, as he wrote in his diary, have looked back on his time at Rugby "with any sensations of pleasure" (*Life* 30),[48] but he performed well in his studies, especially mathematics. He was one of the winners of the Lower Mathematics Prize (awarded to three students each half-year) for four half-years in a row. Nor were the prizes reported in the school lists the only ones he won. In an 1847 letter to her sister, Charles's mother notes that at the end of the first half-year of 1847 he came home with "two handsome Prize Books! one gained last Christmas, *Arnold's Modern History*— the other *Thierry's Norman Conquest* just *now* gained for having been the best in Composition (Latin & English Verse & Prose) in his Form during the Half."[49] In October 1849, Charles wrote to his sister Elizabeth, "in reply to your question, I do get a prize, value one guinea. I have chosen for it Butler's Analogy in 2 vols. . . . As to the other prize, I am not yet decided" (*Letters* 7). One of these prizes was the Divinity Prize, for which he chose the two-volume set of the works of Joseph Butler. So, in the eight half-years Dodgson attended Rugby, he won prizes in at least seven, and those prizes totaled no fewer than eight, including at least four in math, one in composition, and one in divinity. The prizes outside divinity and mathematics are not recorded in the school lists, and were likely form prizes, such as his 1847 composition prize, rather than school-wide prizes. Lest there be any doubt that Charles had fully embraced the religious education available to him at Rugby, in December 1849 Dr. Tait wrote to the boy's father, "his examination for the Divinity prize was one of the most creditable exhibitions I have ever seen" (*Life* 29).

There has been some confusion about when Dodgson left Rugby, caused by Collingwood's comment that Dr. Tait "was headmaster during the whole of the time Charles was at Rugby, except during the last year, during which Dr. Goulburn held that office" (*Life* 26). Rev. Edward Meyrick Goulburn did not take over the headmastership from Tait until the spring of 1850, but the school lists make it clear that the second half-year of 1849 was Dodgson's final half-term. Even Dodgson himself misremembered his Rugby departure, writing in his diary for 1855, as quoted by Collingwood, of his "three years" at Rugby (*Life* 30). The school lists make clear that he was there for eight half-years (February 1846–December 1849). He matriculated at Oxford on 23 May 1850, and in the months before that examination must have studied at home in Croft.

Rev. Charles Dodgson did not send his next two sons, Wilfred and Skeffington, to Rugby. Neither attended a public school, though both did eventually follow their brother to Christ Church (Wilfred became a land agent and Skeffington a parochial priest). The youngest son, Edwin, did attend Rugby, and his eldest brother, Charles, came up to the school in April 1860 to help his fourteen-year-old brother get moved in. It was the only time Charles recorded revisiting his school.

In Headmaster Tait's letter to Rev. Charles Dodgson of December 1849 he wrote of Charles the son, "I fully coincide with Mr. Cotton's estimate both of his abilities and upright conduct" (*Life* 29). Cotton had been Dodgson's tutor throughout his years at Rugby, had been his Fifth Form master, and had awarded him two mathematics prizes and the divinity prize.

In the last sermon Dodgson heard Tait preach at Rugby, the headmaster returned to the theme of self-examination, with particular reference to a topic Dodgson had first learned about from his father, the proper use of the Sabbath.

> Are we more alive than we were a short time ago to the great value of our own and of one another's souls? Are we endeavouring all we can with God's aid to help those around us to live more seriously? Do we feel more than we did before how great a responsibility attaches to all our privileges and means of influencing each other? . . . There remains a Sabbath rest for the people of God, and the Christian Sunday is but a type of that rest and a preparation for it. Are our Sundays spent with the general seriousness which will make them with God's blessing a real help in our religious progress?[50]

Charles sat again in his study. He was older now, and more a protector of those who were teased than a victim of teasing himself, but he still enjoyed the quiet solitude this tiny retreat provided him. He had been reading from the scriptures, as he did every evening, and now turned to the book of prayers and devotions that Mr. Cotton had written for the boys. He opened to the evening prayer and read aloud—though by now he could have recited the words from memory:

O Almighty God, I thank Thee that Thou hast added to my life another day, and thereby given me a fresh opportunity of turning heartily to Thee, and of devoting to Thy glory the talents which Thou hast entrusted to me. But I confess to Thee, O Father, with shame, that I have not used this opportunity as I should have done, but have sinned against Thee in thought, word, and deed.

And here, where the words in the book exhorted him to "confess the sins of the day," Charles did his best to enumerate his faults. He had not worked as hard as he might have, he had wasted time in taking a walk and reading a chapter of a novel. He had given short shrift to his scripture reading.

My only hope is in Thy mercy, and in the merits of our Lord and Saviour, Jesus Christ. Grant to me, for His sake, Thy Holy Spirit, to cleanse the thoughts of my heart by His holy inspiration, to assure me of Thy forgiving love, and to give me both the power and the will to love Thee in return.

And, forasmuch as Thou hast made the night for man to rest in, grant that the sleep which I now hope to enjoy maybe consecrated, to Thy service, by refreshing my wearied body, and enabling me to do Thy will more faithfully when I wake. Help me now also to call to mind the sleep of death, which must one day come upon me; and give me Thy grace so to follow Christ in life, that I may also pass with him through death to His glorious resurrection. Grant that my sins may be so done away in me now by the blood of Christ, and by the power of His Spirit, that, from this my mortal body, there may hereafter rise a glorious body, fitted to dwell for ever with Thee, Father, through Him who died to save us. Thy most dear and blessed Son, Jesus Christ our Lord. Amen[51]

· FIVE ·

Come to Years of Discretion

Charles knelt at the altar rail of Rugby Chapel. The bishop's hands pressed on his head, and he did his best to concentrate on the importance of the moment. His baptismal vows were now his own, and the hands that lay upon him were connected to a chain of hands laid upon heads that reached all the way back to the Apostles. He truly felt connected to the church historical, as well as to an inner faith that had grown and deepened during his time at Rugby—tempered by the realities of sickness, death, and suffering. The bishop spoke the now familiar words: "Defend, O Lord, this thy child Charles Lutwidge with thy heavenly grace, that he may continue thine for ever; and daily increase in thy holy Spirit more and more, until he come unto thy everlasting kingdom, Amen."

The Book of Common Prayer describes confirmation as the rite in which "children, being now come to the years of discretion, and having learned what their Godfathers and Godmothers promised for them in Baptism, they may themselves, with their own mouth and consent, openly before the Church, ratify and confirm the same." Charles Lutwidge Dodgson's confirmation almost certainly took place on Tuesday, 1 June 1847, in the chapel at Rugby School.

Rev. Charles Dodgson, the father, had a strong interest in confirmation; at least as early as 1839, he published his *A Plain Catechism, Intended Chiefly for the Instruction of Young Persons before Confirmation.* Oddly, only a single copy (of the twelfth edition) of this pamphlet appears to have survived, though it was advertised as late as 1867 and had reached a twenty-fifth edition by 1856.[1] An 1856 review in the *Literary Churchman* called the piece "in many ways a useful tract, [that] should only be given to candidates who have sufficient time to look out the numerous texts quoted."[2] Dodgson understood this, and in 1841 published *Confirmation: An Appendix to A Plain Catechism,* a collection of the "numerous [biblical] texts quoted."

The Book of Common Prayer requires candidates for confirmation to be able to "say the Creed, the Lord's Prayer, and the Ten Commandments; and can also answer to such other Questions, as in the short Catechism are contained." But Rev. C. Dodgson did not think this was enough. In his *Controversy of Faith,* he wrote of the sad state of confirmations in the eighteenth century, using a hypothetical parishioner as his "hero":

> At the age of fourteen, his parents took him to a neighbouring town to be confirmed. The Curate of the Parish called at the house the day before; and telling him that he supposed he could say his catechism, presented him at the same time with a ticket for confirmation.
>
> The church was intolerably crowded; and he was unable to see or hear much that was going on. At one part of the Service, he thought he heard the words "I do" from a few young persons near the Bishop. At length the ceremony was over, and he was glad to escape. . . .
>
> [Later, when he became a priest] at the time of Confirmation, he was always considered in the Parish rather strict with the young persons; for his rule was to give no one a ticket who could not repeat the Creed, the Lord's Prayer, and the Ten Commandments; and many of the parents told him that in *their* time there was not so much trouble about being confirmed.[3]

This lax practice was part of what Dodgson called the "the alarming state of degeneracy and decay" in the eighteenth-century church. In 1841 he listed the "increasing veneration for . . . the holy rite of confirmation" as one of the remedies for that decay.[4]

Judging from Dodgson's *Plain Catechism,* he required his parishioners to learn more than the Creed, Lord's Prayer, Ten Commandments, and catechism before receiving their ticket to confirmation. That catechism in the Book of Common Prayer consists of twenty-four questions and occupies about three pages. Dodgson's twenty-page *Plain Catechism* consists of 121 questions in eight sections, concerning Confirmation, God the Father, God the Son, God the Holy Ghost, the Ten Commandments, Prayer and more particularly the Lord's Prayer, and the Sacraments.

Each section consists of a series of questions and answers, with scriptural references at the end of each answer. At the end of most sections is a paragraph headed "Application," consisting largely of inward-looking questions to be asked by the prospective confirmand. A typical example is the "Application" paragraph at the end of the section on the Holy Ghost:

> Let me look into my own heart and consider what it is by nature—Is it not full of sinful thoughts and desires? Have I any power of myself to cast away these thoughts? Is it not then a great mercy that God has given me His Holy Spirit, to cleanse my heart from sin, to lead me in the way of righteousness, and to strengthen me against the temptation of the devil?—But am I striving to follow this Holy Spirit, or do I resist and rebel against Him? Is my heart growing better, or is it growing worse? If I continue to rebel against the Spirit, God will take it from me, and leave me without His help; and then how dreadful will be the danger of my soul![5]

The twenty-eight religious subjects the Dodgson children studied may have been a rough draft for Dodgson's *Plain Catechism*. Of the seventy-nine scriptural citations used to support these subjects, thirty-three appear in *Plain Catechism;* those quotes are drawn from twenty-one of the twenty-eight subjects. There is a major overlap between the subjects on the Dodgson children's cards and those covered in *Plain Catechism*. Probably published when he was seven, *A Plain Catechism* may have been the next step in Charles Lutwidge Dodgson's religious education.

Rev. C. Dodgson wrote that the confirmand must "*confirm* . . . the promises . . . made for me at my Baptism," and that those promises are, "That I should believe all the Bible teaches, that I should obey God's commandments, to resist the temptations of the Devil, and to keep myself from wicked works, words, and thoughts" (3).

As he prepared for his own confirmation, C. L. Dodgson likely recalled his father's words in the "Application" paragraph of this "Confirmation" section of *Plain Catechism:* "How am *I* prepared for confirmation? Have I thought seriously about it? I am going to make a solemn promise to God; God will hear my promise; he will know the thoughts of my heart, when I make it. Do I understand what the promise is? Do I sincerely desire to *keep* it? Let me consider what a serious thing I am going to do, and wicked I should be if I were to do it without thought or preparation!" (4).

In every section of *Plain Catechism,* Rev. Charles Dodgson expanded on what the prayer book requires of confirmands. In "Concerning God the Son," for instance, he asked questions not only on the life, death, and resurrection of Christ, but on the theological details of redemption, leading to questions such as "What is repentance?" and "What is faith?" Dodgson assumed that his readers had already learned the prayer book catechism; his *Plain Catechism* was intended to augment, not replace, that catechism. In his section on the Ten Commandments, for instance, he asked twenty questions (compared to three in the prayer book), often spending several on a single commandment.

Dodgson cited scripture from the New Testament that offered a Christian interpretation and context for the Hebrew laws. His answer to "What may you learn from the sixth Commandment?" (Thou do no murder),[6] is: "To hurt nobody by word or deed, nor to give way to angry passions, and to bear no hatred or ill-will against any of my fellow creatures" (11), and his scripture citations included Matthew 5:21, 22: "Ye have heard that it was said by them of old time, Thou shalt not kill . . . But I say unto you, That whosoever is angry with his brother without a cause shall be in danger of the judgment."

While the questions on baptism in *Plain Catechism* were less pointed than those Dodgson posed as examining chaplain, the scripture verses he cited clearly point toward the high church view of baptism: that regeneration, justification, and sanctification all take place at infant baptism. Of the eleven scripture passages Dodgson cites in his 1850 *Controversy of Faith* in making the case for the high church view of baptism, five are also cited in *Plain Catechism*.

At the end of *Plain Catechism,* Dodgson added "A Prayer to be used by a young person":

O Lord, who hast promised to give thy Holy Spirit to them that ask thee, grant to me, I beseech thee, the help and comfort of that Holy Spirit, that I may be defended against the temptations of the Devil, and preserved from evil thoughts, words, and works. Teach me, by the same Spirit, to know and to confess my own unworthiness, to repent truly of my sins, and to seek pardon and salvation through Christ who died to save me. Teach me to love and obey thy Holy Word; make me day by day a better Christian while I continue in this world, and finally receive me into thine everlasting kingdom in Heaven, for the sake of Jesus Christ thy Son our Saviour. Amen. (20)

In 1842, while still incumbent at Daresbury, Dodgson defended Bishop Longley's practice vis-à-vis confirmation. An article published in the *Dublin Review* accused Longley of dispensing with the individual laying on of hands, due to the great numbers of confirmands. As Longley's chaplain,

Dodgson wrote a response to this charge, explaining that it was only the individual repetition of the bishop's words at confirmation which sheer numbers had necessitated dispensing with, not the laying on of hands.[7]

At least four times during his oldest son's childhood, Dodgson hosted a confirmation at his own church: Daresbury parish records show expenditures for "Ringers on Confirmation Day" in October 1832, May 1839, and May 1842.[8] Young Charles would certainly have been old enough to remember the latter two occasions. On Monday, 21 October 1844, Bishop Longley confirmed 167 children at St. Peter's, Croft, but it is unlikely Charles Lutwidge Dodgson was among them. Even if he did return from school in Richmond for the special occasion, he was only twelve, and the usual age of confirmation was fourteen or fifteen. Charles may have attended Bishop Longley's confirmation service the following day at the parish church in Richmond. Some of his schoolmates were among the confirmands, and he had probably heard the confirmation sermons of Rev. Scott Surtees in Richmond Church that led up to the occasion. Charles, however, was almost certainly confirmed by Henry Pepys, bishop of Worcester, in the chapel of Rugby School on 1 June 1847.

Thomas Arnold instituted the practice of holding confirmation for Rugby boys in the school chapel and arranged for confirmation at Rugby every two years: "The boys were prepared by himself and the other masters in their different boarding-houses, who each brought up their own division of pupils in succession to the communion table on the day of the ceremony."[9]

In his "Address before Confirmation," Arnold speaks of confirmation as a tool against the evils then inherent in the public schools:

> If you strive . . . to walk by the light of the Spirit, you will be bold and decided in thinking for yourselves, and in doing what you yourselves approve, without caring for the opinion of your companions. And as the public opinion among boys, as well as men, is swayed by the influence of decided characters, so two or three individuals, steadily and quietly acting as they think right, will in a short time be like a leaven, to leaven the whole mass.[10]

For most Rugby boys, confirmation was also the doorway to the Communion table; generally, only those who had been confirmed partook of the sacrament at Eucharistic services in the school chapel. There may have been exceptions, as seen in an episode from *Tom Brown's School Days* in which

Tom's friend, East, confesses that he has not been confirmed, not wanting to do so, as he felt some boys did, merely to get ahead at the school. Tom takes East to "The Doctor," who gives the boy permission to take Communion and comes up with a plan for him to be confirmed soon. The episode not only gives a sense of the relation between confirmation and Holy Communion at Rugby, but it also indicates that not all students approached confirmation as a holy religious rite; some participated only to curry favor.

Although no records of Charles Lutwidge Dodgson's confirmation survive, there are several reasons to deduce he was confirmed at Rugby on 1 June 1847. First was his age. From his father's writings we know that the age of fourteen was common in the eighteenth century (his hypothetical confirmand in *Controversy of Faith* was fourteen); from the book of instruction for Rugby boys preparing for confirmation we know that in the 1840s at that institution, the age was fifteen or sixteen. Charles Lutwidge Dodgson was still at school in Richmond when confirmation took place at Rugby on 15 May 1845, and "the chapel was crowded in every part, and the reverent demeanour and attention of the boys . . . was most striking,"[11] but two years later, as a fifteen-year-old student at Rugby, he would have been the perfect age for confirmation.

While the records of Henry Pepys, bishop of the Diocese of Worcester in which Rugby lay, do not record a confirmation at that time, we know from the evidence of Archibald Campbell Tait's manuscript sermons and addresses that either Pepys or some other bishop held a confirmation in the Rugby School chapel on 1 June 1847. Headmaster Tait delivered an "Address to the Candidates for Confirmation" on 31 May 1847 in which he stated, "It is no exaggeration to say that tomorrow you are to take a more important step than [in] any of your past lives."[12] And, on 6 June 1847, his address titled "First Sunday after Confirmation" included the words, "Two hundred of you within the last week deliberately set your hands to the plough [and were] . . . confirmed last Tuesday."[13]

Between 25 April and 16 May 1847, Headmaster Tait preached four sermons on confirmation from the pulpit of the Rugby School chapel. He published these sermons to "circulate among the candidates" for confirmation.[14] The book apparently survives in only two copies, both at the Lambeth Palace Library. Its rarity and its Rugby imprint point to its being circulated *only* among that year's candidates for confirmation. At the time of his death, Charles Lutwidge Dodgson had a copy of this book in his library—a copy bearing not only his autograph but also his markings throughout. He also owned a copy of George Cotton's *Instructions in the Doctrine and Practice of Christianity, Intended Chiefly as an Introduction to Confirmation,* a book written by a Rugby master and used to prepare Rugby students for confirmation. Dodgson's copy was marked inside the front cover, "Dodgson, Sch. House," indicating he owned it while at Rugby.

All this points to the conclusion that Dodgson was confirmed in the Rugby chapel with roughly two hundred of his schoolmates on 1 June 1847. His preparation for that confirmation consisted of more than just listening to sermons by the headmaster and reviewing his father's *Plain Catechism.* While the house heads were not solely responsible for the preparation of the confirmands, they certainly participated in the process. In his *Religious Teachings,* Henry Highton, then assistant master at Rugby and a house head, included two addresses on confirmation which he had delivered exclusively to the boys of his house.[15] But a significant part of preparation for confirmation came at the hands of George Edward Lynch Cotton.

Cotton was master of the Fifth Form during Dodgson's Rugby years, having come to Rugby as an assistant master in 1836, when Thomas Arnold was still headmaster. He served as Dodgson's tutor throughout his years at Rugby. Headmaster Tait dedicated his book of sermons preached at Rugby to Cotton, noting in the introduction, "much aid received from him . . . especially by his ministrations in the school chapel" (*Lessons* [iii]). In defending Rugby against a charge of lax religious teaching in 1849, Tait wrote, "If you really wish to know whether the charge you have made against the School is unfounded, I beg to refer you to such books as I have distinctly recommended in the School, *e.g.* to Mr. Cotton's admirable book of *Prayers and other Helps to Devotion,* or to his short work on Confirmation."[16] Dodgson owned copies of both these books and kept them until his death. In a scrapbook he kept as an adult, Dodgson pasted a picture of Cotton, clipped from his obituary.[17] It was Cotton who, through his book and through personal instruction, prepared many Rugby boys for their confirmations and in this context likely worked with Dodgson.

Cotton was born in 1813, in Chester. Educated at Westminster School and at Trinity College, Cambridge, he was a member of the evangelical party that dominated that university at the time. In 1836 Thomas Arnold appointed him as an assistant master at Rugby. In the memoir of Cotton's life, his wife, Sophia, writes, "It is not too much to say that there was none of all the direct pupils of Dr. Arnold on whom so deep and exclusive a mark of their master's mind was produced as on Cotton."[18]

It is easy, in reading the account written by Arthur Penrhyn Stanley of Cotton's personality during his Rugby days, to see how Charles L. Dodgson might have been attracted to the master, for there were strong similarities between the two men, though they were separated by nearly twenty years.

> His keen and boyish sense of life's mirthful side never left him. He was often the most amusing and laughter-moving of companions. There was a natural and quiet flow of genial humour that overran and freshened, like a mountain spring, the dry places and arid relations, the numbing cares and anxieties, of scholastic life. But with all this he was never frivolous or self-indulgent: the vein of ceaseless humour which played beneath an exterior somewhat grim and saturnine was combined with an intensity and earnestness of religious life which formed the chief feature in his character. The pastoral relation in which a clergyman should stand to his pupils was never out of his sight. To deepen and quicken the Christian side of public school life was the deliberate purpose of his life.[19]

Cotton pursued this purpose not only through the writing and publishing of two books which became standard texts in public schools for generations of students and taking charge of preparing Rugby boys for confirmation, but also by giving religious addresses to the members of his house on Sunday evenings and preaching on occasion in the school chapel. In all of these capacities he would frequently have dispensed advice to the boys, and we can see him, in a fictionalized guise, doing exactly that in the pages of Thomas Hughes's *Tom Brown's School Days*, where he appears as the "young master":

> You are mixing up two very different things in your head, I think, Brown . . . and you ought to get clear about them. You talk of "working to get your living," and "doing some real good in the world," in the same breath. Now you may be getting a very good living in a profession, and yet doing no good at all in the world, but quite the contrary, at the same time. Keep the latter before you as your one object, and you will be right, whether you make a living or not.[20]

In his book intended to prepare students for confirmation, Cotton was quick to point out, in language similar to that used by Rev. C. Dodgson in discussing the role of examining chaplain, that "a book can rarely make such an impression on the heart as is produced by the teaching of a true Christian friend; and it is impossible in a treatise like this to give explanations of the different minute points which suggest difficulties to different persons, and for which the help of a teacher whom they can freely question is quite necessary."[21]

For Charles Lutwidge Dodgson, both Cotton and Tait served as this teacher. Both men, unlike Charles's high church father, stood near the evangelical end of the doctrinal spectrum, and while Tait felt school boys should not dwell upon sectarian divides, Charles cannot have helped noticing some differences between the views of his teachers and those of his father, especially during those private discussions of "different minute points."

The two texts which give the best insight into Charles's preparation for confirmation are Tait's *Four Sermons Connected with Confirmation* and Cotton's *Instructions in the Doctrine and Practice of Christianity*. While religious instruction, prayer, preaching, and worship were constants at Rugby, the specific process of preparation for confirmation took about six to seven weeks.[22] During those weeks in April and May 1847, Charles studied Cotton's text and first heard, and then read, Tait's sermons.

Cotton describes his book as "[beginning] with a short explanation of Confirmation itself, which is followed by a series of chapters on the different heads treated of in the Church Catechism; and the whole concludes with a very short sketch of the grounds on which Christianity claims to be considered as divine revelation, intended to lead the student to trains of thought which are developed in larger treatises" (*Instructions* vi).

Those heads, which were also treated by Rev. Charles Dodgson in his *Plain Catechism,* are the baptismal vows (including the Creed and the Ten Commandments), prayer (including the Lord's Prayer), and the sacraments of baptism and Communion. To each of his chapters (three on baptismal vows) Cotton appends a prayer or prayers, and a series of questions for review. Cotton makes a point in his introduction to state that his book was "fitted for young persons of the educated classes. . . . Books on the subject of Confirmation have generally been written by parochial clergymen, and are therefore in their style and manner chiefly adapted to the minds of those with whom such clergymen have most intercourse, the children of the poor" [v].

Cotton's book covers the same basic information as Rev. Charles Dodgson's *Plain Catechism,* but it goes into greater depth and, in some cases, adapts its material specifically for the public school audience. There is no doubt Cotton was attuned to this audience—what we now call adolescent boys. In reviewing the baptismal promises made to "repent of and renounce three classes of sins; those suggested by the World, the Flesh and the Devil" (21), Cotton took the opportunity to warn against sins especially prevalent among school boys—swearing, lying, idleness, succumbing to peer pressure, and sins of the flesh, in which he included "the indulgence of impure thoughts" (24). In discussing the Ten Commandments, he listed six "obstacles to their keeping God's Commandments" to which the young are especially prone: "selfishness, vanity and the love of applause, carelessness, weakness, faults of temper, and the desire to indulge bodily appetites" (57).

On the subject of prayer, Cotton, before offering his own parsing of the Lord's Prayer, wrote that "when a person who is anxious to observe the vow made for him in his Baptism, begins to put his good intentions into practice, he soon finds that he is weak and helpless, and will therefore be desirous to seek for aid elsewhere, that is, he will betake himself to prayer" (67).

A life of prayer, wrote Cotton, means doing more than "express[ing] to [God] our wants merely in the evening and the morning." Christians should "make it a rule, in the course of our daily work, to consecrate some few minutes to God, and pray for His help" (69–70). He offered instruction for how to pray, making a distinction between prayers for temporal blessings and those for "improvements in holiness and Christian feeling" (76). In the first case, he wrote, "We shall never pray for a temporal blessing without the reservation, 'if Thou, O Father, seest that it is good for me to have it'" (72). Then, "He will either grant us what we ask, or give us grace and strength to bear His refusal" (74).

> But when we turn from petitions for temporal blessings, to prayers for improvement in holiness and Christian feeling, we find ourselves at once in the midst of those gifts which Christ died and rose again to procure for us, and for which, therefore, we may ask, with the fullest confidence that God will grant us what we ask. Here we must remember that two things are necessary for the accomplishment of our prayers: perseverance and watchfulness. . . . Hence with our prayers should be combined a strict self-examination, that so we may trace the commission of open and flagrant sins to the existence of some hidden evil in our characters, against which it is especially needful to watch and pray. . . . Neither must we forget that with all our prayers for ourselves, supplications for others also must be united. (76–80)

On the question of whether prayer should be codified—read word-for-word from a prayer book—or should flow spontaneously, Cotton wrote that the Lord's Prayer was "intended by our Lord to be used in the actual words in which it occurs in Scripture, yet his chief design in giving it was to provide us with a kind of fountain of prayer, from which we may draw copious supplies for longer and more particular devotions" (81).

And elsewhere he wrote, of one of his own chapter-ending prayers, "a form has been provided; but it will be better for him to adopt it rather as a guide and model for his devotions, than as furnishing the exact words in which he ought to pray" (13). In Charles L. Dodgson's adult prayer life, he used words modeled on printed prayers but adapted to his own particular use.[23]

On the subject of baptism, Cotton's teachings varied from those Charles may have received from his father. While Cotton did not explicitly challenge the high church view of baptism, he never used the words "sanctification" or "justification," never explicitly stated that grace is received by all at baptism, and never mentioned regeneration. Baptism, Cotton wrote, changes one's state but not one's nature: "This can only mean that we are admitted to the privileges and blessings of Christianity, not that we are made holy" (100). Cotton sums up his thoughts on baptism with a warning that points toward a *via media* between the high church and evangelical positions: "First a caution as to the danger of unduly valuing it, but imagining that Baptism in itself will communicate holiness to us; secondly, a warning against the error of depreciating it into a mere ceremony to which no special blessings are attached" (108).

"Admission to Communion," wrote Cotton, "is the only outward result of our Confirmation" (117), and in his discussion of Communion is an implicit dismissal of doctrinal views held by the elder Charles Dodgson, who rejected the idea that Christ's words in instituting Communion, "This is my Body," etc. "imply a *merely* metaphorical comparison. . . . I hold . . . that the words are *not* literal, but figurative: but that, *besides and beyond the figure,* they contain a *mystery* also: and it is the adoption of the figure, *to the exclusion of the mystery,* which constitutes the view which I condemned."[24]

Cotton did not directly attack the view that the elements of Communion are more than a figurative representation of the Body and Blood of Christ, but when discussing the words of Christ in John 6:54 ("Whoso eateth my flesh, and drinketh my blood, hath eternal life"), he wrote, "It must be plain to any one who reads this chapter, and compares it with other parts of our Lord's teaching, that his words here are figurative, and intended to express by the strongest possible metaphor, the necessity that our souls should depend upon Him for sustenance" (Cotton, *Instructions* 108).

As in the case of baptism, Cotton offered a definition of Communion that left room for interpretation, writing that, for communicants, eating Christ's Body and drinking His Blood is "becoming imbued with the divine principles of life and holiness, and the strength to conquer sin, which they would receive from communion with him. *To eat His Flesh* seems especially to refer to a heartfelt appreciation of the blessings of His Incarnation: *to drink His Blood* is to realize the benefit, derived from the shedding of that Blood on the Cross" (111).

Cotton warned that "we deny that the Communion is of any benefit to us whatever, or Christ's Body and Blood in any sense received by us, unless we go to that Sacrament in earnest faith" (112–13), but he also pointed out that if we wait until we are in a sinless state to approach the Communion table, we will never do so. He also emphasized the way in which Communion can build community—especially within the walls of a school. As to the long-term benefits of regular Communion, Cotton was explicit: coming to Communion in true faith and repentance, and in a true sense of community, will make communicants feel "gradually that it is more and more impossible for them to sin" (117).

Cotton admitted that his final chapter, "Reasons for Believing," dealt with its topic in only the most perfunctory way, but briefly he made the case for the truth of Christianity. He showed how Christianity supplies the individual's need to answer the question, "How shall I, unclean and polluted as I am, approach a pure God, of whose existence and holiness my reason convinces me?" (128–29) and that both the history of the religion and the internal and external evidence of the truth of its scriptures provide a strong argument for its acceptance. In the course of his argument, Cotton wrote of how Christ came into the world because it had fallen into an appalling state of immorality. In making this point, he provided his schoolboy readers a possible reason for their study of classical writings: "Let him take for example the writing of Horace, as a specimen of the thoughts and feelings of an educated Roman who lived just before the coming of our Lord. The unblushing profligacy, the gross selfishness, the utter indifference to anything really lofty and virtuous which distinguishes his Satires and Epistles, are the characteristics, not of him only, but of the whole spirit and feeling of the time" (128).

In summarizing this chapter, Cotton returned his emphasis to the individual, writing: "But the real proof that Christianity is true, is not intellectual, but moral. The great, the convincing evidence, which must abide with us in every difficulty and doubt, suggested to our understanding, is the evidence of Christ's Spirit, influencing and purifying our hearts. [The Christian] sees no difficulty half so great, as the belief that God should have left His creatures in utter wickedness, without any adequate means of knowing His will, because that is repugnant to those two ideas of love and justice, which form an essential part of his conception of God" (148–49).

Love and justice undoubtedly formed an essential, even *the* essential, part of Charles Lutwidge Dodgson's conception of God. And when he encountered difficulties, as he would, he returned to these two pillars. "In the Gospel it is revealed to us that God's essential attribute is love" (36), wrote Cotton, a belief Dodgson clung to for the rest of his life.

Cotton finished his book with a list of steps to be taken by those confirmands who "feel desirous to avail themselves of the opportunity which that ordinance affords them, of leading lives more distinctly and avowedly religious than they have yet done" (155). His steps towards a holier life were:

1. Praying privately.
2. Setting apart Sunday for "the increase of our religious knowledge and elevation of our religious feelings."
3. Reading religious books.
4. Befriending those who are "anxious to lead a holy life."
5. "Setting apart special times for examining the state of the heart."
6. Giving money for the relief of the poor.
7. Having "some kind and friendly intercourse with the poor."
8. Endeavoring through Communion with God and serious thought to "discipline and guide" their minds to believe that "we are placed on earth for higher objects than our own gratification." (155–59)

Throughout his life Dodgson would make an effort in almost all of these areas to approach closer to what he saw as the ideal Christian life.

On four consecutive Sundays in April and May 1847, at services in the Rugby School chapel, Headmaster Tait preached directly to the candidates for confirmation. The sermons were titled "Confirmation," "Baptism," "Baptismal Vow," and "The Eucharist."

Tait defined confirmation as "a solemn act of prayer and of blessing, preceded by an earnest declaration on the part of the young that they fully understand now the responsibilities which devolve onto them as baptized Christians, and that by God's help they will labour to live up to them" (*Four Sermons,* 11–12).

Tait warned of the dangers of delaying confirmation, saying, "A boy may say, I will not be Confirmed yet; I will take my pleasure a little longer in the thoughtlessness of childhood; but he cannot stop his body's growth, and neither can he stop his soul's: for good or for evil it is growing daily. . . . If God shall say, 'Thou fool, this night thy soul shall be required of thee,'[25] will it be the better or the worse, think you, that you have put off solemn rites . . . to a more convenient season?" (12–13).

The deaths of schoolmates in the previous year must have made this thought, of suddenly being called upon to meet one's maker, very real to any Rugby boy who heard this sermon. The citation from Luke, combined with the allusion to Acts 24:25 ("When I have a convenient season I will call for thee") maintained meaning for Charles Lutwidge Dodgson throughout his life. In his preface to his 1889 novel *Sylvie and Bruno,* he wrote a passage paraphrasing this sermon on confirmation he heard more than forty years earlier: "A man may fix his own time for admitting serious thought, for attending public worship, for prayer, for reading the Bible: all such matters he can defer to that 'convenient season', which is so apt never to occur at all; but he cannot defer, for one single moment, the necessity of attending to a message, which may come before he has finished reading this page, 'this night shall thy soul be required of thee.' "[26]

Tait's second warning to the confirmands of Rugby was that they not regard confirmation "as a matter of course" (*Four Sermons* 13).

The question which the Lord Jesus Christ on the Confirmation day will ask each of you, must be, how is it with your hearts? Have you really examined them with great thoughtfulness? Have you really prayed for strength where you find yourselves to be weak and yielding? Are your tempers and your ordinary habits in your daily life more regulated on Christian principles? Have you really made new resolutions, and by God's help begun to act on them? Is your childish knowledge of Christ, and of the things of Christ, daily expanding to a more thoughtful acquaintance with Him? And do you take the means to make it thus grow daily, by really praying, by reading your bible earnestly, by great attention and many efforts to be serious in the house of God? If you do not make these efforts by God's help, your Confirmation will be a vain ceremonial. (13–14)

"We cannot . . . understand our Confirmation rightly," said Tait, "without some definite conception of the nature of our Baptism" (18). Tait implicitly argued against the high church doctrine of baptismal regeneration, writing, "It is not true that any mysterious change of nature has been wrought on the soul of the unconscious infant by Baptism" (18). "Our Baptism is not an isolated act," he wrote, "but an admission to the Church. Its effects were not intended to be the blessing of a moment, acting with miraculous power and then ceasing, but gradually operative through our whole lives" (22).

Tait encouraged prospective confirmands to think on their baptism, which he acknowledged was a "much disputed subject" (23):[27] "I do not see how you can think of any purpose of your Baptism, without considering what the privileges are to which it has introduced you" (23). And he ended his sermon on baptism by reminding the boys of the "thousands of baptized infants . . . who are never taught to pray—for whom the weekly return of the Lord's day brings no holy association; who scarcely ever hear the name of Christ, except when it is blasphemed. . . . And as we think of their case, we shall understand better the blessedness of our own" (25–26).

Tait's third confirmation sermon was on "The Baptismal Vow," which he saw "as a statement of the requirements of a Christian's life. Viewed in its threefold aspect, first, as a struggle with the evil spirit, with the ways and customs and bad examples of evil men, and with our own evil desires; secondly, as a faithful acceptance from the heart of all that Christ teaches us; and thirdly, as a quiet course of obedience to Christ's holy law" (28).

Living such a life, said Tait, requires "the grace of God's Holy Spirit" (28): "The one thing above all others of which the Confirmed are concerned to make sure is, that they have practically and really entered on a true Christian life. . . . Think of this, all of you, who are preparing for Confirmation. The real preparation must be that which is carried on in secret and by yourselves. . . . No one acts wisely whose Confirmation passes without his having made some marked change in his mode of living" (30–31).

Tait's dissection of the threefold life of the Christian—rejecting sin, believing and accepting the teachings of Christ, and living a holy life—illustrates much about life at Rugby and the life which Tait hoped awaited the prospective confirmands. On the rejection of sin, he wrote:

If the world about us . . . adopts low maxims . . . if it teaches, e.g. that indolence and idleness are no sins—that you may spend the Sunday here like any other day, following your ordinary pursuits, except while you are in Church, or restrained by other outward regulations—reading the commonest books of worldly interest, or giving up the whole Sunday evening to unprofitable senseless talk—if it teaches, e.g. that there is no harm in wasting your time daily, and debasing your minds, by poring over those low books, published from the lowest press, to suit the tastes of the lowest minds. . . .—if it would

hold up those who are more conscientious than their fellows to ridicule . . .—
if it would teach that there is no harm in wasting money, which might be used
in God's service, on selfish indulgence, or in contracting debts against your
parents' wish . . . you are no real Christian if you do not steadily use all your
influence to introduce a better state of things. (33–34)

On the topic of belief, Tait warned his students against common forms of
unbelief—from excessive dogmatism, "holding . . . as articles of faith, what
Christ never taught" (35), to "universal doubt . . . [a] dangerous temptation
for enquiring minds" (36). But these "unbeliefs," said Tait, are more likely to
come later in life. To his schoolboy charges he said, "This is your great trial of
unbelief—to have a full conviction of the reality and importance of the amusements or business in which you are here engaged, but not to look beyond
these to your great work as Christ's redeemed, and to the soul's purest pleasures—to know and feel that you have a body, and allow in words that you have
a soul, but never fully grasp the thought that the soul is your real selves" (37).

Finally, Tait addressed briefly the need for a life of holiness—"the word
has its real fulfillment only in the life of Christ. . . . May we learn daily more
clearly to understand how great a thing it is to be a Christian" (38).

Tait's final confirmation sermon was on the subject of "The Eucharist,"
since "the Lord's Supper is the natural sequel of your Confirmation" (43).
He called the Eucharist "the outward sign of a heavenly influence which is
communicated to the faithful soul. . . . Those who approach [Christ] in this
rite faithfully, will receive rich supplies of that grace which His body broken
and His blood shed did produce. . . . These are rich blessings, amounting
to nothing less at last than the soul's becoming completely holy, completely
fitted to enjoy the society of the Father and of Christ in heaven" (40–41).

By the time of this sermon on 16 May 1847, the preparation for confirmation had been underway at Rugby for five weeks, and Tait was earnest in
the warning he laid before the candidates: "If there be any here, who seek
to be Confirmed and to receive the Lord's Supper and yet deliberately to
live in sin, I warn them in God's name not to rush upon destruction . . . it
is better not to have put on the mockery of holy professions, than to receive
the symbols of Christ's most holy body and blood with unclean hands" (43).

Those who were "sincere in [their] desire to become earnest Christians,"
Tait urged to take Communion "frequently, and never to turn away when an
opportunity offers" (43, 45). Nor, said Tait, should the state of mind necessary for Holy Communion be one which is reached only on those occasions.

"The requisites which the Catechism mentions—sorrow for sin and stead-fast purpose of amendment, a lively faith in God's mercy through Christ, a thankful remembrance of His death, and charity—these if they be in the mind at all must be habitual" (46).

Like Cotton, Tait leaned away from high church teachings and focused particularly on the needs of the boys of Rugby School. Tait laid emphasis, too, on the need to make a true change in one's life at the time of confirmation: "Whatever has been your habit of praying and reading the bible hitherto, see that for the future you secure more time for such exercises of devotion" (31).

Charles Lutwidge Dodgson walked from the altar rail of Rugby School chapel back to the pews where he sat with the rest of the boys in his house. He had now taken on for himself the vows that his Aunt Lucy and his god-fathers had taken at the time of his baptism. Then, they had renounced "the devil and all his works" and had affirmed a belief in the words of the Creed. Now that renunciation and that belief belonged to him alone. The weeks of preparation with Mr. Cotton and Mr. Tait had led to this. Charles slipped back into the pew, a confirmed Christian.

SIX

This Thy Table

Charles Lutwidge Dodgson knelt again at the altar rail of the Rugby Chapel. He had confessed his sins, and Dr. Tait had pronounced his absolution. Now, Charles held his hands in front of him, palms up, his right hand resting on his left. He felt the dry wafer pressed into his hand, and he raised it to his lips. As he ate, he heard, for the first time addressed to him, the words: "The Body of our Lord Jesus Christ, which was given for thee, preserve thy body and soul unto everlasting life. Take and eat this in remembrance that Christ died for thee, and feed on him in thy heart by faith with thanksgiving." A moment passed, and then the cup was raised to his lips, and he drank.

On Sunday, 6 June 1847, the members of the Rugby student body who had been confirmed the week before were welcomed to the communion rail of the school chapel, and Charles Lutwidge Dodgson likely took his first communion. Earlier in the service, headmaster Tait had particularly addressed those boys who might feel, for whatever reason, unworthy of the sacrament, saying, "It is not a good commence of that new life which you have publicly declared you desire to enter, within a few days to turn away as publicly from the Communion. A man who is not a habitual communicant is habitually disobeying Christ."[1]

Rev. Charles Dodgson the father viewed preparing Christians for the Eucharist as one of the central roles of education. In 1841 he said the "plan [of the education system] is to train that child, from the first moment it is able to think, and to know, as a son of that church with which it is hereafter to come into full communion; to train it for confirmation; to train it for the reception of the holy sacrament."[2] But what exactly was, in the eyes of Rev. Charles Dodgson, the "holy sacrament"?

According to the catechism in the Book of Common Prayer, the Eucharist is "an outward and visible sign of an inward and spiritual grace . . . ordained . . . for the continual remembrance of the sacrifice of the death of Christ, and of the benefits which we receive thereby. [T]he inward part, or thing signified [is] The Body and Blood of Christ, which are verily and indeed taken and received by the faithful in the Lord's Supper. [T]he benefits [are] the strengthening and refreshing of our souls by the Body and Blood of Christ, as our bodies are by the bread and wine."[3]

Clearly this definition leaves room for interpretation. On the one hand, the Body and Blood of Christ are referred to as "the thing signified," which leaves open the possibility that the elements are symbols only. On the other hand, the catechism clearly states that the Body and Blood are "verily and indeed taken and received," leading to the doctrine of real presence.

The Thirty-Nine Articles state that "the bread which we break is partaking of the Body of Christ; and likewise the Cup of Blessing is a partaking of the Blood of Christ. Transubstantiation (or the change of the substance of Bread and Wine) . . . is repugnant to the plain words of Scripture . . . and hath given occasion to many superstitions. The Body of Christ is given, taken, and eaten, only after an heavenly and spiritual manner. And the mean whereby the Body of Christ is received and eaten in the Supper is Faith."[4]

Rev. Charles Dodgson stated his own interpretation of the Church of England's position on the Holy Communion in an 1853 sermon when he said: "The Church of England does not pretend to determine the mode, in which the Body and Blood of Christ are present in the Lord's Supper. . . . [S]he is content with repudiating the Romish notion of Transubstantiation . . . and with affirming that 'the Body of Christ is given, taken, and eaten in the Supper, only after a heavenly and spiritual manner,' . . . but in no way defining what the 'manner' *is,* to which the terms 'heavenly and spiritual' are applied."[5]

The Church of England may have been vague on the exact nature of Christ's presence in the Eucharist. Charles Dodgson, however, expressed in this sermon his belief about part of what happens at the altar rail—an aspect of Dodgson's personal Eucharistic theology that would have been especially relevant to his son, and to any of the Rugby boys who may, as Headmaster Tait guessed, have felt unworthy.

"The view which I would venture to propose," said Dodgson, "is briefly this: that the consecration, the due administration, and the faithful reception of the Bread and Wine, constitute virtually one act, to which, in its entire and undivided state, and not to any detached portions of it, the Sacramental Presence of the Body and Blood of Christ is attached" (14–15). Thus the sacramental presence, for Dodgson, depended as much on the person receiving Communion as on the priest administering it. "There is no sacramental presence of the Body and Blood of Christ," he posited, "previous to and independent of the act of eating and drinking" (20).

In his 1868 *Charge Delivered to the Clergy and Churchwardens of the Archdeaconry of Richmond,* Archdeacon Dodgson expanded on this view of the Eucharist while objecting to ritualists who would add to the Communion service symbols and gestures of adoration of the bread and wine, believing Christ to be present within them. Dodgson dismisses this doctrine of "Real Presence" as not differing in any essential way from Transubstantiation: "The real essence of the error lies in ascribing a local presence to the Body of our Lord, whatever be the nature and manner of it, in a defined space, and under a substantial form—'on the Altar,' as it is said, and 'under the form of bread and wine.' . . . But the Church of England, in her 28th Article, expressly teaches that 'the mean whereby the Body of Christ is received and eaten is Faith.' Where therefore there is no Faith, there can be no reception."[6] By rejecting the local presence of Christ in the bread and wine independent of the faith of the recipient, Archdeacon Dodgson dispensed with claims by the ritualists that the priest conducted a sacrifice during the service and that the elements themselves were deserving of outward signs of adoration.

Rev. Charles Dodgson's *Plain Catechism* shows more precisely what young Charles may have been taught about Communion by his father: "While our *bodies* eat the bread and drink the wine, our *souls,* in a *spiritual* manner, partake of the Body and Blood." Our souls thus receive the benefit of "the grace of God's Holy Spirit, to comfort them, and to strengthen them against the power of sin" (17).

> Some [neglect the Lord's Supper] because they are careless of their souls, and do not think about Christ; and some because they are afraid. . . . They feel they are sinners and therefore not fit to come . . . [but] we go to the Sacrament to *remember Christ's death,* and the single reason why we should remember it and be thankful for it is, *because we are sinners.* . . . Since then we are *continually* sinners . . . before we come to the Lord's Supper . . . we must *repent* truly of our sins, or else we cannot draw any comfort or hope of salvation from the death of Christ. (18)

In summarizing the section in the *Plain Catechism* about the Lord's Supper, Dodgson wrote: "Begin the habit of attending the Lord's Supper as soon as you have been confirmed. It is your Saviour's invitation—how then can you refuse to attend it? It is your Saviour's command—how then can you dare to disobey it? . . . Begin it in the season of youth, health, and strength, and then you will find the comfort of it in the time of old age, of sickness, and of death" (20).

The question of the sinfulness of unworthily receiving the sacrament may have been in the minds of some Rugby boys that morning in 1847. Rev. Charles Dodgson addressed this issue in his sermon "What Do the Wicked Eat and Drink in the Lord's Supper?" He claimed that the worthy recipient was required for the sacramental presence of Christ, thus the unworthy recipient did not receive Christ, but merely bread and wine. In his *Plain Catechism,* Dodgson described those who were unworthy as "Those who receive the Sacrament without thinking *seriously* about it, who do not desire to repent of their sins, and who have no care for the salvation of their souls."[7]

Dodgson expanded on his thoughts about the Eucharist in two sermons on "The Sacraments of the Gospel," preached in Ripon Cathedral on 3 January and 17 January 1864. Dodgson preached in favor of what he called a "high view" of the sacraments—a view that rankled his more evangelical colleagues. "There would seem to be in some men," said Dodgson, "a sort of earnest desire . . . to give prominence to the *secondary* characters of these Sacraments, as signs, seals, badges, and tokens . . . and to slur, if not altogether pass over, their *primary* and essential character, as special means and effectual instruments ordained of God."[8]

Dodgson cited the twenty-fifth, twenty-seventh, and twenty-eighth Articles in opposing those who hold this low view of the sacraments, and an unbiased reading of these Articles seems to support his view: "The language of the Articles exalts to the highest the nature of the Sacraments, and that of the Services [i.e., the Book of Common Prayer] has always been thought to be even more full and explicit than the Articles in this respect" (54). Dodgson accused low churchmen of separating what the catechism calls the "outward and visible sign" of the sacraments from its true meaning—the "inward and spiritual grace." He described the Eucharist as

an act of thankful remembrance of the sacrifice of the death of Christ; . . . a renewal of our covenant with God; . . . a token of the love and union, which we should have one with another as Christians. But, beyond and above all this, let us remember that it is "the holy Communion of the Body and Blood of our Saviour Jesus Christ;" and that "the benefit is great," is wondrous, is incomprehensible, "if with a penitent heart and lively faith we receive that holy Sacrament; for that then we spiritually eat the flesh of Christ and drink His Blood: then we dwell in Christ, and Christ in us; we are one with Christ, and Christ with us."[9] (56)

In his second sermon on the sacraments, Rev. Charles Dodgson parried two objections put forth by low churchmen to the high church view: "The first is, that such Preaching tends to corrupt in the hearers the simplicity of their Faith in Christ. . . . 'Teach your people,' it is said, to look to the Spirit of God . . . not to the representation of it in the Lord's Supper; to the exercise of Faith, not to the performance of outward acts of service." To this objection Dodgson claimed, "Trust in the Sacraments . . . does not interfere with the exercise of Faith in the Author of those Sacraments" (61).

The other objection was "that the doctrine of Sacramental grace tends to create false and indolent security." If grace can be renewed by partaking of the Lord's Supper, the argument went, why bother living a godly life? "What more constraining motive to holiness," wrote Dodgson, "what more powerful check upon sin, than the thought that the Spirit of Holiness hath once been imparted to us?" (63).

Though these sermons were preached nearly twenty years after Charles Lutwidge Dodgson's first Communion,[10] Rev. Charles Dodgson likely held those same beliefs during the years he educated his son at Daresbury and Croft—that the primary characteristic of the Lord's Supper, the bestowing of God's grace, was the most important; that with that grace came the responsibility to live a holy life; that Christ's body and blood were spiritually present in the elements but there was no real local presence on the altar; that the faith and worthiness of the recipient was a necessary part of the sacrament and of the presence of Christ in it; and that the worthiness of the recipient was dependent upon his repenting of his sins. All these things would have been in Charles's mind as he prepared to receive the elements.

It is perhaps telling that in his twenty-four *Sermons for the People*, Rev. Scott Surtees, preaching before Charles Lutwidge Dodgson when the boy was at Richmond School, did not specifically teach about sacraments. Nonetheless, in Sermon VI, which Dodgson may have heard, Surtees mentioned the Lord's Supper while enumerating certain doctrines of the Roman Catholic Church as having "added to the word of God, traditions of their own."[11] While Surtees's remarks are more by way of condemning Roman Catholic doctrine than elucidating Anglican doctrine, they nonetheless give some insight as to the sort of teaching young Charles may have received from the pulpit in Richmond.

"They pretend that at the will of their priests, they can bring down from heaven the Son of God, and turn the bread and wine by consecration into the very body and blood of Christ. . . . When at the first institution of this holy sacrament, he said 'this is my body' and 'this is my blood,' it is plain he used figurative language . . . did not our Lord often use figurative language on other occasions. Did he not say, 'I am the door' [John 10:9], 'I am the vine' [John 15:5], 'I am the way?' [John 14:6]."[12]

Clearly Surtees advocated a more low church, evangelical view of the sacrament. In fact, Rev. Charles Dodgson, in his 1864 sermons on the sacraments, uses some of the same language that Surtees uses here in setting out what he considers the faulty evangelical argument, writing that "those who hold that . . . the Lord's words, 'This is my Body; this is my Blood,' are to be understood in just the same way as His expressions, 'I am the vine,' 'I am the door;' . . . stand in heretical opposition to that Catholic Faith, which the Church [of England] believes herself to hold" (*Sacraments* 55).

By the time Charles Lutwidge Dodgson arrived at Rugby, he had been exposed to both his father's high church view of the Lord's Supper and a lower church interpretation of the sacrament, calling Christ's language, and by implication the entire sacrament itself, figurative. At Rugby he would receive teaching on the sacrament of the Lord's Supper from both the headmaster, Archibald Campbell Tait, and George Edward Lynch Cotton.

In his chapter on the Lord's Supper in *Instructions in the Principles and Practice of Christianity*, Cotton sets himself in the evangelical school of interpretation, writing that when Christ, in John 6, said that the "heavenly food of eternal life" was "to be obtained by eating His Body, and drinking his Blood," "His words here are figurative, and intend to express by the strongest possible metaphor, the necessity that our souls should depend upon Him for sustenance" (118).

Cotton's description of the true nature of the Communion was echoed by Rev. Charles Dodgson years later, the difference being that Dodgson went on from a paraphrase of Cotton's position to add a further set of clauses. Cotton wrote: "[The disciples] were to keep this feast together as a commemoration of His death, a symbol of their union with Him, a means of strengthening and preserving this union, and a communion of love and Christian fellowship with one another" (121). But Dodgson, after listing these same benefits, goes on to say, "But, beyond and above all this . . . it is 'the holy Communion of the Body and Blood of our Saviour Jesus Christ;' and . . . we spiritually eat the flesh of Christ and drink His Blood" (*Sacraments* 56).

Cotton argued against the literal presence of Christ's Body and Blood in the elements, saying, "For, of course, if the bread and wine were actually changed into the Body and Blood of Christ, these would be received by the wicked as well as by the faithful" (*Instructions* 123), but Rev. Charles Dodgson dispensed with this objection by stating that the faith of the receiver of Communion is an integral part of the presence of Christ.

Cotton did encourage his charges to approach the Communion rail in the proper frame of mind. "If anyone goes to the Lord's Supper carelessly," he wrote, "irreverently, or profanely, that which is to the true Christian a savour of life unto life, becomes to him a savour of death unto death" (123).

But, like Rev. Charles Dodgson, if for different theological reasons, Cotton did not wish to scare off Christians from the sacrament. "To those who imagine they are too sinful to go [to Communion]," he wrote, "we reply that if they really and truly feel themselves to be sinful, and are desirous not to continue so, they are in a state of mind exactly fitted for the profitable reception of the ordinance; whereas, if they wait till they are not sinful, they certainly will never go at all" (125).

Cotton extended the metaphor of feeding on Christ, writing, "Not indeed that the Communion is the only way of our so feeding upon Him; to pray, and humbly meditate on His goodness and His love, to read His Holy Word . . . are all, in their measure, means of feeding upon him" (124). In discussing the Communion as a symbol of mutual Christian love, Cotton wrote, "as the Spirit of that feeding on Christ which the Communion represents, ought to pervade every part of our daily life, so also should the spirit of love which it expresses, extend through all our dealings with every one for whom Christ died" (126). And in discussing Communion as "the only outward result of our Confirmation," Cotton wrote, "The best test by which we may know whether we are really partakers of Christ in Communion, is to try and observe whether our conduct shows that we daily feed upon his Body and Blood." To Cotton, feeding on Christ was a daily activity and the Communion "one of the chief and holiest means" (127).

Rugby's headmaster, Archibald Campbell Tait, occasionally spoke to his boys on the topic of the sacrament, both in Sunday-morning chapel and in the talks he gave in School Hall on Sunday evenings. Communion was, at the time, celebrated every two months at Rugby during term time. "I know of no reason why this should be so," said Tait, "except that a more frequent repetition . . . might lead you to look upon [it] as too common a matter and too much a thing of course. This would certainly be a great evil."[13]

Tait repeatedly urged confirmed boys to partake of the sacrament. In November 1849, he told his boys: "I must say a few words tonight in preparation for the communion. For those of you who were confirmed last summer it is of much importance that you should none of you turn away from this. . . . For it may be asked for what purpose were you confirmed if not to follow up your good professions."[14]

But no boy was forced. On Easter Sunday 1849, Tait said, "190 is a large number of communicants in a school like ours where the matter is left . . . to the free decision of each of yourselves."[15]

Two of Tait's sermons on the Eucharist are included in his 1850 book *Lessons for School Life*. Though we cannot be certain that Charles Lutwidge Dodgson heard these two sermons, we do know that Tait often repeated sermons and that the doctrines and ideas he professed from the pulpit at Rugby were unwavering, so Charles would certainly have heard words similar to these from his headmaster.

While Tait did not explicitly address the question of high church versus low church interpretations of the sacrament, he referred to the bread and wine at the Last Supper as "symbols of His body and blood" (*Lessons* 327) and spoke of the Eucharist in these words: "In the Lord's Supper the faithful soul, drawing near with reverence, is, by the Holy Spirit's influence, more closely united to its Saviour; made more to resemble Him in will and desire; rendered less capable of being ever separated from Him; and thus sustained and strengthened for life everlasting" (274).

Tait spoke of Communion as an act of community, saying it was "natural for friends to wish to receive this rite together" and calling it a "great act of social worship" (326–27). Tait devoted the most time, however, to directly addressing his boys about their own state of mind and heart during Communion and the importance of preparing for the sacrament.

It is well that, by diligent preparation, the heart and feelings should be solemnized. . . . how many [of you], from their very age and character, are naturally indisposed to any solemn thoughts. Our life would go very badly; our souls would be daily becoming more estranged from God, if we were not at times imperatively called upon to pause that we may review our state. . . . [This] self examination is not only to make us serious, it is to make us know ourselves. . . . [W]hat we reckon lighter sins, are more difficult for us to detect: They may be lying hid in the dark corners of our hearts . . . and require a vigorous self-examination to drag them to the light. . . . It is not only necessary to know ourselves, but to resolve by God's help to improve. (276–78)

As an adult, Charles Lutwidge Dodgson would, if he did not remember Tait's exact words, continue to take solemnly the sacrament and to use it as an opportunity to "resolve by God's help to improve." At Croft on 2 October during the Long Vacation of 1864, he wrote in his diary: "Communion Sunday. May God grant that I in sincerity 'repent of my sins, and intend to lead a new life.'[16] For Jesus Christ's sake." Two years later, he attended Communion at the high church St. Mary Magdalene in Oxford and wrote, on 1 July 1866, "Oh for grace to partake of that holy mystery more faithfully, more penitently, with more real resolve of amendment of life!" On 26 May 1872, after Communion at the University Church of St. Mary's, he wrote, "Oh that the grace I have sought in that most Holy Sacrament might show itself in my life!"

Charles Lutwidge Dodgson mentions Communion thirty-six times in his diaries, and these not infrequent mentions indicate a reverence for the rite and a need to partake. In 1888, when laid up with a bad knee, he asked one of the canons of Christ Church to come to his rooms and administer Communion. And he remained aware of confirmation as the entry to the Communion table. In 1890, his child-friend Isa Bowman, who had recently been confirmed, was staying with him at Eastbourne, and on 14 September he wrote in his diary: "Isa and I went to the early Communion at St. Saviour's. It was a real pleasure to have this new and yet closer link between us."

As a deacon, Dodgson occasionally assisted with the Eucharist, recording in his diary thirteen times when this happened. He did this for the first time at the Priory Church in Great Malvern, where he was visiting, on 17 August 1862, several months after his ordination. On 9 February 1863, Dodgson attended the Vere Street Chapel in London, where the incumbent was the renowned Christian Socialist Frederick Denison Maurice: "There was Communion, and as there seemed to be no one to help him, I sent him my card, and offered to help. This lucky accident led to my making his acquaintance."[17] Dodgson's task as a Eucharistic minister, as is often the case with a secondary or tertiary minister, was most frequently to administer the cup; on 21 April 1867, he wrote: "Went to St. Mary's and was asked by Burgon to help in administering the Communion. . . . I was rather nervous about it, as

I had never administered the Bread before, and feared I should not be able to remember the words." Eight of the times Dodgson records assisting with Communion occurred during the period from 1862 to 1867, when he seemed to be still actively considering the possibility of proceeding to the priesthood.

As to Charles Lutwidge Dodgson's beliefs on the theology of the Eucharist, he left us little in the way of evidence, but we do have a passage from a transcribed sermon he delivered in 1887. Here, in discussing the miracle of salvation, he wrote: "How was this marvel to be wrought now? By blending the divine with the human nature. In itself unexplainable, the Lord unfolded this truth to His disciples under many parables. The vine, nourishing with its own vigour the branches.[18] The head and the body, the one necessary to the life of the other.[19] And, chiefest of all, closer, more intimate relationship—the Holy Eucharist of His own institution, Flesh and Blood."[20]

Here, Dodgson seemed to say that the Eucharist was a parable, and he referred to the same metaphorical language that Scott Surtees had used to argue for the low church interpretation of the sacrament. However, Dodgson went on to describe Communion as "A figure, revolting to the mind in its carnal sense, yet chosen by the Lord to enforce the doctrine He would inculcate. For as the morsel of bread and drops of wine become incorporated with and absolutely part of this physical frame, so in a wider, deeper, truer sense, does the worshipper receive the spiritual body and blood of Christ, which, commingling with and interfusing the spiritual frame gradually purifies it, daily fashioning it more and more to the Divine likeness."[21]

There are two essential aspects to the Communion service—what happens to the bread and wine and how the ceremony itself is performed. It is likely, since Headmaster Tait was a low churchman, that the Communion service young Charles attended on 6 June 1847 was celebrated with the minimum of ceremony prescribed by the rubrics of the Book of Common Prayer. But Charles would, by adulthood, certainly have been familiar with the ritualistic practice of some in the high church movement.

While Charles's father was firmly entrenched in the high church party, he was not an extreme ritualist. That group sought to instill the divine services, and in particular the Eucharist, with acts of ritual that had been stripped away either at the Reformation or since. These included the priest facing eastward; the elevation of the host; choral services, where much of the service is sung by the choir; mono-toning certain prayers and readings; the use of lighted candles, elaborate vestments, and incense; and other similar innovations. Those opposed to these forms of ritual referred to them as Romish or as Popery.

Despite his high church leanings, Rev. Charles Dodgson did not go as far down the road of ritualism as many who came after him. In an 1851 sermon, he bemoaned "how far decay in faith and doctrine may be traced to laxity and negligence in matters of ritual observance."[22] But here Dodgson refers not to Eucharistic vestments, candles, or choirs, but to the Church's "provisions for daily Confession, and Prayer, and Thanksgiving, and the hearing of the Word; its series of Festivals and Fasts, designed for keeping in memory the works of God's grace in redemption, and the lives and deaths of His holiest Saints and Martyrs."[23]

The following year, in his sermon "Ritual Worship," Dodgson laid out his views in a historical context:

> The Church of England, in the early ages of her Reformation, did by such authority abolish many and retain many of the ceremonies, which she had before observed. The changes were made advisedly, and on sound and sober principles; and the system which resulted ought to have been, as it was unquestionably designed to be, a source of unity and peace among all members of her Communion. That it has not proved so in our own days, was owing first to a long course of sinful neglect and indifference, for which Clergy and Laity were alike responsible: and afterwards to an hasty and misguided zeal, which effectually opposed a return to unity and order, by rejecting the only principles, on which it was possible that order and unity should be established.[24]

Dodgson believed the restoration of rituals that had fallen away due to laxity in the eighteenth and early nineteenth centuries was beneficial, but the restoration of rites and rituals that had been stripped away at the time of the Reformation was not. He used the term "Ritual Worship" to refer primarily to a recognition of the importance of the regular celebration of the rites and rituals enumerated in the Book of Common Prayer and observance of the calendar of feasts and fasts. In his *Charge Delivered to the Clergy* of May 1866, Dodgson specifically condemns some ritual practices:

> Far different is the view, which I take of those ceremonial practices, which some have added to the use of these vestments. The Rubric respecting ornaments cannot possibly be construed to sanction them. I speak of such as are unquestionably connected with some of the worse Romish superstitions: the bodily gestures used towards the consecrated elements in the Lord's Supper: the uplifting of them before the people, a thing expressly forbidden even

in the first Book of Edward the sixth: the scattering of incense during the Hymn of Mary the Virgin: such practices as these are not only not enjoined, but are, I conceive, virtually prohibited by the Law.[25]

During his preparation for ordination, Charles Lutwidge Dodgson likely both heard and read Bishop Samuel Wilberforce's *Addresses to Candidates for Ordination* in which Wilberforce stated, speaking of moderation on this question: "And this same principle applies with even greater force to our vestments in the sanctuary, and to the adoption in our services of rites which, however they may be justified by the letter of long-sleeping laws, are strange and novel in the eyes of our people. I have no hesitation in saying to you that it is better in these matters to acquiesce for a while in a long-established custom of deficiency than to stir our people up to suspicion and hostility by the impetuous restoration of a better use."[26] Wilberforce took a middle road—his high church inclinations did not allow him to strictly forbid ritual worship, but he pointed out that if it made people uncomfortable, it may not be the best way to proceed.

In Charles Lutwidge Dodgson's library at the time of his death was a copy of *The Directorium Anglicanum,* compiled by John Purchase and edited by Frederick George Lee. This was the handbook for high church ritualism, giving detailed instructions on how to celebrate the Holy Communion and other rites and ceremonies of the church. It is possible that he inherited this book (his copy was printed in 1865) from his father, but he may have been familiar with its contents. This book sought to return the Eucharist as the central act of Christian worship and dealt with such controversial issues as the celebrant facing eastward, the wearing of Eucharistic vestments, the placement of candles on the altar, and so on. But the presence of a book in one's library is clearly no indication that the owner is in sympathy with its contents. In the years when the debate on ritual in worship in the Church of England raged most strongly, Dodgson made it clear he opposed the ritualists.

Dodgson's public writings about his distaste for ritualism came after his father's death, but, as he wrote in a letter of 1885, "My dear father was a 'High Church' man, though *not* a 'Ritualist'" (*Letters* 586). Nonetheless, in the years immediately following his ordination, Charles Lutwidge Dodgson actively sought out some of the highest of Oxford churches in which to preach, assist, and worship (see see pp. 183–85 in this volume). Why did he then turn so harshly against the ritual movement? Certainly one reason is that Dodgson felt the movement had gone too far, as he says in the preface to *Sylvie and Bruno Concluded* (see p. 120 in this volume).

Dodgson's foreign journey with his friend Henry Parry Liddon in 1867 may also have contributed to his feelings about ritualism. For the first time in his life, Dodgson got a regular look into the services and rituals of the Roman Catholic and Eastern churches, and he did not like what he saw. Liddon records in his diary that Dodgson thought Russian religion "too external," and Dodgson's own diary shows his disdain for ritual. At his first experience at a Catholic church in Brussels on 14 July 1867 he showed both an ignorance of and a dislike for genuflection, the Sanctus Bell, and the Rosary all in a short passage, writing in his diary, "the whole body of priests etc. were continually going up in little processions, kneeling for about a second before the altar (quite too short a time for any act of devotion) and returning to their places. Attention was called to the chief points in the service by a shrill bell . . . the man next to me was . . . counting off his prayers with a string of beads. . . . [I]t was very difficult to realize it as a service for the congregation to join in—it all seemed to be done *for* them."

This was Dodgson's chief complaint about ritualism—it reduced the congregant to the role of spectator. Of a service in St. Petersburg on 28 July, Dodgson wrote, "the more one sees of these gorgeous services, with their many appeals to the senses, the more, I think, one learns to love the plain, simple (but to my mind far more real) service of the English church." On 28 August in Warsaw, he wrote of visiting "several churches, chiefly Roman Catholic, which contained the usual evidence of wealth and bad taste, in the profuse gilding, and the masses of marble carved into heaps . . . of ugly babies meant for cherubs." By Sunday, 1 September, Dodgson, unable to locate the English church in Dresden, accompanied Liddon to the Roman Catholic Church only for "a few minutes to hear the music."

We see his continued prejudice against Roman Catholic ritual in an entry in his diary from 5 April 1885, when he attended St. Mary's Guildford: "I helped Mr. Beloe with the midday Communion at St. Mary's. But I do not intend to do so again, as I much dislike the observances with which he concluded the service (e.g. washing the cup, and his fingers in it, and then drinking the water!) which savour too much of Romanism." The following day, Dodgson "Called on Mr. Beloe, and had a long chat, about the ritual observed here."

By the 1880s Dodgson had no qualms about making his distaste for ritualism public, writing about or at least alluding to it in a letter to the press, in a sermon at Guildford, and in the *Sylvie and Bruno* novels. In his 1887 sermon, he laid out the centerpiece of his objections clearly, saying, "The Church Services of the present day are in every sense so attractive in comparison with those of former times (when if a man went to church at all, he went to worship God) that there is danger—great danger—of our becoming mere formalists, of putting outward beauty of structure, of adornment, of external reverence, in the place of that inward spiritual grace of holy devotion, without which it is impossible to offer up acceptable worship."[27]

Dodgson had already gone on the attack against ritualism in a letter to the *St. James's Gazette* published on 30 December 1881. Dodgson accused the evangelical Church Association of giving the ritualists of England, especially those associated with the high church English Church Union, exactly what they wanted with their cries to imprison those practicing ritualism.[28] Dodgson signed this letter "Lewis Carroll," something he did when he wanted to use his fame to forward a cause. "Does any sane man suppose that any persecuted Ritualist does not thankfully seize the opportunity of posing as a martyr?," he wrote.[29]

Dodgson took the ritualists to task not so much for violating an act of Parliament as for disobeying their bishops: "'[Mr. Green is] in prison,' so chorus the delighted English Church Union, 'because he conscientiously refuses obedience to a secular court!' It is a mere waste of breath to point out to these impassioned orators that he also refuses obedience to his ecclesiastical superior, the Bishop whom he has solemnly sworn to obey. . . . They have discovered a new and most astonishing axiom in morals—that whatever you are ordered to do by anyone to whom you owe no allegiance you may rightly refuse to do, even if it also be ordered by a lawful authority."[30]

In driving home this point, Dodgson rewrote a section of the Ordination service to quote from what he called a "Revised Version of the English Prayer Book." He copied the question posed word-for-word from the original, but added parentheticals to the answer.

Q. Will you reverently obey your Ordinary, and other chief Ministers, unto whom is committed the charge and government over you; following with a glad mind and will their godly admonitions, and submitting yourself to their godly judgments?

A. I will reverently obey them (when they order that which I desire to do); I will gladly follow their godly admonitions (when they admonish those who oppose me); and I will submit myself to their godly judgments (whensoever and wheresoever they will submit their godly judgments to me). (12)

That Dodgson rejected ritualism, and saw it as not just outside the low and broad church movements but as a corruption of the high church movement as well, can be seen in this scathing paragraph:

The only consolation, which the Protestant portion of the English Church (under which title I include all, whether High, Low, or Broad, who hold to the principles of the Reformation) are likely to find in the present miserable state of things, is the thought that now at last we have a crucial test as to whether Ritualism is or is not suited to the genius of the English nation. "You have had every chance," they can now say to the Ritualists: "your choral services have charmed our ears, your rich vestments our eyes, and even your incense our noses! And now you have the darling wish of your heart: you are persecuted: you can appeal to the ineradicable instinct which ever impels John Bull to side with the persecuted, be he right or wrong. Fortune can do no more for you: you must stand or fall by your present chance: if persecution will not popularize Ritualism, nothing will!" (12)

In *Sylvie and Bruno,* published in 1889, Dodgson puts words into the mouth of his character Arthur Forester—and in 1893, in the preface to *Sylvie and Bruno Concluded,* he writes of this passage, "I admit that I am much in sympathy with Arthur" (xix). We can assume, then, that he was also in sympathy with the narrator, in the passage leading up to Arthur's speech. Arthur has just returned from a church service:

The service would have been pronounced by any modern aesthetic religionist—or religious aesthete, which is it?—to be crude and cold: to me, coming fresh from the ever-advancing developments of a London church under a *soi-disant* "Catholic" Rector, it was unspeakably refreshing.

There was no theatrical procession of demure little choristers, trying their best not to simper under the admiring gaze of the congregation: the people's share in the service was taken by the people themselves, unaided, except that a few good voices, judiciously posted here and there among them, kept the singing from going too far astray.

There was no murdering of the noble music, contained in the Bible and the Liturgy, by its recital in a dead monotone, with no more expression than a mechanical talking-doll.

No, the prayers were *prayed,* the lessons were *read,* and best of all the sermon was *talked.* . . .

"Yes," said Arthur, apparently in answer to my thoughts, "those 'high' services are fast becoming pure Formalism. More and more the people are beginning to regard them as 'performances,' in which they only 'assist' in the French sense. And it is *specially* bad for the little boys. They'd be much less self-conscious as pantomime-fairies. With all that dressing-up, and stagy-entrances and exits, and being always *en evidence,* no wonder if they're eaten up with vanity, the blatant little coxcombs!" (272–74)

The reference to "murdering of the noble music, contained in the Bible and the Liturgy, by its recital in a dead monotone," is especially interesting, given that Dodgson, on 21 May 1865, assisted at a service at the Tractarian St. Paul's Church in Oxford. "Helped again at St. Paul's," he wrote in his diary, "this time by reading the lessons and Litany, the latter I tried to mono-tone, with pretty fair success." The younger Charles Lutwidge Dodgson, as seen in chapter 10 in the analysis of his preaching habits, was at least a little more in sympathy with some aspects of the ritual movement than the man of middle age. He gave some justification for this change in the preface to *Sylvie and Bruno Concluded,* writing, "while freely admitting that the 'Ritual' movement was sorely needed, and that it has effected a vast improvement in our Church-Services, which had become dead and dry to the last degree, I hold that, like many other desirable movements, it has gone too far in the opposite direction, and has introduced many new dangers" (xix).

Because in services with higher levels of ritual, much of the service was sung, the choir naturally took on a larger role, and the congregation, instead of saying certain prayers and canticles, found themselves listening to the choir singing these parts of the service. Dodgson articulated his feelings about "'Choristers,' and all the other accessories—of music, vestments, processions, &c.,—which have come, along with them, into fashion,"[31] in the preface of *Sylvie and Bruno Concluded:*

> For the Congregation this new movement involves the danger of learning to think that the Services are done *for* them; and that their bodily *presence* is all they need contribute. And, for Clergy and Congregation alike, it involves the danger of regarding these elaborate Services as *ends in themselves,* and of forgetting that they are simply *means,* and the very hollowest of mockeries, unless they bear fruit in our *lives.*
>
> For the Choristers it seems to involve the danger of self-conceit, . . . the danger of regarding those parts of the Service, where their help is not

required, as not worth attending to, the danger of coming to regard the Service as a mere outward form—a series of postures to be assumed, and of words to be said or sung, while the *thoughts* are elsewhere—and the danger of "familiarity" breeding "contempt" for sacred things. (xix–xx)

Stuart Dodgson Collingwood recalled that Dodgson "would not, for example, stand up in church when the choir entered, because he feared it made the choristers self-conscious and proud."[32]

Dodgson had one other interesting thought about the Communion service, on the question of whether the laity could administer the rite. In his 1880 Bampton Lectures, Edwin Hatch wrote, "It is clear from [the Ignatian Epistles] that . . . the celebration of the Eucharist without the presence of a Church officer was not of itself invalid."[33]

Dodgson wrote to Hatch on 26 December 1887: "There is a question, that interests me, raised in your book on the Early Church, and that is about the lawfulness of administering Holy Communion by laymen. *A priori,* I can see nothing in the service—not even in the prayer of consecration—(I except the absolution which raises *another* question) but what a layman might say" (*Letters* 689).

Whether Hatch replied, either in person or by letter, we do not know, but here we see Dodgson, just months after he reentered the field of preaching after a twenty-year absence, taking a controversial view of the subject in even suggesting that a lay celebration would be lawful.

On an August evening in 1895, with the late-summer sun still high in the sky, Charles Dodgson took the chalice from Rev. William Hewett. He had agreed to assist with Communion at this service, something he rarely did these days. Turning to the altar rail, he waited for Reverend Hewett to distribute the bread, going over in his mind the words he would soon be saying—words he had heard so many times before. He lowered the cup to the lips of a communicant and spoke in a clear voice: "The Blood of our Lord Jesus Christ, which was shed for thee, preserve thy body and soul unto everlasting life. Drink this in remembrance that Christ's Blood was shed for thee, and be thankful."

· SEVEN ·

Diligent Attendance

Charles Lutwidge Dodgson sat in a railway carriage rumbling north toward his family home at Croft. In his hand, he held a copy of the Oxford University Statutes—rules that would govern his life for at least the next several years. He would not enter into his life at Oxford for several months, but he had already begun to look over the statutes. As the lush landscape scrolled past the window, he read: "It is enacted, that all doctors, masters, graduates, and scholars, shall diligently attend the divine offices, or solemn prayers, according to the liturgy of the Church of England, and the sermons publicly delivered before the University."[1]

In May 1850, Charles Lutwidge Dodgson traveled to Oxford to matriculate at the university. He would become an undergraduate at the college of Christ Church, his father's college and the largest of the Oxford colleges.

> [At Oxford] the students undergo a matriculation examination in the first instance, and become members of the University before they are members of any college. . . . In practice, no doubt, a man has generally chosen his college before he goes up, and his matriculation takes place under the guidance of the college tutor; still, the matriculation is a University and not a college proceeding. It is the University that requires subscription to the Thirty-Nine Articles, although the college tutor very often undertakes the task of examining them to the youthful student and removing difficulties if any are expressed.[2]

Once Dodgson had passed his matriculation examination, he was ready for the formal ceremony that would make him a member of Oxford University—a distinction he would hold for the rest of his life. On 23 May 1850, he knelt before Frederick Charles Plumptre, vice chancellor of the university, in the anteroom of the Convocation House and swore to uphold the statutes of the university. At the end of the ceremony, the vice chancellor presented Dodgson with a copy of those University Statutes.[3]

But matriculation was not merely an academic ceremony; it had a religious component as well. As part of his matriculation Charles was required to sign his name to the Thirty-Nine Articles of Religion, the outline of the Anglican faith. Though reform was on the way, no dissenters, Roman Catholics, or nonbelievers were welcome in the Oxford of 1850.

Dodgson spent his undergraduate years in an Oxford where the fires of Tractarianism still smoldered. John Henry Newman had left the Church of England for the Roman Catholic Church five years earlier, nor was he alone. In his library, Dodgson had an 1878 pamphlet titled *Rome's Recruits,* which listed the names of hundreds of distinguished English men and women who had converted to Roman Catholicism.

While John Keble had, in 1835, taken up work as a parish priest in Kent, E. B. Pusey still lived at Christ Church when Dodgson arrived. He was Regius Professor of Hebrew and a canon of Christ Church Cathedral, and it is likely that young Dodgson saw Pusey often in chapel and elsewhere in the college.

Though Oxford would undergo great reforms during Dodgson's nearly fifty-year residency there, in 1850 the university was still firmly rooted in its traditional role as training ground for the clergy. Richard William Church describes the Oxford that had only just begun to fade away in the face of reform when Dodgson arrived.

> Oxford had always been one of the great schools of the Church. Its traditions, its tone, its customs, its rules, all expressed or presumed the closest attachment to that way of religion which was specially identified with the Church, in its doctrinal and historical aspect. Oxford was emphatically definite, dogmatic, orthodox, compared even with Cambridge, which had largely favoured the Evangelical school, and had leanings to Liberalism. . . . Its Tutorial system, of its lectures and examinations, implied . . . a considerable amount of religious and theological teaching. . . . The colleges . . . were for the most part, in the intention of their founders, meant to educate and support theological students on their foundations for the service of the Church.[4]

The extent to which Oxford, in the early 1850s, was still a school for clergy can be seen in the fates of those Christ Church men who took their B.A. on the same day as Dodgson. Of the thirteen men, eight, including Dodgson, were later ordained, one wished to be ordained but was not for medical reasons, two became lawyers, and two became soldiers.

Following several months of preparation at Croft, Charles Lutwidge Dodgson arrived at Oxford on 24 January 1851 to begin his university education. Only two days later he was called back to Croft after the unexpected death of his mother. Like his own father a generation before, he began his Christ Church education with the pall of maternal loss and a keen awareness of the transience of life hanging over him.

Though a member of the university, Dodgson's undergraduate education was at the hands of his college and consisted of tutorials and lectures. Dodgson left little record of his undergraduate years. Certainly, in the broad demarcation of Oxford undergraduates as either readers or nonreaders, Dodgson was a reader. His seriousness about his studies is evident in a letter to his sister Elizabeth at the beginning of the Long Vacation of 1852: "Before I left Oxford I had a long talk with Mr. Gordon, and one with Mr. Faussett on the work of the Long Vacation: I believe about 25 hours' *hard* work a day *may* get me through all I have to do" (*Letters* 20).

Dodgson's religious life during this period consisted of worship and education. Worship meant mandatory attendance at daily college chapel during term time. The pattern of college worship during Dodgson's undergraduate years was thus:

On ordinary week-days, Latin Prayers were always said at the College services. They were not abolished until the end of 1861.[5] . . . On Sundays and Holy Days there were Surplice Prayers; the Holy Communion was celebrated once a month after the Choral Matins: its proper place no doubt, but involving a service of nearly two hours' length before breakfast. College sermons were not known; but when the Dean or a Canon preached in his turn before the University, the sermon always took place at Christ Church and not at St. Mary's.[6]

Dodgson took attendance at chapel seriously. Just over a month after he began his undergraduate education he wrote to his sister: "I have to record a very sad incident, namely my missing morning chapel. . . . I have had no imposition, nor heard anything about it. It is rather vexatious to have happened so soon, as I had intended never to be late" (*Life* 49). In addition to morning chapel at 8:00 a.m. and evening chapel at 9:00 p.m. each day,

"There is a choral service in the cathedral morning and evening throughout the year; [7] on the mornings of Sundays and holydays at 8 a.m., on other days at 10 a.m., and in the afternoon at 4:00."[8]

To these regular daily and Sunday services must be added the weekly university sermons, preached by heads of the colleges and other officials in rotation either at the university parish church of St. Mary's in High Street or, when the task fell to the dean of Christ Church or one of the cathedral canons, in the Cathedral of Christ Church. This was Dodgson's main opportunity to hear sermons, for, at Christ Church, "At the bishop's ordination a sermon is preached in the choir, and as in all other college chapels on Easter day; with these exceptions, there is no sermon preached in Christ Church" (773–74).

Thus during his undergraduate years, Dodgson would have attended, at a minimum, chapel on each weekday, Matins on Sunday (with Holy Communion once a month), and the weekly preaching of the University Sermon. This pattern continued during term time, barring illness or infirmity, for the rest of his life. He also often heard visiting preachers, sometimes recording his impressions of them in his diary. Living in a foundation that was also a cathedral, he would have been able to attend daily morning and evening services sung by the choir as well. On occasion he read one of the lessons at chapel.

Dodgson would not, as an undergraduate, have attended theological lectures by the university professors. Rather, he would have studied divinity as part of his daily work within his college. As E. B. Pusey explained:

The theological instruction of those educated for Holy Orders in Oxford is not, and has not, I suppose, ever been given by the divinity professors; it has practically been given by the tutors. . . .

The study of divinity is in this way spread over the three years of the steady under graduate's life. Such students, as a matter of course, would not continue their classical studies on the Sunday, and would read divinity. In my own time, and since, the tutors have often on the Sunday given lectures in the New Testament. The student would thus have one seventh of his time as a religious act, free for theological study, besides whatever might be given to it amid the employments of the week. (790)

In addition to tutorials that covered (along with classical studies) matters of divinity, there was, according to an 1853 letter from Germain Lavie, the registrar of Christ Church, "a Divinity lecture delivered in the lecture room to the undergraduates of the college by virtue of a private benefaction" (774).

There are few records of Dodgson's specific studies in divinity during his undergraduate years, but he would have made a careful study of scripture and theology. In 1852 he wrote to his sister that he had that day to "get up work on the Acts of the Apostles, 2 Greek Plays, and the Satires of Horace" (*Letters* 22).

Some of the only evidence of Dodgson's thinking during his undergraduate years is a trio of short essays he read aloud in Hall. These pieces were chosen as the best weekly theme by a Christ Church man on a moral subject and read aloud at a Saturday-afternoon gathering of the college. Though in penning these essays Dodgson was responding to a particular assignment, they nonetheless, as the only surviving documents from his undergraduate years that touch on moral subjects, are worth examining. What emerges from them is not surprising, given Dodgson's upbringing—a vision of the world as divided into good and evil and an understanding of the endowments of mankind as capable of being used for the promotion of either. But here he takes a more mature view of the relationship between good and evil than what, perhaps, he learned from the devotional cards of his childhood.

His first essay, on the subject of beauty, was delivered just a few months into his undergraduate career, on 22 November 1851. Dodgson argued that the ability to perceive beauty is limited to humankind and that the "highest and grandest" form of beauty can be found "in the divine form and features of man." But he stops short of claiming that the faculty of perceiving beauty is endowed upon men by God, saying only that "we have no means of knowing." It is easy to understand his hesitancy here for he goes on to briefly explicate the dual nature of beauty. On the one hand, he writes, the pleasures derived from perceiving beauty are "among the highest, the most ennobling, and the most enduring which our nature is capable of receiving." However, he also notes that the "sense of love and admiration for the object in whom this Beauty is perceived" is wholly unjust as the possession of Beauty is "beyond the will and control of the individual admired."[9]

On 22 May 1852, Dodgson read an essay on the subject "Nothing aids us which may not also injure us." He wrote, "Alike within us and without us . . . there is nothing that is not alloyed with some mixture of evil, nothing that the wayward genius of man has not at some time or other wrested to his own hurt. The fault lies not in the things themselves which are thus abused, but in the abuser; it was of his own free choice that he sought out the evil in them, and not the good" (Cohen, *Lewis Carroll* 536–37).

Dodgson presents a view of man who is not only inherently sinful but also possessing of free will: "We may not then, in judging of any faculty, consider only the good it is capable of doing, but also the evil to which it is liable, remembering that, however mighty it may be as an instrument of good, abuse will make it as mighty an instrument of evil" (537).

The final of the three essays is undated, but Morton Cohen has suggested that the handwriting puts it closer to the 1851 essay on beauty than to the 1852 essay. The subject this time was "To despise fame is to despise merit." Dodgson generally sees fame as a factor that drives men toward good deeds, writing, "This it is which upholds the student through long days and nights of incessant toil, which enables him to persevere in obscurity, in poverty, and in distress, content to bear all so that his name may be known here-after as a mighty philosopher, as a discoverer of the hidden things of science, or as one who has benefited mankind by the result of his labours."

Yet, again, Dodgson sees the dichotomy of good and evil in the pursuit of fame, noting that it can drive men to "deeds of reckless folly and excess, if not to worse crimes." He advises a middle path, writing, "we may run into extremes in both directions, either paying too much respect to the opinion of men, or in utterly disregarding it" (537–38).

On Christmas Eve 1852, Dodgson was made a Student of Christ Church[10] on the nomination of his father's old friend E. B. Pusey. This was no mere nepotism, however. As Dodgson's father wrote to him: "I cannot desire stronger evidence than [Pusey's] own words of the fact that you have *won*, and well won, this honour for *yourself*, and that it is bestowed as a matter of *justice* to *you*, and not of *kindness* to *me*" (*Life* 53–55). On 18 December 1854, Charles Lutwidge Dodgson received his bachelor's degree and on 5 February 1857, his master of arts degree. After receiving the honorary appointment of Master of the House, he was made mathematical lecturer at Christ Church beginning in Michaelmas Term of 1855, a position that gave him financial independence and that he would hold until 1881.

During his years of study at Oxford, Dodgson met one of his closest friends, and a man who would become an advisor on religious topics, Henry Parry Liddon. Liddon had arrived at Christ Church four years prior to Dodgson and held a number of positions in and near Oxford for many years, including, from 1854 to 1859, vice principal of Cuddesdon College, the theological training school established by Bishop of Oxford Samuel Wilberforce. Liddon became a leading figure in the Church of England, being made a canon of St. Paul's in 1870, and brought the high church ideals of the Tractarians to a wide popular audience. He was a close disciple of Pusey and Keble, reviving their Anglo-Catholic ideas of the previous generation in his sermons.

In 1867, Dodgson would embark on his only foreign journey in the company of Liddon—a trip through Europe to Russia which included near daily visits to churches and many discussions about religion, ceremony, etc.—but long before that the two men were close, and Dodgson often sought advice on religious matters from Liddon. Over the years he consulted him about ordination, about finding a church in which to assist with the service, about learning to read Hebrew, and about matters of reverence in the Christ Church Common Room.

Dodgson frequently attended lectures and sermons by Liddon, including his 1867 Bampton Lectures. Liddon provided one of many influences on Dodgson and was probably the most catholic-leaning of Dodgson's close friends. While Dodgson did not always agree with Liddon on matters of ritual, he had a deep affection and respect for him and felt comfortable consulting him on matters of faith. When Liddon died in 1890, Dodgson wrote in his diary on 10 September: "My dear old friend, Dr. Liddon, died yesterday. It is a heavy loss, to many friends, and to the whole English Church."

Though now studying far from home, Charles returned to Croft for most of his vacation time, so remained under his father's influence.[11] Likely he heard his father preach both at St. Peter's Church in Croft and, beginning in 1852, in the early weeks of each year when the family was in residence there, at the cathedral in Ripon. One sermon preached by his father that may have influenced Charles was "Do the First Works," preached at Ripon Cathedral on Trinity Sunday 1851. Here, Rev. C. Dodgson warned a group of newly ordained priests against the dangers of letting the church slip into degeneracy:

> The first error which I would notice, as being not unfrequent in public preaching . . . is the desire of *simplifying*, as it is termed, the system of Christian Teaching, partly by selecting a few doctrines as the sole topics of instruction, and partly by attempting to divest these of all *mysterious* character. . . . The simple and ignorant, thus trained and instructed, will suppose that the partial teaching, to which they have been confined, contains all that it is needful for any to believe or know. . . .
>
> Another error, and one which grows directly out of the former, is that of habitually suppressing in Ministerial Teaching . . . positive doctrinal

statements of the Church, that they may not offend the inveterate preju-
dices . . . of certain classes of our hearers.[12]

Rev. Charles Dodgson wrote that the remedy lay "not by lowering the standard to the level of the popular mind, but by raising the tone of the popular
mind to the level of the yet unmutilated standard."[13]

Near the end of his life, Charles Lutwidge Dodgson echoed his father's
concerns about simplifying church doctrine, complaining in his diary on
21 April 1896 of the preaching of Cyril Fletcher Grant, then incumbent at
Guildford: "His chief aim seemed to be to reduce to 'commonplace' (his
favorite word) all the doctrines of Christianity: and he made several extraordinary assertions . . . which I earnestly hope will not be believed."

In February 1854, Rev. Charles Dodgson gave a speech to a meeting in
Ripon of the Society for the Employment of Additional Curates in Populous Places. He defended the need for additional clergymen in the country's most populous areas. In speaking about the growth of population and
the ebbing of religion in the great cities of England, Dodgson asked: "Did
they not see how much time and zeal were appropriated by men for the
accumulation of wealth? Had they not seen and did they not still see how
large bodies of manufacturers and persons engaged in other branches of
business were raising up building above building and warehouses above
warehouses, and doing everything that was possible for the purpose of carrying out some great worldly interest, yet all the while forgetting the Great
Giver of all good, to whom they were wholly indebted for all the wealth
they possessed?"[14]

Dodgson lays blame for the lack of religion and the general state of degeneracy among urban populations directly at the feet of the men driving the
Industrial Revolution. His son always showed a much greater affinity for the
countryside than for urban life, enshrining that pastoral vision of England
in *Alice's Adventures in Wonderland.*

Shortly before Charles Lutwidge Dodgson received his bachelor's degree, his father became archdeacon of Richmond. He delivered his first
charge as archdeacon in May 1855. Along with remarks on a variety of
church business, Dodgson spoke of the need not to bow to public opinion.
"It is often cast as a taunt and reproach upon the clergy," he said, "that they
do not move with the spirit of the age. . . . [W]e may thank God that it is
so. Amidst all the transient variations which are ever flitting over the face of
human affairs, it seems to have been ordained, in the wisdom and love of

God, that mankind shall possess, in His visible Church on earth, an object fixed in its position and immutable in its character."[15]

Years later, an Oxford colleague would say of Charles Lutwidge Dodgson that a sermon he gave was preached "by one who held to the faith of his childhood, undisturbed by the learning or the criticism of any later age."[16] Like his father, he believed in the importance of maintaining that "noble vessel," God's Church on Earth, on a straight course, whatever winds of change might blow.

At five minutes until midnight on the last day of 1857, Charles Lutwidge Dodgson sat in his small room on the third floor of the Croft Rectory writing in his diary. The moon had just passed full, and its light streamed in through the window above the bed. "What do I propose as the work of the New Year?," he wrote. He knew well what the first item on the list needed to be, though it had vexed him so that he hesitated for a moment before writing it. Yet surely in this coming year he must decide; he must take some action. And so he wrote, the scratch of the pen the only sound in the room as the new year arrived: "Reading for Ordination at the end of the year, and settling the subject finally and definitely in my mind."

· EIGHT ·

Learning and Godly Conversation

Charles sat in the pews of Christ Church Cathedral, his college chapel where he had attended hundreds of services over the past eleven years. Yet none of those services had been as momentous as this. Rev. James Woodford, examining chaplain to the bishop of Oxford, Samuel Wilberforce, had just ascended the pulpit to preach a sermon in which he addressed those waiting to be ordained to Holy Orders. In a short time, Charles would be a deacon in the Church of England, but the road to this day had been long.

Charles Lutwidge Dodgson delayed ordination for many years. Twelve other Christ Church men received their B.A. degrees on the same day as Dodgson (18 December 1854). Of the seven who proceeded to Holy Orders, all had been ordained deacon by 1857. Dodgson waited another four years, and did not even complete a course of theological lectures (two such courses were required prior to ordination) until 1856. He never proceeded to priests' orders.

Dodgson first mentions his ordination in his surviving diaries on 13 March 1855. In an outline of his planned reading, he writes "Divinity reading for Ordination . . . should take precedence of all other." At this time he intended to present himself for ordination, yet it would be another six years before he did so.

The terms of Dodgson's Studentship at Christ Church required he take Holy Orders, so if he planned to continue the life he had set out for himself of mathematical tuition and residence in the college, he would have to be ordained. In a letter to his cousin William Wilcox in 1885, Dodgson explained his history with respect to ordination:

When I was about 19, the Studentships at Christ Church were in the gift of the Dean and Chapter—each Canon having a turn: and Dr. Pusey, having a turn, sent for me, and told me he would like to nominate me, but had made a rule to nominate *only* those who were going to take Holy Orders. I told him that was my intention, and he nominated me. . . .

When I reached the age for taking Deacon's Orders, I found myself established as the Mathematical Lecturer, and with no sort of inclination to give it up and take parochial work: and I had grave doubts whether it would not be my duty *not* to take Orders. I took advice on this point (Bishop Wilberforce was one that I applied to), and came to the conclusion that, so far from educational work (even Mathematics) being unfit occupation for a clergyman, it was distinctly a *good* thing that many of our educators should be men in Holy Orders.

And a further doubt occurred. I could not feel sure that I should ever wish to take *Priest's* Orders. And I asked Dr. Liddon whether he thought I should be justified in taking Deacon's Orders as a sort of experiment, which would enable me to try how the occupations of a clergyman suited me, and *then* decide whether I would take full Orders. He said "most certainly"—and that a Deacon is in a totally different position from a Priest: and much more free to regard himself as *practically* a layman. So I took Deacon's Orders in that spirit. And now, for several reasons, I have given up all idea of taking full Orders, and regard myself (though occasionally doing small clerical acts, such as helping at the Holy Communion) as practically a layman. (*Letters* 602–3)

We have no reason to doubt these statements; however, Dodgson does not explain *why* he felt he did not want to take priests' orders or why, in the light of the counsel received from Wilberforce and Liddon, he took so long to be ordained a deacon. His nephew and biographer provides a little more information:

[H]is mind was very much exercised on the subject of taking Holy Orders. Not only was this step necessary if he wished to retain his Studentship, but also he felt that it would give him much more influence among the undergraduates, and thus increase his power of doing good. On the other hand, he was not prepared to live the life of almost puritanical strictness which was then considered essential for a clergyman, and he saw that the impediment of speech from which he suffered would greatly interfere with the proper performance of his clerical duties.

The Bishop of Oxford, Dr. Wilberforce, had expressed the opinion that "the resolution to attend theatres or operas was an absolute disqualification for Holy Orders," which discouraged him very much, until it transpired that this statement was only meant to refer to the parochial clergy. He discussed the matter with Dr. Pusey, and with Dr. Liddon. The latter said that "he thought a deacon might lawfully, if he found himself unfit for the work, abstain from direct ministerial duty." And so, with many qualms about his own unworthiness, he at last decided to prepare definitely for ordination. (*Life* 74)

While no specific reference to attendance in theaters has been located in any of Wilberforce's writings, Collingwood's analysis of the situation provides a good starting point. The truth of Dodgson's hesitation may have been more complicated than a desire to attend the theater and a concern about his speech difficulties and more deeply seated in the feelings of unworthiness mentioned by Collingwood.

The issue of attendance at the theater cannot be isolated from Dodgson's general enjoyment of worldly pleasures. In his *Addresses to the Candidates for Ordination,* Bishop Wilberforce described the temptations of the academic clergyman—"the common temptation to a life of indolent and easy self-indulgence, whether in its grosser form of enjoying every day plenty of food and plenty of amusement, or in its subtler form of living for mere intellectual excitement."[1] While this may not seem an apt description of Dodgson's life at Oxford, this and other statements in Wilberforce's addresses hint that proceeding to priests' orders would certainly mean a significant change in his lifestyle. Dodgson's "amusements" at the time were many—his love of art galleries, his hobby of photography, his enjoyment of travel, his frequent social visits, and his attendance at the theater.

Speaking of the spirit of love in which a clergyman must work, Wilberforce wrote, "when it is real it will lead to the self-denying abandonment of ease, favourite pursuits, and of pleasant company" (93). He warns of "gratifying freely a taste for literature, or exercise, or any other pursuits which would draw us aside from our chief purpose" (109) and of "too free an indulgence in lawful pleasures" (131). "Men who wish to lower for themselves the ministerial standard reason backwards," he writes. "They say, Such and such amusements . . . moderately enjoyed, are clearly not wrong in a layman . . . why then should they be wrong in a clergyman?" (174). But Wilberforce wrote that pastimes which, "though not actually wrong, [were] yet manifestly unsuitable to our office" (216).

All this might add up to the "life of almost puritanical strictness" to which Collingwood referred, and Wilberforce certainly had the authority to enforce such strictness. The final question from the ordination service reads, in the order for ordaining deacons, "Will you reverently obey your Ordinary, and other chief Ministers of the Church . . . following with a glad mind and will their godly admonitions?" Wilberforce was Dodgson's "Ordinary," and in commenting on this question the bishop stated, "When, therefore, we are bidden by a competent authority to do anything or to leave it undone, we have at first sight simply one course, and that is to obey" (264).

Likely his bishop's strictures against worldly amusements played a role in Dodgson's foot-dragging prior to ordination and in his unwillingness to proceed to priests' orders. While Dodgson changed some of his habits following his ordination—recording prayers in his diary with more frequency and preaching sermons—he did not abandon his pursuit of worldly amusements.

Wilberforce also frequently warned against idleness, which he called a "great snare" (158). "Idleness, I need scarcely remind you, is the fruitful parent of almost every other fault" (193). Entries in Dodgson's surviving diaries prior to his ordination show his concern on this topic. On New Year's Eve 1856, he wrote, "I am afraid that lately I have been even more irregular than ever, and more averse to exertion," and on 1 September 1857, "One good result at least, springs out of my former habits of indolence, and that is a continual spurring motive to work, as a kind of self-retribution for so much lost time." On the final day of that year, he wrote as one of his New Year's resolutions, "Constant improvements of habits of activity, punctuality, etc."

Dodgson was also concerned about his ability to conduct religious arguments, something he had so often seen his father do publicly. Here Dodgson may have specifically been looking toward possible life as a priest, for the service of ordination for priests in the Book of Common Prayer includes some questions not in the service for deacons, one of those being, "Will you be ready, with all faithful diligence, to banish and drive away all erroneous and strange doctrines contrary to God's word?" Although the deacon's ordination service does not include this question, Bishop Wilberforce wrote, in his *Addresses to the Candidates*, "To all ranks of our body this duty specially belongs" (82), and went on to say:

It belongs to those of us for whom God's providence has marked out as our post an academic life. For you, my brethren, are indeed set on the watchman's tower: to your eyes lie open the distant plains: you can see, if you will, what are the dangers which are threatened in the future by the early indications of the mind of the rising generation: you have leisure and endowments, and all the accumulated stores of the past for this very purpose, that you may, whenever need is, send forth champions armed duly for the conflict from your strongholds of calm observation, of ancient truth and of Christian learning. (82–83)

But Dodgson had serious doubts about his abilities in this arena. On 2 February 1857, after an argument with his younger brother Wilfrid, who had matriculated at Christ Church, Oxford, the previous May, he wrote in his diary:

> In the evening Wilfred and I had a long argument about college duties, he supporting the theory that each man should judge for himself on each particular college rule, whether he should obey it or not, and ignoring the principle of submission to discipline which would make him obey all alike. My arguments ended as all viva voce argument seems to me to do, in returning to the starting point. . . .
>
> This also suggests to me grave doubts as to the work of the ministry which I am looking forward to, if I find it so hard to prove a plain duty to one individual, and that one unpractised in argument, how can I ever be ready to face the countless sophisms and ingenious arguments against religion which a clergyman must meet with!

Dodgson's feelings of unworthiness for ordination may also be related to what his father taught about the responsibilities and burdens of the clergy: "To feed the flock of Christ—to spread the knowledge of the Gospel of salvation—to lead the sinful soul to the Saviour of sinners—to instruct the ignorant, to encourage the faint-hearted, to console the afflicted—to maintain moreover the dignity and purity of the Church, to which we belong, against the secret inroads of heresy, and the open attacks of avowed hostility—such is the task, which has devolved upon us."[2]

Later in the same sermon Rev. Charles Dodgson warned that "the habits, the conversation, the outward demeanour, of the Christian Minister . . . should be in keeping with the peculiar character of the office which he fills" (25–26). In 1838, he spoke of clergy as "having no longer power over themselves; as having sealed an irrevocable bond of self-resignation; as having for ever renounced selfish interest, pursuits, advantages, and pleasures."[3]

As archdeacon of Richmond, Rev. Charles Dodgson, in May 1859, described an ideal member of the parochial clergy:

> One steady friend ever at hand to teach, to counsel, to help, and to comfort; ever treading the same humble, quiet, Heaven-doted, self-denying course of doing good, in the Parish Church, in the Parish School, in the poor man's home, in the retreat of the mourner, by the bed of the sick and dying; a living impersonation of the Church, for which he ministers; teaching all around him to love and serve her, by the very earnestness and reality, with which he loves and serves her himself.[4]

Charles L. Dodgson may also have been humbled by his father's career in the church. By the time Charles was wrestling with the issue of taking Holy Orders, his father held not just the living of Croft and a canonry at Ripon, but also the offices of archdeacon of Richmond and of chancellor of the Diocese of Ripon.

A final reason for Charles Lutwidge Dodgson's qualms about taking Holy Orders may be found in words of both his father and his bishop on the subject of ordained clergy submitting to the church doctrine. "The doctrines of the Church of England," wrote his father, "are the doctrines of her Ministers. On every point, on which she has declared herself, the right of private judgment . . . is no longer theirs."[5] Bishop Wilberforce echoed these words in his *Addresses to the Candidates,* writing, "remember also, that the decisions of your Church must settle the question for you as her minister" (72).

While there is no evidence that Dodgson was, in the 1850s, wrestling with his own disagreement with matters of church doctrine, later in life he stood contrary to established doctrine on at least two issues—the remarriage of those who have been divorced and the doctrine of eternal punishment (see pp. 247–48 and 263–73 in this volume).

While it is impossible to state unequivocally Dodgson's reasons for delaying his ordination as a deacon and eschewing ordination as a priest, it seems a combination of issues, some practical and some deeply personal, led to these decisions. The teachings of his bishop that a clergyman, and especially a priest, must give up worldly pleasures and pastimes; his concern that his speech hesitation might interfere with his reading of divine services; his guilt about what he perceived as his own idleness and indolence; his concern that he would be unable, by argument, to defend the church against its enemies; his fear that he would not live up to the standards set by his father in both word and example; and his doubts about certain professed doctrines of the Church of England—all these factors may have contributed to "qualms" that Dodgson felt. Nonetheless, in 1855, he took the first steps in what would be a six-year journey toward ordination as a deacon.

In his plan of reading in his diary for 13 March 1855, Dodgson wrote: "Divinity: keep up Gospels and Acts in Greek, and go on to Epistles. . . . Divinity reading for Ordination: this should take precedence of all other, I must consult my Father on the subject. Other subjects; Scripture History, Church Architecture. . . ." Whether he consulted with his father on the subject of what to read for ordination, he did not record, though certainly, as an examining chaplain, Rev. Charles Dodgson would have had thoughts on the subject. At Croft during the Easter Vacation on 5 April 1855, C. L. Dodgson wrote, "I began reading Burton's Lectures on Church History," and two weeks later, on 18 April, "As to Divinity reading, I shall at present keep to Burton's History of the Church,[6] and Scripture History."

One of the requirements for ordination for university men was attending at least two courses of lectures delivered by the university professors of divinity. Each course consisted of eighteen lectures, and to receive a certificate of completion one had to attend at least sixteen. C. L. Dodgson attended three such courses, though not without a false start. When he returned from his Easter Vacation, during which he had been reading for ordination, he recorded in his diary on 1 May 1855, "went to Heurtley's first lecture on the Creed," referring to the first of a series of lectures delivered by Lady Margaret Professor of Divinity Charles Abel Heurtley. However, Dodgson did not attend enough of the lectures that Lent Term 1855, and he began again more than a year later in Michaelmas Term 1856, attending enough of the lectures for Professor Heurtley to sign the form indicating Dodgson had completed the course.

Charles Abel Heurtley, previously a Fellow of Corpus Christi College, was appointed Lady Margaret Professor of Divinity in 1853—a post he held for forty-two years until his death in 1895. Attached to the post was a canonry at Christ Church, so Dodgson had likely known Heurtley since the former's undergraduate days. Heurtley's character was marked by "grave earnestness, modest dignity, refined and unobtrusive courtesy. . . . He was of a profoundly Christian temper, and, though himself of a somewhat narrow school of evangelical theory, he was a harmonious element in a Chapter containing the most widely contrasted members."[7]

Heurtley's primary text for his lectures on the Creed was *An Exposition of the Creed* by John Pearson, a book first published in 1659 and still, in the 1850s, standard reading for those studying for Holy Orders. Pearson's work explicates a single paragraph—the Apostles' Creed, the shortest and simplest of the three creeds to which allegiance is demanded in Article 8 of the Thirty-Nine Articles. The book was published in two volumes—the first being Pearson's exposition of nearly five hundred pages and the second more than three hundred pages of notes, including passages in Greek and Hebrew. In his introduction Pearson described his method:

> First, to settle the words of each Article according to their antiquity and generality of reception in the Creed. Secondly, to explicate and unfold the terms, and to endeavour a right notion and conception of them as they are to be understood in the same. Thirdly, to shew what are those truths which are naturally contained in those terms so explicated. . . . Fourthly to declare what is the necessity of believing those truths, what efficacy and influence they have in the soul, and upon the life of the believer. Lastly . . . briefly to deliver the sum of every particular truth, so that every one, when he pronounceth the Creed, may know what he ought to intend, and what he is understood to profess, when he so pronounceth it.[8]

Dodgson had spoken the Creed regularly since childhood and studied its parts as a child and in preparation for confirmation. But never had he delved into the Creed in such depth. Pearson's style, as his early nineteenth-century editor Edward Burton wrote, was "rugged and antiquated, even for the age in which he lived" (v). At the end of his explication of each of the articles, Pearson gave a simple summary, rendered in the first person, of what the speaker of that article professed. An example is this summary of the belief professed in the second article, "which was conceived of the Holy Ghost":

> I assent unto this as a most necessary and infallible truth, that the only-begotten Son of God, begotten by the Father before all worlds, very God of very God, was conceived and born, and so made man, taking to himself the human nature, consisting of a soul and body, and conjoining it with the Divine in the unity of his Person. I am fully assured that the Word was in this manner made flesh, that he was really and truly conceived in the womb of a woman, but not after the manner of men; not by carnal copulation, not by the common way of human propagation, but by the singular, powerful, invisible, immediate operation of the Holy Ghost, whereby a Virgin was beyond the Law of nature enabled to conceive, and that which was conceived in her was

originally and completely sanctified. And in this latitude I profess to believe in Jesus Christ, *which was conceived by the Holy Ghost.* (209)

Pearson's views were high Anglican, and, by the time Dodgson was reading them in the 1850s, some were beginning to seem old-fashioned. As one reviewer of an 1810 abridgement of Pearson's book wrote, "Considering . . . the advances which have been made in biblical erudition and sound criticism since Bishop Pearson's time, it would have been preferable, in our opinion, to have written a new exposition of the Creed."[9]

Among those doctrines put forth by Pearson which Dodgson would see challenged in his lifetime was that the world was created "not more than six, or at farthest seven thousand years" ago (*Exposition* 86). Pearson's view of judgement stands in stark contrast to the emphasis at the time of the Reformation on redemption by faith not works. He writes that at the time of judgment Christ "shall judge them all according to their works done in the flesh" (361). And on the final page of his treatise, Pearson stated a doctrine which Dodgson would come to disbelieve, the doctrine of eternal punishment: "The unjust after their resurrection and condemnation shall be tormented for their sins in hell, and shall so be continued in torments for ever" (472).

Pearson's summary of "I believe in the Holy Ghost" is perhaps especially pertinent in showing the relationship of man to the divine in everyday matters which Dodgson was taught and which, in many ways, permeated his belief. "I believe," Pearson wrote, "this infinite and eternal Spirit to be . . . the immediate cause of all holiness in us . . . illuminating the understandings of particular persons, rectifying their wills and affections, renovating their natures . . . leading them in their actions, directing them in their devotions, by all ways and means purifying and sanctifying their souls and bodies" (393).

Those who attended Heurtley's lectures on the Creed read not only Pearson but also several supplementary texts, including writings on the Creed by Isaac Barrow[10] and Thomas Jackson.[11] From the works of the early church fathers, Heurtley chose the writings of the late fourth-century theologian Rufinus, St. Augustine's *De fide et symbolo* (*Treatise on Faith and the Creed*), and writings of Cyril of Jerusalem, all of which included explications of the Creed.

William Ince wrote of Heurtley as a lecturer that "his natural shyness and nervousness of manner made lecturing very oppressive to him at first, especially with a large class of forty or fifty men; but he took a lively interest in the work, and thus succeeded, after some experience, in imparting a like interest to his listeners."[12]

Dodgson took the lectures seriously and wrote in his diary on 15 November 1856: "I think of devoting my hour in the Library on Mondays, Wednesdays and Fridays, to reading Pearson for Heurtley's lectures. I shall thus have the advantage of having all the original authorities round me to refer to."

After the false start with Heurtley in May 1855, Dodgson, in Lent Term 1856, attended his first full series of theological lectures—delivered by Regius Professor of Divinity William Jacobson. He would ultimately attend two sets of Jacobson's lectures.

William Jacobson was vice principal of Magdalen Hall when he was made Regius Professor of Divinity in 1848. The position came with a canonry at Christ Church, and Jacobson served until 1865, when he became bishop of Chester. On arriving at his canonical residence within Christ Church in 1848, Jacobson had not only a wife but six children (though at least three died in childhood). The family resided on the east side of Tom Quad adjacent to the gateway leading to the Hall, so Charles Lutwidge Dodgson could hardly fail to notice them during his early years at Christ Church. His diaries for the first half of 1857 include several references to social engagements at which Jacobson was present. Dodgson's father's patron, Charles Thomas Longley, was a lifelong friend of Jacobson.

Jacobson's public lectures as Professor of Divinity focused on his favorite subject, the Book of Common Prayer. The delivery of these lectures, in the Latin Chapel of Christ Church Cathedral, has been variously described in terms which may reveal more about the listeners than the lecturer. While some called them "a mere list of books," and one cited the weight of all the books he recommended as "five and a half tons," others felt differently. "Jacobson's lectures were of the greatest importance," wrote one who heard him, "and would have ranked in the highest class of excellence had they been delivered in a course in a German University."[13]

Another wrote that Jacobson "was highly communicative and perfectly delightful: expressing his individual opinion and personal sentiments, without reserve. . . . Next to the largeness of his knowledge, his singular fairness,—the absence in him of prejudice and partisanship,—was what used to strike us most. . . . It was a great help *to be shown* (as well as to hear about) the præ-Reformation Service books: to have the place pointed out to one where the germ of a Collect is to be found; or to have one's attention directed to an important rubric in some forgotten 'Use.'"[14]

Stone baptismal font now
standing outside All Saints
Church, Daresbury. (Photograph
by Charlie Lovett)

Rev. Charles Dodgson
(father of Charles Lutwidge
Dodgson). (Photograph
by Charles Lutwidge
Dodgson, 1856; Gernsheim
Photography Collection,
Harry Ransom Center,
University of Texas at Austin)

Original building of Richmond Grammar School. (From Christopher Clarkson, *The History of Richmond* [Richmond: Thomas Bowman, 1821])

Archibald Campbell Tait. (Engraving by D. J. Pound from a photograph by J. J. E. Mayall, 1862)

George Edward Lynch Cotton. (From Sophia Anne Cotton, *Memoir of George Edward Lynch Cotton* [London: Longmans, Green, 1871])

Ritualistic celebration of Eucharist. (From Frederick George Lee, *Directorium Anglicanum* [London: Thomas Bosworth, 1865])

Great Quadrangle, Christ Church, as it appeared on C. L. Dodgson's arrival in 1850. (Engraving by J. Le Keux after F. Mackenzie [Oxford: Parker, 1833])

Bishop Samuel Wilberforce.
(Engraving by D. J. Pound from a
photograph by J. J. E. Mayall, 1858)

Watercolor by Charles Lutwidge Dodgson of the three Liddell sisters (1862).
(Lovett Collection)

Interior of Christ Church Cathedral, Oxford. (Uncredited photograph from an 1877 album assembled by Charles Lutwidge Dodgson)

Interior of Rugby chapel, where C. L. Dodgson was confirmed and received his first communion in 1847. (From the *Illustrated London News* [22 November 1862], after George Barnard; Lovett Collection)

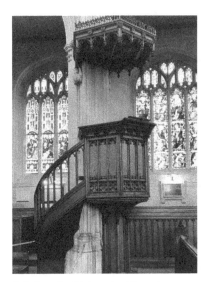

Pulpit at the University Church of St. Mary's from which Charles Lutwidge Dodgson preached. (Photograph by Charlie Lovett)

Grave of Charles Lutwidge Dodgson (Lewis Carroll). (Photograph by Charlie Lovett)

Dodgson appears not to have attended Jacobson's public lectures but rather two series of private lectures. On 26 February 1856, Dodgson "went to the first of Jacobson's lectures," yet Jacobson's public lectures for that term began on 31 January. On 5 May 1857 he wrote in his diary, "Went to the first of Jacobson's private course of lectures on the Prayer-book." The private lectures took place in Jacobson's rooms, and one former pupil recalled that "any one coming to a private lecture a little before the time, was pretty sure to find him standing at his upright desk absorbed in study; the floor strewn with toys, and Burton, his favourite child, (if one child could be called a favourite where all were so fondly loved,) crying "Who!" to a little wooden horse. Two volumes of Augustine set on end were observed to afford commodious stabling, while 'Lamb on Articles' left nothing to be desired in the way of a roof."[15]

One might easily imagine the pleasure which Dodgson, on entering Jacobson's rooms for his first private lecture on 26 February 1856, would take in such a scene, fond as he was of children and play. The happy picture would not have greeted him when he attended Jacobson's lectures the following year, for poor Burton died on 20 September 1856. Despite the domestic scene, "[Jacobson] would take as much pains with a class consisting of two or three men as if twenty had been present: was always cheerful, always indulgent, always evidently fond of his work; never anxious to get rid of us."[16]

The second course of Jacobson's lectures Dodgson attended focused on the Book of Common Prayer, and the first likely took as its subject the writings of the early church fathers. For these lectures Jacobson took as his textbook the *Scriptorum ecclesiasticorum opuscula* of Martin Joseph Routh,[17] a collection of patristic writings edited by the former president of Magdalen College and including works by Hippolytus, Tertullian, Irenaeus, Cyprian, Polycarp, and others. One student wrote of these lectures: "I should find it hard to describe the advantage it was, under his guidance, to acquaint oneself with such choice samples of patristic Antiquity. He had the subject at his fingers' ends. There was no time wasted. But O how fast the hour seemed to slip away!"[18]

To be ordained, Dodgson required certificates of completion from two courses of theological lectures; from early 1856 through mid-1857 he obtained three such certificates, yet he would wait more than three years before he took any further direct action toward ordination. On New Year's Eve 1857, he wrote in his diary "What do I propose as the work of the new year? Reading for Ordination at the end of the year, and settling the subject finally and definitely in my mind." In March 1858, the surviving diaries break off for a period of four years.

As early as 3 August, the notice for the bishop of Oxford's December 1861 ordination, when Charles Lutwidge Dodgson would enter the order of deacons, was announced in the papers: "The Bishop of Oxford has given notice that he will hold a general ordination at Christmas."[19]

Dodgson, in Croft at the time, may not have seen this notice. In any case, he thought in early August that he would submit himself for ordination in September, and he wrote to the diocesan registrar on 5 August: "I am intending to offer myself at the Bishop of Oxford's examination in September, to be ordained Deacon. I gave his Lordship notice of this about 4 months ago. Would you kindly inform me what else is necessary (of papers to be sent in, etc.) before presenting myself for examination, and when and where I ought to appear?" (*Letters* 50).

Dodgson did not take Holy Orders in September, but in December. There are two possible reasons for this: he may have decided not to return south from Croft until after 22 September, when the ordination service was scheduled (Michaelmas Term did not begin until October 10). Also Bishop Wilberforce held his September ordination service at the parish church of Lavington, Sussex, about eighty miles south of Oxford. Dodgson would be among those ordained on 22 December 1861 at Christ Church Cathedral, in his own college.

In accordance with canon 34, Dodgson, before his ordination, had to present "Letters testimonial" of his "good life and conversation."[20] This he did, submitting the required letter on 9 December 1861, less than two weeks before the scheduled ordination.

> To the Right Reverend Father in God Samuel by Divine
> Permission Lord Bishop of Oxford.
>
> Whereas our well beloved in Christ Charles L Dodgson Master
> of Arts Student of Christ Church in the University of Oxford
> hath declared to us his intention of offering himself as a candidate
> for the Sacred Office of a Deacon and for that end hath requested
> of us letters testimonial of his learning and good behaviour we
> therefore whose names are hereunto subscribed do testify that
> the said Charles L Dodgson having been personally known to us
> for the last three years, hath during that time lived soberly and
> honestly; nor hath he at any time, as far as we know and believe,

maintained or written anything contrary to the doctrine and discipline of the Church of England and moreover we think him a person worthy to be admitted to the Sacred Order of Deacons. In witness whereof we have hereunto set our hands this ninth day of December in the year of our Lord one thousand eight hundred and sixty one.

> Henry Liddell, Dean
> Charles W. Sandford, Censor
> F. H. Joyce, Censor[21]

Canon 35 stipulates that "The Bishop, before he admit any person to holy orders, shall diligently examine him in the presence of those Ministers that shall assist him at the imposition of hands." Samuel Wilberforce, the bishop of Oxford, made his examinations a sort of spiritual retreat, hosting all the candidates for ordination at Cuddesdon—the theological college he had founded opposite the bishop's palace a few miles from Oxford in 1854. These retreats lasted several days, and to such a retreat Dodgson traveled in December 1861.

The Cuddesdon examination of December 1861 was especially crowded. The bishop of Oxford's office sent a letter to several of the candidates asking that they secure lodgings in Oxford and travel to Cuddesdon each day "owing to the unusual number of Candidates" for ordination.[22] Dodgson was not one of the men who received this letter, however, so he stayed at Cuddesdon for the duration of the retreat. A notice in the *Ecclesiastical Gazette* referring to Bishop Wilberforce's preparation of candidates for ordination states that "The Examination of the Candidates will commence at Cuddesdon Palace, on Thursday, the 19th of December, at ten o'clock."[23] Other accounts of Bishop Wilberforce's preordination retreats make it clear that they lasted the whole of the Ember Week;[24] likely this notice refers not to the entire retreat but to the actual examinations, which would have come toward the end of the week. In all likelihood, Dodgson arrived at Cuddesdon on Monday, 16 December 1861 and remained there through Saturday, 21 December. Wilberforce's biographer described the examination retreat:

> Each day of the Ember Week the Bishop himself, at the morning and evening services, spoke, generally from the lessons for the day, on the work and life which was then beginning with those who heard him. . . . The great principle

that governed the arranging of these seasons, was first the securing of a bright social intercourse among all brought together by them. Every meal was taken at the palace with the Bishop and his chaplains, and the Bishop was unwearied in his efforts to make all at their ease, and to promote a pleasant, all-including conversation. Spiritual preparation rather than the mere examination, was made the dominant idea outside the hour of necessary recreation. The questions were never printed, but given out orally. . . . They aimed at bringing out not mere intellectual knowledge, but the principles on which the candidates would be likely to administer their parishes, and to teach their flocks. . . . This was the time for a close searching into character and motives; for words of rebuke or encouragement; sometimes for rejection.[25]

John William Burgon gave a further sense of the proceedings:

The days at Cuddesdon were days which Candidates for the Ministry found it impossible ever to forget, or rather which they learned to look back upon ever after with gratitude and secret joy. The examination was felt to be in every sense a reality. The Candidates . . . were brought daily within the sphere of the Bishop's influence; in the private chapel of the palace, besides listening every day to a short address, they received on the eve of their Ordination a Charge which for persuasiveness and power certainly seemed far superior to anything of the kind they were ever invited to listen to in after years. . . . At the private interview the Bishop showed himself really acquainted with the man before him; and blending the language of affection with the dignity of his office, contrived to establish a permanent relation between himself and the candidate which might easily ripen afterwards into friendship, but could not possibly be forgotten or ignored. . . . To every candidate, before the imposition of his hands, he presented a copy of the Holy Scriptures, with a short inscription on the fly-leaf.[26]

The retreat at Cuddesdon in December 1861 took place in the shadow of the death of Prince Albert, husband of Queen Victoria, who had died just days earlier, on 14 December. Bishop Wilberforce had been a friend to Albert and participated in the funeral at Windsor the day after he ordained Dodgson. James Woodford, who preached the sermon at Dodgson's ordination and was one of Wilberforce's examining chaplains, wrote, "I remember, as though it were yesterday, the ordination of Advent, 1861—how the whole Ember week at Cuddesdon, usually so bright notwithstanding the work, was darkened by the shadow of the Prince Consort's death. . . . I was to preach the Ordination sermon, and [Wilberforce] was especially anxious that the subject should not go unmentioned, however difficult it might be to weave it into an address to the candidates."[27]

Because Bishop Wilberforce did not print his examination questions, what he asked Charles Dodgson during their private interview is not known. However, there are two clues about the examination, the first being the required reading list advertised in the bishop's announcement of the ordination:

The Bible
The Greek Testament
Richard Hooker's *Ecclesiastical Polity,* Book 5
John Pearson's *An Exposition of the Creed*
Augustine's *On Christian Doctrine,* Book Four
James Craigie Robertson's *Sketches of Church History*
John. J. Blunt's *Sketch of the Reformation in England*

The list shows a clear understanding of how the Anglican clergyman ought to approach matters of faith and doctrine. First comes the Bible and the Greek testament. In the Thirty-Nine Articles, in the service of ordination, in Rev. Charles Dodgson's writings, and in Bishop Wilberforce's sermons, the message is delivered again and again: "Holy Scriptures containeth all things necessary to salvation: so that whatsoever is not read therein nor proved thereby, is not to be required of any man."[28] Rev. Charles Dodgson pointed out that such proving is, of course, subject to differences of opinion among churchmen. Whence then do they seek guidance? First in the authorized Formularies of the Church of England—the Book of Common Prayer and the Thirty-Nine Articles. For a full understanding of these, a study of the English Reformation is necessary (hence the presence of John James Blunt's book on the list) as well as a familiarity with the great Anglican divines. Wilberforce was particularly fond of both Pearson (whose book he called a "perfect library of divinity") and Richard Hooker, recommending "his profound and most instructive examination of the whole Ecclesiastical Polity of the Church, grounding that polity, as he profoundly does, on the great corner-stones of Christian doctrine."[29] Hooker's book is primarily concerned with matters of church governance but also, through strong theological and philosophical arguments, refutes the position of

Puritanism. "Where the meaning of [the formularies] is also disputed," writes Rev. Charles Dodgson, "the doctrine of the Primitive Church . . . becomes not only a legitimate subject, but the only remaining subject, for inquiry amongst Churchmen."[30] Hence the two remaining books on the list, Augustine of Hippo's *De doctrina christiana* (*On Christian Doctrine*) and James Craigie Robertson's *Sketches of Church History during the First Six Centuries.* Augustine wrote that ministers must discover the truth of God's Word in the scriptures, preach that truth to the people, and defend that truth from attack. Book 4 of *De doctrina christiana,* the part specifically required by Wilberforce, speaks largely about the art of preaching. Taken as a group, these books contained the major elements of learning for one in need of determining matters of doctrine in the Church of England.

The second surviving clue about Dodgson's examination for ordination is a written deacon's examination taken by Henry John Bulkeley, who was ordained by Bishop Wilberforce on 27 May 1866. Why Bulkeley submitted a written examination rather than the usual oral examination is not known, but his papers, in the Oxfordshire Diocesan Archive, reveal the specifics of a Wilberforce examination.

Bulkeley's examination was divided into five sections: Church History, Doctrinal, Old Testament, New Testament, and translations from Latin into English of a passage from Augustine's *Doctrina christiana* and from Greek into English of individual words. While only Bulkeley's answers survive, the scope of the questions is easy to intuit.

The "Church History" section began with two questions about the early church, one about Justin Martyr and one about St. Jerome. In his answer to the first question, Bulkeley described early Christian worship in some detail—no doubt from his reading of Robertson's *Sketches of Church History.* The next few questions concerned the English Reformation—Bulkeley writing that, "The English Church merely returned to the doctrines of the Primitive Church, which had been corrupted by Rome."[31] Question 5 in this section focused on the Book of Common Prayer, and the examinee was expected to know which parts were newly written and what the sources for other parts were. The final complete answer in the "Church History" section related to the schism between the Eastern and Western churches. Clearly, each section of the examination was timed, because another answer breaks off midsentence.

The "Doctrinal" section was in two parts with a total of twelve questions. In the first part, Bulkeley answered questions on the nature of the incarnation, the ordering of the Trinity, the inspiration of the sacred writers, the acts and writing of the apostles and of St. Paul, and the nature of Holy Scripture. Question 2 came directly from Hooker and concerned what Hooker described as "the threefold gift bestowed on Christ,"[32] that being the gifts of Generation, Union, and Unction. In the second part, Bulkeley again cited Hooker in the answer to a question about Christ's body and the doctrine of real presence in the Eucharist. The ensuing questions concerned the nature of miracles, baptism, original sin, and the sacrificial nature of the Eucharist.

The "Old Testament" section of the examination required not just a knowledge of that portion of scripture, but some degree of interpretation and historical context. Some answers are almost purely factual ("Nadab, the son of Jeroboam, the son of Nebab was murdered by Baasha," etc.), whereas others required making connections rather than just repeating facts—for instance, an answer comparing Christ and Isaac. The twelve "New Testament" questions likewise required interpretation of the scriptures. The questions focused mostly on the Gospels with a few referencing Acts and the Epistles and no mention whatsoever of Revelation.

To pass his examination in December 1861 Charles Lutwidge Dodgson needed first an in-depth knowledge of the Bible and especially of the Gospels. Wilberforce wanted more than mere identification of quotes or recitation of facts. He expected an ability to apply the Bible to church doctrine, to make connections between the Old and New Testaments, and to express and defend personal views based on the evidence of scripture. Wilberforce clearly took his published reading list seriously. Of the five books on the list apart from scripture, Bulkeley quotes two directly in his answers (Pearson and Hooker). Two others (Robertson's *Sketches of Church History* and Blunt's book on the English Reformation) clearly formed the basis of the questions on church history. And the Latin translation exercise was drawn from Augustine's *On Christian Doctrine*.

In the years leading up to his ordination, Dodgson's reading of divinity had waxed and waned—after a flurry of entries about reading divinity in 1855, on 12 November 1856 he wrote, "I want time for some Divinity reading, which is at present entirely dropped," and on the last day of that year, "As to the future, I may lay down as absolute necessities, Divinity Reading." Reading for Ordination is again on his list of goals at the end of 1857. But he certainly must have been well prepared for this examination. He had studied scripture not only in English but in Latin and Greek, and he had read and studied Pearson's book on the Creed for Heurtley's series of divinity lectures. He owned an edition of the complete works of Richard Hooker, edited by John Keble. He had read and studied early church history and the reformation—during the Easter Vacation of 1855, he read Burton's lectures on ecclesiastical history. On 5 February 1856, he wrote about his proposed system of reading and under the topic "History," wrote, "I believe the best way is to take one single point (I shall begin with the reformation), and get it up thoroughly, and so on."

While Dodgson could have seen the advertisement for the December ordination as early as August 1861 and had plenty of time to familiarize himself with the specific books required by Wilberforce, he likely already knew this list. Wilberforce had been bishop of Oxford since 1845, and Dodgson had been contemplating ordination for at least six years. At least as early as March 1859, Wilberforce published the same list of books.[33]

One of the best records of the happenings at Cuddesdon in December 1861 comes in the form of Bishop Wilberforce's addresses, delivered at "successive ordinations." Dodgson probably heard these thirteen addresses during his stay at Cuddesdon, and he owned a copy of the published version, printed in 1860 under the title *Addresses to the Candidates for Ordination on the Questions in the Ordination Service.*[34] Wilberforce's talks were based on the questions posed to ordinands during the services of Ordination in the Book of Common Prayer—questions that differed somewhat for priests and deacons.

Of Wilberforce's thirteen addresses, while all were relevant in some ways to anyone contemplating Holy Orders at any level, only five focused on questions included in the deacon's service. Those questions were:

Do you trust that you are inwardly moved by the Holy Ghost to take upon you this Office and Ministration, to serve God for the promoting of his glory, and the edifying of his people?

Do you think that you are truly called, according to the will of our Lord Jesus Christ, and the due order of this Realm, to this Ministry of the Church?

Do you unfeignedly believe all the Canonical Scriptures of the Old and New Testament?

Will you diligently read the same unto the people assembled in the Church where you shall be appointed to serve?

Will you apply all your diligence to frame and fashion your own lives, and the lives of your families, according to the Doctrine of Christ; and to make both yourselves and them, as much as in you lieth, wholesome examples of the flock of Christ?

Will you reverently obey your Ordinary, and other chief Ministers of the Church, and them to whom the charge and government over you is committed, following with a glad mind and will their godly admonitions?[35]

Within Wilberforce's remarks, most of which were aimed at prospective parochial priests, were some specific instructions for academic clergy and for deacons. The first question, concerning the inward call, Wilberforce called the most "perilous." Dodgson had to either aver, in front of his bishop and his God, that he felt "inwardly moved" by the Holy Spirit to take Holy Orders or give up his position at his college. Wilberforce said the "words cannot be unsaid; [the] vows cannot be read backwards" (*Addresses* 4). While he did not directly address the position of academics who must take Holy Orders to maintain their positions, he did note that, "It is not to be thought that a man is moved inwardly by the Holy Ghost to undertake it, when he enters upon it merely because it is an honourable profession, and has attached to it a certain rank, respectability, or endowment; or because his friends have designed him for it; still less, because he has a family living waiting for him; or has good prospects of preferment; or, least of all, because he is unfit for any other business or calling" (7).

Wilberforce went on in his first address to describe the peculiar position of the academic clergyman—a position Dodgson envisioned for himself.

Preachers of the word, indeed, when thereto licensed, you will be at once; and those who are engaged in tuition will find their flock amongst their pupils: as God's ministers, charged with the training of their fellow Christians, you must be far more than mere lecturers, or teachers of philosophy. Yet, still your duties and your temptations differ in many points from those of others. You have far more time, far fewer interruptions, than men who are labouring to supply the pressing spiritual necessities of populous parishes. And your duty seems to be defined by these facts: you should live much in devotion. . . . And, further, you should be deep students of theology. It is for you to maintain amongst us a high tone of Christian learning. (15–16)

Wilberforce's words in his address on "Diligence in Prayer" certainly resonated with Dodgson, and chapter 11 examines how the instructions in this address formed part of the structure on which Dodgson hung his prayer life. This address is one of three in a row that outline the life of the mind expected from a clergyman: "Diligence in Prayer," "Diligence in the Study of Holy Scripture," and "Diligence in Study." In the last of these, added in the second edition of the book, also published in 1860, Wilberforce outlines a course of study of scripture and theology to be pursued throughout the life of the clergyman and building on those books he required all the candidates for Holy Orders to read.[36]

Scattered throughout these addresses is a vision of what Wilberforce expected in the life of a clergyman—strictness, sacrifice, prayer, study, and example, all equally applicable to a deacon or a priest and to academic or parochial clergymen.

The clergyman should have "Some desire, at least, to live nearer to Christ in employment and pursuit than worldly callings render possible" (7). "We must live more and more in secret intercourse and direct communion with Him; we must often retire, at least in thought and aspiration, from business, pleasure, nay, even from outward service itself, into the sacred shrine of His presence" (32–33). The clergyman must have "a deep inward love of souls learned beneath the Cross of Christ: . . . when it is real it will lead to the self-denying abandonment of ease, favourite pursuits, and of pleasant company" (93). "The virtuous life of a clergyman is the most powerful eloquence to persuade all that see it to reverence and love, and, at least, to desire to live like him" (212).

Wilberforce warned against idleness, against "party zeal," against sloth and self-indulgence, against interpreting scripture "perversely" when "the voice of the Church is clear." Rather the clergyman must lead a life of self-denial, prayer, and study; he must have "a daily consistency of life, a manifested spirituality of mind, gravity, sincerity, uncorruptness and habitual soundness of speech" (124).

Wilberforce's addresses may not have been the only public lectures Dodgson heard during Ember Week at Cuddesdon. James Russell Woodford, one of the examining chaplains, gave a series of three ordination lectures during the ordination retreat at Cuddesdon in May 1861. Woodford was at the December retreat and may have delivered these or similar lectures. They certainly reflect some of the ideas of one of the bishop's examining chaplains.

In the first of his lectures, "Personal Influence," Woodford spoke of the dual nature of the priest or deacon—he is an instrument of God and thus his office is "essentially divine," but "the success of our ministry depends mainly upon what we are ourselves."[37] Woodford, like Wilberforce, reminded ordinands that, according to the rubric in the Book of Common Prayer, "all Priests and Deacons are to say daily the Morning and Evening Prayer either privately or openly,"[38] noting that "these services are designed first and foremost not for the laity, but for the clergyman himself" (15).

In the second lecture, "Strength of Will," Woodford instructed candidates to have "one single object, and that 'to do God's work in the world'" (27). "Strength of will, built upon singleness of purpose, reality of character, faith in God's Church as His recognized instrument, is that at which we should aim" (30). The third lecture, "The Parish Priest A Ruler," was focused strictly on the leadership necessary to be an effective parochial minister.

Dodgson's week at Cuddesdon comprised at least two services a day with sermons, lectures, and addresses from Bishop Wilberforce and most likely also his examining chaplains Richard Trench and James Woodford; private examination by the bishop; and daily meals with nearly fifty fellow candidates for Holy Orders,[39] including three of his fellow Christ Church men—Offley Henry Cary, Frederick Pember, and Francis Hayward Joyce. He may have had Cary and Pember as pupils—both matriculated at Christ Church in 1855, the year Dodgson became mathematical lecturer. Joyce had been at Christ Church since before Dodgson's arrival and frequently entered into the latter's diaries. As junior censor of Christ Church, Joyce had signed Dodgson's letters testimonial required for ordination.

Before the ordination service on Sunday, 22 December, Dodgson, according to his certificate of ordination, "freely and voluntarily subscribed to the Thirty-Nine Articles of Religion and to the three articles contained in the thirty-sixth Canon."[40] Under the requirements of Canon Thirty-Six, he spoke these words:

> I, Charles Lutwidge Dodgson, do solemnly make the following declaration; I assent to the Thirty-Nine Articles of Religion, and to the Book of Common Prayer, and of Ordering of Bishops, Priests, and Deacons; I believe the doctrine of the United Church of England and Ireland, as therein set forth, to be agreeable to the Word of God: and in public prayer and administration of the Sacraments, I will use the form in the said book prescribed, and none other, except so far as shall be ordered by lawful authority.[41]

Charles Dodgson knelt before the high altar of his college chapel, the Cathedral Church of the Diocese of Oxford. On his head rested the hands of

Bishop Samuel Wilberforce, whom Dodgson had known for many years. The bishop spoke the words, "Take thou Authority to execute the Office of a Deacon in the Church of God committed unto thee; In the name of the Father, and of the Son, and of the Holy Ghost. Amen."

Charles rose an ordained clergyman in the Church of England.

· NINE ·

Fresh from God's Hands

Charles L. Dodgson took another pull on the oar as the warm summer sun shone down on his white trousers. Three sets of eager eyes stared at him, as three little girls waited breathlessly having shouted out the command, "Tell us a story." He had not the least idea how to begin, but that didn't worry him. He had often invented extempore stories for the benefit of these children. Today, he thought, he'd trying sending his heroine down a rabbit hole and see what happened.

"Very well," he said. "Alice was beginning to get very tired of sitting by her sister on the bank, and of having nothing to do."

For Charles Lutwidge Dodgson, bringing happiness to a child was a near religious experience. In 1886, describing why he wrote the story of *Alice's Adventures Under Ground,* he wrote: "Those for whom a child's mind is a sealed book, and who see no divinity in a child's smile, would read such words in vain: while for anyone that has ever loved one true child, no words are needed. For he will have known the awe that falls on one in the presence of a spirit fresh from God's hands."[1]

His letters reveal he maintained this belief in the near divinity of children throughout his life. In 1877, he wrote: "how much nearer to God, than our travel-stained souls can ever come, is the soul of a little child" (*Letters* 267). In 1885, he mused: "Next to what conversing with an angel *might* be—for it is hard to imagine it, comes, I think, the privilege of having a *real* child's thoughts uttered to one" (*Letters* 607). In 1892: "It is *good* for one (I mean, for one's spiritual life, and in the same sense in which reading the Bible is good) to come into contact with such sweetness and innocence" (*Letters* 905). And in 1893: "It is very healthy and helpful to one's own spiritual life and humbling too, to come into contact with souls so much purer, and nearer to God, than one feels oneself to be" (*Letters* 980).

Even his practice of photographing children *sans habille* (which has been called a habit by critics, though he did it only a few times) was closely linked to this idea of children as unfallen creatures. In a letter to the mother of Gertrude Chataway, he wrote, "with a child like your Gertrude, as simple-minded as Eve in the garden of Eden, *I* should see no objection (provided she liked it herself) to photographing her in Eve's original dress" (*Letters* 253). Of two of his young models photographed in a full state of undress, he wrote, "Their innocent unconsciousness is very beautiful, and gives one a feeling of reverence, as at the presence of something sacred."[2] For Dodgson, innocence, love, and divinity all came together in the person of a child.

Dodgson first told the story of Alice's adventures to Alice Liddell and her sisters Edith and Lorina, the children of Henry George Liddell, dean of Christ Church, on 4 July 1862, during a rowing trip up the River Isis from Oxford. The inspiration of that summer afternoon became *Alice's Adventures Under Ground*, a manuscript book that he illustrated for Alice, and later expanded into *Alice's Adventures in Wonderland*, published in 1865. Six years later, he published the sequel *Through the Looking-Glass and What Alice Found There*. Dodgson only ever claimed the books as nonsense stories. As to their religious nature, he wrote, "I can guarantee that the [Alice] books have no religious teaching whatever in them—in fact, they do not teach anything at all" (*Letters* 548).

Yet when we write, and especially when we tell extempore stories, we draw, consciously or unconsciously, on all our experience, what we have read and what we know, what we value and who we are. As Dodgson himself wrote of *The Hunting of the Snark*, "words mean more than we mean to express when we use them" (*Letters* 548). While Dodgson undoubtedly told the story only as a flight of nonsense to please a smiling child on a summer's day, the centrality of religion in his life and his view of his child audience as linked to the divine, may have manifested themselves in the text. And though Dodgson himself claimed the books provided no religious "teaching," he never said they contained no undertones of religion.

Dodgson came to storytelling from two backgrounds. First were the didactic and moralistic stories of his childhood, which he both embraced and rejected in *Alice*. He used their frank style of narration, their curious child as central character, and their veneration of the pastoral; he rejected and even parodied their overt moralizing and the constant kowtowing of the child to adult authority.

The other story Dodgson had heard and read daily since childhood was the story of scripture and of the liturgy of the Church of England. Whether the stories of the Old Testament, the life of Christ, or the story of Christian life told through the services and sacraments in the Book of Common Prayer, Dodgson rarely went a day in his life without reading or hearing part of this great story, and its presence in his life informed nearly everything he did. The results of his moment of greatest artistic inspiration—that boat trip of 1862—contain many elements of this story. While Dodgson did not intend to write a religious text, parallels to religious life could not help but sneak into his narrative, coming as it did from the most authentic part of his being.

In 1862 religious matters were much on Dodgson's mind. He had been ordained deacon on 22 December 1861 and could now participate in the life of the church in a variety of new ways. In the months leading up to the 4 July river trip, he was aware of and even, in a small way, participated in religious controversies; he preached his first sermon; and he began to explore the possibility of offering regular assistance at a church in Oxford. Even his daily worship experience transformed during this period, as the daily college chapel services he attended at Christ Church ceased, at the end of 1861, to be read in Latin and were read in English.[3]

In late 1861 and early 1862, Dodgson waded into the waters of religious controversy in which his father had been swimming for many years. On 20 November 1861, he made his first speech in Congregation, during the debate over whether to raise the salary of Benjamin Jowett, Regius Professor of Greek. Jowett's salary was fixed at the ancient rate of £40 per annum, and the chief objection to raising it came from those opposed to Jowett's liberal theological opinions, most dramatically articulated in the controversial volume *Essays and Reviews,* published in 1860. Though Dodgson did not state an opinion on either Jowett or *Essays and Reviews,* he did rise to beg that the two issues of the salary and Jowett's unorthodoxy be kept separate. Two days later he issued his first Oxford squib, *The Endowment of the Greek Professorship,* a comic response to suggestions made by Rev. Drummond Chase. While Dodgson expressed no theological opinion, just weeks before his ordination, he was keenly aware of religious controversy.[4]

Essays and Reviews included seven papers by leading liberal churchmen of the day. Condemned by many as heretical, the book sold in large number and sparked widespread controversy. Dodgson owned a copy of *Aids to Faith; a*

Series of Theological Essays by Several Writers Being a Reply to "Essays and Reviews."[5] The editor, William Thomson, had been a Fellow at Queen's College, Oxford, and was an acquaintance of Dodgson. In the introduction he wrote, "The writers . . . desire to set forth their reasons for believing the Bible, out of which they teach, to be the inspired Word of God, and for exhorting others still to cherish it as the only message of salvation from God to man."[6]

One of those who wrote for *Essays and Reviews* was Rowland Williams, whose article "Bunsen's[7] Biblical Researches" denied "the predictive character of Old Testament prophecies."[8] Williams was vicar of Broad Chalke, in the Diocese of Salisbury, and as a result of his paper, the high church bishop of Salisbury, Walter Kerr Hamilton, brought charges against Williams for maintaining "certain erroneous, strange, and heretical doctrines, positions, and opinions."[9]

On 1 February 1862, an anonymous attack on Bishop Hamilton appeared in *Punch* in the form of a poem titled "The Shepherd of Salisbury Plain,"[10] which accused Hamilton of unfairness in the Williams case, saying:

> Our Shepherd's a piper—his sheep if they bleat,
>   Must bleat to the tune of his pipe.[11]

Dodgson clipped out a copy of this poem and pasted it into a scrapbook (now at the Library of Congress), so he was certainly aware of the controversy. He may have written a response to this poem, in the form of a set of verses with the same meter and rhyme scheme as those in *Punch*.[12] The handwriting of this piece leaves some room for doubt that it is by Dodgson, but it may have been, and the level of wit and the views similar to his father's expressed in the piece argue in favor of his having written it. Author or not, Dodgson's logical mind and his father's high church teachings would have led him to admire the stinging rebuke about ordination vows, which foreshadows his own argument against the ritualists (see pp. 116–21 in this volume):

> But supposing this sheep, when he entered the fold,
>   Had solemnly taken a vow
> To shape all his bleats to one definite mould,
>   Pray what can be said for him now?
> Must the rules we hold binding to business and trade
>   Be ignored in the Church's domain?
> And need promises never be kept that are made
>   To the Shepherd of Salisbury Plain?

On 8 June 1862, less than a month before the boat trip, Dodgson preached what was probably his first sermon, at St. Andrew's Church in Sandford-on-Thames. Four days later, he wrote in his diary "I think of getting some Sunday duty in Oxford next term." It had been five and a half months since his ordination, and in the weeks before the river trip Dodgson began to embrace the possibilities and responsibilities of being a deacon.

The Sunday before the river trip, 29 June 1862, began Commemoration week at Oxford, with its various festivities and ceremonies. On Sunday morning, Dodgson attended the University Church of St. Mary's for the morning service and to hear E. B. Pusey preach. "The church was literally crammed, hundreds of persons being unable to obtain admission."[13] Pusey's sermon, titled "The Lord is My Light," explored the omnipresence of God and His love. "He intimately pervades all, inflows into all, sustains all,"[14] said Pusey, whose words reflected C. L. Dodgson's principal belief about God: "He loves thee with His whole Being; for God is Love" (50).

Given that Dodgson was about to have what has since been called an inspiration of genius, Pusey's words seem especially relevant:

> There is nothing human, in which man is so borne out of himself, which is so little dependent on himself, in which he can give so little account of himself, in which the highest activity and passivity of the soul are so blended, as in the conceptions, inventions, combinations, discoveries of Genius. . . . The mind moves and is moved; darts forth, yet not by an act of its own will. . . . Even in lesser degrees of ordinary men, if they have a keener thought, a more glowing word, if words or conceptions throng upon the soul, they are conscious that it "comes to them," as they would say, i.e. it is not of their own power or will, but it is given to them. (42–43)

Pusey's words are remarkably similar to those used by Dodgson in later years to explain his writing of the *Alice* stories. In his article "Alice on the Stage," published in 1887, he recalled: "In writing it out, I added many fresh ideas, which seemed to grow of themselves upon the original stock; and many more added themselves when, years afterwards, I wrote it all over again for publication: but . . . every such idea and nearly every word of the dialogue, *came of itself.* . . . 'Alice' and the 'Looking-Glass' are made up almost wholly of bits and scraps, single ideas which came of themselves."[15]

Perhaps, when the words flowed so freely as Dodgson wove his story to the Liddell sisters on that summer's day, he recalled what Pusey had said about divine inspiration and realized he was experiencing just such a moment.

What led to Dodgson's moment of divine inspiration? Certainly the inquisitive children and the beautiful day on the river, but there is a larger context. Friday, 4 July 1862, was a moment of calm in the midst of end-of-term business. Dodgson had had a friend (Francis Home Atkinson) staying with him since 27 June and had been a busy host. On 5 July the two men would depart for a few days in London, where Dodgson would visit the International Exhibition that was drawing tens of thousands of people a day. They had attended Commemoration on Wednesday, along with three to four thousand others. Being on the river with just his friend Robinson Duckworth and the three Liddell sisters must have been a serene interlude. Dodgson's recent foray into preaching certainly drove home the idea that he would need to have skills as an extempore speaker if he moved forward with his clerical life; Pusey's words about divine inspiration perhaps echoed in his head; in his listeners he saw creatures "fresh from God's hands." While Charles Lutwidge Dodgson set out to do nothing more than entertain three bright children with a nonsense story when he "sent his heroine straight down a rabbit-hole,"[16] it is not surprising that the story that became *Alice's Adventures in Wonderland* had elements of Dodgson's religious life beneath its surface.

Even the name Lewis Carroll may have had an ecclesiastical inspiration. When contributing some verses to the magazine *The Train* in 1856, Dodgson decided to adopt a pseudonym and sent several possibilities to the editor, Edmund Yates. Two of these were Louis Carroll and Lewis Carroll, both derived from loose Latinizations of his Christian names Charles Lutwidge. He explained the derivation thus: "Ludwidge=Ludovic=Louis." (He did not point out that Charles Latinized to "Carolus" hence "Carroll.") Yates chose Lewis Carroll. In the north transept of Christ Church Cathedral, a building Dodgson entered nearly every day during term time, is a memorial to Charles Lewis Atterbury, who came to Christ Church in 1796 and died in 1823. The memorial, printed in Latin, begins with the name: "Carolus Ludovicus Atterbury." Might this memorial have given him the idea for his famous pseudonym?

For many of the bizarre creatures that populate Wonderland, one also need look no further than the ecclesiastical settings where Dodgson spent so much time. From the gryphon carved into the Daresbury pulpit, to a grinning stone cat in the church at Croft, the youthful Charles Dodgson encountered a menagerie of strange creatures in the churches he attended, and several of these reappeared in Wonderland. Perhaps most remarkable is a medieval misericord in the choir of Ripon cathedral, where Charles frequently worshiped during his holidays from 1853 to 1868. The carving shows a gryphon chasing two rabbits, one of whom is disappearing down a rabbit hole.

In a larger sense, *Alice's Adventures Under Ground* has Christian underpinnings: it posits more than one plane of existence, begins with a fall, and ends with a resurrection. *Under Ground* and *Wonderland* begin with a fall into darkness, just as the Christian story begins with man's fall into sin. All three *Alice* books (*Under Ground, Wonderland,* and *Looking-Glass*) end with Alice waking from a dream; and what is sleep if not a milder form of death, and waking but a milder form of resurrection? The metaphor of waking from sleep as rising to eternal life began for Dodgson in the Rugby sermon of A. C. Tait and continued in his own Easter Greeting (see pp. 166–67 in this volume). Like that of a Christian, Alice's "resurrection" is preceded by a scene of judgment, much expanded in *Wonderland* from the few sentences of courtroom antics in *Under Ground.*

As with Christianity, one thing that seems to be required for a full participation in the life of Wonderland is a belief in the impossible. Dodgson builds upon this idea in *Looking-Glass,* when the White Queen tells Alice she can "believe six impossible things before breakfast," but even in *Under Ground,* we find Alice quickly adapting to the idea that she can believe things that defy science and common sense, "For you see, so many out-of-the-way things had happened lately, that Alice began to think very few things indeed were really impossible" (7).

If *Under Ground* and *Wonderland* have a central question, it is that posed by the caterpillar: "Who are you?" Alice's constant search for identity reflects the essential question of all religion: "Who are we?" In his *Addresses to the Candidates for Ordination,* Bishop Wilberforce worded it thus: "Let this, then, be your question,—what am I?"[17] The question is posed most directly to Alice by the caterpillar who can be seen as an examiner (or even, as Dodgson's father, an examining chaplain). But it is not only here that Alice questions her own identity. In *Under Ground,* when Alice has picked up the nosegay and gloves, she thinks: "I wonder if I was changed in the night? Let me think: was I the same when I got up this morning? I think I remember feeling rather different. But if I'm not the same, who in the world am I?" (13). Later, when she fails to properly recite "How doth the Little," she imagines being summoned back to the surface: "Who am I then? answer me that first" (16).

Others seem as confused by Alice's identity as she is. The White Rabbit mistakes her for Mary Ann. When her neck is so long that she is mistaken for a serpent, she tells the pigeon "rather doubtfully" that she is a little girl. In *Wonderland* this shaky identity is further challenged by the pigeon, who tells her that if little girls eat eggs, then "they're a kind of serpent" (73).

As the Christian becomes more certain of his identity in the universe through the process of reading scripture, worship, learning, and prayer, so Alice becomes more aware of and in control of her identity as she makes her way through *Under Ground.* From a confused child uncertain of everything she encounters at the beginning of the book, she matures into a confident young woman who knows exactly what surrounds her ("nothing more than a pack of cards") and is in no way intimidated by it. She apparently passes her "examination" with the caterpillar and is given the food that will enable her to control her size—in much the same way that when Dodgson had passed through the studies prior to his confirmation, he was granted access to the Communion table.

If the examination by the caterpillar and subsequent access to life-altering food can be seen as a sort of confirmation, there are other, even more direct, allusions to Christian rites and sacraments in the book. It is a short leap indeed from the words Alice finds printed on top of a cake and on the label of a bottle—"Eat Me" and "Drink Me"—to the words that Dodgson heard every time he partook of Holy Communion: "Take, eat, this is my Body which is given for you. . . . Drink ye all of this; for this is my Blood." Rev. Charles Dodgson wrote of baptism and Communion that they are "special means and effectual instruments ordained by God, whereby He is pleased to convey . . . some of His highest and most precious gifts and graces."[18] In other words, Holy Communion leads to a real change in those who receive it worthily. Likewise when Alice partakes of the contents of the bottle and of the cake, she undergoes a real (and in her case quite visible) change.

Near the beginning of *Under Ground,* still young and innocent by Wonderland standards, Alice falls into the pool of tears and is symbolically "baptized." Baptism, said A. C. Tait to the prospective confirmands of Rugby, constituted admission into the great Christian Society. Likewise, the pool of tears is Alice's admission into the society of Wonderland. She falls into it alone, having had only the briefest glimpse of another creature underground to that point; she exits a member of a large community of "birds and animals."

Another question that crops up in Wonderland and is central to Christianity is, "What happens after life?" While Alice never articulates these exact words, she does give thought to death and what follows. "First, however, she waited for a few minutes to see whether she was going to shrink any further: she felt a little nervous about this, 'for it might end, you know,' said Alice to herself, 'in my going out altogether, like a candle, and what should I be like then, I wonder?'" (*Under Ground* 8–9).

On page 16 of *Under Ground*, Alice drops the nosegay (it becomes a fan in *Wonderland*) "just in time to save herself from shrinking away altogether." In *Looking-Glass,* Dodgson returns to this topic, at one point using the same candle metaphor: "If that there King was to wake," says Tweedledum, in chapter 9, "you'd go out—bang!—just like a candle!" (81). And the inevitability of death is driven home in Alice's discussion with the Gnat in chapter 3:

> "Supposing it couldn't find any?" she suggested.
> "Then it would die of course."
> "But that must happen very often," Alice remarked thoughtfully.
> "It always happens," said the Gnat. (59)

Even in the poems that frame the published versions of the *Alice* books we find religious symbolism and a melancholia tied to the inevitability of death. In the prefatory verses to *Wonderland,* Dodgson tells the story of the book's genesis and, in the final stanza, compares it to a religious artifact:

> Alice! A childish story take,
>   And, with a gentle hand,
> Lay it where Childhood's dreams are twined
>   In Memory's mystic band.
> Like pilgrim's wither'd wreath of flowers
>   Pluck'd in a far-off land. [ix]

In the prefatory verses to *Looking-Glass* we find Dodgson, in the midst of a poem nostalgic for the days of Alice's childhood (she was nineteen when *Looking-Glass* was published), using the metaphor of sleep for death:

Come, hearken then, ere voice of dread,
  With bitter tidings laden,
Shall summon to unwelcome bed
  A melancholy maiden!
We are but older children, dear,
Who fret to find our bedtime near. [x]

The epilogue verse to *Looking-Glass* ends with the haunting line, which drives home the connection between earthly life and dreaming (and by implication resurrected life and waking) at the same time echoing the words of Archibald Campbell Tait: "Life what is it but a dream?" (224).

Significantly, the most overt religious symbolism in the *Alice* books exists in *Under Ground*. *Wonderland* copies and expands upon this (especially the judgment scene), but none of the entirely new scenes and characters in *Wonderland* ("Pig and Pepper," "A Mad Tea Party") seems to have any particularly strong Christian underpinnings. *Looking-Glass* may repeat or restate the religious ideas in *Under Ground*, but no new religious ideas are introduced. In writing *Looking-Glass,* Dodgson was not laden with a preexisting manuscript as in the case of *Wonderland,* a manuscript that was an almost exact record of the extempore story told on 4 July 1862. It is only in this extempore story that we find Dodgson, perhaps even unbeknownst to himself, accessing the deepest wells of his being—wells that included the Christian story.

While Dodgson maintained the *Alice* stories themselves had no religious teaching, their success gave him a pulpit from which he could address the congregation he most desired to reach—children.

In his preface to the 1886 facsimile of *Alice's Adventures Under Ground,* Dodgson quoted extensively from letters sent to him by his friend Ellinor Feilden. Feilden was married to an Oxford man, and her daughter, Helen, was a photographic subject of Dodgson. The correspondence with Ellinor apparently began many years before 1886, for Dodgson mentions it in a letter to Helen in 1876. At the time of the letters Ellinor was "a lady-visitor at a Home for Sick Children."[19] She wrote, "How I do wish that you . . . [would] write a book for children about GOD and themselves, which is *not* goody, and which begins at the right end, about religion, to make them see what it really is" (vii).

In 1876, Dodgson wrote to Helen Feilden: "Give my kindest regards to your Mother. I have thought many times of her letter, but feel no hope of writing such a book as she suggests" (*Letters* 251). Ten years later, in a correspondence with Mrs. Feilden about the preface to *Under Ground,* he wrote: "I may perhaps some day try to write such a book for children as you want: but I feel about it much as David did about building the temple."[20] In the end, Dodgson did not write a book for children about God, but he did take advantage of his books for children to send his child readers what amounted to, in some cases, almost mini-sermons.

In his 1869 collection *Phantasmagoria,* Dodgson included a poem titled "Christmas Greetings. [From a Fairy to a Child]," written in 1867. He issued the poem separately in 1884, reprinted it in the 1886 edition of *Under Ground,* and thereafter it was included in most printings and editions of his books for children. The central three stanzas (of five), are the crux of the matter:

> We have heard the children say—
>   Gentle children, whom we love—
> Long ago, on Christmas Day,
>   Came a message from above.

> Still, as Christmas-tide comes round,
>   They remember it again—
> Echo still the joyful sound,
>   "Peace on earth, good-will to men!"

> Yet the hearts must childlike be
>   Where such heavenly guests abide:
> Unto children, in their glee,
>   All the year is Christmas-tide! (*Phantasmagoria* 194)

Here again Dodgson makes a direct link between children and the divine— one who wishes to see the true meaning of Christmas at any time of year need only look to a child.

Though "Christmas Greeting" was written in 1867 and first published in 1869, the first religious message to be included in one of Dodgson's *Alice* books was a little pamphlet titled *To All Child-readers of "Alice's Adventures in Wonderland,"* dated Christmas 1871 and probably distributed in copies of *Alice* and *Looking-Glass* (published in a first edition of nine thousand copies in December 1871).

At Christmas time a few grave words are not quite out of place, I hope, even at the end of a book of nonsense. . . .

To all my little friends, known and unknown, I wish with all my heart, "A Merry Christmas and a Happy New Year." May God bless you, dear children, and make each Christmas-tide, as it comes round to you, more bright and beautiful than the last—bright with the presence of that unseen Friend, Who once on earth blessed little children—and beautiful with memories of a loving life, which has sought and found that truest kind of happiness, the only kind that is really worth the having, the happiness of making others happy too![21]

Dodgson often returned in his correspondence to the theme that true happiness only came in making others happy. He wrote to his niece and goddaughter, Edith, on the subject (see p. 22 in this volume). On 9 April 1893, he wrote to Edith Miller: "I *am* truly thankful when God grants me the happiness of helping others (as I think he has granted in *your* case) in the battle we all have to fight. I can see no harm in your being happy in your present surroundings, and in having found some genuine work to do for God and for others" (*Letters* 952).

He wrote to Gertrude Chataway on 30 August 1893, consoling her on the death of her mother: "I think there is no higher privilege given us in this life than the opportunity of doing something for *others*, and of bearing one another's burdens, and praying, one for another. And I believe, and *realise* it more as life goes on, that God hears, and answers, our prayers for *others*, with a special love and approval that does not belong to prayers offered for *ourselves*" (*Letters* 971).

Both Edith Miller and Gertrude Chataway were former child-friends now grown. Dodgson seemed to have a special willingness to open up about matters of religion to adults whom he had known as children.

On 8 July 1895, Dodgson wrote to Lilian Moxon, whom he had not known as a child. She had written Dodgson a letter in which, apparently, she alluded to heaven as the "goal" of human existence. Dodgson replied: "But the taking 'heaven' as our goal seems to me a motive of the same kind as taking *earthly* happiness as our goal. To me it seems that to *give* happiness is a far nobler goal than to *attain* it: and that what we exist for is much more a matter of *relations to others* than a matter of *individual* progress: much more a matter of helping others to heaven than of getting there ourselves" (*Letters* 1067).

In a correspondence with his friend Ellen Terry, Dodgson considered whether it was selfish to take pleasure in bringing happiness to others, writing, "While it is hopelessly difficult to secure for *oneself* even the smallest bit of happiness, and the more trouble we take the more certain we are to fail, there is nothing so easy as to secure it *for somebody else*: so that, if only A would aim at B's happiness, and B at C's, and so on, we should *all* be happy, and there would be little need to *wait* for heaven: we should *have* it" (*Letters* 488).

Then, on 13 November 1890, after Terry agreed to give acting lessons to Dodgson's child-friend Isa Bowman, he wrote:

> [A]ll, that is really *worth* the doing, is what we do for *others?* Even as the old adage tells us, "What I spent, that I lost; what I gave, that I had." Casuists have tried to twist "doing good" into another form of "doing evil," and have said "you get pleasure yourself by giving this pleasure to another: so it is merely a refined kind of selfishness, as your own pleasure is a motive for what you do." I say "it is *not* selfishness, that my own pleasure should be a motive so long as it is not *the* motive that would outweigh the other, if the two came into collision." . . . I am very sure that God takes real *pleasure* in seeing his children happy! And, when I read such words as "looking unto Jesus, the author and finisher of our faith, who *for the joy that was set before him* endured the cross,"[22] I believe them to be *literally true*. (*Letters* 813)

In an undated and unfinished essay on "Pleasure," Dodgson probed again at the question of pleasure as a motive for our actions: "The wise, however, who propose to themselves virtue as the mark they are chiefly to aim at, perceive that true pleasure consists in its attainment, and in the consciousness of inward purity. So that although they do not take it all as a motive for action, yet they do more surely and constantly obtain it and more thoroughly enjoy it, than do those who blindly aim at pleasure, believing it to be good in itself and think that way best, which appears to lead straight to their object."[23]

The search for true happiness also came into play when Dodgson was asked about the meaning of his 1876 poem *The Hunting of the Snark*, which he always insisted was only nonsense. In 1884 he wrote: "Whatever good meanings are in the book, I am very glad to accept as the meaning of the book. The best that I have seen is by a lady . . . that the whole book is an allegory on the search after happiness."[24] Of course the *Snark* ends in tragedy, with the vanishing of the Baker. Here happiness is pursued for itself alone, and thus, Dodgson might say, the search is doomed from the start. Happiness can only be found in making others happy.

Dodgson's second religious pamphlet for children, the 1876 *An Easter Greeting to Every Child Who Loves "Alice,"* received much wider distribution than his first. First issued on 1 April 1876 (Easter fell on 16 April that year), the pamphlet was reprinted many times and is often found tipped into copies of the first edition of *The Hunting of the Snark,* which was published simultaneously. The text was printed in *Alice's Adventures Under Ground* (1886) and *The Nursery Alice* (1889) as well as in the People's Editions of the *Alice* books (published beginning in 1887, these sold well for the rest of Dodgson's life and through much of the twentieth century). Here Dodgson proclaimed the joy of resurrection and new life in terms he hoped would go straight to the hearts of his youthful readers:

> Do you know that delicious dreamy feeling when one first wakes on a summer morning, with the twitter of birds in the air, and the fresh breeze coming in at the open window—when, lying lazily with eyes half shut, one sees as in a dream green boughs waving, or waters rippling in a golden light? It is a pleasure very near to sadness, bringing tears to one's eyes like a beautiful picture or poem. And is not that a Mother's gentle hand that undraws your curtains, and a Mother's sweet voice that summons you to rise? To rise and forget, in the bright sunlight, the ugly dreams that frightened you so when all was dark—to rise and enjoy another happy day, first kneeling to thank that unseen Friend, who sends you the beautiful sun?
>
> . . . I do not believe God means us thus to divide life into two halves—to wear a grave face on Sunday, and to think it out-of-place to even so much as mention Him on a week-day. Do you think He cares to see only kneeling figures, and to hear only tones of prayer—and that He does not also love to see the lambs leaping in the sunlight, and to hear the merry voices of the children, as they roll among the hay? Surely their innocent laughter is as sweet in His ears as the grandest anthem that ever rolled up from the "dim religious light" of some solemn cathedral? . . .
>
> This Easter sun will rise on you, dear child, feeling your "life in every limb," and eager to rush out into the fresh morning air—and many an Easter-day will come and go, before it finds you feeble and gray-headed, creeping wearily out to bask once more in the sunlight—but it is good, even now, to think sometimes of that great morning when the "Sun of Righteousness shall arise with healing in his wings."[25]

Surely your gladness need not be the less for the thought that you will one day see a brighter dawn than this—when lovelier sights will meet your eyes than any waving trees or rippling waters—when angel-hands shall undraw your curtains, and sweeter tones than ever loving Mother breathed shall wake you to a new and glorious day—and when all the sadness, and the sin, that darkened life on this little earth, shall be forgotten like the dreams of a night that is past![26]

It is no coincidence that the first paragraph echoes the sentimental style of the final passages of *Wonderland*. Here, waking from a dream is no mere subconscious allusion to resurrection; in *Easter Greeting*, Dodgson completed the metaphor he began in *Under Ground*. The comparison began with the words of Archibald Tait in his 1846 sermon: "What is life? Is it all a dream?" It continued through the dream narratives of *Under Ground* and *Wonderland*. It was teased out further in the final line of the poetic epilogue to *Looking-Glass*: "Life, what is it but a dream?" And in *Easter Greeting*, earthly life is compared to "ugly dreams that frightened you so when all was dark," and resurrection to new life in Christ becomes that time when "sweeter tones than ever loving Mother breathed shall wake you to a new and glorious day."

Following the publication of *Easter Greeting*, Ellinor Feilden wrote to Dodgson in a letter recorded in the preface to *Under Ground:* "I want you to send me one of your Easter Greetings for a very dear child who is dying at our Home. She is just fading away, and 'Alice' has brightened some of her weary hours in her illness, and I know that letter would be such a delight to her." After Dodgson sent the letter, inscribed for "Minnie," Mrs. Feilden wrote back, "I am quite sure that all these children will say a loving prayer for the 'Alice-man' on Easter Day: and I am sure the letter will help the little ones to the real Easter joy" (vi–viii).

That Dodgson could bring both comfort and the Good News to sick and suffering children must have been extremely gratifying. He often gave copies of his books to children's homes and hospitals, and he wrote in the *Under Ground* preface, "I can truly say that no praise . . . has ever given me one hundredth part of the pleasure it has been to think of sick children in hospitals (where it has been a delight to me to send copies) forgetting, for a few bright hours, their pain and weariness—perhaps even putting up a childish prayer (and oh, how much it needs!) for one who can but dimly hope to stand, some day, not quite out of sight of those pure young faces, before the great white throne" (vi).

In this same introduction Dodgson quotes extensively from an Ellinor Feilden letter in which she describes what she sees of children's relationship with God in the hospital where she works. That Dodgson would quote her letter so extensively and in such a prominent spot in a publication largely aimed at children surely indicates he was in sympathy with her thoughts— that children should see God as a cause for rejoicing, not as a cause for fear. Feilden wrote:

> I get quite miserable very often over the children I come across: hardly any of them have an idea of really knowing that God loves them, or of loving and confiding in Him. They will love and trust me, and be sure that I want them to be happy, and will not let them suffer more than is necessary: but as for going to Him in the same way, they would never think of it. They are dreadfully afraid of Him, if they think of Him at all, which they generally only do when they have been naughty, and they look on all connected with Him as very grave and dull: and, when they are full of fun and thoroughly happy, I am sure they unconsciously hope He is not looking. I am sure I don't won-der they think of Him in this way, for people never talk of Him in connection with what makes their little lives the brightest. If they are naughty, people put on solemn faces, and say He is very angry or shocked, or something which frightens them: and, for the rest, He is talked about only in a way that makes them think of church and having to be quiet. As for being taught that all Joy and all Gladness and Brightness is His Joy—that He is wearying for them to be happy, and is not hard and stern, but always doing things to make their days brighter, and caring for them so tenderly, and wanting them to run to Him with all their little joys and sorrows, they are not taught that. I do so long to make them trust Him as they trust us, to feel that He will "take their part" as they do with us in their little woes, and to go to Him in their plays and enjoyments and not only when they say their prayers. I was quite grateful to one little dot, a short time ago, who said to his mother "when I am in bed, I put out my hand to see if I can feel Jesus and my angel. I thought perhaps in the dark they'd touch me, but they never have yet." I do so want them to want to go to Him, and to feel how, if He is there, it must be happy. (vii–viii)

Three years after the publication of *Under Ground,* Dodgson became even more overt in his printed religious messages for children, incorporat-ing a variety of religious content into his two-part novel *Sylvie and Bruno* (published in 1889 and 1893). Though both its heft and content might belie the fact, Dodgson intended *Sylvie and Bruno* as a children's book. He mixed religious ideas not just into prefatory matter but into his text. "It is written," he wrote in the preface to the first volume, "in the hope of supplying, for the children whom I love, some thoughts that may suit those hours of innocent merriment which are the very life of Childhood; and also in the hope of suggesting, to them and to others, some thoughts that may prove, I would fain hope, not wholly out of harmony with the grave cadences of Life."[27]

In the dedicatory poem of the first volume, he returned to the metaphor of life as a dream. The ever-present threat of death, which pervades the novel and is mentioned explicitly in the preface, is here alluded to poetically:

Is all our Life, then, but a dream
Seen faintly in the golden gleam
Athwart Time's dark resistless stream?

Bowed to the earth with bitter woe,
Or laughing at some raree-show,
We flutter idly to and fro.

Man's little Day in haste we spend,
And, from its merry noontide, send
No glance to meet the silent end.[28] (vii)

Dodgson used this inevitability of death as his excuse for mixing the grave and the gay, words of nonsense with words of religious thought, writing in the preface:

To [some] such a mixture will seem, no doubt, ill-judged and repulsive. . . . with youth, good health, and sufficient money, it seems possible to lead, for years altogether, a life of unmixed gaiety—with the exception of one solemn fact, with which we are liable to be confronted at *any* moment, even in the midst of the most brilliant company or the most sparkling entertainment. A man may fix his own times for admitting serious thought, for attending public worship, for prayer, for reading the Bible: all such matters he can defer to that "convenient season," which is so apt never to occur at all: but he cannot defer, for one single moment, the necessity of attending to a message, which may come before he has finished reading this page, "this night shall thy soul be required of thee." (xvi–xvii)

In the same preface, Carroll provided descriptions of several "books desirable to be written" (xiii), including a child's Bible, a book of selections from the Bible designed for memorization, and a similar book of secular texts.[29] His description of a child's Bible shows he took Ellinor Feilden's words to heart: "One principle of selection, which I would adopt, would be that Religion should be put before a child as a revelation of *love*—no need to pain and puzzle the young mind with the history of crime and punishment" (xiii).

The preface to *Sylvie and Bruno Concluded* finds Dodgson elaborating on the comments made by his characters on the questions of the morality of hunting for sport, the place of choristers in holy worship, and the present quality of preaching. Of his characters' opinions on these topics (the specifics of which are dealt with elsewhere in this study), Dodgson wrote, "I do *not* hold myself responsible for *any* of the opinions expressed by the characters in my book. They are simply opinions which, it seemed to me, might probably be held by the persons into whose mouths I put them, and which were worth consideration."[30]

Even when denying that the thoughts on serious subjects in the book are his own, he equivocated, saying they are "worth consideration." Later in the preface he admitted that, in the case of sermons and choristers, he was "very much in sympathy" with the views expressed by his character Arthur Forester. Dodgson also wrote of how *Sylvie and Bruno* was written—by collecting a mass of ideas and incidents over many years. Why would he have collected, preserved, and published thoughts on serious religious subjects with which he himself was wholly out of harmony? It is hard to imagine the views on serious subjects expressed by his characters, and especially by his unnamed narrator, as anything other than closely paralleling his own.

So, what of those thoughts "not wholly out of harmony with the grave cadences of Life" that Dodgson introduced into his final children's books? In the two volumes of *Sylvie and Bruno* comments and plot developments of a serious nature are woven throughout the text, but in nearly a dozen places the actions stops for what can perhaps best be described as sermonettes. Some of these are on social issues such as hunting for sport, charity, or teetotalism; some are on distinctly religious topics such as sin, temptation, the Sabbath, prayer and free will, and even ritualism. On all of these topics, Dodgson's conclusions are considerably subtler and more complex than the clear black-and-white morals presented by his own childhood reading. Most of these digressions are considered elsewhere in this study, but an example of Dodgson's application of both humor and logic to a serious topic may be seen in his treatment of teetotalism. Dodgson was a moderate drinker, known to enjoy a glass of sherry at luncheon. In *Sylvie and Bruno Concluded,* the unnamed narrator both condemns immoderate drinking and defends moderate drinking with the words that drink is "Only a curse . . . when it is used wrongly. Any of God's gifts may be turned into a curse, unless we use it wisely" (72). Later in the same volume, the doctor and romantic hero Arthur Forester encounters a teetotaler and deals with him with typical Carrollian wit and logic. First Arthur parries the man's "Teetotal Card," showing how much money is spent on alcohol with his own "Anti-Teetotal Card" showing how much is earned by the same sales. Then the man reads a newspaper cutting:

> To the Editor. Sir, I was once a moderate drinker, and knew a man who drank to excess. I went to him. "Give up this drink," I said. "It will ruin your health!" "You drink," he said: "why shouldn't I?" "Yes," I said, "but I know when to leave off." He turned away from me. "You drink in your way," he said: "let me drink in mine. Be off!" Then I saw that, to do any good with him, I must forswear drink. From that hour I haven't touched a drop!

To this, Arthur replies with a "letter" of his own:

> To the Editor. Sir, I was once a moderate sleeper, and knew a man who slept to excess. I pleaded with him. "Give up this lying in bed," I said. "It will ruin your health!" "You go to bed," he said: "why shouldn't I?" "Yes," I said, "but I know when to get up in the morning." He turned away from me. "You sleep in your way," he said: "let me sleep in mine. Be off!" Then I saw that to do any good with him, I must forswear sleep. From that hour I haven't been to bed! (139–41)

There is room to doubt that a child interested in fairy stories would also have the patience to read such a digression, and those on ritualism, the problems of preachers, the nature of free will, and sin and temptation are considerably less humorous, but Dodgson nonetheless used his status as well-respected children's author as an opportunity to "preach" on a wide variety of topics to the children of England.

Dodgson did not, in these books, abandon what he saw as the central message of Christianity. Especially in his religious dealings with children,

Dodson laid a heavy emphasis on the view of God as all-loving and all-caring—one who rejoices in our happiness. More than anything, Dodgson wished that religion, to a child, would be a source not of dreariness and drudge but of joy and that when children thought of God they would think first not of vengefulness or anger, but of love.

This view of love as the central quality of God is embedded in the *Sylvie and Bruno* story, and especially in the fairy heroine, Sylvie. Sylvie is the child as Dodgson truly believes the child to be: "for I think," he wrote in the preface to *Under Ground,* "a child's *first* attitude to the world is a simple love for all living things" ([v]). So it is with Sylvie—ceaselessly giving and unselfish, deeply moved by the plight of her fellow creatures, always thinking of others' happiness before her own. In chapter 6 of *Sylvie and Bruno,* the Fairy King gives Sylvie a choice between two lockets: one inscribed "All Will Love Sylvie" and one inscribed "Sylvie Will Love All." "It's *very* nice to be loved," says Sylvie, "but it's nicer to love other people!" (77). She chooses the latter locket.

In the final chapter of *Sylvie and Bruno Concluded,* Dodgson returned to the locket, and to the twin Christian themes of resurrection and love. The chapter, titled "Life out of Death," begins with the discovery that Dr. Arthur Forester, thought to have died nobly while ministering to the medical needs of an isolated village, has in fact survived—a resurrection made all the more joyful by Lady Muriel's love for Arthur. In the final pages, Sylvie discovers that what she thought were two lockets are really only two sides of the same jewel. "Sylvie will love all" is a message inextricably intertwined with "All will love Sylvie." And so that the child reader could be reminded of the source of that love that binds Muriel to Arthur and Sylvie to all, Dodgson ended the saga with this passage:

"SYLVIE WILL LOVE ALL—ALL WILL LOVE SYLVIE," Bruno murmured, raising himself on tiptoe to kiss the 'little red star.' "And, when you look *at* it, it's red and fierce like the sun and, when you look *through* it, it's gentle and blue like the sky!"

"God's own sky," Sylvie said, dreamily.

"God's own sky," the little fellow repeated, as they stood, lovingly clinging together, and looking out into the night. "But oh, Sylvie, what makes the sky such a darling blue?"

Sylvie's sweet lips shaped themselves to reply, but her voice sounded faint and very far away. The vision was fast slipping from my eager gaze: but it seemed to me, in that last bewildering moment, that not Sylvie but an angel was looking out through those trustful brown eyes, and that not Sylvie's but an angel's voice was whispering

"It is Love." (410–11)

Significantly the word "love," like other references to the deity, is capitalized. Here in a single passage is the notion that children are unconditionally loving, that they are the closest things to angels we are likely to encounter in this world, and that the nature of God—as creator and redeemer—is Love.

In two of Dodgson's final published pieces, he continued to tell children (and their parents) that religion need not be an unpleasant chore and that God is first and foremost a God of love. One of these was the introduction to his cousin E. G. Wilcox's book for children, *The Lost Plum-Cake*. Dodgson's argument here that young children should be allowed to read a book during sermons so that they do not come to dread church as tedious, is quoted above (p. 46). The other item was an address he made to children at St. Mary Magdalene Church, St. Leonards-on-Sea on 3 October 1897.

On 22 August 1897, Dodgson, during his annual Long Vacation sojourn to Eastbourne, recorded in his diary that he had, "a new experience. At Mr. [William Henry] Hewett's [the vicar of Christ Church, Eastbourne] request I went to his 'Children's Service,' at 3, to talk to from 200 to 300 children. I put no text to it, but simply told them, with a few additions, the allegory of the little boy's day's walk along the hill-range. (I have now called him 'Victor,' and his little brother 'Arnion'). I left it unfinished, promising more another day."

The following week he continued the story. In a letter to his sister Louisa on 1 September 1897, Dodgson elaborated on this novel experience, writing that it was "an *extremely* interesting task. There were about 100 boys and 200 girls. I took no text but merely told them a story (an allegory I devised years ago) with *very* few words of explanation. It took about 20 minutes. I had to leave it unfinished, and went and told them another piece last Sunday. And *still* it is unfinished. It grows on my hands. Perhaps I shall print it some day. And now I have undertaken to go over to St. Leonard's, and tell it at the Children's Service at St. Mary Magdalen's" (*Letters* 1136).

Rev. William Henry Hewett wrote of these addresses that their purpose was "to illustrate the temptations to which children are exposed, and to teach them how they may be avoided and conquered. The addresses were delivered with deep feeling; at times the speaker was scarcely able to control his emotions, especially when speaking of the love and compassion of the Good Shepherd."[31]

Dodgson was, just months from the end of his life, doing in person what he had been doing in print for decades: speaking to children on religious topics. And he did it by combining his skills as storyteller with his deep personal faith.

The first talk at Christ Church, Eastbourne, began what was perhaps the most intensive period of formally addressing children in Dodgson's life. From 22 August to 18 October, he gave four addresses at children's services and spoke seventeen times to groups of children in schools in Eastbourne, St. Leonards, Brighton, and Guildford. He described the first of these school sessions (which consisted largely of teaching mathematical games and puzzles and telling stories such as "Bruno's Picnic" from *Sylvie and Bruno*) as a "new experience." Rev. Robert Allen[32] of nearby St. Leonards invited Dodgson to speak both at schools and at church. On 26 September, Dodgson addressed the Children's Service at the Harvest Festival at Christ Church; Eastbourne and he repeated the talk (with the addition of an anecdote about Jenny Lind) at a similar service in St. Leonards a week later. Luckily, this talk was preserved in the St. Leonards parish newsletter. It shows a storyteller, collector of anecdotes, author of dream literature, and a man who believed the most important religious messages he could share with children were the loving nature of God and the importance of kindness to his creation. Love and kindness—near the end of his life Dodgson may have been remembering words from the beginning of his life, from the twenty-eight "subjects" that he studied as a child. The address is worth quoting in full:

A little girl named Margaret went to a Harvest Festival Service one Sunday. The Church was beautiful with flowers and fruit and sweet music of thanks-giving. And the preacher spoke of God's great love and goodness in giving us everything that we possess, and that we must try to show our thankfulness to Him by offering of our best to Him in return. Some of us—and especially the children—perhaps thought they had nothing to give, or worthy to offer, to God, but the preacher said that God would accept even a little deed of love, or a simple act of kindness to one of His creatures, and that children, especially, could do these if they would try.

When the service was over and the people had gone away, little Margaret lingered in the churchyard thinking about what the preacher had said, and a lark started up from her feet and sang soaring into the blue sky with such gladness that Margaret said to herself, "Ah, he is trying to thank God as well as he can—how much I wish there were something that such a little girl as I could do too!"

She sat down on the grass in the sunshine to think, and presently she noticed a rose-bush growing near, and that the roses were hanging their heads, quite withered in the sun for want of water. So she ran to the brook, and making a cup of her hands dipped them into the water and ran and threw the water on the roses. She did so again and again, and the rose revived.

Little Margaret then walked on till she passed a cottage where a baby was sitting on the doorstep and crying sadly because his toy was broken. It was a paper windmill, and the sails had become all crumpled up and would not go round any more. Margaret took the toy from the baby and straightened out the sails, and a wind came by and turned them round merrily, so that the baby stretched out his hands and laughed for joy.

Then little Margaret thought she must go home, but as she passed the brook again she saw a little brown bird struggling in the water. He had fallen in and was being drowned, and growing weaker in his struggles. So Margaret caught hold of a bough, and stretching as far as she could, with her other hand she lifted the little bird out of the water and laid him safely on the bank.

And now she began to feel very tired, and at last reached her home. She climbed up to her room, and lay down on her little bed, very white and still, and closed her eyes. And then she said to herself: "I think this must be dying—yes, I am dying—and soon I shall be dead." And her friends came in and said, "Ah, she is dying, poor little Margaret!"

But a rose that was growing outside by the garden path heard it, and began to grow, and climbed and grew till it reached the window, and crept in through the window into the room, and crept all round the walls and little bed till there were wreaths of lovely roses filling the room with their sweetness. And the roses bent over Margaret's little pale face till her cheeks began to take a faint colour too. And just then a soft wind came blowing in at the window and fanned her face, and a little brown bird outside began to sing so prettily, that Margaret smiled, and opened her eyes and . . . well, she was still sitting on the grass outside the Church, in the soft sunshine—for it was a dream![33]

I read this story in a book, and put it by to tell you, dear children, this afternoon; but now I will tell you three stories of love and kindness. For—

"He prayeth well, who loveth well
Both man and bird and beast."

Some forty years ago there was a great singer, named Jenny Lind, and her voice and her singing were so beautiful that people who heard her felt as if they were listening to an angel. And they would go in crowds, and pay any money, to hear her sing.[34]

On one occasion when she was singing at Manchester, she was caught by the rain during her morning walk and she took shelter in a poor little cottage, where a poor old woman lived alone. Jenny Lind talked kindly to her at once, and the poor old woman (of course not knowing who she was) told her about the wonderful Singer, who, "she was told was going to sing that afternoon," and how everybody was "mad" to hear her, and how very very much she wished that she could hear her too. But that of course was impossible "for a poor old body like me!" Then Jenny Lind told the old woman that she was the Singer, and said she, "and I will sing to you." So then and there, in that poor little cottage, the great Singer sang three or four of her sweetest songs, and gave the poor old woman the desire of her heart.[35]

Again—a man walking along a country lane heard such a fluttering and chirping in the hedge that he stopped to look what it could be; and he saw that a young bird had fallen out of its nest, and its wings having caught on a thorn, it was hanging helpless. The mother bird was close to it fluttering and crying with all her might, but powerless to release her little one. She did not move as the man gently lifted the young bird and replaced it in the nest, but then instantly hopped on to the nest herself, and spread her wings over her little ones without a trace of fear, but in perfect confidence in the person who had come to her aid.

And now one more true tale, and this of a child's kindness to one of God's creatures. You will, I think, all have heard of Florence Nightingale. Hers is a name to make all English hearts beat warm as long as they exist:—one of England's noblest women, for she was the first who thought of going to nurse our poor wounded soldiers on the battlefield.

From her childhood Florence Nightingale was always wanting to help and heal those in pain, and her first patient was a dog! She was but a child when one day she met a shepherd whom she knew, and he was in great distress because his faithful old dog, that had served him for so many years, was near his end. Some cruel boys—or I would rather say, thoughtless boys—had stoned the poor old dog, and he was so much hurt that he had only just been able to drag himself home to die! He was well-nigh worn out, but "Now he's done for, and I must do away with him," said the shepherd, as he led the child to the cottage to show her the dog, and then he went sadly away to get the means of putting him out of his misery.

Florence Nightingale sat down beside the poor suffering creature, her kind heart full of pity. Presently she saw some one pass the door who she knew understood all about animals, and calling him in, she showed him the dog. After examining him, her friend said, "Well, he's very bad, but there are no bones broken; all you can do is to wring out some cloths in hot water and lay them on the wounds, and keep on doing that for a long time." And the child set to work at once, lighted a fire, boiled the water, and persevered in her work for many hours, and to her joy the old dog began to get better and better. When the shepherd came home, Florence Nightingale said to him, "Call him, oh! do call him;" and so he called the old dog, who got up and greeted his master.[36]

> "He prayeth best, who loveth best
> All things both great and small;
> For the dear God who loveth us,
> He made and loveth all."[37]

And now, dear children, I want you to promise me that you will each one try, every day, to do some loving act of kindness for others. Perhaps you have never really tried before; will you begin to-day—the beginning of a new week? Last week is gone for ever; this week will be quite different. As you rub out the sums on your slate that have not come right, and begin all over again, so leave behind the disobedience, or selfishness, or ill-temper of last week, and begin quite fresh to try your very best, every day, to do what you can towards fulfilling God's law of love.[38]

His diary for 3 October 1897 gives a sense of Dodgson's primary intention in crafting this address: "it ended with three real stories—of kindness to 'man, and bird, and beast.'"

Throughout his career, Dodgson used the success of the *Alice* books and his position as a children's author as platforms from which to address children on religious subjects, and in those writings, and in his private letters, he returned again and again to the same points: there needn't be a separation between grave and gay; the central aspect of God is love; the greatest happiness comes in making others happy; children should delight in God's love, rather than fear his wrath; and worship and Sunday observance should enhance that delight for children, not become a drudgery that leads them to resent God.

He did not know, as he looked across the faces of the children and the eager eyes waiting for him to speak, that this would be his last chance to impart some words of a religious nature to a group of children. He only knew that he saw the shining faces of those fresh from God's hands; he hoped he might be able to teach them something of that God and of his love and kindness, but it seemed equally likely that he, and not his audience, would be the greater recipient of God's gifts on that day, for he was in the company of that purity next to angels that could only be found in children.

· TEN ·

Preach the Gospel

Charles L. Dodgson looked out over the small congregation gathered for the Whitsunday evening service in the narrow chancel of the Parish Church of St. Andrew. He had risen early that morning in Oxford and walked several miles through the Thames Valley, first to morning service at Iffley, then to dine with his friend William Henry Ranken at Radley, then to Sandford-on-Thames, where Ranken was the incumbent and where Dodgson now prepared to do something he had never done before—preach a sermon. He had written out headings to remind him of what he wished to say, and, with the afternoon sun streaming through the windows, he began. He found he had to refer to his headings almost constantly, but he managed to avoid words and phrases that tended to trigger his speech hesitation. As he stepped from the pulpit a half hour later, he wondered what his father would have thought.

Within months of his ordination, Charles Lutwidge Dodgson would preach his first sermon, but his career as a public speaker had begun years earlier. As an undergraduate he read out three essays in Hall (see pp. 126–27 in this volume). He had taught classes at the Croft National School in 1855. In that same year he became Mathematical Lecturer at Christ Church.

On 31 May 1856, Charles read out another paper in Hall for the annual Gaudy dinner, a reunion of old Christ Church men. Each year a member of the college wrote and read an essay about a distinguished member of Christ Church. Henry George Liddell, who had become dean of Christ Church in January that year, asked Dodgson to write a paper about Richard Hakluyt, who came to Christ Church in 1570. Hakluyt was a lifelong student of naval history and collected and published accounts of voyages. In summarizing the life of this man who contributed to science not through original work but

179

through collecting, translating, and editing the works of others, Dodgson echoed his father's first published sermon, preached in 1837.

Rev. Charles Dodgson the elder said that "the deference universally paid to splendid talents, and the eminence to which they so often rapidly attain, is proof of their comparative rarity, and a proof, therefore, that the great mass of good must be produced by the aggregate force of those, whose single efforts may seem to be of little value and efficacy."[1]

Nineteen years later, his son concluded his speech at Christ Church Gaudy with these words: "The genius of an original writer, like the enterprising zeal of a first discoverer, or the resistless energy of a conqueror, is apt to dazzle the eyes of those that look on: and they too easily overlook the heavier toil and almost equal abilities which belong to those that come after, and whose part it is to collect and shape the stray efforts of genius, to record for time to come the results of discovery, to secure and perpetuate the gains of conquest."[2]

Charles L. Dodgson continued his career as a public speaker when, on 21 November 1859, he addressed the Ashmolean Society at the museum of the same name, "on the introduction of a fourth co-ordinate into Algebraical Geometry."[3] The Ashmolean Society, founded in 1828, was devoted to the study of natural history. The following year, on 26 November, he gave another talk to the society, "On the Continuity of Daylight."[4]

On Tuesday, 9 April 1861, before Dodgson had determined he would be ordained at the end of that year, he gave his first public speech for adults that dealt, though in an oblique way, with religion. He spoke at the opening of the Ore Working Men's Institute in a suburb of Hastings, in which town he was probably visiting his maiden aunts Margaret and Henrietta Lutwidge at the Easter holidays. As one of the speakers at its opening said, the Working Men's Institute was established to give workingmen a place to read, better themselves, and purify their characters.

Dodgson delivered a speech, which he later published under the title "Feeding the Mind,"[5] though there were some differences between the published version and that which the workingmen of Ore heard. Dodgson spoke on how people should, through their choice of reading, feed and nourish their minds with the same care as they do their bodies through their choice of food. He advised listeners to avoid "unwholesome novel[s]" but rather to choose wholesome reading "in *proper amount*" to avoid "*mental gluttony.*" "We must not consume too many kinds [of reading] at once," he said, and must "allow *proper intervals* between meal and meal." He advised mentally "making up . . . knowledge into proper bundles, and ticketing them." At the end of the published version of this paper, Dodgson wrote: "If it has given any useful hints on the important subject of reading, and made you see that it is one's duty, no less than one's interest, to 'read, mark, learn, and inwardly digest,' the good books that fall your way, its purpose will have been fully answered."

While "Feeding the Mind" may not, at first glance, seem religious in nature, there are several hints that Dodgson saw it as at least a semi-religious talk. The phrase "read, mark, learn, and inwardly digest" comes from the Collect for the Second Sunday in Advent in the Book of Common Prayer. Dodgson submitted "Feeding the Mind" for publication in the *Oxford Magazine and Church Advocate,* which called itself a "periodical of general character, in which Church of England principles are recognized as the ruling authority."[6] Finally, in a newspaper account of Dodgson's talk, we find words echoing his father's sermon of 1837: "[Mr. Dodgson] concluded by . . . remembering that every one is accountable to one Heavenly Father for the talents committed to him."[7]

Dodgson almost certainly gave his first proper sermon on the evening of Sunday, 8 June 1862, at Sandford-on-Thames, a village about three and half miles down the river from Christ Church. The vicar was an old friend of Dodgson's, William Henry Ranken, a Corpus Christi man whom Dodgson had known at least since the two were part of a group who read mathematics with Professor Bartholomew Price at Whitby during the Long Vacation of 1854. On 7 June 1862, Dodgson wrote in his diary: "Walked with Ranken and undertook to preach for him the evening of tomorrow (Whitsunday) at Sandford." Dodgson had a dinner party that evening and recorded that he was "too sleepy to prepare the sermon afterwards." The next morning he "was called at 7, and lay awake an hour thinking of the sermon, and after breakfast wrote out the headings." Before the evening service at Sandford, he "got about another hour to think over the sermon." He did not write the sermon out, only an outline of "headings" to prompt himself. "I found I had to refer to the headings constantly," he wrote in his diary. "It lasted, I should think, half an hour."

Dodgson chose as his text 2 Corinthians 13:14, a verse known in the Church of England as the Grace, which concludes both Morning and Evening Prayer: "The grace of the Lord Jesus Christ, and the love of God, and the communion of the Holy Ghost, be with you all. Amen." As he did for no other sermon, Dodgson wrote the "headings" in his diary, and they give a good sense of the general structure of the sermon, especially given that he preached on Whitsunday, or Pentecost, the day the church remembers the Holy Spirit descending on the Apostles.

The first heading makes a good title for a sermon preached on this day and this verse: "Mystery of communion of God with man." Under this, Dodgson wrote five subheadings: "Separation by sin, Baptism, Believing and realizing, Traveller, Shipwreck." He began with the fact that God and man are separated from one another by sin but that Holy Baptism can bridge that gap. Perhaps "Traveller" and "Shipwreck" referred to some allegorical story.

The second heading reads, "Difficulty of realizing this communion," and the subheads are "Bunyan's Pilgrim's Progress, Children in garden, Visible and invisible dangers, Church attendance and prayer, man's praise." While the reference to *Pilgrim's Progress* is not specific, the book is about the sins of man being a barrier between man and God. One can imagine many possible stories about children in a garden and many visible and invisible dangers that prevent man from communing with God. Not surprisingly, Dodgson encouraged church attendance and prayer. The reference to "man's praise" might refer to the danger of becoming too taken up with praise received from others rather than listening to the voice of God.

The third major heading is "Difference between those who realize it and those who do not." Here Dodgson was unequivocal in his subheads: "Honesty, Prayer, True repentance, Christ's words to Thomas." The first three were, to Dodgson, the path to communion with God. "Christ's words to Thomas" referred to the words Christ spoke to his disciple after Thomas insisted on seeing Christ's wounds before believing in the resurrection: "Blessed are they that have not seen, and yet have believed" (John 20:29).

The fourth major heading, "Blessedness of so realizing it," is followed by "Constant communion with God, Guidance in difficulty, Comfort in sorrow," specific reasons why one should strive for communion with God.

Finally, the fifth heading reads, "Means of realizing it." Dodgson gave the means in two simple words, "Prayer" and "Action." Following the word "Action," he wrote, "John 7." The seventh book of John finds Christ teaching in the temple and disagreement among the people about who he is. He says, "Yet a little while am I with you, and then I go unto him that sent me. Ye shall seek me, and shall not find me: and where I am, thither ye cannot come" (John 7:33–34). In discussing the "mystery of communion of God with man," Dodgson ended with this chapter of John in which Christ slips into Jerusalem to be with the people but is not recognized by all. This outline is the only surviving detailed piece of evidence about Dodgson's early sermons.

Over the next five years, from 8 June 1862 until 10 March 1867, Dodgson preached on at least thirty-eight occasions. He was especially active in 1865, preaching twenty-one times. Then, from March 1867 there followed a period of almost twenty years when he did not preach a single sermon. He resumed preaching in January 1887 and preached at least thirty-six times between then and his death in January 1898. It is convenient to divide his sermons into those preached from 1862 to 1867 (the early sermons) and those preached from 1887 to 1897 (the later sermons).

The thirty-eight early sermons may be divided into three categories: those preached for friends and acquaintances at small parishes, mostly in the countryside near Oxford; those preached for his father or for friends near Croft; and those preached in Oxford. Only one of these sermons does not fall into these categories—that preached in 1863 in aid of the Curates' Aid Society[8] at Wintringham, Lincolnshire, when Dodgson and his sister Fanny were visiting there.

In a city filled with a variety of parishes, Dodgson preached nearly all his early Oxford sermons at parishes where the rector was distinctly high church, and in some cases strongly Tractarian. This pattern began in February and March 1863, when he preached at two suburban churches—the Iron Church in Cowley, and St. Thomas Becket in Osney.

Richard Meux Benson, the incumbent at Cowley, was a high churchman who went on, in 1865, to found the first religious order of monks in the Anglican Church since the Reformation. Dodgson took the evening service for Benson on Ash Wednesday (18 February 1863), preaching and performing his first baptism.

Two and half weeks later, he preached at another bastion of the high church, St. Thomas Becket, in Osney. The vicar, Thomas Chamberlain, was a "a staunch Tractarian, [who] introduced daily services, candles on the altar, the eastward position in celebrating Holy Communion, and, in 1854, Eucharistic vestments."[9] On Sunday 8 March 1863, Dodgson took the afternoon service, preaching and reading the lessons. "I was annoyed at finding that I hesitated a good deal in the first lesson," he recorded in his diary, "but I got on better afterwards."

His next foray into Oxford preaching was not in the suburbs but in the city itself, at a church built in the 1830s by supporters of the Oxford Movement. "Preached for Hackman at St. Paul's," he wrote in his diary. "My first sermon in Oxford, to the largest congregation I have yet addressed, 300 or 400 I should think." Under Alfred Hackman, the vicar of St. Paul's from 1844 to 1871, that church became a center of Tractarianism. Dodgson returned to preach at St. Paul's, a neoclassical building across from the Oxford University Press, three times in 1865.

Dodgson preached twice more in Oxford during the early period. On Easter Day, 1 April 1866, he attended the 8:00 a.m. Holy Communion service at St. Mary Magdalene. He assisted the curate officiating, who then asked if Dodgson would preach at the afternoon service: "I undertook a short sermon, never having had so short notice for preparation. I gave about 1½ hours to it altogether. It lasted longer than I expected, about 16 minutes." St. Mary Magdalene was perhaps the most well-known of the Oxford high churches. Its then vicar, Richard St. John Tyrwhitt, was a Student of Christ Church and friend of Dodgson, who records in his diary several instances of discussions with Tyrwhitt about religious and supernatural matters. Tyrwhitt, as rector of St. Mary Magdalene, "was sympathetic to some of the teachings of the Oxford Movement, but not to its ritual."[10] Dodgson had attended St. Mary Magdalene at least once before (on 5 June 1864) and chose to make his Easter Communion at this moderate high church in 1866.

When he wasn't preaching for friends or family, in the early years Dodgson preached almost exclusively at high church parishes. The same is true of his churchgoing in Oxford during this period. While he attended chapel at Christ Church and church at the University Church of St. Mary the Virgin regularly as required, he sometimes ventured to other Oxford parishes, almost exclusively high church ones. Including visits at which he assisted or preached, he records in his diary prior to the death of his father in 1868, among high church parishes: four visits to St. Mary Magdalene, seven to St. Paul's, and one to the new parish of St. Philip and St. James', a ritualistic parish where the "elaborately carved reredos and other altar decoration gave the impression of a Roman Catholic church."[11] In the same period he records, among lower church parishes, only three visits—two to St. Giles's (once to hear his friend Liddon preach) and one to St. Aldate's, the closest parish to Christ Church.

His other direct involvements with Oxford parish churches in this period were an attempt to teach at the church school of St. Aldate's in 1856—an experiment that lasted only about a month—and his desire to find a place to regularly help with Sunday services. "For some while I have been thinking about getting Sunday-duty, but cannot decide on which church to offer my help to, St. Giles's and St. Paul's are both attractive," he recorded in his diary on 11 June 1862. Though Liddon advised St. Giles's, Dodgson appears to have taken no immediate action. Three years later he apparently decided to pursue helping at St. Paul's. On 10 February 1865, he wrote, "I am obliged to give up my idea of helping at St. Paul's as I find intoning is necessary," referring to the high church practice of chanting portions of the service. Yet, three months later, on 21 May, he wrote, "Helped again at St. Paul's, this time by reading the lessons and Litany, the latter I tried to monotone, with pretty fair success." He preached his three sermons at St. Paul's around this time, on 14 May, 4 June, and 18 June, so possibly he was helping there on a regular basis. Though the parish enters his diary only once more, when he preached on 15 October of that year, his work at St. Paul's seems the closest Dodgson ever came to identifying with an Oxford parish outside the university, and St. Paul's was among the most high church of Oxford parishes.

Dodgson gave up not only preaching in 1867. In the just over five years from his ordination until April 1867, he assisted with services outside his college, in the role of deacon, at least twenty-three times, excluding services at which he preached. This generally meant reading the service (whether Morning or Evening Prayer) or assisting with Communion. In the twenty years during which he did not preach, he records assisting with services only five times, including two family events (his brother Wilfred's wedding and his aunt Lucy's funeral). Sometime between 1866, when his frequency of preaching curtailed dramatically, and 1868, by which time it had stopped altogether, Dodgson considered that his experiment of taking deacon's orders had come to an end, with the conclusion that he not only did not wish to proceed to priests' orders but wanted to regard himself as "practically a layman." Why did Dodgson give up preaching and other parochial activities in 1867? To hazard a guess, one must consider the end of Dodgson's "experiment" in a broader context.

First, there is the question of Dodgson's intention, or nonintention, to proceed to priests' orders. After his ordination as a deacon at the end of 1861, Dodgson made no immediate move to proceed to priests' orders. Nearly a year later, on 21 October 1862, he wrote in his diary:

Called on the Dean to ask him if I was in any way obliged to take Priests' Orders. (I consider mine as a Lay Studentship). His opinion was that by being ordained Deacon I became a Clerical Student, and so subject to the same conditions as if I had taken a Clerical Studentship, viz. that I must take Priests' Orders within four years from my time for being M.A. and that as this was clearly impossible in my case, I have probably already lost the Studentship, and am at least bound to take Priests' Orders as soon as possible. I differed from this view, and he talked of laying the matter before the electors.

Dodgson may not have been so quick to "differ from this view" had he any desire to quickly take priests' orders. The following day he wrote, "The Dean has decided on not consulting the electors, and says he shall do nothing more about it, so that I consider myself free as to being ordained Priest."

But Dodgson did not immediately and finally give up all thought of becoming a priest. Not only did he continue preaching, but two weeks later he wrote about trying to get Sunday duty at a local church. Three years later, on 13 August 1865, his diary indicates that he still seriously contemplated priests' orders:

I will take this week for ascertaining the relative rate at which I will read the various books for Ordination, and I will record opposite the time given to each.

The books I intend reading are:

(1) O.T. History—begin with Joshua.

(2) N.T. begin with Philippians.

(3) Hooker V.

(4) Pearson

(5) Robertson's Church History

(6) Blunt on the Reformation

The books Dodgson lists are all from the list required by Bishop Wilberforce of those wishing to be ordained in the Diocese of Oxford—the same books Dodgson studied to pass his deacon's examination. This declaration that he would continue to read for priest's ordination was followed by the most concentrated period of preaching in his life—seven sermons in ten weeks.

On 14 April 1867, in one of the many prayers he records in his diary (see pp. 211–15 in this volume), Dodgson mentioned the subject of ordination: "To have entered into Holy Orders seems almost a desecration, with my undisciplined and worldly affections." Dodgson echoed the words of Bishop Wilberforce in his *Addresses to the Candidates,* where he frequently spoke of setting aside worldly things. This lamentation comes just weeks after he preached his final sermon of the early period, but the sermons had been coming more sparsely for some time before this. After preaching twenty-two sermons in 1865, he preached only one in 1866 and one in 1867. Did Dodgson simply lose interest in proceeding to priests' orders, finding that he liked being "practically a layman"? Or did something else happen?

He did hint, in an 1873 letter to the speech therapist Henry Frederick Rivers, that his hesitancy to take up clerical duties was not wholly unrelated to his speech problems: "These failures [of speech] have rather deferred the hope I had formed of being very soon able to help in Church again, for if I break down in reading to only one or two, I should be all the worse, I fear, for the presence of a congregation" (*Letters* 194).

While it seems most likely that the reasoning above concerning Dodgson's delaying his ordination as a deacon and not proceeding to priests' orders was playing out gradually in his life, there were three major events that occurred around this time which may have influenced his abandonment not just of the idea of the priesthood but of virtually all clerical work.

First was the publication on 18 November 1865 of *Alice's Adventures in Wonderland.*[12] By the autumn of 1866, Dodgson began to see that this might be a profitable enterprise. "By the end of 1867 I hope to be about clear, if not actually in pocket by it," he wrote in his diary on 3 September. Did Dodgson foresee a career as a writer of books for children and works of humor? Certainly from the early success of *Wonderland,* he pursued such a career, following it up with the humorous verse collected in *Phantasmagoria* (1869); the *Alice* sequel *Through the Looking-Glass* (1871); *The Hunting of the Snark* (1876); the *Sylvie and Bruno* books (1889, 1893); and a plethora of games, puzzles, and verses. Is it possible that Dodgson decided, in the early years after the publication of *Wonderland,* that he wanted to pursue such a career and felt writing humorous works for children was incompatible with the sober and serious life of a clergyman?

The next major event in this period was Dodgson's only foreign journey, his 1867 tour through Europe to Russia in the company of his friend, the high churchman Henry Parry Liddon. Dodgson had sought advice from

Liddon on the subject of ordination, and now they spent nearly two months together, visiting churches and monasteries, attending services at a wide variety of places of worship, and speaking on religious topics.

These discussions became arguments on at least five occasions. Dodgson did not record these arguments in his highly detailed diary, which remained at all times a travel journal he might share with family and friends. Liddon, however, did mention them in his diary. "A long argument with Dodgson afterwards about the obligation of the daily Service,—an obligation which he fiercely contested,"[13] he wrote on 20 July when the pair were in Berlin. The obligation of the daily service is stated clearly in the Book of Common Prayer: "All Priests and Deacons are to say daily the Morning and Evening Prayer either privately or openly."[14] Bishop Wilberforce lamented that the duty was "too generally neglected,"[15] but why would Dodgson "contest" this obligation? And how did the subject come up? Might they have been discussing the life of a clergyman and its requirements?

Over the next few weeks Liddon recorded in his diary "a long argument with Dodgson" (12–13) on 28 July; "A great argument with Dodgson on the character of Russian religion—he thought it too external, etc." (27) on 13 August; "a warm argument with Dodgson about Prayers for the Departed" (28) on 14 August; and "Some discussions with Dodgson in the evening. He thought the Roman Catholic church like a Concert-room—and went out. Dislikes the name Catholic because it connected us with Rome" (40) on 1 September. Were these discussions with Liddon a reminder to Dodgson of what the life of a clergyman entailed and that it was a life he did not want for himself?

Finally came the most significant personal event of this period, the unexpected death of Charles's father, Archdeacon Charles Dodgson, on 21 June 1868. The archdeacon had been Dodgson's primary religious teacher for the first twelve years of his life, and doubtless a significant influence in later years. His place in the moderate high church movement may have influenced his son to attend the high churches of Oxford. He seems to have desired his son to follow him into parochial work. On 21 August 1855, Charles received a letter from his father with advice about saving money: "I will just sketch for you a supposed case, applicable to your own circumstances, of a young man of twenty-three, making up his mind to work for ten years. . . . Suppose him at the end of the ten years to get a Living enabling him to settle" (*Life* 61).

Following his father's death, wrote Collingwood, "it seemed to him at first as if a cloud had settled on his life which could never be dispelled"

(*Life* 133). Collingwood cited a letter Dodgson wrote to Edith Rix "long after the sad event" which gives some insight into the events immediately following the archdeacon's death and the scar that death left on his son. Edith had sent Dodgson an illuminated text, and he replied: "That text is consecrated for me by the memory of one of the greatest sorrows I have known—the death of my dear father. In those solemn days, when we used to steal, one by one, into the darkened room, to take yet another look at the dear calm face, and to pray for strength, the one feature in the room that I remember was a framed text, illuminated by one of my sisters, 'Then are they glad, because they are at rest; and so he bringeth them into the haven where they would be!'" (*Life* 132).[16]

This illuminated text had been made by Dodgson's sister Louisa, and he hung it in his bedroom in the family's new home in Guildford.[17] It is easy to see Charles Lutwidge Dodgson being of two minds about his father's death. First, he was deeply depressed, and so not inclined to take on any tasks that put him before the public, such as preaching or assisting at church services. He may have even experienced a sort of crisis of faith—not enough to keep him from church as a worshipper or prevent him from prayer, but perhaps enough for him to finally and fully abandon the idea that he was or would ever be, anything more than "practically a layman." But it is also possible that Dodgson felt liberated not just from the archdeacon's high church tendencies but from his wish that his son go into parochial life.

Dodgson's falling away from the path of a clergyman may have been a result of a combination of all these factors—his original doubts about his own worthiness, his interest in pursuing a career as a children's writer, his concerns about the duties of the clergy following two months' journey with Liddon, and the sudden death of Archdeacon Dodgson. In any case, during the time between the publication of *Alice's Adventures in Wonderland* on 18 November 1865 and the death of his father on 21 June 1868, Dodgson severely curtailed and then essentially ceased his preaching and clerical work. He never again mentioned reading or preparing for ordination as a priest.

After Dodgson's decision, whether sudden or gradual, to not only give up being ordained a priest but even to abstain from those duties allowed to a deacon, there followed a period of nearly twenty years when he lived essentially as a layman. The vows he had taken to become a deacon could not be retracted, and he continued to be addressed, officially, as "Rev. Charles L. Dodgson," but only rarely, and only after he had begun preaching again, did he actually sign a letter "Rev. Charles L. Dodgson."[18]

In the second half of the 1880s, Dodgson began to think about again taking on some of the privileges of a deacon. He had, on three occasions between 1867 and 1887, assisted with Communion and had once come close to giving a sermon. In his diary for 4 June 1881, he wrote:

> As Prout[19] was sent for yesterday to his brother in London (who died) Salwey[20] undertook to take the service for Binsey for him, and I volunteered to help him, and prepared a short sermon. But I am not destined to deliver it, as Prout returned this evening. It is some relief to one's nerves, as I was looking forward with terror to the ordeal. It is years since I have tried preaching.

Dodgson did not note the source of his terror, but having fallen out of the habit of preaching, he did not, at this time, wish to resume. But in 1887, resume he did. St. Mary's, the church in Guildford where the Dodgson family worshiped, was just around the corner from the family home, the Chestnuts, where most of Dodgson's sisters lived following a move there after the death of Archdeacon Dodgson; thus it was almost like a home parish to Dodgson. In 1885 a new rector arrived, Arthur Sutton Valpy. On 1 November 1886, Dodgson called on Valpy and "had a long talk with him: and gave a sort of promise to try and preach sometime."

Two months later, on 2 January 1887, Dodgson preached at St. Mary's. "I took the headings, written, in my pocket, but did not refer to them," he said. Dodgson would preach regularly for the rest of his life, delivering at least thirty-six sermons over the next ten years. Twelve of these he preached at St. Mary's Guildford, but his choice of where to preach the others reveals a significant shift in his attitude from the period of the early sermons. Then, with his high church father still alive and the possibility of becoming a priest not completely removed from his mind, he had preached at some of Oxford's highest churches. Now, he sought out more broad church opportunities, even preaching in places that were not technically churches. At the same time, he wrote of his disdain for ritualism. The high church young man had become a broad churchman by middle age.

He preached his first Oxford sermon of this new period at Oxford High School. He most frequently preached at the special Sunday-evening service for college servants held in the Latin Chapel of Christ Church Cathedral. In both cases he sought out not high church services, but places where he might touch the lives of the less educated—especially in the case of the servants' service. He first preached at this service on 19 May 1889 and preached there eleven times in the next four and a half years. "Once more I have had the privilege of preaching at the 'College Servants' Service," he wrote on 9 November 1890. "Once more I have to thank my Heavenly Father for the great blessing and privilege of being allowed to speak for Him! May he bless my words to help some soul on its heavenward way. I preached at the College Servants' Service," he recorded on 3 April 1892.

After this period of fairly regular preaching at the College Servants' Service, Dodgson stopped what seemed to have been a pleasant duty, but an entry in his diary on 24 April 1896 explains why:

> Wrote to Warner[21] about the College Servants' Services, which it appears he manages. I had written to the Dean (Paget) about my not having been asked to preach for 2½ years. I now find that Warner has tried to make it more *parochial*, and mostly preaches himself, and asks those who have had parochial experience. He now asks me to preach on May 10. But this is clearly out of regard for *my* feelings. I wrote that I think things had better go on as they are now, and preachers *not* asked, who, like myself, have had no parochial experience.

Dodgson still, on rare occasions, assisted friends in small parishes—preaching on 3 July 1892 for his cousin Arthur Wilcox at Spelsbury; on 16 April 1893 at Nettlecombe when visiting his old friends Mary Seymour and her sister Isabel; twice in May 1893 at Alfrick, where his brother Skeffington was curate; and once at Cassington, where fellow Christ Church Student Robert Faussett was rector. But the majority of his sermons of the late period, outside St. Mary's Guildford, reached out to communities that might be seen as underserved or undereducated. We see this not just in his preaching at Oxford High School and the College Servants' Service, but in his sermons in and around Eastbourne, the seaside town where he spent the bulk of his Long Vacations from 1877 until his death.

On 10 September 1893, he preached his first Eastbourne sermon at the Ocklynge Mission-Room. "It is fitted up so that it can be used as a chapel," he wrote in his diary, "but it serves as a school also. . . . The room seemed full: perhaps 200 were there." He preached again at the mission room the following Sunday and a third time on 7 October 1894, on which occasion he also assisted with Holy Communion. The mission room was a project of the parish church of St. Mary's, Eastbourne—a sort of stopgap measure to serve the growing suburbs until a proper church could be built.

On 29 September 1895, he preached at the evening service for the Harvest Festival at Westham, near enough to Eastbourne that he walked home afterward. The vicar, Howard Hopley recorded: "Our grand old church was crowded, and, although our villagers are mostly agricultural labourers, yet they breathlessly listened to a sermon forty minutes long, and apparently took in every word of it. It was quite extempore, in very simple words, and illustrated with some delightful and most touching stories of children" (*Life* 328–29).

On several occasions in 1897, as detailed above, he gave addresses (he did not call them sermons) at children's services at Christ Church, Eastbourne, and in Hastings. This is the pattern of these later sermons— Dodgson preaching at a school and a mission room; speaking to children, college servants, and agricultural workers, all in lieu of seeking out Sunday-morning appointments at high churches in Oxford. Not surprising, then, that one of Dodgson's friends described him as "broad—as broad as Christ" (*Life* 284). Dodgson never forgot or completely renounced the high church views of his father—they would always be a part of him. But he certainly broadened his outlook. Collingwood quotes a letter from 1882, five years before Dodgson resumed preaching, in which he talks about this transition from high to broad:

> My dear father was what is called a "High Churchman," and I naturally adopted those views, but have always felt repelled by the yet higher development called "Ritualism."
>
> But I doubt if I am fully a "High Churchman" now. I find that as life slips away (I am over fifty now), and the life on the other side of the great river becomes more and more the reality, of which this is only a shadow, that the petty distinctions of the many creeds of Christendom tend to slip away as well. (*Life* 340)

In January 1886, he wrote to Edith Rix: "(I hope you won't be *very* much shocked at me as an ultra 'Broad' Churchman) . . . what a person *is* is of more importance in God's sight than merely what propositions he affirms or denies" (*Life* 250–51).

In a letter to his sister Elizabeth in 1894, when explaining his argument against eternal punishment (see pp. 266–67 in this volume) he wrote of the three premises he laid out: "Those who believe (1) and (2), and deny (3) (which is *my* case) are usually called *Broad Church*. Those who believe

(1) and (3), and deny (2) (which is the case with Edwin)[22] are mostly *High Church*" (*Letters* 1045).

He makes a similar statement in a letter of 1885—claiming to be a high churchman, but then essentially admitting to have adopted a more broad church outlook, writing: "I myself belong to the 'High Church' school. My dear father was a 'High Church' man, though *not* a 'Ritualist,' and I have seen little cause to modify the views I learned from him, though perhaps I regard the holding of different views as a less important matter than he did. As life draws nearer to its end, I feel more and more clearly that it will not matter *in the least,* at the last day, what *form* of religion a man has professed" (*Letters* 586).

On three occasions in the last two years of his life, Dodgson preached at the University Church of St. Mary's in Oxford. On 6 December 1896, the curate in charge, Rev. Sydney Baker, a chaplain of Christ Church, had asked for Dodgson's assistance with the evening service, and Dodgson delivered a sermon. "It was indeed a privilege to be thankful for—" Dodgson wrote in his diary, "but a formidable task: I had fancied there would be only a small audience, and the church was full, as well as the West Gallery, and the North one partly filled as well. . . . The sermon lasted about 18 minutes."

The last two sermons Dodgson delivered in Oxford, both in 1897, were at evening services for university men at St. Mary's. As he explained in his diary for 7 March 1897:

> There is now a system established of a course of six sermons at St. Mary's, each year, for University men only, and specially meant for undergraduates. They are preached, preceded by a few prayers and a hymn, at 8 ½. This evening ended the course for this term: and it was my great privilege to preach. It has been the most formidable sermon I have ever had to preach: and it is a great relief to have it over. I took, as text, Job. XXVIII. 28, "And unto man he said, The fear of the Lord, that is wisdom," and the prayer in the Litany, "Give us an heart to love and dread thee." It lasted about three quarters of an hour.

Henry L. Thompson described Dodgson's preaching this sermon, recalling, "the erect, gray-haired figure, with the rapt look of earnest thought; the slow, almost hesitating speech; the clear and faultless language; the intense solemnity and earnestness which compelled his audience to listen for nearly an hour, as he spoke to them on the duty of reverence, and warned them of the sin of talking carelessly of holy things."[23]

A few months later, Dodgson preached at the same service, delivering his final sermon on 24 October 1897. This time he took for his topic a doctrine on which he held a strong opinion—eternal punishment (see pp. 263–73 in this volume). In arguing against the doctrine, he chose as his text verses 11–12 of Psalm 103:

> For look how high the heaven is in comparison of the earth: so great is his mercy also towards them that fear him.
>
> Look how wide also the east is from the west: so far hath he set our sins from us.

One member of the congregation wrote "The hard thinking of many years was so evident in every sentence that he uttered in his musical and somewhat slow words."[24]

How was Charles Lutwidge Dodgson taught to preach? First by the words and example of his father, some of whose thoughts on the topic are recorded in his sermon "Preach the Gospel":

> Let us define an Evangelical Preacher simply as one who preaches the Gospel of Jesus Christ, to the exclusion of every other system of teaching opposed to or unsanctioned by it. . . .
>
> The essential character, therefore, of a Preacher is that of a herald and a messenger. . . . His task is not that of the Philosopher in his lecture, to propound and vindicate theories; nor that of the Orator in the assembly, to invent popular and persuasive arguments: he is simply commissioned to deliver a message. . . .
>
> The object of such a Preacher must be the same as the object of the Gospel itself,—to lead the sinner to Christ.[25]

His first schoolmaster, James Tate II, wrote about preaching in a note dated 9 November 1851. Likely Tate did his best to illustrate to his charges such passionate, personal preaching.

> I (J.T.) like a sermon which seizes me with ineluctable interest—arouses, pierces, scrutinizes, connects, remodels, smooths, comforts me. I love to feel my very heart probed and anatomized.
>
> I love to feel a new heart creating in me meanwhile my old spirit renewing.[26] For impurity—cleanness! . . . For ignorance—discernment and

knowledge! For lukewarmth—zeal! For apathy—love! For this barrenness of indifference—the fruit of belief! . . . For fears—laughter! For earth, heaven!! Such preaching . . . answers in my judgement the end of preaching.[27]

Bishop Samuel Wilberforce, too, had advice on preaching to offer to candidates for ordination, telling them to "Set your people before you in their numbers, their wants, their dangers, their capacities; choose a subject, not to shew yourself off, but to benefit them; and then speak straight to them, as you would beg your life, or counsel your son, or call your dearest friend from a burning house, in plain, strong, earnest words. . . . Let every sermon be one subject, well divided and thoroughly worked out; and let all tend to this highest purpose, simply to exalt before your people Christ crucified."[28]

Both Rev. Charles Dodgson and Bishop Wilberforce spoke of preaching a specific theology based not just on the Gospel but on the creeds and the formularies of the Church of England. What did Charles Lutwidge Dodgson believe constituted good preaching? He was frank about the responsibilities of the preacher when the character of Arthur discusses a sermon in *Sylvie and Bruno*. "I must say," says Arthur, "that our preachers enjoy an enormous privilege—which they ill deserve, and which they misuse terribly. We put our man into a pulpit, and we virtually tell him 'Now, you may stand there and talk to us for half-an-hour. We won't interrupt you by so much as a word! You shall have it all your own way!' And what does he give us in return? Shallow twaddle, that, if it were addressed to you over a dinner-table, you would think 'Does the man take me for a fool?'" (277).

In the preface to *Sylvie and Bruno Concluded,* Dodgson admitted to being "much in sympathy" with Arthur, and commented on sermons in general, "In my opinion, far too many sermons are expected from our preachers; and, as a consequence, a great many are preached, which are not worth listening to; and, as a consequence of *that,* we are very apt *not* to listen."[29]

In his comments about preachers in his diaries and letters, Dodgson described what he did and did not like in a sermon and its delivery. He complained several times about a speaker who was either dull or inarticulate. "[H]is delivery is very monotonous," he wrote of one preacher on 25 February 1855. "It seemed a good sermon but his delivery is bad," read the verdict on 15 March 1857. Of an aging John Keble he wrote, on 24 May 1864, that he gave a "nervous and feeble delivery, but a beautiful sermon." And of one service on 20 August 1882 he wrote, "There was a long anthem, of which not one articulate word could be heard: and in Mr. Whelpton's sermons the ends of many of the sentences were in the same plight." Another sermon on 19 August 1888 he described as "recited on one note, a most wearisome performance" and of another preacher he wrote, on 26 September 1897, "his *tone* is wearisomely 'sing-song.'"

Not only delivery, but content also sometimes brought Dodgson's condemnation. "Sermons too evangelical," he wrote of a parish church on the Isle of Wight on 31 March 1883. The new rector of Guildford, Cyril Fletcher Grant, who came to the parish in 1895, came in for particularly harsh criticism in Dodgson's diaries. On 21 April 1896, Dodgson recorded that he "heard three sermons from the new Rector, Mr. Grant, in which his chief aim seemed to be to reduce to 'commonplace' (his favourite word) all the doctrines of Christianity: and he made several extraordinary assertions (e.g. that the work of our salvation seemed to our Lord 'trivial' and 'not worth talking about,' and that our hope of salvation rests not so much on the love of God as on His self-interest, regarding us as property that has been lost) which I earnestly hope will not be believed."

Dodgson suggested a method for dealing with a poor, or poorly delivered, sermon in a letter to Edith Rix on 14 February 1886, writing: "I fear I agree with your friend in not liking all sermons. Some of them, one has to confess, are rubbish: but then I release my attention from the preacher, and go ahead in any line of thought he may have started: and his after-eloquence acts as a kind of accompaniment—like music while one is reading poetry" (*Letters* 621).

In praising specific preachers and sermons, he most often called the former "eloquent" and "earnest" (as well as "powerful" and "interesting") and the latter "striking" and "beautiful" (along with "excellent" and "wonderful").

He was attuned to whether a speech was actually a sermon—that is, did it take as its basis a passage of scripture, and was it Christian in nature? "A sermon," wrote Dodgson in an 1896 letter to Harry Furniss, "has for its subject-matter 'holy things'" (*Letters* 1090). Of one preacher he wrote, on 15 November 1866, "His preaching is eloquent and impressive, though rather more like a speech than a sermon," and of another on 12 May 1878, "It was a very able and eloquent lecture on 'War,' but *not* a Christian sermon, I thought."

Dodgson felt humor was out of place in a sermon. When, in May 1887, he heard then Bishop of Ripon William Boyd Carpenter deliver a sermon as part of his Bampton Lectures at St. Mary's, Oxford, he wrote to the bishop that, "I feel very sure that the 2 or 3 sentences . . . which were distinctly *amusing* (and of which *one* raised a general laugh) went far to undo, in the minds of many of your hearers, and specially among the *young* men, much of the good effect of the rest of the sermon" (*Letters* 677).

Dodgson seemed to prefer sermons that at least sounded extempore rather than being read from a text. Of one, on 15 November 1856, he complained, "it was delivered without a book, but evidently learnt by heart," and another on 28 May 1882 he praised as "a very remarkable extempore sermon."

He also feared, as he said in his own sermon of 2 January 1887 (see pp. 200–203 in this volume) the danger of a sermon becoming a performance—the goal, he felt, of both worship and sermons, should be "inward spiritual grace of holy devotion."[30]

Not surprisingly, Dodgson felt it important to use good logic when composing sermons, so as to be sure one's arguments would stand in the face of skeptics. In a long letter to his nephew Stuart Dodgson Collingwood dated 29 December 1891, he wrote:

> You have never studied technical Logic, at all, I fancy. It would have been a great help: but still it is not indispensable: after all, it is only the putting into rules of the way in which *every* mind proceeds, when it draws valid conclusions: and, by practice in careful thinking, you may get to know "fallacies," when you meet with them, without knowing the formal *rules*. . . .
>
> At Eastbourne, last summer, I heard a preacher advance the astounding argument "We believe that the Bible is true, because our holy Mother, the Church, tells us it is." I pity that unfortunate clergyman, if ever he is bold enough to enter any Young Men's Debating Club, where there is some clear-headed sceptic who has heard, or heard of, that sermon. I can fancy how the young man would rub his hands, in delight, and would say to himself, "Just see me get him into a corner, and convict him of arguing in a circle!" (*Letters* 878–79)

The preparation of sermons and the lead-up to their being preached caused Dodgson some anxiety, but his belief in the importance of what he was doing above and beyond his own comfort ruled the day. In a letter of 6 May 1890, he wrote to a schoolmistress on the topic of his "some day having a few *serious* words" with some of the elder girls: "Physically, all such coming out of one's-self, so to speak, is a terror to me: sometimes, when I have undertaken to preach a sermon, I feel, as the time gets near, as if I really *could* not face it, and must get myself excused: and I have to say to myself 'what *does* it matter what *you* feel about it? If you can say anything helpful to other immortal souls, that is the only thing that *really* signifies'" (*Letters* 788).

Some of this anxiety came from the seriousness with which Dodgson approached the task of preaching. "I do feel that preparing [sermons] takes a good deal *out* of me, in the way of vital force," he wrote in a letter in 1891. "But I would not have it otherwise: it is work that, if it is to do any good, needs that one should put one's whole self into it" (*Letters* 837). Some of his concern and stress came, however, as he explained in a letter of 1 February 1891 to Edith Blakemore, from his speech hesitation:

> A sermon would be quite formidable enough to me, even if I did *not* suffer from the physical difficulty of hesitation: but, with *that* super-added, the prospect is sometimes almost too much for my nerves. This last Xmas, I undertook to preach at Guildford (where my sisters live); and, as the day drew near, I felt so entirely despondent that I went to the Curate's house, to ask him to bring a sermon with him, in case I should feel unequal to preaching. Luckily for me, he wasn't at home; and I didn't go again, but made up my mind to face it, and make the best of it. And, when I got into the pulpit, all the difficulty seemed to have vanished, and I hardly once hesitated! (*Letters* 821–22)

Despite this anxiety, Dodgson wrote in a letter to his brother Wilfred, "I always feel that a sermon is worth the preaching, if it has given *some* help to even *one* soul in the puzzle of Life" (*Letters* 946). On 1 September 1897, Dodgson, hard at work on the sermon he was to deliver to Oxford undergraduates, wrote to his sister Louisa. The man who, in 1885, had described himself as "practically a layman," now said that he was "most glad to have some distinctly *clerical* work" (*Letters* 1136).

Several of Dodgson's contemporaries left reminiscences about his style of preaching, though it appears all these came from the later sermons. "His preaching was remarkable for its simple earnestness and apt cleverness of phrase,"[31] wrote fellow Christ Church Student Frederick York Powell. Michael Sadler, Steward of Christ Church, recalled, "He wept when he came to the more serious parts of his sermons" (60). Corpus Christi Scholar Claude Blagden wrote of one of Dodgson's sermons at the University Church of St. Mary's: "The church was thronged, but those who expected fireworks were doomed to disappointment. What they did hear was a plain, evangelical sermon of the old-fashioned kind, preached by one who held to the faith of his childhood, undisturbed by the learning or the criticism of any later age" (63). Another Christ Church Student, Thomas Banks Strong, wrote, "His sermons were picturesque in style, and strongly emotional; there could be no doubt that they came from real and sincere devotion; he delivered them slowly and carefully, and he held his audience" (39).

Dodgson did not write out his sermons, although he sometimes did write out headings to remind him of what he wished to say. As his child-friend Beatrice Hatch recalled: "He knew exactly what he wished to say, and completely forgot his audience in his anxiety to explain his point clearly. He thought of the subject only, and the words came of themselves. Looking straight in front of him he saw, as it were, his argument mapped out in the form of a diagram, and he set to work to prove it point by point, under its separate heads, and then summed up the whole" (105).

Especially in his later years he often repeated favorite sermons for new audiences. On 11 February 1894, when he preached at Cassington, he wrote, "Preached the morning service on Luke XI.4 (I have already preached it five times)."

He never published his sermons, but his surviving writings on reverence and eternal punishment do give us a good idea about his final two sermons preached at the University Church of St. Mary's (see pp. 236–39 and 263–73 in this volume). One complete record of one of Dodgson's sermons for a general congregation does survive. In July 1900, a religious journalist named Charles T. Bateman published an article in a short-lived periodical called *The Puritan* titled "'Lewis Carroll' as a Preacher." Bateman wrote, "At Guildford Mr. Dodgson occasionally preached at St. Mary's Church, and by courtesy of a clergyman the following notes of a sermon delivered on the commencing Sunday of 1887 are here reproduced for the first time."[32] This was the first of Dodgson's later sermons, preached on 2 January 1887 and taking as its text Mark 10:51—"And Jesus answered and said unto him, What wilt thou that I should do unto thee? The blind man said unto him, Lord, that I might receive my sight." The sermon was likely reconstructed by Arthur Sutton Valpy, vicar at Guildford in 1887, from notes he took at the time. Valpy may also have worked from Dodgson's own notes, for Dodgson wrote in his diary of this sermon, "I took the headings, written, in my pocket, but did not refer to them." As the only surviving complete sermon by Dodgson in *any* form, and one that has not been reproduced since its publication in *The Puritan* in 1900, it bears reprinting in full.

The Church Services of the present day are in every sense so attractive in comparison with those of former times (when if a man went to church at all, he went to worship God) that there is danger—great danger—of our becoming mere formalists, of putting outward beauty of structure, of adornment, of external reverence, in the place of that inward spiritual grace of holy devotion, without which it is impossible to offer up acceptable worship.

And the sermons of to-day share in the same perilous tendency. The loss of novelty, of sensation, of something to startle, assails both preacher and hearers. In my own experience I have heard remarks passed upon the order and arrangement of services, not sparing the sermon, its matter and delivery—in the tone and spirit of visitors at opera or theatre. "How did you like this or that?" "What did you think of him?" "Wasn't it horrid?"

I feel this danger. I feel it especially, coming among you for the first time. Lay aside, I pray you, this spirit of shallow criticism. Let us remember that we are fellow-sinners together in a suffering world; fellow wanderers together in the rich garden of God's word; fellow-seekers together for some lesson out of that word for our mutual comfort and encouragement.

I was reading the other day in the Gospel by St. Mark of the coming to Jesus of blind Bartimaeus, chap. x. ver. 51. He was met by the question "What wilt thou that I shall do unto thee?" The sense of unutterable need drove the blind beggar to make his supplication—and he was met half-way.

The thing which makes life so sorrowful—at times so oppressive—is not *disease*. Tortured frames find heaven in the temporary lull of pain. Sick beds have been places of martyrs for the faith. Strong ones have come away stronger for a sight of such triumph out of weakness. Halos of glory have floated around suffering heads. It is not *death*. When we lay down the heavy head, to ache no more; as we fold the tired hands into repose; as we look our last upon the beloved features from which already the kind angel is smoothing away each lingering trace of pain—it is in the joyful hope of meeting them again. It is neither of these which rob us of all peace. It is the burden of *sin*—unrepented, unforgiven sin. Our own sin and the sin all around us.

Is it possible that there is anyone here who has not felt more or less this anguish of sin in all its loathsomeness, clinging to and defiling the garments of the soul? The being severed from those better, holier than ourselves, shut out from sharing their inner joys, knowing ourselves contaminated, cut off from communion with a holy God. This, this is what makes life unendurable, and I think this sense of the unbearable weight of sin seems to have fallen upon the lower orders of creation. There are instances of some of the most faithful and sensitive of our dumb, domestic friends, whose tender hearts have broken under the intolerable load of displeasure in those the brute counts worthy of his worship and service.

Life is an enigma, and when we see the innocent perishing for the guilty, gross injustice, unblushing tyranny, the cruel dark corners of the land, some are tempted to cry aloud, "Where is the God of love?" But the problem is not to be solved here. Hereafter in the full fruition of Love the riddle of sorrow shall be read to comprehending ears, and the mystery of incongruity made plain to comprehending eyes. *Here*—Faith and Patience must be watchwords.

Is there no mitigation of this pain? No balm for this woe? Is the evil incurable? Hope sounds in the voice of Him who is saying, "What wilt thou?"

We all wish to be happy. But how? In ancient legend and fairy tale the prevailing idea was ever that of some happiness to be secured by the attainment of a wish. Honour, fame, riches—usually riches. Now it is not what we *fancy,* but what we *want,* that will make us happy. Our needs, not our notions, will be supplied in answer to this question, "What wilt thou?" Would Bartimaeus have been satisfied with anything else than sight? Would beauty, luxury, wealth, have compensated for open eyes? And can a sin-laden world be satisfied with anything short of a release from sin? Can a soul be content until it has received salvation? What is salvation? So incomprehensible a thought, that no figure of speech can adequately convey its breadth and depth and height. God, the creator. Man, the hopeless debtor. Christ discharging that debt. Is that all? If sin be left to accumulate fresh liabilities, is that salvation? Or, God, the just judge—man, the guilty criminal—Christ, the penalty bearer. If sin be left to stain the conscience anew, is that salvation? Could we appear in His presence with joy merely because our debts have been paid, our punishment borne? Ah, no, Christ's salvation is far beyond all this. It is to take us out of sin and self—by His blood to cleanse, by His spirit to sanctify, so that we may look forward to a day when we too shall be absolutely sinless—nothing to come between us and holiness. This is what He has done for us. This is why He was born and grew and lived and taught and died and rose again. This is why we hear His voice "What wilt thou?" How was this marvel to be wrought now? By blending the divine with the human nature. In itself unexplainable, the Lord unfolded this truth to His disciples under many parables. The vine, nourishing with its own vigour the branches.[33] The head and the body, the one necessary to the life of the other.[34] And, chiefest of all, closer, more intimate relationship—the Holy Eucharist of His own institution, Flesh and Blood. A figure, revolting to the mind in its carnal sense, yet chosen by the Lord to enforce the doctrine He would inculcate. For as the morsel of bread and drops of wine become incorporated with and absolutely part of this physical frame, so in a wider, deeper, truer sense, does the worshipper receive the spiritual body and blood of Christ, which, commingling with and interfusing the spiritual frame gradually purifies it,[35] daily fashioning it more and more to the Divine likeness.

Our sustaining hope is to become like Him. No longer to be impure, cruel, proud, selfish, jealous, and shallow; but clean, kind, tender-hearted, upright, and noble. This is a full salvation. Is this what we want? "What wilt thou?" "Lord, if Thou wilt Thou canst make me clean." Two wills are necessary— God's and man's. And He willed not that anyone should perish. What is our will—yours and mine? A new year stretches out before us. What is our will concerning the record of the future? Every life has its book. Upon the pages of the past year there are dismal stains and dark blots of thought, word, and deed which we would fain wash out with our tears. It cannot be. What is done can never be undone. It may be repented of. It may be cancelled by the Divine reckoner, but God Himself, if He would, could not undo it. Some in this church have turned over many pages in their life-book,—upwards of threescore and ten,—some are but just entering upon the roll. But none, old or young, can say when the last leaf will be turned, and they see the solemn words—The End.

Before us lies a clean, fair page; what shall be written there? It is within our power to decide. Shall the year, now in its infancy, find as it wanes that the entries are unsullied with spot or stain? Or will the Recorder have had to weep over the dark evidence of misspent days, weeks, and months?

"What wilt thou?" Sin repented, forgiven, blotted out. Power so to live Godward and manward that at the crisis of our passage from Here to the Hereafter, we shall not shrink from the face of Him who is both willing and "able to do exceeding abundantly above all we can ask or think."[36] (532–34)

The sermon can be divided into five sections: introduction, text, problem or question, answer, and action. The introduction was a warning against what Dodgson saw as the dangers of ritualism and of treating a church service, including the sermon, as a performance. He stated the text simply, noting he was "reading the other day in the Gospel of Mark." Without explicitly exhorting his congregation to scripture reading, he casually set an example. Then came the problem and question, one he dealt with in his first sermon in 1863. We are, he said, "cut off from communion with a holy God" by our own sin. He ended this section with a series of questions: "Is there no mitigation of this pain? No balm for this woe? Is the evil incurable?" Then came the answer, nothing less than an analysis of the nature of salvation through Jesus Christ, which Dodgson described thus: "It is to take us out of sin and self—by His blood to cleanse, by His spirit to sanctify, so that we may look forward to a day when we too shall be absolutely sinless—nothing to come between us and holiness." Likely this first Sunday service of the year included Holy Communion, because of Dodgson's emphasis on the Eucharist as the "chiefest" means toward this sanctification. Finally, came his suggestions for action, and here he took advantage of the new year as a time for self-reflection and renewal. "Before us lies a clean, fair page; what shall be written there? It is within our power to decide." In conclusion, Dodgson returned to his text, "What wilt thou?"

Obviously this sermon was meant for a parochial audience—simpler, shorter, and less intellectually challenging than, for instance, his final sermon, "Eternal Punishment," given to a congregation of Oxford undergraduates, but probably a good example of the sorts of sermons Dodgson preached, especially in the later period from 1887 to 1897 that began with this sermon.

Rev. Charles Lutwidge Dodgson ascended the steep stairs to the pulpit of the University Church of St. Mary the Virgin. For nearly fifty years he had listened to sermons preached from this pulpit, from which John Henry Newman had launched the Oxford Movement. In the pews below and in the galleries above him sat a throng of undergraduates of the university, along with many of his colleagues. Unlike when he delivered his first sermon, he was no longer an obscure Oxford don. Most everyone in the congregation knew that the famous Lewis Carroll was about to preach. He could see his logical argument, laid out before him almost as if the words hung in the air. He began with what he had been taught as a child and believed ever since, the central axiom of his own faith—God is perfectly good.

· ELEVEN ·

Diligence in Prayer

Twenty-four-year-old Charles knelt in prayer on the hard floor of his room in the family home at Croft Rectory. The cold seeped in through the window frame above his head. His watch showed a quarter past midnight. The new year 1857 had begun. On his bed lay his diary, the ink on the latest entry barely dry: "I do trust most sincerely to amend myself in those respects in which the past year has exhibited the most grievous shortcomings, and I trust and pray that the most merciful God may aid me in this and all other good undertakings. Midnight is past: bless the New Year, oh heavenly Father, for thy dear Son Jesus Christ's sake!"

There were three aspects to Charles Lutwidge Dodgson's prayer life—private prayer, about which we know very little; prayer in the context of worship services, primarily from the Book of Common Prayer; and written prayers recorded in his diary.

How was Charles Lutwidge Dodgson taught to pray in the years of his education? Among the twenty-eight subjects the Dodgson children were encouraged to study were several related to prayer:

14. If our repentance is sincere, we shall confess, and forsake all sin, and wickedness.
18. Men are commanded and encouraged to pray to God.
19. God will hear our prayers if they are offered up thro' the merits of Jesus Christ.
20. God will give his Holy Spirit to those who desire and pray for his help.
21. The Holy Ghost will guide us in the way to Heaven and strengthen us against sin.

These together with the services in the Book of Common Prayer and the handwritten Dodgson family prayer book form the basis of Dodgson's prayer life as a child. The family prayers, probably composed by his father, proceed, as previously noted, through six stages: (1) thankfulness for blessings, (2) acknowledgment of sinfulness, (3) asking forgiveness through Christ, (4) request for guidance, (5) request for blessings, and (6) request for help in serving God and man. These six types of prayer crop up often in Charles Lutwidge Dodgson's adult diaries, especially the admission of sins, asking for forgiveness, and request for help in doing God's work. Even in short prayers, he could address several of these topics, as in this diary prayer from 22 July 1866: "I thank God for grace and strength given me, and pray Him to pardon my sins, and help me to serve Him better, for Jesus' sake. Amen."

Rev. Charles Dodgson's *Plain Catechism* contains specific instruction on the subject of prayer. In his "Application" after the section on prayer and the parsing of the Lord's Prayer, he writes:

> Is it not a great blessing to be allowed to pray to God, and to know that He will hear me? But what use do I make of this blessing? Do I say my prayers to God every day? [A]nd when I pray, do I pray with my heart as well as with my mouth? When I pray that God will forgive my sins, do I really repent of them and wish to forsake them? When I pray for His Holy Spirit to make me a better Christian, do I really desire and intend to follow that Spirit? When I pray for future mercies, does my heart and life shew that I am really thankful for those God has already given me?—Let me remember that God sees my heart, and that He will not hear my prayers, if they are not sincere.[1]

Within the *Plain Catechism* we also find some of what Rev. Charles Dodgson would have taught his son about prayer: that we pray through Jesus Christ and not in our own names because "we are sinners, and cannot deserve or expect that God should give us anything for our own sakes," and that we ought to pray especially for such things as "concern the soul" and for the needs of others (13). At the end of the *Plain Catechism*, we find a prayer that was echoed in many of Charles Lutwidge Dodgson's diary prayers when he admitted to sin and unworthiness and prayed to lead a holier life:

> O Lord, who hast promised to give thy Holy Spirit to them that ask thee, grant to me, I beseech thee, the help and comfort of that Holy Spirit, that I may be defended against the temptations of the Devil, and preserved from all

evil thoughts, words, and works.—Teach me, by the same Spirit, to know and to confess my own unworthiness, to repent truly of my sins, and to seek for pardon and salvation through Christ who died to save me—Teach me to love and to obey thy Holy Word; make me day by day a better Christian while I continue in this world, and finally receive me into thine everlasting kingdom in Heaven, for the sake of Jesus Christ thy Son our Saviour. Amen. (20)

In the notebook of Charles's Richmond headmaster James Tate II is a passage on prayer that reveals the sort of thoughts Tate might have shared with his students. "How is it that the Heathens of old . . . were so religious in praying and sacrificing?," wrote Tate. "And . . . so also the Roman Catholics of this day. While we Scripturals are found so lukewarm, so prayerless, so thrifty of aught like sacrifice? Is it not because we feel required of us a devotion of soul, and inwardness of supplication, an abnegation of self?"

At Rugby, Archibald Campbell Tait, at the beginning of the half-year on 22 August 1847, told his students that prayer was a direct means "for gaining that deeper sense and feeling of religion which we all grievously want. . . . Are we placed in new and difficult positions of responsibility? There is no way by which we can gain firmness and strength to fulfill these responsibilities but by prayer. Are we conscious of our weaknesses and of the difficulty we shall find in resisting the temptations to which we have often before yielded? Our strength is . . . in prayer."[2]

A month later, on 22 September, Tait spoke again about prayer, saying, "I should advise all of you then to consider . . . what your prayers are. I confess last summer when the approach of Confirmation made me acquainted with the forms of prayer [used] by many of you I was surprised to find with some here the forms you [used] were beneath your age and suited rather to children. Examine your prayers therefore . . . and ask yourselves whether they be sufficient to give you a real and full . . . intercourse with God."[3]

Also at Rugby, under the religious tutelage of George E. L. Cotton prior to his confirmation, Dodgson read the section on prayer in Cotton's *Instructions in the Doctrine and Practice of Christianity*. Cotton discussed four types of prayer—prayers for temporal blessings, prayers for holiness, intercessions for others, and the Lord's Prayer as a model for prayer. Cotton linked prayer with self-examination, something seen in Dodgson's diary prayers. Cotton wrote of the need for regular prayer: "A life of prayer implies something deeper than a mere petition for God's blessing in the evening and in the morning. . . . [W]e shall make it a rule, over the course of our daily work, to consecrate some few minutes, and pray for His help . . . remembering that a Christian is bound to hallow every occupation to his Master's glory."[4]

Temporal blessings, wrote Cotton, should never be prayed for "without the reservation, 'if Thou, O Father, seest that it is good for me to have it'" (79). "But when we turn from petitions for temporal blessings, to prayers for improvement in holiness and Christian feeling, we shall remember that these are Christ's especial gifts to his people. . . . For these, therefore, we may pray, with the fullest confidence that God will grant us what we ask" (84).

Often prefaced with an acknowledgment of sin, the overwhelming majority of Dodgson's diary prayers were "prayers for improvement in holiness," as just a few of the scores of examples will show: "Oh God help me to begin a holier and better life! For thy son Jesus Christ's sake. Amen" (16 December 1863); "Lord, let Thy holy day, now beginning, be to me the beginning of a holier life" (22 December 1866); "Oh merciful Father, forgive me my past sins: help me to begin a holier and better life, for without Thy help I can do nothing" (26 May 1867); "May God bless this day to me as the beginning of a holier and better life! For Jesus' sake. Amen" (20 November 1869).

Of intercession for others, Cotton wrote: "It must be our constant endeavor to . . . pray for blessings on our country, on the whole church of Christ, on all who are in danger, necessity, and tribulation, to ask God to have mercy upon all men" (89).

Another view of how Cotton taught Dodgson how to pray at Rugby comes from the prayer book that Cotton prepared for the Rugby Boys, *Short Prayers and Other Helps to Devotion*. This contained prayers for many occasions, but those used most often were the first two, prayers for morning and evening. The prayer for morning contains concrete examples of what Cotton taught about prayer in *Instructions in the Doctrine and Practice of Christianity*. Here Cotton set an example of how to pray for holiness and forgiveness and to offer intercessions for others. Here, too, are echoes of themes from Dodgson's earliest childhood education—especially the idea that God is with us at all times:

> O Lord and heavenly Father, by whose great mercy I have spent this night in peace, and awake this morning refreshed and strengthened, incline my heart now to seek Thee, and teach me how to pray. Let thy Spirit, O Lord, pour His light upon my mind. Forgive me, for Jesus Christ's sake, all the sins and evil thoughts of the past night, and of my whole former life: forgive all my ingratitude, perverseness, and hardness of heart; and may this new morning

which Thou hast permitted me to see, make me feel more deeply that I must work while it is day, since the night cometh when no man can work. Keep me throughout this day, by Thy Holy Spirit, from the sins which Thou knowest most easily beset me; especially from forgetfulness of Thee and of my own soul, from selfishness and passion, from idleness and sloth, from evil thoughts and evil words; and enable me to fulfill my duties in this place with energy and perseverance, endeavouring always to consecrate them all to Thy glory. Be with me in my work and my enjoyments alike; and may neither estrange my heart from Thee, who art the giver of all good, and the source of all happiness.

Bless, O Lord, all my relations and friends. Bless this School, and those who are set over it. Bless especially my own chosen friends in it. May this day be spent in peace by all of us, even in the peace which Thou givest, and which passeth all understanding. And May Christ our Lord be amongst us by his Spirit to preserve us from all sin, and keep us ever pure, and faithful, and loving. Hear me, O Lord, I beseech Thee, through the same Jesus Christ our Saviour. Amen.[5]

Samuel Wilberforce devoted one of his *Addresses to Candidates* to the question, "Will you be diligent in prayer?" He said prayer should not simply be a formal recitation, but must go deeper into a relationship with God. "For true diligence there must be . . . that full application of the heart and mind; that lifting up of the soul to God; that drawing out of the affections after Him; that cleaving of the desires to Him; that ardour and yet that patience; that humility and yet that boldness, which time cannot measure."[6]

Again and again, Wilberforce repeats the idea of prayer as communion with God, not simply a litany of needs. True prayer is "real, secret, undisturbed, concentrated communion with God" (156). "And as prayer attains to its true character of reaching forth after God, there should be an absolute forgetting of self" (154).

Wilberforce, like Cotton, wrote of the need for prayer to be a regular habit. He warned of many factors that might hinder regular prayer—from too much idleness to too much busyness—and that "we can no more pray aright than do anything else aright, unless in practice our separate acts grow up into habits" (160). Like Cotton, too, he says that watchfulness and self-knowledge must be a part of prayer: "The man who would indeed, in his hour of prayer, find the presence of God, and hold communion with his Lord, must live in habitual watchfulness; must taste lightly and with self-recollectedness even of lawful pleasures" (164).

Dodgson prayed publicly or privately from the Book of Common Prayer on most days during term time and frequently, if not daily, during vacations. As an ordained deacon in the church, he was required to say daily Morning and Evening Prayer either privately or openly, and though he contested that obligation in a conversation with H. P. Liddon and, for much of his adult life, considered himself "practically a layman," he attended regular services at which these offices were said, and, at times at least, he said these services, or something similar to them, privately, especially in family gatherings. Collingwood states that Dodgson's final illness, in January 1898, was serious enough "to prevent him from following his usual habit of reading family prayers" (*Life* 347). This seems to have been his regular practice when with his family after the death of his father in 1868. His child-friend Ethel Arnold recalled that during a visit to Guildford, "Mr. Dodgson read family prayers before breakfast each morning."[7] Whether these family prayers took the form of one or both of the daily offices is unknown, but likely they would have drawn from the prayer book.

The Lord's Prayer was certainly part of both Dodgson's public *and* private prayer. He learned this by heart at an early age. Explications of the Lord's Prayer are included in the catechism in the Book of Common Prayer, in his father's pamphlet *A Plain Catechism,* and in the teachings of his Rugby master George Cotton, who wrote that the Lord's Prayer is "the model of all our supplications, and the summary to which all can be reduced" (*Instructions* 89).

The offices of Morning and Evening Prayer were central to Dodgson's public prayer life. Each begins with a sentence or two of scripture, followed in both services by the identical Exhortation (a call to confession), then the Confession itself, and the Absolution. Then comes the Lord's Prayer and a short series of responses. Following the responses, the psalm or psalms appointed for the day are said. The psalms are appointed in a cycle so if one attends both Morning and Evening Prayer for an entire month, all 150 psalms will be said. Up to this point, the two services are identical. Following the psalms are a selection of canticles, or songs from scripture, alternating with readings from scripture. Both services have two scripture readings. After the final canticle is the Apostles' Creed. This is followed by another set of responses, the repetition of the Lord's Prayer, and three collects, the first being the Collect of the Day. The collects are followed by four prayers. The collects vary between the Morning and Evening Prayer services—at Morning Prayer there are collects for Peace and Grace; at Evening Prayer for Peace and for Aid Against all Perils—but the prayers are identical: For the Queen's Majesty, For the Royal Family, For the Clergy and People, and A Prayer of St. Chrysostom. Both services end with the Grace (2 Corinthians 13): "The grace of our Lord Jesus Christ, and the love of God, and the fellowship of the Holy Ghost be with us all evermore."

Central to both these services is the confession of sin, a prescribed part of the daily religious life of all Anglicans. Most days of his adult life, Dodgson would read or say these words once or twice:

> Almighty and most merciful Father; We have erred, and strayed from thy ways like lost sheep. We have followed too much the devices and desires of our own hearts. We have offended against thy holy laws. We have left undone those things which we ought to have done; And we have done those things which we ought not to have done; And there is no health in us. But thou, O Lord, have mercy upon us, miserable offenders. Spare thou them, O God, which confess their faults. Restore thou them that are penitent; According to thy promises declared unto mankind in Christ Jesu our Lord. And grant, O most merciful Father, for his sake; That we may hereafter live a godly, righteous, and sober life, To the glory of thy holy Name. Amen.

In addition to the daily offices of Morning and Evening Prayer, Dodgson attended, less often but still regularly, the service of Holy Communion. Here, again, the Confession is an integral part of the service. One must confess one's sins before coming to the table of Christ.

In the Anglican worldview, man is by nature sinful and will commit sins, even in the brief interval between one day's Morning Prayer and Evening Prayer. These sins must be acknowledged and confessed, and a resolution be made for amendment of life. The priest declares forgiveness of the penitent in the Absolution. Then, a few hours later, it all happens again. In Dodgson's confession of sins in his diary prayers, he often acknowledged not that he had "done those things which he ought not to have done" but rather that he had "left undone those things which he ought to have done." He often referred to his "sins and omissions," prayed to spend his time more in the service of God, and prayed for better habits. His confessions seemed aimed not at some great sin committed but at the desire to live a more holy life. He expressed this best, perhaps, in his New Year's Eve prayer of 1869: "At the close of another year, I give thanks to our Heavenly Father, who has mercifully borne with me, and spared me in life and health, yet to do something, I trust, more than I have yet done, in His service, and for the good of my fellow creatures."

While Dodgson, in his diary prayers, most often prayed in generalities, explicating neither his sins nor his plans for a better life, sometimes, especially in the years just after his ordination, these prayers allow a glimpse into his self-perceived weaknesses and plans for reform. He generally mentions these shortcomings as a sort of introduction to the prayer itself as in this entry from 9 March 1863: "I seem to have been living in a constant hurry of business, and yet neglecting much, and especially all religious duties. Oh God, I pray thee, for Jesus Christ's sake, to help me to live a more recollected, earnest and self-denying life. Oh help me to break the trammels of evil habits, and to live better and better year by year. For Jesus Christ's sake, Amen."

A similar example comes on 21 May 1867: "Began reading the 'Epistle to the Galatians' in Greek. I have much neglected one means of grace, the reading of the Bible, and desire, with God's help, to begin a better course. Help me, oh Lord, for Thy dear Son's sake, to turn to Thee in true penitence for my sins, and lead me in the right way! For Jesus' sake. Amen."

On 6 February 1863, he made a plan to address those things he had "left undone" followed by a short prayer: "My habits of life need much amendment, and I am grievously neglecting means of grace. With God's help I desire to begin (1) daily reading and meditation on the Bible (best before chapel), (2) after Common Room, clearing off arrears of lecture-work before doing anything else, (3) denying myself indulgence in sleep in the evenings, (4) methodically preparing outlines of sermons. Oh God, I repent of my past life. I long to do better. The spirit is willing. Help Thou the weak flesh, for Jesus Christ's sake. Amen."

This prayer is also an example of something Dodgson did occasionally, especially in the early years of the diary prayers—quoting or alluding to a text, most often the Bible (in this case Matthew 26:41, "Watch and pray, that ye enter not into temptation: the spirit indeed is willing, but the flesh is weak"). In other prayers he quotes or paraphrases Ecclesiastes 9:10 ("Whatsoever thy hand findeth to do, do it with thy might"); Corinthians 9:27 ("But I keep under my body, and bring *it* into subjection: lest that by any means, when I have preached to others, I myself should be a castaway"); Psalm 39:13 ("O spare me, that I may recover strength, before I go hence, and be no more"); and Psalm 51:10 ("Create in me a clean heart, O God; and renew a right spirit within me"). On multiple occasions he quoted from the Exhortation and the Confession in the Communion service in the Book of Common Prayer and once he paraphrased the prayer of Richard of Chichester.[8] At the end of 1863, he added a prayer to another set of reflections and resolutions:

> Here, at the close of another year, how much of neglect carelessness, and sin have I to remember! I had hoped, during this year, to have made a beginning in parochial work, to have thrown off habits of evil, to have advanced in my work at Ch. Ch.—how little, next to nothing, has been done of all this! Now I have a fresh year before me: once more let me set myself to do some thing worthy of life "before I go hence, and be no more seen."
>
> Oh God, grant me grace to consecrate to Thee, during this new year, my life and powers, my days and nights, myself. Take me, vile and worthless as I am: use me as Thou seest fit: help me to be Thy servant; for Christ's sake. Amen.

The phrase "vile and worthless as I am" has been used to argue that Dodgson had some great secret sin, but again he was merely quoting another source—in this case a devotion before Holy Communion from a book of services for the Canonical hours for Anglicans called *The Hours of the Passion*. The devotion with the phrase "vile and worthless as I am" is translated from the French priest and writer Claude d'Arvisenet (1755–1831) and is not so different from the words "miserable offenders" which Dodgson applied to himself every time he said the Confession at Morning or Evening Prayer.

The diary prayers are few and far between in the years prior to Dodgson's ordination—only three prayers are in the surviving volumes of the diaries between 1855 and 1861. There is a single prayer in May 1862, and then, beginning on 12 June 1862, just days after he preached his first sermon, begins a period of fairly regular diary prayers—eleven in 1862; twenty-one in 1863; twelve in 1864; fifteen in 1865; seventeen in 1866; eleven in 1867; and ten in 1868. Following the year of his father's death, the prayers taper off. There are eleven in 1871, but in no other year after 1868 are there more than seven, and by 1873, the maximum number is down to three. After 1892, the diary prayers cease altogether. The reduction of the diary prayers more or less aligns to Dodgson's general reduction in the number and length of diary entries, but, as with his preaching, there is a concentration of diary prayers in the years following his ordination as a deacon and preceding the death of his father, years in which he still considered the possibility of proceeding to the priesthood.

The vast majority of the diary prayers respond to a particular time or event. Of 151 prayers in the diary, thirty mark twenty different new years; another twenty-five are on other specific days mentioned in the prayer—Good

Friday and other Holy Days, half or quarter year, beginning of a month or week; twenty-eight come at the beginning or end of term; five are on Dodgson's birthday. So, fully 58 percent of the prayers are primarily calendar driven. Another forty (or 26 percent) respond to a specific event, such as taking Communion, having a religious conversation, reading a religious book or passage, embarking on travel, personal events such as the death of his father and the resignation of his lectureship, and public events such as the meeting of the Church Congress or a service for the Prince of Wales. Of the remaining 16 percent of diary prayers, several are directly related to his religious life—resolutions to read the Bible more diligently, looking for Sunday duty, trepidation about preaching; several relate especially to the proper use of free time, and about twenty (or just over 13 percent of the total) are for no particular reason or season.

Dodgson explained the preponderance of calendar-driven prayers, and many of those inspired by events such as departing for a journey, in a comment in his diary on 20 June 1862: "Any change is a good opportunity for change in life," and further on 5 June 1866, "All change of life is favourable for a change of religious life."

With a few exceptions, Dodgson's diary prayers are no more than a sentence or two and include either a confession of sins, a desire to lead an amended life, or both. He often prayed to serve God better, to do God's will, to put his sins behind him, and to lead a new and holier life. All this came directly from the Book of Common Prayer and from what he was taught about prayer. Typical examples include:

Oh God help me to live a better and more earnest life. (17 May 1862)

Once more I pray to God to help me lead a more thoughtful and Christian life. (12 June 1862)

Lord, have mercy on me, a sinner. Forgive me and take me back to thy fold, for Jesus Christ's sake. Amen. (24 June 1867)

O merciful Father, pardon the many sins of the past year, and help me to serve thee better in the time to come, for Jesus' sake. Amen. (31 December 1871)

Father, forgive me, and help me to spend the remnant of my days as in Thy sight! (30 January 1892)

While most of the prayers are a sentence or two long, and many even shorter, some of the early New Year's prayers are longer and exhibit a pattern that crops up often even in the shorter prayers—reflection, resolution, and request. Dodgson looked back on past sins and omissions, he resolved to lead a better life, and he asked for God's forgiveness, blessing, and assistance. An example is his diary entry for 31 December 1857:

> Five minutes more, and the Old Year comes to an end, leaving how many of its promises unfulfilled. As a last deed for it, I have begun on the opposite page a scheme which occurred to me the other day, by which I hope in future to save a great deal of waste time. . . . What do I propose as the work of the New Year?

> 1) Reading for Ordination at the end of the year, and settling the subject finally and definitely in my mind.

> 3) Constant improvements of habits of activity, punctuality, etc.

> On all which and other good works I pray God's blessing in this first hour of 1858.

Most of the prayers are short and generic, but on rare occasions Dodgson crafted a more carefully thought-out prayer. Two of these prayers stand out, written just months apart, in the period when Dodgson was tapering off his preaching but still had possibly not entirely given up thoughts of the priesthood. Might he have been practicing the art of prayer? The first came on 5 June 1866:

> Gracious Lord, send Thy Holy Spirit to dwell in this sinful heart, to purify this corrupt affection, to warm into life this cold love for Thee, to strengthen this failing faith, to lead back from the wilderness this wandering sheep, to make real my repentance, my resolutions to amend my struggles against the temptations of the devil, and the inclinations of my own sinful heart. Grant this for Jesus' sake. Amen.

And the other came eight months later, on 2 February 1867:

> Oh merciful Father, I come before Thee, a sinner: be merciful to me for Thy dear son's sake! Strengthen my weakness; raise me from the dust; lead me in

Thy way! Oh grant me the great blessing that I may look back on this night as the beginning of better things—that so when Thou shalt call me, I may welcome the call, knowing that though I have long wearied Thy patience and love by my sins, yet that the precious Blood of Jesus has washed away those sins, and that Thou hast graciously forgiven me "all that is past." God be merciful to me a sinner. For Jesus' sake. Amen.

One consideration in evaluating Dodgson's diary prayers must be the habits of other Victorian clergyman. Recording prayers and confessions in a diary was not unusual at the time. Archibald Campbell Tait, during the years he served as Dodgson's headmaster at Rugby, kept a private journal completely in the form of prayers. These show some of the same concerns (forgiveness of sin and amendment of life) expressed by Dodgson. On 4 September 1849, Tait wrote: "Oh Lord receive this morning my humble confession of deep sin. I find it very difficult to fix my thoughts. They wander from thee while I am praying. Oh Lord . . . deliver me from this great sin."[9] On 25 April 1847, he, like Dodgson fifteen years later, quoted 1 Corinthians 9:27: "How can I preach to others if I be myself a castaway?"[10] (Dodgson wrote on 24 July 1862, "God grant . . . I may not, when I have preached to others, be 'myself a castaway'" and three years later, on 18 October 1865, "Grant, O Lord, that I may so live that I be not, while I preach to others, myself a castaway!")

The diaries of Dodgson's friend H. P. Liddon contain self-deprecating prayers similar to Dodgson's. On 18 April 1861, Liddon wrote: "Feel very unequal to preaching at St. Paul's to-morrow, both spiritually and physically. O Lord Jesus, help me—a poor sinner."[11] And on 26 January 1866, on the subject of writing his Bampton Lectures: "O, Lord, help me, though most unworthy."[12]

Arthur Hugh Clough, at Oxford just before Dodgson, frequently described his sins in his diary, and that document gives a good sense of the sort of sins that might be committed within the confines of the Oxford scholarly life:

17 June 1838: "During University Sermon let myself run into all sorts of foolish and conceited fancies."[13] 25 April 1839: "Wasted a vast deal of time & read very slovenly. . . . This is not serving God" (110); 19 October 1839: "I see too much society. It is pure vanity of one kind or another that gives me pleasure in it and desire for it" (123).

While the diaries contain the best record of Dodgson's prayers, they reveal only part of his prayer life. Daily private prayer was certainly a part of

Dodgson's entire life. In a letter of 26 April 1891, relating the story of how he fainted in chapel, he wrote, "The two tutors . . . noticed that I did not get up, but concluded I was only going on in private prayer a little longer than usual" (*Letters* 837). And Claude M. Blagden, a Christ Church undergraduate in the 1890s, wrote that, "We used to see [Dodgson] kneeling devoutly in Cathedral at the College prayers."[14] Remaining in private prayer after morning chapel appears to have been a regular habit.

For Dodgson, prayers for the needs of others held a special place, and while he rarely mentioned these prayers in his diary, he did refer to them in his letters. In a letter "To an Invalid," he wrote, "I always pray specially for my friends 'who are in trouble'" (*Letters* 880). To Edith Miller on 9 April 1893, he wrote: "I have not forgotten my promise to pray for you. I have done so ever since, morning and evening. There are a good many names that I specially mention: and yours has been one" (*Letters* 952). Most tellingly, he wrote to Gertrude Chataway, 30 August 1893, when her mother was on her deathbed: "I think there is no higher privilege given us in this life than the opportunity of doing something for *others,* and of bearing one another's burdens, and praying, one for another. And I believe, and *realise* it more as life goes on, that God hears, and answers, our prayers for *others,* with a special love and approval that does not belong to prayers offered for *ourselves.* In that hope I pray for you, and your father and sister, to give you in your sorrow the peace and strength that only He can give" (*Letters* 971).

The following week, referring to the time of Mrs. Chataway's funeral, Dodgson, in a letter to Gertrude, wrote, "I did remember you at 3 ½ on Saturday: and I shut myself up in my room, and thought of you, and prayed for you all" (*Letters* 972).

In an 1886 letter, Dodgson wrote: "I wonder if I shall seem to you utterly heretical in confessing that I not only pray for God's mercy on all the departed, but also on all in rebellion against Him. That includes 'evil spirits'" (*Letters* 633). In a letter to his sister Elizabeth in 1894, he explained why he prayed for those in rebellion against God:

> *I* constantly pray to God to have mercy on all who are in rebellion against him (I don't believe He ever has, or ever will, give up all hope that such beings may *yet* repent), and that certainly includes all the rebel angels. It is almost inconceivable to me that *any* being, capable of free will, can rebel *for ever. Some* day he *must* realise, one would think, the love of God, and the hatefulness of sin. And there may be a time, in the ages to come (I constantly

pray to God to bring it on, *if it be possible*), when *all* created wills shall have learned to hate sin. (*Letters* 1045)

Dodgson also wrote to his sister Elizabeth about prayers for the dead and for "sinless beings" such as angels.

"Prayers for the dead" I need not say much about. Though I can't go so far as Dr. Liddon, who held that the English Church distinctly *enjoins* it,[15] I can't see that she anywhere *forbids* it. And, whatever the *Church* holds, *I* think it a good practice, quite consistent with the will of God.

But why do you *limit* such prayers to the *one* subject of *sin?* When we pray for *living* friends, we don't so limit our prayers. *Sinless* beings (such as angels, for instance) are surely capable of receiving *blessings* from God: and surely blessings are a fit subject for prayer? (*Letters* 1042)

In a letter of 26 December 1889 to Mary Brown, Dodgson wrote: "God has given [man] means for learning what is his duty, such as prayer, reading the Bible, etc., and these means he ought to use" (*Letters* 772). Prayer then was a way of discerning God's will. He continued, "When you are puzzled go and tell your puzzle to your Heavenly Father . . . and pray for guidance, and then do what seems best to *you,* and it will be accepted by Him."

Dodgson also saw prayer as a protection against evil, as he explained in a letter of 15 December 1881 to Mrs. F. W. Richards: "I trust your boy will grow up as good as you now find him. The habit of prayer will be the best of all safe-guards for him as he gets into the world and comes to know the sin around him" (*Letters* 448).

Dodgson addressed the subject of unanswered prayers in a letter of 1885, writing: "About answered and unanswered prayer: we certainly are not au-thorised to ask that *miracles* should be worked for us. The Apostles were, but it is not a general permission—also . . . we should only ask *anything* of our own devising, *hypothetically,* i.e. *if* it be good (which we cannot know). I have had prayers answered—most strangely so sometimes—but I think our heavenly Father's loving-kindness has been even more evident in what He has *refused* me" (*Letters* 606–7).

Dodgson looked deeper into the issue of what prayers can be answered, the relationship between prayer and free will, and how prayer was relevant in a society that had turned toward science as the explanation for the natural world in a passage in *Sylvie and Bruno.*

"Would you—would you mind my telling you something [Eric] said about *prayer?* It had never struck me in that light before."

"In what light?" said Arthur.

"Why, that all Nature goes by fixed, regular laws—Science has proved *that.* So that asking God to *do* anything (except of course praying for *spiritual* blessings) is to expect a miracle: and we've no right to do *that.*" . . .

"I will begin by asking 'Why did you except *spiritual* blessings?' Is not your mind a part of Nature?"

"Yes, but Free-Will comes in there—I can *choose* this or that; and God can influence my choice. . . . Human Free-Will is an exception to the system of fixed Law. Eric said something like that. And then I think he pointed out that God can only influence Nature by influencing Human Wills. So that we *might* reasonably pray *'give us this day our daily bread,'* because many of the causes that produce bread are under Man's control. But to pray for rain, or fine weather, would be as unreasonable as—" she checked herself, as if fearful of saying something irreverent.[16]

. . . Arthur slowly replied "*Shalt he that contendeth with the Almighty instruct him?*[17] Shall we 'the swarm that in the noontide beam were born,'[18] feeling in ourselves the power to direct, this way or that, the forces of Nature—of *Nature,* of which we form so trivial a part—shall we, in our boundless arrogance, in our pitiful conceit, *deny* that power to the Ancient of Days? Saying, to our Creator, 'Thus far and no further. Thou madest, but thou canst not rule!'? . . . If you would *know* the power of Prayer—in anything and everything that Man can need—*try* it. *Ask, and it shall be given you.*[19] I—*have* tried it. I know that God answers prayer!"[20]

In the cold stone surroundings of Christ Church Cathedral, Charles knelt in prayer long after morning chapel had ended. He prayed for forgiveness of his sins and amendment of life. He prayed for those whom he knew were ill or in distress. But when these petitions had ended, he tried, as he did whenever he knelt in private prayer, to commune with God, to sense God's purpose for his life and work, to sift through, with God's guidance, the complexities of a world of good and evil so that he might, with God's blessing, do what was right.

· T W E L V E ·

In His Holy Ways

Charles rose from the place where he had knelt, only a few feet away from the spot on which he had been ordained as a deacon by Bishop Wilberforce so many years ago. He still attended chapel each morning during term time, he still spent time each day in private prayer, but as he walked down the aisle of the empty cathedral and his footsteps echoed in the winter morning's gloom, he knew that there was much more than this to leading a holy life.

Charles Lutwidge Dodgson's holy life was defined by many factors—his insistence on reverence for things sacred; his prayer life; his attendance at regular worship; his reading the Bible and works of theology; his writings on various topics related to religion; and his advice and comments, mostly surviving in his letters, to friends and family members—and occasionally to the general public—on religious matters. His faith rested on strong pillars, learned since childhood and carefully considered and logically thought out as an adult. It affected every aspect of his life from his work in mathematics and logic to his love of the theater. His faith caused him to reflect deeply on issues as varied as vivisection, divorce, and suffering. And it made him a generous, thoughtful, nonjudgmental man, always eager to put the needs of others before his own.

"No one who knew him could doubt . . . that his religion was a great reality to him, controlling his thoughts and actions in a variety of ways," wrote his Oxford colleague Thomas Banks Strong. "His power with children, which he could not fail to know was great, was a matter of serious responsibility in his mind, and he regarded it, rightly, as in a true sense part of his 'work.'"[1] Strong's assessment of Dodgson as a "kind and thoughtful devout Christian man" is far from singular.

Claude Martin Blagden called Dodgson "very simple and sincere in his religion" (65), while Christ Church colleague Henry Lewis Thompson wrote, "He was in truth a deeply religious man, almost a puritan in strictness; always on the guard against the intrusion into the conversation of any expression which savoured in the least degree of light estimation of Divine truth" (53). Dodgson's fellow Christ Church undergraduate George James Cowley-Brown took issue with Dodgson being called a Puritan but did remember him as an "unaffectedly religious man" (62). Dodgson's friend Isa Bowman, whom he knew as both a child and a young woman, recalled him as a "deeply religious man,"[2] while another former child-friend, Beatrice Hatch, wrote: "He took a serious view of life and had a very grave vein running through his mind. The simplicity of his faith was very beautiful" (Cohen, *Interviews* 108).

His nephew and biographer, Stuart Dodgson Collingwood, wrote: "He was essentially a religious man in the best sense of the term, and without any of that morbid sentimentality which is too often associated with the word; and while his religion consecrated his talents, and raised him to a height which without it he could never have reached, the example of such a man as he was, so brilliant, so witty, so successful, and yet so full of faith, consecrates the very conception of religion, and makes it yet more beautiful" (*Life* 78). His private library also attests to the importance of religion in his life. He had more than four hundred religious titles in his library, or close to 20 percent of the total.

What were the pillars upon which his holy life rested? Some are clear in his education and upbringing, but his own words also define the cornerstones of his belief. In a letter to an unidentified recipient, he wrote, "Most assuredly I accept to the full the doctrines you refer to—that Christ died to save us, that we have no other way of salvation open to us but through His death, and that it is by faith in Him, and through no merit of ours, that we are reconciled to God; and most assuredly I can cordially say, 'I owe all to Him who loved me, and died on the Cross of Calvary'" (*Life* 340).

In a letter to an unnamed agnostic with whom Dodgson carried on a correspondence in the 1890s, he asserted additional truths on which he based his faith: "(1) The world is full of sin: sin causes misery: sin needs a remedy. *If* it were true that God had provided a remedy, which man could not reason out for himself, a revelation would be necessary. This would need miracles to attest it. So miracles would be *probable*. (2) God *has* provided a remedy, and *has* thus revealed it" (*Letters* 1150–51). On this subject of Christ as the remedy for the sinfulness of man, Dodgson wrote to his friend Ethel Arnold on 7 February 1888:

Perfect obedience would no doubt suffice, and make human life all it is meant to be, *if* it were possible. But it is *not* possible—or, at any rate, no human being (except Jesus Christ) has ever achieved it. Hence, since no act of obedience, in *one* thing, can take away the guilt of disobedience in another thing, and as human pain, however willingly borne, is not enough to cleanse us, we need the help of that awful mystery, of God taking our nature, and expiating our guilt, and rendering, for us, the perfect obedience which we fail to render for ourselves. Thus the question "What must I do to inherit eternal life?" was answered, even by our Lord himself in words very like that text from Micah, because He had not yet died; it was answered, *after* His death, in quite other terms—"*Believe on the Lord Jesus Christ, and thou shalt be saved.*"[3] (*Letters* 696)

Another truth on which much of Dodgson's belief and therefore actions and writings rested he stated in his essay "Eternal Punishment" simply as "God is perfectly good." He went on to write:

The grounds on which this claims our assent, seem to be, first, certain *intuitions* (for which, of course, no *proofs* can be offered), such as "I believe that I have Free-Will, and I am capable of choosing right or wrong; that I am responsible for my conduct; that I am not the outcome of blind material forces, but the creature of a being who has given me Free-Will and the sense of right and wrong, and to whom I am responsible, and who is therefore perfectly good. And this being I call 'God.'"

And these *intuitions* are confirmed for us in a thousand ways by all the facts of revelation, by the facts of our own spiritual history, by the answers we have had to our prayers, by the irresistible conviction that this being whom we call "God" *loves* us, with a love so wonderful, so beautiful, so immeasurable, so wholly undeserved, so unaccountable on any ground save His own perfect goodness.[4]

In this passage Dodgson also touches on his belief in free will and how free will can separate man from God through sin. He elaborates on this in an 1889 letter to Mary Brown:

I believe, *first and before all,* that there is an absolute, self-existent, external, distinction between Right and Wrong. Now put side by side with this the theory that "God is almighty." If any one points out the contradiction, and says "if you grant Him to be *almighty,* you must grant that He can make

Right into Wrong, and Wrong into Right," I reply "if, as it seems, the two are contradictory, I must of course deny *one*. But I do not follow your bidding, and deny the *first:* no, I hold that *independently* of *all* else: I deny the *second:* I say 'God is *not* almighty, in this sense.'"

. . . Secondly, I believe I am responsible to a *Personal Being* for what I do.

Thirdly, I believe that Being to be *perfectly good*. And I call that perfectly good Being "God." (*Letters* 746–47)

In a later letter to the same recipient, he writes:

> I will try to put clearly what seems to me to be the position of each human being. God has given him conscience (that is an intuitive sense of "I ought," "I ought not"), and this he ought to obey: God has given him means for learning what is his duty, such as prayer, reading the Bible, etc., and these means he ought to use. . . . If, having duly used all those means, he then does *what seems to him right,* that is right, in the sight of God, whatever the resulting act may be. (*Letters* 772)

And, in an 1893 letter to an unnamed invalid, he writes again of sin and free will: "I feel sure that you believe, as I do, that the *whole* of our nature is Divine in the sense of being created by God. Its going wrong is, of course, our *own* choice, and not God's doing" (*Letters* 951).

One other belief on which much of Dodgson's holy life rested was that the "truest kind of happiness, the only kind that is really worth the having, [is] the happiness of making others happy too!"[5] The idea that work for others and prayer for others lead to a much richer life than work or prayer for oneself returned again and again in Dodgson's letters (see p. 164 in this volume). He believed that all people were interconnected and interdependent. In an 1891 letter to his niece Edith, he wrote:

> Of course it is *possible* to imagine a world where no such interaction was designed. For instance, Adam *might* have been left to live his life without a partner. Very likely he would have found that none of the beasts and birds needed his help or even his sympathy; and that they could get on, on the whole, better *without* his interference than *with* it. But what a dull existence it would have been! With no chance for self-denial, or industry, or usefulness, or anything that might bring him the words "Well done, good and faithful servant"—nothing to do but store up *knowledge,* for his own benefit. (*Letters* 827)

Here Dodgson's mature faith is connected to his father's earliest sermons. In 1837, Rev. Charles Dodgson wrote that God had "joined together the whole body [of mankind] by a bond of mutual dependence."[6]

The bedrock principles on which Dodgson built his faith, in addition to the tenets of the Creed, were the extrinsic existence of right and wrong, the free will of man, the redeeming power of Christ, the limitless love of God, and the joy of doing work for others and for God in a world in which we are all interdependent. He saw each day as an opportunity to do such work, whether the education of young minds, the creation of art, the amusement and comfort of children, or his more direct religious work such as preaching the Gospel, reading and studying scripture and theology, writing on moral and social issues, and guiding others by personal example, letters, and spoken advice.

Dodgson saw even his work in mathematics and logic as "work for God." In an 1894 letter to his sister Elizabeth, he wrote, of his proposed three-part work on symbolic logic, "*One* great use of the study of Logic (which I am doing my best to popularise) would be to help people who have *religious* difficulties to deal with, by making them see the absolute necessity of having clear *definitions,* so that, before entering on the discussion of any of these puzzling matters, they may have a clear idea *what it is they are talking about*" (*Letters* 1041).

Two years later, writing to his sister Louisa of the same project, he said: "The book will . . . be a help to religious thoughts, by giving *clearness* of conception and of expression, which may enable many people to face, and conquer, many religious difficulties for themselves. So I do really regard it as work for *God*" (*Letters* 1100). In the introduction to *Symbolic Logic Part I,* he wrote that the book would "give you a clearness of thought—the ability to *see your way* through a puzzle . . . and, more valuable than all, the power to detect *fallacies,* and to tear to pieces the flimsy illogical arguments, which you will so continually encounter in books, in newspapers, in speeches, and even in sermons."[7]

In 1895, Dodgson paid seven guineas to have four thousand copies of his detailed advertisement for this book, a pamphlet titled *A Fascinating Mental Recreation for the Young: Symbolic Logic,* inserted into copies of *Crockford's Clerical Directory.* He hoped to reach clergymen responsible for educating children, for he described *Symbolic Logic* as a healthy and educational pastime for the young, noting that its study was not merely an end in itself but something that could help a student "to get *clear* ideas, to make *orderly* arrangement of his knowledge, and, more important than all, to detect and unravel the *fallacies* he will meet with in every subject he may interest himself in."[8]

His wrote his book of mathematical puzzles, *Pillow Problems,* in order, he said, to help readers banish "worrying" subjects from their minds. By focusing one's attention on mathematical challenges, there would be no room left for such thoughts. In the introduction he wrote:

> There are mental troubles, much worse than mere worry, for which an absorbing object of thought may serve as a remedy. There are sceptical thoughts, which seem for the moment to uproot the firmest faith: there are blasphemous thoughts, which dart unbidden into the most reverent souls: there are unholy thoughts, which torture with their hateful presence the fancy that would fain be pure. Against all these some real mental *work* is a most helpful ally. That "unclean spirit" of the parable, who brought back with him seven others more wicked than himself, only did so because he found the chamber "swept and garnished," and its owner sitting with folded hands. Had he found it all alive with the "busy hum" of active *work,* there would have been scant welcome for him and his seven![9]

Dodgson also connected Bible reading to banishing unholy thoughts when he wrote in his diary on 18 March 1889, "Another 'book' has occurred to me, to bring out as 'Lewis Carroll': select passages of the Bible, to be learned by heart (or conned over by old people) printed in large *readable* type, such passages as would do to say over to oneself, in sleepless nights, etc." Dodgson wrote to Alexander Macmillan on 31 May about this, but neither it nor the "Child's Bible" he suggested was ever published. Nonetheless, he continued to think the project a good idea. In the preface to *Sylvie and Bruno,* published on 13 December of that same year, Dodgson included, in a list of books "desirable to be written,"

> a book of pieces selected from the Bible—not single texts, but passages of from 10 to 20 verses each—to be committed to memory. Such passages would be found useful, to repeat to one's self and to ponder over, on many occasions when reading is difficult, if not impossible. . . .
>
> Thirdly, a collection of passages, both prose and verse, from books other than the Bible. . . .

These two books of sacred, and secular, passages for memory—will serve other good purposes besides merely occupying vacant hours: they will help to keep at bay many anxious thoughts, worrying thoughts, uncharitable thoughts, unholy thoughts.[10]

Dodgson's idea to publish a book of Bible excerpts was, of course, not just a way to banish unholy thoughts but also a means of scripture study, another important part of his religious life. Dodgson owned no fewer than twenty Bibles in English, Latin, Greek, and Hebrew. He owned an annotated Bible, Bible concordances, Bibles dictionaries and glossaries, and volumes of Bible commentary, history, chronology, and criticism. His library speaks of someone who took the study of scripture seriously.

Like his prayers, much of Dodgson's reading and study of scriptures took place in private (excepting of course that he heard scripture read at every worship service he attended), and so we have little concrete record of his habits. His frequent allusions to and quoting of scripture in his letters and serious writings show a man with a thorough knowledge of the Bible, and this must have been the case for him to pass his ordination examination in 1861.

In his diaries, most of his mentions of Bible reading concern not doing enough, though he did note, on 24 February 1858, "Began a system [which I hope to continue] of Scripture reading before chapel." But on 26 November 1862, less than a year after his ordination, he wrote: "I have given almost no time to Bible-reading, etc. lately. Oh God help me to live a holier life, for Christ's sake. Amen." On 6 February 1863, he wrote, "With God's help I desire to begin . . . daily reading and meditation on the Bible," and four years later, on 21 May 1867, "I have much neglected one means of grace, the reading of the Bible, and desire, with God's help, to begin a better course."

Later in life, when he spent his Long Vacations at Eastbourne, he often had young girls come to visit him, and Bible reading was part of the daily routine. Isa Bowman, recalling her habits with Mr. Dodgson at Eastbourne, wrote that after breakfast they always "read a chapter out of the Bible. So that I should remember it, I always had to tell it to him afterwards as a story of my own."[11] On 2 September 1886, Dodgson wrote in his diary, "Marie and I, after a little Bible reading . . . spent the morning on the beach," and on 18 August 1887, "Irene [Barnes] and I had a walk before breakfast. Then a little Bible reading together." And in a letter of 1 July 1892, he wrote to the mother of his child-friend Polly Mallalieu, then visiting at Eastbourne,

"I shall be very glad to have Polly's company to church: and hope we may be allowed to read a little of the Bible together, as I love to do with my young friends" (*Letters* 912).

Perhaps Dodgson's feelings about Bible reading are best summed up in his letter of 1 June 1892, when he writes to the mother of his child-friend Enid Stevens of his recent visit with Enid, "It is *good* for one (I mean, for one's spiritual life, and in the same sense in which reading the Bible is good) to come into contact with such sweetness and innocence" (*Letters* 905).

Although Dodgson's religious beliefs were strongly held, he was also accepting of those who did not share those beliefs, and he felt each person must act according to the dictates of their own conscience. Writing to Ellen Terry of the scene in *The Merchant of Venice* in which Shylock is forced to become a Christian, he said, "To all Christians now (except perhaps extreme Calvinists) the idea of forcing a man to abjure his religion, whatever that religion may be, is . . . simply horrible" (*Life* 182–84).

"You and I will never *argue,* I hope, on any controverted religious question," he wrote to Edith Rix in 1886, "though I do hope we may see the day when we may freely *speak* of such things, even where we happen to hold different views. But even then I should have no inclination, if we did differ, to conclude that my view was the right one, and to try to convert you" (*Life* 250–51). In an 1890 letter to an invalid, he wrote, "More and more I am becoming content to know that Christians have *many* ways of looking at their religion, and less confident that my views must be right and all others wrong, and less anxious to bring everybody to think as I do" (*Letters* 809).

This open-mindedness was not limited to generalities; Dodgson allowed all people to judge a particular issue according to their own conscience. To Mrs. Henry George Liddell he wrote in 1891: "I refused all *Sunday* invitations, on principle (though of course allowing to others the same liberty, which I claimed for myself, of judging that question)" (*Letters* 870). And in an 1891 letter to Winifred Stevens, on the subject of whether she should see the play *The Dancing Girl,* he wrote: "*Please* don't suppose I shall think the worse of you, in the smallest degree, if you do choose to do so. I form my own views in the matter, for my own guidance: and I most fully recognise the clear right that others have to form contrary views, and to take a contrary course" (*Letters* 875).

Dodgson believed that what is sinful for one man is not necessarily sinful for another. In an 1897 letter to an unidentified recipient on the subject of repeating "irreverent" stories, he wrote: "The misinterpretation I would guard against is, your supposing that I regard such repetition as always *wrong* in any grown-up person. Let me assure you that I do *not* so regard it. I am always willing to believe that those who repeat such stories differ wholly from myself in their views of what is, and what is not, fitting treatment of sacred things, and I fully recognise that what would certainly be wrong in *me,* is not necessarily so in *them"* (*Life* 337–38).

Not just in his private correspondence and conversation did Dodgson maintain this openness but in his public writing as well. He wrote in 1894 to his sister Louisa: "That is the line I am taking, in the book, on religious difficulties, that I am gradually composing—not so much to prove one view of a thing right, and another wrong, as to get *both* views *clearly stated"* (*Letters* 1044). And in the preface to *Sylvie and Bruno,* he wrote, of attendance at the theater, "If the thought of sudden death acquires, for *you,* a special horror when imagined as happening in a *theatre,* then be very sure the theatre is harmful for *you,* however harmless it may be for others" (xix).

Dodgson offered religious counsel to friends, family members, and even strangers. He preferred, in the case of religious disputation, to correspond in writing rather than by having a conversation. In an 1897 correspondence with an agnostic, he wrote, "I think conversation a very *bad* way of conducting such a discussion as I supposed you were willing to enter on . . . as it is impossible to remember accurately what has been said. . . . If you really would like to discuss these matters, I should be most happy to do so. But it must be by letters."[12]

Dodgson's primary reason for preferring correspondence in disputations was accuracy. If all of the argument is written down, one side cannot misquote the other. But Dodgson also expressed, in his diary, an early aversion to face-to-face arguments on religious and moral points when he entered into a dispute with his brother Wilfred over college duties on 2 February 1857: "My arguments ended as all viva voce argument seems to me to do, in returning to the starting point. This also suggests to me grave doubts as to the work of the ministry which I am looking forward to, if I find it so hard to prove a plain duty to one individual, and that one unpractised in argument."

But in general he preferred religious discussion to religious argument, and he was always ready to dispense advice when asked (and equally ready to keep quiet when not asked). In an 1889 letter to his friend Mary Brown, he wrote of the privilege of offering such advice: "I find it one of the many pleasures of old age (I think at 57 I may call myself an old man?) to be allowed to enter into the inner lives, and secret sorrows, of child-friends now grown to be women, and to give them such comfort and advice as I can. It makes me very humble in view of one's own need of guidance and unfitness to guide, and very thankful to God for thus letting one work for Him" (*Letters* 772).

Especially in his later years, Dodgson often offered religious guidance. He carried on correspondence with an unnamed invalid and with an unnamed agnostic, with whom he tried to use deductive logic to explain the tenets of Christianity. He wrote to his friend Mary Brown responding to her questions about death and eternal punishment and corresponded with his sister Elizabeth on the same topic. He offered guidance to his niece Edith and frequently wrote to friends and family to offer blessings or prayers on occasions both happy and sad.

Dodgson also expressed his holiness in his generosity; his bank account shows contributions to many charitable institutions and gifts to family members. He was thoughtful in his charity and, over the years, developed certain ideas about how and why charity should be effected. "He was a man who thought it right to see that his charity was well bestowed," wrote his Christ Church colleague Frederick York Powell, "and he took care to see what he gave was given in quarters where it would reach those he wished to benefit" (Cohen, *Interviews* 41).

Dodgson wished the recipients of his charity to be in genuine need. On his frequent London visits, he had no way to tell if beggars were genuinely in distress or merely plying a trade of alms-seeking. On 1 March 1882, he made a contribution to the Society for the Suppression of Mendacity. The society provided donors with a booklet of tickets they could give to beggars in lieu of money. The ticket directed the beggars to the offices of the society, which would determine if they were in genuine need. Dodgson contributed to the society every year for the rest of his life.

Dodgson also supported the Charity Organisation Society, a precursor of modern social work, which tried to identify real needs and differentiate among the "deserving poor" and the "undeserving poor." In addition to auditing charitable organizations and making reports available to the public, the society set out to help charitable individuals solve the problem of whether those appealing for money did so truthfully.

Dodgson was concerned with motive when it came to charity. Charitable acts, he thought, should be done for wholly selfless reasons. He never made a public show of his private generosity—either to his family members or to charitable organizations. While his name did, on occasion, appear in the press in lists of donors to institutions, this was likely done without his direction. His letters and even his diary make scarce mention of any giving. In a letter to Emily Drury Wyper, a former child-friend, he wrote on 10 November 1892: "I have . . . special objections to bazaars connected with charitable or religious purposes. It seems to me that they desecrate the religious object by their undesirable features, and that they take the reality out of all charity by getting people to think that they are doing a good action, when their true motive is amusement for themselves" (*Life* 310).

He echoes this theme in *Sylvie and Bruno,* when Arthur is speaking about selfishness: "The very last charity-sermon I heard was infected with it. After giving many good reasons for charity, the preacher wound up with 'and, for all you give, you will be repaid a thousandfold!' Oh the utter meanness of such a motive, to be put before men who *do* know what self-sacrifice is, who *can* appreciate generosity and heroism! Talk of Original *Sin!*" (276).

From the beginning of his bank register in 1856 until early 1882, Dodgson's charitable contributions by check were infrequent and haphazard, though he may have made cash donations or sent postal orders that have left no record. Most often he responded to some immediate demand. On 14 November 1863, he donated £5 5s. to the Lancashire Relief Fund, set up the previous year to aid cotton workers put out of work by the cotton blockade during the American Civil War. On 19 October 1871, he donated £2 to the Small-Pox Fund, started in February of that year to assist the Sisters of St. Saviour's Priory in East London in their care for those stricken with the disease. On 18 February 1876, he gave £5 to an organization to prevent animal cruelty. And on 27 September 1878, he sent £5 to the Abercarne fund to help with the relief efforts after a mine explosion in that Welsh town.

These were not his only charitable contributions prior to 1882—he made four annual contributions to the National Society (see p. 29 in this volume) beginning in 1872—but his bank register shows no regular pattern of contributions and rarely more than two or three gifts to charities each year.

But in early 1882, that all changed. Dodgson had resigned his mathematical lectureship at the end of 1881, writing in his diary on 18 October that he hoped "to do some worthy work in writing—partly in the cause of Mathematical education, partly in the cause of innocent recreation for children, and partly, I hope (though so utterly unworthy of being allowed to take up such work) in the cause of religious thought." He gave his final lecture on 30 November.

In early 1882, Dodgson was organizing his new life. On 7 February, his friend Walter Watson came for a visit, leaving on 23 February. The following day, Dodgson wrote six checks to charities, and he wrote another four on 27 and 28 February. Then, on 1 March, he wrote checks to twenty-two charitable institutions. This habit, of writing a large number of checks for charitable donations in the course of a few days or less, continued for the rest of his life. He usually undertook the task in the first few days of the year.

Dodgson supported at least fifty different charitable organizations during his lifetime. His bank register lists about 650 separate charitable contributions, totaling more than £900, more than £100,000 in today's money. These contributions went to hospitals and other forms of medical care, often serving the poor (27 percent) and to general aid for the poor (24 percent). Another 20 percent went to organizations helping women and children, with a significant portion of this assisting "fallen" women. Religious outreach counted for another 12.5 percent and care of animals, 6 percent. The remainder was distributed among organizations dealing with public sanitation, education, morals, beautification, and disaster relief.

A look at some of the specific institutions to which Dodgson gave reveals the open-mindedness of his support. He gave regularly to the London Female Penitentiary and Guardian Society, where penitent "fallen women" were cared for and given useful employment, job training, and religious instruction. Another recipient of his charity, the Society for the Rescue of Young Women and Children, stated its object as "the reformation of openly immoral women, and the guardianship and training of young girls exposed to danger."[13] He was also a regular contributor to Lock Hospital, a clinic for the treatment of venereal diseases.

There is no doubt that Dodgson's generosity was a direct extension of what had become, by the 1880s, his Christian broad-mindedness. He believed charity should be generous but not foolish, careful but not judgmental, thoughtful, organized, and, above all, selfless.

Another area in which Dodgson's holiness manifested itself in daily life was in his relationship to the theater. In an age when theatergoing by clergymen was still frowned upon by many, Dodgson was a lifelong lover of the stage, attending the theater in London and elsewhere regularly from his earliest days of adult independence until the end of his life.

Dodgson saw himself as a member of what he called "a large class of the British Public who attend theatres and take an intelligent interest in plays, keenly enjoying all the good they find in them, and resenting with equal keenness all that is bad or even worthless."[14] He promoted the ideals of a theater which could raise the moral consciousness. In 1882, supporting a proposed School of Dramatic Art, he wrote, "The Stage is (as every play-goer can testify) an engine of incalculable power for influencing Society: and every effort to purify and ennoble its aims seems to me to deserve all countenance that the great, and all the material help that the wealthy can give it."[15]

Dodgson's friend and sometime advisor H. P. Liddon took a different view, and his attitude, and that of other like-minded clergymen, may have been part of what drove Dodgson to a Christian-based defense of the theater. Liddon wrote: "Certainly we must all agree that if the Stage could be enlisted in the cause of Religion and Morality, or even so influenced as not to oppose that cause, it would be an immense gain to the Church of Christ and to mankind at large. But at the risk of seeming faint-hearted, I must avow my belief that this happy result is quite impossible."[16]

Dodgson's writings on the theater include letters to the press about children acting onstage, his article "The Stage and the Spirit of Reverence," and an unpublished essay on stage dress. In all of these he took a distinctly Christian view of the theater.

In his unpublished essay (dated 22 November 1885) titled "On Dress," Dodgson explored not just what constitutes decency in theatrical dress but the entire relationship between sin and sinner in a theatrical context:

> [The] plain facts are:—God has implanted sexual desires and has laid down conditions under which they are innocent, and blessed by Him—other conditions, under which they are sinful and accursed. It seems that God forbids us to arouse or encourage these desires, except for the object, for which he gave them, marriage. And the real distinction between sin and innocence, in pictures, dramatic representation, dress, etc., etc. is whether it stimulates such sinful feeling, or not. The case of the *agent,* and of the *receiver,* must be kept distinct. First, as to the *agent:* if a picture is painted, or an attitude taken, or a dress worn, *with the intention* of causing sinful desires, this is sin in the agent, whatever the actual effect. Again, if these things are contemplated, with the consciousness that they are stimulating such passions, this is sin in the spectator, whatever were the agent's motives. And so, conversely, if the spectator have no such feelings, he is innocent, though the agent may have had sinful motives: but the remaining case hardly seems true—we can hardly say that a painter is innocent, so long as he did not *intend* to suggest evil thoughts, even though the actual effect of his picture be, in average cases, to suggest them: here the distinction, between this and the other cases seems to be that he *ought* to have foreseen the natural and *probable* effects of his work.

This seems to give a very simple test as to stage-dress. Take first the agent—whether actor or dramatist: if the dress be designed, or worn, with the knowledge that a *probable* result, with average spectators, is the rousing of sinful feelings, it is, in him or her, sinful—even if no such effect follows. . . .

But the . . . spectator is in a totally different position. "A" may find in the picture etc., nothing but innocent thoughts: and he enjoys it without sin, though the painter may have *meant* evil. In the very same picture, "B" may find sensual thoughts suggested to him. *His* duty is plain—to go away, or to look at it no more. . . .

The censor of the stage should take this rule to guide him. If, from a common sense point of view, anything on the stage is calculated to attract vicious people, or suggest evil to the *average* mind of an innocent young person, it should be stopped. It is a *practical* question, and each case must be judged not by a fixed rule, but on its merits.[17]

In 1887, Dodgson entered into the public debate about a proposed bill to ban children under ten from acting on the professional stage. In a letter, signed "Lewis Carroll" and published in the *Sunday Times,* he responded to the claims that such a career would cause children physical, intellectual, and moral harm. Under the category of moral harm, he wrote:

Take first "immorality, whether of general tone or particular passage, in the play itself." Ignorance of the ways of the world, and of the meaning of most of the words they hear, is a protection enjoyed by young children, and by them only. The evil itself is undeniably great—though less, I believe, in this age than in any previous one—but it is almost wholly limited to the adult members of the company and of the audience.

Take next "the encouragement of vanity, love of dress," &c. Here, again, the danger is distinctly greater in the case of adults. Children are too deeply absorbed in attending to their stage "business," and in observing the discipline enforced in all well-conducted theatres, to have much opportunity for self-consciousness.

Take, lastly, the gravest and most real of all the dangers that come under the category of "moral harm," viz., "the society of profligate men." For adult actresses this danger is, I believe, in well-conducted theatres, distinctly less than it would be in most of the lines of life open to them. Here again the good people, who see such peril in the life of an actress, seem to be living in a fool's paradise, and to fancy they are legislating for young ladies who, if they did not go on the stage, would be secluded in drawing-rooms where none but respectable guests are admitted. Do they suppose that attractive-looking young women, in the class from which the stage is chiefly recruited, would be safer as barmaids or shopwomen from the insidious attentions of the wealthy voluptuary than they are as actresses?[18]

Dodgson's most public and passionate defense of the stage came in his 1888 article "The Stage and the Spirit of Reverence," where he wrote of the stage, at its best, as a place where all that is good and holy can be held up and honored and that which is evil and sinful can be laid bare. Dodgson wrote that stage audiences themselves have the capability of being "reverent," not only hissing with disgust at evil but also showing "equally keen sympathy with self-denial, generosity, or any of the qualities that enoble human nature."[19] He gave as an example the performance of Mr. Samuel Anderson Emery as a factory owner in *All That Glitters Is Not Gold.* [20]

> I well remember how he "brought down the house," when speaking of the "hands" employed in his factory, with the words "And a' couldn't lie down to sleep in peace, if a' thowt there was a man, woman, or child among 'em as was going to be cold and hungry!" What mattered it to us that all this was fiction? . . . We were not "reverencing" that actor only, but every man, in every age, that has ever taken loving thought for those around him, that ever "hath given his bread to the hungry, and hath covered the naked with a garment."[21] (287)

The inclusion of a biblical quotation shows that Dodgson felt the ability of the theater to evoke an emotional response to goodness among the audience was closely tied to his religious beliefs.

While most of the theater Dodgson found objectionable was that which failed to live up to his standards of reverence, there was one other category he avoided, and that was theater that represented the story of the Gospels. He had no wish to see realistic stage representations of the life of Christ. In 1881, he wrote to Helen Feilden:

> Many thanks for your history of the "Ober-Ammergau Passion-Play." I am very much interested in reading accounts of that play: and I thoroughly believe in the deep religious feeling with which the actors go through it: but would not like to see it myself. I should fear that for the rest of one's life the

Gospel History and the accessories of a theatre would be associated in the most uncomfortable way. I am very fond of the theatre, but I had rather keep my ideas and recollections of it *quite* distinct from those about the Gospels. (*Letters* 417)

If one of Dodgson's reactions to the divide between his love for the theater and its condemnation by many whom he respected was to defend the institution both publicly and privately, another was to police the stage. As shown above (p. 19), he wrote to a theatrical manager to take issue with the jesting treatment of the subject of baptism, but this was far from an isolated incident. Dodgson was quick to call out managers and playwrights when he thought a play fell short of the mark.

On 16 January 1874, Dodgson attended a performance of *Richelieu*, starring Henry Irving. There followed a farce called *A Husband in Clover*, featuring Virginia Bateman, a friend of Dodgson, in the role of Lydia. Early in the play, Bateman, reading from a diary, said, "Damn Bunbury." Dodgson wrote to object to the unnecessary use of the oath but apparently received no reply.

He had a similar reaction to a holiday pantomime of *Whittington and His Cat* at the Avenue Theatre, London, which he saw on 1 January 1883. In his diary he recorded: "[It] had only one blot—a piece of indecent fun in the harlequinade (about which I wrote same day to the stage manager)." Receiving no answer, he wrote to the *Times, Daily News, Morning Post, Standard,* and *St. James's Gazette.* "May God bless my small attempt to promote good, and help me myself to watch against evil," he wrote in his diary on 14 January. The following day, 15 January, he "heard from Ward, who has been to the 'Avenue' and found nothing wrong: so telegraphed to the various papers to withdraw my letter." Perhaps the offending piece of indecency had been removed as a result of Dodgson's objection; perhaps Ward simply took no offense.

His boldest move in this effort was asking Ellen Terry in January 1880 to persuade Henry Irving to change the ending of Shakespeare's *The Merchant of Venice*. Dodgson objected to the moment when Shylock, a Jew, is forced to convert to Christianity. Irving did not alter the Bard.

Dodgson also took pains to screen plays he considered taking young people to (or even attending alone) to be sure they were not objectionable. He laid out the Christian argument for such careful screening in an 1892 letter to Alfred Richard Henry Wright. He had met Wright and his family on a train and had sent a book to the eldest Wright child. He "got a strange letter from her father, who teaches his children that no true Christian can attend theatres" (*Diaries,* 23 April 1892). In response, Dodgson wrote to Mr. Wright:

> The main *principle,* in which I hope all Christians agree, is that we ought to abstain from *evil,* and therefore from all things which are *essentially* evil. This is one thing: it is quite a different thing to abstain from anything, merely because it is *capable* of being put to evil uses. Yet there are classes of Christians (whose *motives* I entirely respect), who advocate, on this ground only, total abstinence from
>
> (1) the use of wine;
>
> (2) the reading of novels or other works of fiction;
>
> (3) the attendance at theatres;
>
> (4) the attendance at social entertainments;
>
> (5) the mixing with human society in any form.
>
> All these things are *capable* of evil use, and are frequently so used, and, even at their best, contain, as do *all* human things, *some* evil. Yet I cannot feel it to be my duty, on that account, to abstain from any one of them. . . .
>
> *I* say as to the theatres, to which I often take my young friends, "I take them to *good* theatres, and *good* plays; and I carefully avoid the *bad* ones." In this, as in all things, I seek to live in the spirit of our dear Saviour's prayer for his disciples: "I pray not that thou shouldest take them out of the world, but that thou shouldest keep them from the evil."[22] (*Letters* 902)

Dodgson's habit of testing the waters before taking guests, and especially children, to the theater, dated back at least as far as 1871. On 20 July of that year, as he wrote in his diary, he went with his brother Edwin to the Haymarket, where several of the pieces were "very poor, and the wit low and vulgar." He had planned to take some children to the performance, but vowed, "in future I shall not take any children to a London theatre without first ascertaining that the pieces acted are unobjectionable."

Dodgson also carefully read reviews of plays, particularly in the *Theatre,* a monthly journal to which he contributed three essays. In 1891, he wrote to his friend Winifred Stevens:

I'm sorry to say I must give up the plan of going to see *The Dancing Girl*. I had only heard it praised by friends, and had never acquainted myself with the plot. Now, that I have read, in the *Theatre*, a candidly and carefully written notice of the play, I have come to the conclusion that it is not a play I should care to witness, or to take any of my girl friends to.

It is not that I object to the representation of vice, generally, on the stage. A play would be ridiculous which represented human beings as sinless. . . . But there are limits, I hold, to what it is desirable to do in this way: and in this case these limits do not seem to me to have been duly observed. (*Letters* 875)

Dodgson felt so strongly about the need to warn people away from theatrical entertainments he found objectionable that he solicited the support of Thomas Gibson Bowles, editor of *Vanity Fair*, for "a daily fly-sheet (which might be called 'Where shall we go?' or the 'Vanity Fair Play-bill,' or any such name) with a list of all amusements to which ladies might safely be taken, and a warning against objectionable plays."[23]

Though nothing came of this proposal, Dodgson would always carefully consider which plays to see and which to avoid—believing that the best of theater could, as he wrote in his diary on 22 June 1855 after attending the London theater for the first time, "raise the mind above itself, and out of its petty cares."

In his penultimate sermon, preached before the undergraduates of Oxford University, Dodgson took as his topic the "duty of reverence" and "the sin of talking carelessly of holy things," a topic which had occupied him for much of his life. Dodgson felt strongly that holy subjects should not be the subject of jests, jokes, or humorous treatment—whether in print, on the stage, or in conversation. He included among these sacrosanct subjects not only Holy Scripture, the life of Christ, churches and church services, priests and ministers, but also the devil, demons, and hell.

Dodgson responded to irreverence starting as early as the 1850s, when he wrote in his diary on 24 August 1855, "received from Frank Smedley the second number of *Comic Times*. . . . I wrote . . . remonstrating on the use of Bible phrases in several articles of the first number." In 1890, he wrote of his forty years in Oxford common rooms and how during that time, there had been an increase in "anecdotes whose point consists in a comic allusion to some Bible text, or the existence of evil spirits, or the reality of future punishment, or even the name of God."[24] Dodgson wrote in one letter that "jesting on sacred things . . . *must*, I think, tend to make these things less and less real: so that, in fighting against profane talk, one is practically fighting the battle of faith as against unbelief" (*Letters* 693).

His child-friend Ethel Arnold recalled, "Stories of children which even remotely hinged upon Biblical episodes or characters, or even upon any of the hymns in *Hymns Ancient and Modern*, were received always with the severest rebuke to their narrators" (Cohen, *Interviews* 164).

In a bold letter to the Duchess of Albany, Dodgson wrote, of recounting such stories told by children: "Is it not a cruelty (however unintentionally done) to tell any one an amusing story of that sort, which will be for ever linked, in his or her memory, with the Bible words, and which *may* have the effect, just when those words are most needed . . . of robbing them of all their sacredness and spoiling all their beauty?" (*Letters* 748). And in an 1897 letter, he wrote of such anecdotes: "I feel sure that most of them are concocted by people who *wish* to bring sacred subjects into ridicule—sometimes by people who *wish* to undermine the belief that others have in religious truths: for there is no surer way of making one's beliefs *unreal* than by learning to associate them with ludicrous ideas" (*Life* 337–38).

In his 1888 article for the *Theatre*, "The Stage and the Spirit of Reverence," Dodgson laid out his thoughts on reverence in detail. Though he used many examples from the stage, his arguments applied to all sorts of reverence and irreverence—whether in society, in literature, on the stage, or in the pulpit:

> Before narrowing the field of discussion and considering how "reverence" is due subjects connected with religion, I wish to give this word also a broader sense than the conventional one. I mean by it simply a belief in some good and unseen being, above and outside human life as we see it, to whom we feel ourselves responsible. And I hold that "reverence" is due, even to the most degraded type of "religion," as embodying in a concrete form a principle which the most absolute Atheist professes to revere in the abstract. . . .
>
> But the lowest depths of conscious and deliberate irreverence that my memory recalls have been, I am sorry to say, the utterances of *reverend* jesters. I have heard, from the lips of clergymen, anecdotes whose horrid blasphemy outdid anything that would be even *possible* on the Stage. . . .
>
> Places of worship, also, when made subjects of stage representation, are usually treated with perfect propriety: one must turn to the orgies of the Salvation Army, or the ribaldry of the street preacher, to realise how far religion

can be vulgarized, and with what loathsome familiarity the holiest themes can be insulted. . . .

As for ministers of religion, I would not seek to shield them from ridicule *when they deserve it;* but is it not sometimes too indiscriminate? . . . [Gilbert and Sullivan's] clever song "The pale young curate"[25] with its charming music, is to me simply painful. . . .

The comic treatment of such subjects as evil spirits must be regarded from a fresh stand-point. "What reverence," it might fairly be asked, "is due to the Devil, whether we believe that such a being exists or not?" My answer is, that *seriousness* at least is due in dealing with such subjects. . . . [T]he whole subject is too closely bound up with the deepest sorrows of life to be fit matter for jesting. . . .

The same claim, for seriousness of treatment, may be made as to the subjects of Hell and future punishment. . . .

I have never seen Mr. Gilbert's clever play "Pinafore" performed by grown-up actors: as played by *children,*[26] one passage in it was to me sad beyond words. It occurs when the captain utters to oath "Damn me!" and forthwith a bevy of sweet innocent-looking little girls sing, with bright happy looks, the chorus, "He said 'Damn me!' He said 'Damn me!'" I cannot find the words to convey to the reader the pain I felt in seeing those dear children taught to utter such words. (285–94)

Dodgson held clergymen and others associated with worship to a particularly high standard. In his preface to *Sylvie and Bruno Concluded,* he took clergymen to task for retelling comic anecdotes on sacred subjects:

It is, in fact, for its consequences—for the grave dangers, both to speaker and to hearer, which it involves—rather than for what it is *in itself,* that I mourn over this clerical habit of profanity in social talk. To the *believing* hearer it brings the danger of loss of reverence for holy things, by the mere act of listening to, and enjoying, such jests; and also the temptation to retail them for the amusement of others. To the *unbelieving* hearer it brings a welcome confirmation of his theory that religion is a fable, in the spectacle of its accredited champions thus betraying their trust. And to the speaker himself it must surely bring the danger of *loss of faith.* For surely such jests, if uttered with no consciousness of harm, must necessarily be also uttered with no consciousness, at the moment, of the *reality* of God, as a *living being,* who hears all we say. And he, who allows himself the habit of thus uttering holy words, with no thought of their meaning, is but too likely to find that, for him, God has become a myth, and heaven a poetic fancy—that, for him, the light of life is gone, and that he is at heart an atheist, lost in *"a darkness that may be felt."*[27]

In the same preface, Dodgson complained of irreverence among choir members:

> I attended a Cathedral-Service, and was placed immediately behind a row of men, members of the Choir; and I could not help noticing that they treated the *Lessons* as a part of the Service to which they needed not to give *any* attention, and as affording them a convenient opportunity for arranging music-books, &c., &c. Also I have frequently seen a row of little choristers, after marching in procession to their places, kneel down, as if about to pray, and rise from their knees after a minute spent in looking about them, it being but too evident that the attitude was a mere mockery. Surely it is very dangerous, for these children, to thus accustom them to *pretend* to pray? (xx)

Dodgson's notion of reverence was closely related to his feelings about reading and what ought, and ought not, to be read or printed in the press. Beginning in 1882 and through 1890, he made an annual donation to the Pure Literature Society, whose purpose was to point readers and libraries toward wholesome and unobjectionable books and periodicals.

In 1885, William Thomas Stead, editor of the *Pall Mall Gazette,* published a serialized report in order to muster support for "The Criminal Law Amendment Bill," designed to protect young girls from sexual exploitation. Under the title "The Maiden Tribute of Modern Babylon," the first installment appeared on 6 July and included horrifying accounts of "The violation of Virgins . . . Willing and Unwilling," "The London Slave Market," "Strapping Girls Down," and much more. Stead wrote how he purchased a thirteen-year-old virgin for £5 and gave accounts of girls being drugged, raped, beaten, and being forced into prostitution.

The following day, as the second installment of Stead's exposé was hitting newsstands and being snapped up by an eager public, Dodgson wrote to his friend Lord Salisbury, who had recently become prime minister, asking him to take legal steps against Stead. Salisbury did nothing to inhibit Stead, and the publication of "The Maiden Tribute of Modern Babylon" continued. The report accomplished its goal of goading Parliament into finally passing the Criminal Law Amendment Act on 14 August 1885. Stead's stunt of "buying" a young girl, however, landed him in prison for three months. While Dodgson supported the idea of raising the age of consent and of doing everything possible to protect young girls, he objected strongly to publishing details of prostitution and abuse. In an impassioned letter to the editor of the *St. James's Gazette* titled "Whoso Shall Offend One of These Little Ones"[28] and signed "Lewis Carroll," he wrote:

> The question at issue is *not* whether great evils exist—not again whether the rousing of public opinion is *a* remedy for those evils—on these two points we are agreed. The real question is, whether this mode of rousing public opinion is, or is not, doing more harm than good.
>
> And the worst of the danger is that all this is being done in the sacred name of Religion. If we had no other evidence for the existence of a devil, we might find it, I think, in the Argument from Design—in the terrible superhuman ingenuity with which temptation is adapted to the taste of the age. . . .
>
> I plead for our young men and boys, whose imaginations are being excited by highly-coloured pictures of vice, and whose natural thirst for knowledge is being used for unholy purposes by the seducing whisper "read this, and your eyes shall be opened, and ye shall be as gods, knowing good *and evil!*"[29] I plead for our womankind, who are being enticed to attend meetings where the speakers, inverting the sober language of the apostle, "it is a shame even to speak of those things which are done of them in secret,"[30] proclaim that it is a shame *not* to speak of them: who are being taught to believe that they are still within the bounds of true womanliness and modesty, while openly discussing the vilest of topics: and who all too soon prove, by the eagerness with which they turn to what so lately was loathsome to them, that there is but one step from prudishness to pruriency. Above all, I plead for our pure maidens, whose souls are being saddened, if not defiled, by the nauseous literature that is thus thrust upon them.[31]

Dodgson went on to quote a passage from Edward Monro's sermon "Purity of Life," in which Monro drew a close connection between those things we read (or dwell on) and our personal holiness. "By all means, and on all occasions, avoid dwelling on the object of impure sensation. . . . The mere dwelling on its forbidden pollutions, even to combat them, forms evil habits, and withers holiness."[32]

Dodgson expanded on the notion that Satan could use literature or other written material as a means of temptation in a pair of letters written in 1895 to Charlotte Lucy Barber, who ran a girls' boarding school in Eastbourne. Dodgson befriended Mrs. Barber and her seventeen-year-old daughter, May, in October 1894. The following summer he renewed the friendship. Apparently he and May had some discussion on religious topics in the ensuing days, for on 7 August 1895, he wrote to Mrs. Barber:

> I have written a good deal of a letter to dear May on some religious topics about which we had talked, but have been unable to go on with it, as I am much perplexed by seeing what sort of book it is that she has lent me, with the recommendation that it is "the most beautiful book she has ever read." I do most earnestly hope that you wo'n't think I am doing a presumptuous and unwarranted thing in asking how it is that you have allowed her to read such a book. It occurs to me that perhaps I have been mistaken from the first in assuming (which I did as a matter of course) that you and she were members of the Church of England; on which assumption it seemed quite inexplicable that you could have regarded such a book as anything else than bad and most dangerous reading, which denies the essential doctrines of Christianity, and makes out the Gospel history to be a tissue of falsehood. (*Diaries*, vol. 9, 208)

The book in question was the popular 1886 novel *A Romance of Two Worlds,* by Marie Corelli, which explores issues of religion and spirituality and touches on the debate between religion and evolution. It includes a fictional document called the "Electric Principle of Christianity" that sets forth the idea that God "is a Shape of pure Electric Radiance," and that Christ came "in order to establish what has been called an electric communication between God's Sphere and this Earth."[33]

The *Pall Mall Gazette* wrote, "If all this is not blasphemy, and very outrageous blasphemy, then there is no such thing as blasphemy."[34] So Dodgson was not alone in his condemnation of the novel. In his reply to Mrs. Barber's reply, he discussed his beliefs about reading material and temptation in more detail. On 19 August 1895, he wrote:

> I hold that it is wrong for anyone to put himself, unnecessarily, in the way of temptation. If it comes to us in the path of *duty, then* I hold that we may face it, and may trust to God to help us resist it. But if, for some quite

inadequate motive, we put ourselves in the way of temptation, I do not think we have any right to expect God to help us: and, if we fall under it, I do not think we can expect God to make any allowance for the strength of the temptation, as I am sure he *would* do in the case of temptation incurred in the path of *duty*.

. . . I hold that books written by unbelievers, where infidel teaching is presented in attractive colours, *do* constitute a form of temptation which we have no right to put ourselves in the way of, without really good reason.

. . . And I also hold that I should be doing wrong, in letting any one else, over whom I had influence, read it. I have a feeling that that would be even more wrong than reading it myself. There is a terrible responsibility incurred by having influence over others. (*Diaries,* vol. 9, 209–10)

Dodgson believed one must always be on the watch for temptation. In an 1893 letter to Edith Miller, he wrote: "The temptation is sure to come again: and the very freedom from it brings its own special danger—of laying down the weapons of defence, and ceasing to 'watch and pray'" (*Letters* 952).

He also believed that giving in to a small temptation would lead to greater sin in the future. In a letter to the father of one of his child-actress friends, Dodgson chided William Mallalieu for lying about his daughter's height in order to secure an engagement: "Just as the little brook, that looks so trifling if you see it at its source, becomes a great river further on, so the beginning of evil—the regarding falsehood and cheating as mere trifles—which your example may be introducing into your child's life, may become, in future years, the cause of sin and misery for her" (*Letters* 919).

Dodgson expanded on his thoughts on temptation in a passage in *Sylvie and Bruno Concluded* in which Arthur speaks to Muriel. Arthur's view has much in common with Christian Socialism, and may well have been influenced by F. D. Maurice.

One's first thought in reading of anything specially vile or barbarous, as done by a fellow-creature, is apt to be that we see a new depth of Sin revealed *beneath* us: and we seem to gaze down into that abyss from some higher ground, far apart from it. . . .

Think of some other man, the same age as this poor wretch. Look back to the time when they both began life—before they had sense enough to know Right from Wrong. *Then,* at any rate, they were equal in God's sight.

We have, then, two distinct epochs at which we may contemplate the two men whose lives we are comparing. At the first epoch they are, so far as moral responsibility is concerned, on precisely the same footing: they are alike incapable of doing right or wrong. At the second epoch the one man—I am taking an extreme case, for contrast—has won the esteem and love of all around him: his character is stainless, and his name will be held in honour hereafter: the other man's history is one unvaried record of crime, and his life is at last forfeited to the outraged laws of his country. Now what have been the causes, in each case, of each man's condition being what it is at the second epoch? They are of two kinds—one acting from within, the other from without. These two kinds need to be discussed separately.

The causes, acting from *within,* which make a man's character what it is at any given moment, are his successive acts of volition—that is, his acts of choosing whether he will do this or that. (We are to assume the existence of Free-Will).

The causes, acting from *without,* are his surroundings—what Mr. Herbert Spencer calls his "environment." Now the point I want to make clear is this, that a man is responsible for his acts of choosing, but *not* responsible for his environment. Hence, if these two men make, on some given occasion, when they are exposed to equal temptation, equal efforts to resist and to choose the right, their condition, in the sight of God, must be the same. If He is pleased in the one case, so will He be in the other; if displeased in the one case, so also in the other.

And yet, owing to their different environments, the one may win a great victory over the temptation, while the other falls into some black abyss of crime.

Either those men were equally guilty in the sight of God, or else I must give up my belief in God's perfect justice. But let me put one more case, which will show my meaning even more forcibly. Let the one man be in a high social position—the other, say, a common thief. Let the one be tempted to some trivial act of unfair dealing—something which he can do with the absolute certainty that it will never be discovered—something which he can with perfect ease forbear from doing—and which he distinctly knows to be a sin. Let the other be tempted to some terrible crime—as men would consider it—but under an almost overwhelming pressure of motives—of course not *quite* overwhelming, as that would destroy all responsibility. Now, in this case, let the second man make a *greater* effort at resistance than the first. Also suppose *both* to fall under the temptation—I say that the second man is, in God's sight, *less* guilty than the other.

. . . The thought, that perhaps the real guilt of the human race was infinitely less than I fancied it—that the millions, whom I had thought of as sunk in hopeless depths of sin, were perhaps, in God's sight, scarcely sinning at all—was more sweet than words can tell! (120–26)

Reverence was not the only moral, and by extension religious, topic on which Dodgson made his views known in the press. He was involved in an ongoing debate about vivisection,[35] and his arguments went far beyond objecting to animal cruelty—though he did, in *Sylvie and Bruno Concluded*, argue that animals have souls, when the narrator said, "Most religious believers would *now* agree with Bishop Butler,[36] . . . and not reject a line of argument, even if it led straight to the conclusion that animals have some kind of *soul*, which survives their bodily death" (296). Dodgson also objected to vivisection on the grounds that it led to selfishness, that it morally degraded the person performing it, and that it showed the dangers of secularized education.

In an 1875 letter to the *Pall Mall Gazette*, Dodgson asked, "how far may vivisection be regarded as a sign of the times, and a fair specimen of that higher civilization which a purely secular State education is to give us?"[37] Charles's father had advocated for religious-based education from early in his career. In his 1855 charge to clergy, he railed against "the abolition of the test of subscription to the Articles, in the University of Oxford,"[38] and a plan to allow dissenters into the church-established National Schools. The warning against and bemoaning of the gradual withdrawal of the state from the church is a frequent point of Archdeacon Dodgson's charges.

C. L. Dodgson's most compelling argument about vivisection was that it degraded the morality of the operator.

Is the anatomist, who can contemplate unmoved the agonies he is inflicting, for no higher purpose than to gratify scientific curiosity, or to illustrate some well-established truth, a being higher or lower, in the scale of humanity, than the ignorant boor whose very soul would sicken at the horrid sight? For if ever there was an argument in favour of purely scientific education more cogent than another, it is surely this . . . "What can teach the noble quality of mercy, of sensitiveness to all forms of suffering, so powerfully as the knowledge of what suffering really is?"[39]

He reiterated the argument in his article "Some Popular Fallacies about Vivisection" in June 1875, writing that the "evil charged against vivisection . . .

consists chiefly in the effect produced on the operator. . . . We see this most clearly, when we shift our view from the act itself to its remoter consequences. The hapless animal suffers, dies, 'and there an end:'[40] but the man whose sympathies have been deadened, and whose selfishness has been fostered, by the contemplation of pain deliberately inflicted, may be the parent of others equally brutalized."[41] Ultimately, Dodgson concluded that "that the principle of selfishness lies at the root of this accursed practice" (853).

Within Dodgson's arguments about vivisection are embedded some of his feelings about the morality of sport. He intended to write an essay on this topic and include it in the preface to *Sylvie and Bruno Concluded,* but he found it "too big a subject to deal with that way" (*Letters* 977n).

In "Some Popular Fallacies about Vivisection," he reached the conclusion, upon which most of his ideas about sport were based, that "man has an absolute right to inflict death on animals, without assigning any reason, provided that it be a painless death, but that any infliction of pain needs its special justification" (848).

In his 1885 sketch "Vivisection Vivisected," Dodgson wrote: "All pain, inflicted for sport, is abhorrent to me. But I must allow that the question is a mixed one, as to *some* sport. Where, for instance, wild beasts have to be exterminated for the safety of man, it seems almost inevitable that the hunter should enjoy the excitement of the chase. But that is a totally different matter from keeping up the breed of some animals, such as foxes, for the sole purpose of sport. That I don't justify for a moment."[42]

In the preface to *Sylvie and Bruno Concluded,* he added:

I can but look with deep wonder and sorrow on the hunter who, at his ease and in safety, can find pleasure in what involves, for some defenceless creature, wild terror and a death of agony: deeper, if the hunter be one who has pledged himself to preach to men the Religion of universal Love:[43] deepest of all, if it be one of those *"tender and delicate"*[44] beings, whose very name serves as a symbol of Love—*"thy love to me was wonderful, passing the love of women"*[45]—whose mission here is surely to help and comfort all that are in pain or sorrow! (xx–xxi)

On 11 July 1895, Dodgson wrote to his nephew Bertram Collingwood about the first in a series of essays he proposed to write on what his biographer Stuart Dodgson Collingwood called "Religious Difficulties": "Among the books which death prevented Lewis Carroll from completing, the one on which his heart was most set was a collection of essays on religious difficulties, for he felt that, as a clergyman, to associate his name with such a work would be more fitting than that he should only be known as a writer of humorous and scientific books."[46]

In a letter to his sister Elizabeth a few months earlier, on 29 November 1894, he had stated his intention for the essays in this book: "not so much to prove one view of a thing right, and another wrong, as to get *both* views *clearly stated*" (*Letters* 1044).

It was not the first time he considered writing a book on a religious topic. An entry in his diary for 11 April 1880 reads: "Made a few investigations about my first 'subject' to write on (see Cycle-Book), *viz.* 'Miracles—why have they ceased?'" In his diary for 10 September 1887, he wrote: "The idea occurred to me the other day, of writing a book to be called 'The Difficulties of the Four Gospels'—*stating* them fully and fairly, and with such explanations as have been suggested." Neither book made it further than an idea, but Dodgson did set to work on his book on religious difficulties. In his 1895 letter to his nephew Bertram, he outlined the project:

I do not want to deal with any such difficulties, unless they tend to affect life. Speculative difficulties which do not affect conduct, and which come into collision with any of the principles which I intend to state as axioms, lie outside the scope of my book. These axioms are:

(1) Human conduct is capable of being right, and of being wrong.

(2) I possess Free-Will, and am able to choose between right and wrong.

(3) I have in some cases chosen wrong.

(4) I am responsible for choosing wrong.

(5) I am responsible to a person.

(6) This person is perfectly good.

I call them axioms, because I have no proofs to offer for them. There will probably be others, but these are all I can think of just now. (*Life* 327)

A letter to his sister Louisa written from Eastbourne on 28 September 1896 suggests why this project was never completed:

I brought with me here the MSS, such as it is (very fragmentary and unarranged) for the book about religious difficulties, and I meant, when I came here, to devote myself to *that;* but I have changed my plan. It seems to me that *that* subject is one that hundreds of living men could do if they would only try, *much* better than I could, whereas there is no living man who could (or at any rate who would take the trouble to) arrange, and finish, and publish, the 2nd Part of the Logic. Also I *have* the Logic book in my head: it will only need 3 or 4 months to write out; and I have *not* got the other book in my head, and it might take years to think out. (*Letters* 1100)

Dodgson completed only one essay for this proposed book, that on eternal punishment examined in the next chapter. But another essay, not set in type but surviving in a fair copy, might have been intended for the book. In it, Dodgson takes an unorthodox view on the remarriage of divorced people. When a bill to allow such marriages was proposed in the 1850s, Archdeacon Charles Dodgson wrote, "a very large body of Clergy believe, and, as I think, on strong and sufficient grounds, that the parties in such marriages would be 'coupled together otherwise than God's Word doth allow.'"[47]

But Charles Lutwidge Dodgson reached a different conclusion, spurred on by both his logical mind and his friendship with Ellen Terry. Terry was married, at the age of sixteen, to the Pre-Raphaelite painter George Frederic Watts. Less than a year later, the two separated by mutual consent, and beginning in 1868, Ellen lived with Edward Godwin, with whom she had two children. Their relationship ended in 1874, and in 1877, Watts, claiming he discovered the relationship, filed for and received a divorce on the grounds of infidelity. A few months later, Ellen married the actor Charles Wardell.

When Ellen was still legally married to Watts but living with another man, Dodgson felt he could not maintain his friendship with her, and he had no interaction with her for twelve years. But, with Ellen divorced but not yet remarried in 1877, Dodgson wrote a short essay titled "Marriage Service." While Ellen could remarry in a civil ceremony, at the time the Church of England did not allow remarriage after divorce (this was true until 2002); but Dodgson used logic to find reasons for exceptions to this rule.

The first of the two points is that where an oath is of *mutual* obligation, and where its purpose can only be effected when *both* parties observe it, the failure of one of the parties releases the other. . . . it certainly seems a very strong argument to say that the oath to have and hold, love and cherish, presupposes that *both* have taken the oath; that the thing becomes unmeaning when one side has ceased to observe it; and that so, by the act of the one (which of course *is* a breach of the oath and *is sinful*), the other is released from further obligations.

The other point is perhaps only another way of putting this point: it is that when the fulfillment of an oath becomes impossible, the oath is no longer binding—in other words, that it is no sin in God's sight not to do a thing which we cannot do. Now if one of the two parties in a marriage contract has broken it, it seems impossible that the other can continue to do these things: at any rate, to have, to hold, and to cherish, have become impossible, and to love (in the sense intended in the oath) is also impossible.

. . . [I]n which way is the will of God most fulfilled? A and B have entered into these mutual obligations. A has (sinfully, no doubt), broken and abrogated them: B's further fulfillment of them has thereby become impossible: B has two courses to choose between—either to remain unmarried for life, or at least till the death of A, even though the remaining so has no effect whatever on A—or to consider the oath as at an end, and that a second marriage is allowable. The latter course seems to me one that I should not dare to assent to be displeasing to God.

Those who object to *all* re-marriage, even after the *death* of a husband or wife, take a view that seems to me at variance with Scripture as well as with common sense.[48]

The timing of this document, a few months after Ellen Terry's divorce decree and a few before her remarriage, makes it clear Dodgson had her case in mind. A year and a half after her remarriage to Charles Wardell, Dodgson renewed his personal acquaintance with Ellen Terry, and the two continued friends for the rest of his life.

In April 1890, Dodgson wrote a pair of letters to an unnamed invalid, trying to answer the question of why God allows the innocent to suffer pain, and within these letters he summarizes what he sees as the purpose of living a holy life:

It seems to me that, for everyone of us, life is really a sort of school, or training-time, or trial-time, meant *chiefly* for the building up of a character, and of disciplining the spirit, so that by its own free choice of good rather than evil, and of God's will rather than self-will, it may rise to a higher and higher stage of Christian growth, and get nearer and nearer to God, and more and more like Him, and so more fit for higher forms of existence. . . .

Hereafter, in that higher life, looking back on this, I may be able to see clearly that my character needed exactly the training it had: that a healthy, strong, bright life would have been *ruin* to it, and that all these weary hours of suffering were the steps, and the only ones suitable to *me,* for mounting to this better life. . . .

I seem to realise that [pain] is not always (perhaps not *chiefly)* a punishment for *sin,* but has a far more glorious use. . . . May it not be to raise to *higher* glory the soul that is already glorious? to make the good yet better, the pure *more* pure, the saint *more* saintly? (*Letters* 782–84)

He had tried, thought Charles as he lay in the bed, feeling the breath coming with more and more difficulty. He had tried to lead a holy life. He knew that he had often failed—that he had not devoted enough time to reading the Bible or to religious work, that he had enjoyed his leisure activities too much and allowed them to take away time when he could have been doing work for God. But he had tried.

· THIRTEEN ·

Thy Will Be Done

On a cold January day in 1898, Charles lay in bed at the Chestnuts, the family home in Guildford. His sisters, who surrounded him, had propped him up with some pillows. He thought of the words from Luke's Gospel, words he had used in his own preface to *Sylvie and Bruno* not so many years ago: "This night shall thy soul be required of thee." And then his mind turned, peacefully, to a simple phrase by which he had tried to live his life: "Thy will be done."

Like so much else in Victorian England, the process of death, dying, and grief had its own conventions. In his book *Death and the Future Life in Victorian Literature and Theology,* Michael Wheeler enumerated death-bed conventions including the last visit of the doctor or priest, a dying confession or blessing, and the last words, which held great significance to Victorians. Wheeler also cited the singing or reciting of hymns or Bible passages as an important part of the deathbed vigil. Following the death-bed conventions came the funeral with its black plumes and armbands, the burial in a pastoral setting, and the erection of an impressive monument. In death, as in life, Charles Lutwidge Dodgson followed some traditions and defied others.

On 23 December 1897, Dodgson traveled by train from Oxford to the family home at Guildford to spend Christmas and the new year with his family. Hilary Term would begin in Oxford on 14 January, and he likely planned to return to Christ Church in time for that day's Convocation. He seemed in good health on his arrival, and worked hard on his *Symbolic Logic* most days. Here, his nephew Stuart Dodgson Collingwood takes up the story:

An attack of influenza, which began only with slight hoarseness, yet enough to prevent him from following his usual habit of reading family prayers, was pronounced next morning [6 January] to be sufficiently serious to forbid his undertaking [any] journey. At first his illness seemed a trifle, but before a week had passed bronchial symptoms had developed, and Dr. Gabb, the family physician, ordered him to keep his bed. His breathing rapidly became hard and laborious, and he had to be propped up with pillows. A few days before his death he asked one of his sisters to read him that well-known hymn, every verse of which ends with "Thy Will be done." To another he said that his illness was a great trial of his patience. How great a trial it must have been it is hard for us to understand. With the work he had set himself still uncompleted, with a sense of youth and joyousness, which sixty years of the battle of life had in no way dulled, Lewis Carroll had to face death. He seemed to know that the struggle was over. "Take away those pillows," he said on the 13th, "I shall need them no more." The end came about half-past two on the afternoon of the 14th. One of his sisters was in the room at the time, and she only noticed that the hard breathing suddenly ceased. (*Life* 347–48)

Charles Dodgson was certainly aware of the Victorian conventions of death. His death was not sudden; rather he was blessed with having a sense that the end was approaching. Having been given this notice, Dodgson was able to exercise considerable control over his deathbed experience, conforming that experience to many Victorian conventions, including:

The visit from the doctor or priest. Collingwood describes only a doctor's visit. There may have been a visit from Canon Cyril Grant, the rector of St. Mary's Church, Guildford, just around the corner from where Dodgson lay dying at the Chestnuts. However, judging from Dodgson's comments about Canon Grant in his diary (see p. 129 in this volume), we can guess that he preferred to take his final comfort from his family.

The loving attendant. Dodgson's final days were spent in the bosom of family, because he had the good fortune to be taken ill when he was in Guildford among his sisters. He certainly had round-the-clock attendants in the form of those sisters, who had apparently also brought in a nurse.

The singing of hymns. Here Dodgson certainly exerted control, doing exactly what would be expected from a clergyman—a few days before his death Dodgson asked his sister to read him the words of "that well-known hymn, every verse of which ends with 'Thy Will be done.'" It was the first sign that Dodgson knew, or at least felt, that death was impending. The hymn was written in 1834 by Charlotte Elliot and was included in the Church of England's standard hymnbook of the Victorian period, *Hymns Ancient and Modern,* which Dodgson knew well.[1]

Dodgson had turned his thoughts to these words "Thy will be done" from the Lord's Prayer at times of death before. On 22 March 1879, in a letter to Henry Sinclair offering condolences on the death of his wife, Dodgson wrote, "God alone can bind up the wound that He, for reasons beyond *our* understanding, has made: and He alone can enable us to say, even in our deepest sorrow, 'Thy will be done'" (*Letters* 334). Part of death, for Dodgson, was bending oneself to the divine will.

The hymn which Dodgson asked to hear, "My God, My Father While I Stray," looks to the divine will at times of human distress—the loss of loved ones, the loss of possessions, the loss of health. While it contains overtones of resignation to God's will at the time of death, *Hymns Ancient and Modern* omits, from the original version of the hymn, the fifth and eighth verses—verses especially apt for one on his deathbed:

> Should pining sickness waste away,
> My life in premature decay,
> My Father! still I strive to say, "Thy Will be done."

> Then when on earth I breathe no more
> The prayer oft mixed with tears before,
> I'll sing upon a happier shore, "Thy Will be done!"[2]

Dodgson, convinced that he lay dying, turned his mind to the will of God. At the same time, he conformed to the convention of hymn singing, or at least hymn recitation—not, perhaps, because it was conventional but because he knew it could bring comfort. And perhaps he thought not only of his own comfort but also that of his family. They would hear this hymn again soon; they chose it for Dodgson's funeral.

The last words. What were Charles Dodgson's last words? The Victorian obsession for recording last words being what it was, it seems likely that the last words his nephew recorded, "Take away those pillows. I shall need them no more," were the last Dodgson spoke. On the surface they are simple and practical—Dodgson had been propped up with pillows to ease his labored breathing, he was soon to breathe no more, therefore he had no further need of the pillows. But might not Dodgson have been saying that where he was going he would no longer need the trappings of this world—not food or clothing or his physical body, and certainly not pillows?

Up to the time he breathed his last, Dodgson's death was conventional. Wheeler wrote of three other deathbed conventions that occur after the moment of death—the laying out of the corpse in a darkened room, the last visit of the bereaved, and the closing of the coffin. Collingwood mentions none of these in his biography, but they may have occurred in the five days between Dodgson's death on 14 January and his funeral. During this time presumably the family gathered and the body was moved from the deathbed and placed into a plain oaken coffin. The mortal remains of Charles L. Dodgson did not leave the Chestnuts until they were transported a hundred yards or so down the road to St. Mary's Church on the morning of Wednesday, 19 January 1898.

In a document dated 4 June 1873 and headed "Directions regarding my Funeral," Dodgson wrote:

> I request of those who arrange for my Funeral that no Pall[3] may be employed, and that no hat-bands or scarfs may be worn at the Funeral or given to any one. Also that it may be a walking funeral, unless the distance or other cause should make that arrangement inconvenient. Also that the Coffin may be quite plain and simple, and that there be not an inner coffin, unless that be necessary for some reason other than custom.
>
> And generally I request that all the details be simple and inexpensive, avoiding all things which are merely done for show, and retaining only what is, in the judgement of those who arrange my Funeral, requisite for its decent and reverent performance. But this clause is not to override any preceding clause or any subsequent clause.
>
> Further request that no plumes may be carried, either on the hearse, or on the horses, if there be horses. Also that the Coffin be not black, nor covered with cloth.
>
> Also that there be no expensive monument. I should prefer a small plain head-stone, but will leave this detail to their judgement.[4]

Dodgson not only repudiated some of the funeral conventions of the times—plumes, armbands, palls—but also hinted at his primary concern with religious ritualism. In his 1887 sermon at Guildford he had spoken, with respect to the ritual movement in the church, of the "great danger—of our becoming mere formalists, of putting outward beauty of structure, of adornment, of external reverence, in the place of that inward spiritual grace of holy devotion."[5] Here, as early as 1873, was the same concern, as he wrote of avoiding "all things which are done merely for show."

There was another reason Dodgson wished to avoid many of the outer symbols of mourning. In a letter of 5 September 1884, following the death of his uncle Hassard, he wrote: "I suppose I must go to what we make such a gloomy scene, the funeral. Why should we not, at least when an aged Christian is taken, show signs of rejoicing instead of sorrow? I think we treat Death far too much as the end of all things" (*Letters* 550). He clearly wished his own funeral to be no "gloomy scene."

Dodgson's funeral was, according to the *London News*, "wholly in harmony with the simplicity which distinguished him when alive."[6] The family had invited Francis Paget, dean of Christ Church, Dodgson's Oxford college, to assist the local incumbent, Rev. Cyril Grant, with the service. The *London News* described the morning in detail:

> It would be impossible to conceive a more exquisitely simple service, or a more impressive one.
>
> At about half-past eleven o'clock the procession from the old red brick house in which Mr. Dodgson died emerged from the ancient Castle Arch into one of the many quaint byways with which Guildford abounds. A plain oaken coffin, covered with beautiful flowers, and drawn on a hand carriage, was the center of a small group of mourners, who soon reached the gate of the old church of St. Mary's . . . to the tolling of the bell in the square old tower. The body was met by the Dean of Christ Church, Dr. Paget, and the Rector, Mr. Grant, and thence carried into the nave of the church, in which a handful of people were already seated, to the solemn words of the Office for the Dead: "We brought nothing into this world, and it is certain we can carry nothing out. The Lord gave and the Lord hath taken away; blessed be the name of the Lord."[7] Then rose the choir and congregation and sang, "The Saints of God."[8]
>
> The beautiful service, undertaken partly by the Dean, partly by the rector [they were assisted by the curates Rev. A. Kingston and Rev. E. C. Kirwan] was soon ended; there was another hymn ["My God, my Father While I Stray"]; then once more was the body carried out of the venerable interior into the soft balmy air of open day. And thus was it wheeled down the High-street, over the bridge which crosses the sluggish Wey, and thence slowly climbed up the steep, stern slope to the gates of what must be one of the most lovely burying grounds in all England. . . .

But Dean Paget is committing the dead to the earth: "Earth to earth, ashes to ashes, dust to dust"—it is not earth, or ashes, or dust, but chalk, all lumps of hard chalk, which fall upon the coffin. But the chalk has given forth sufficient sustenance to nourish a pine of goodly stature. Its somber boughs, swaying to and fro in the wind, hang right over the open grave, and shelter the bare-headed clergy. The sweet voices of the choir boys now rise:

Peace, perfect peace, in this dark world of sin,
The blood of Jesus whispers peace within—[9]

Words and music mingle with the winds, and are quickly lost to the ear; final prayers, too—and so the service ends, and all that remains of the famous writer is alone on the crest of this Surrey hill.

Of all the elements of Dodgson's death, funeral, and mourning, perhaps the most quintessentially Victorian were the site of the grave and the monument erected by his siblings in Mount Cemetery outside Guildford. High on a hill, with the Surrey landscape laid out below, it is, as that Victorian reporter predicted, a lovely scene in the summer sunshine. In the eighteenth century and before, many graves were placed inside of English churches, but the nineteenth-century cult of the pastoral led to the convention of interment in a pastoral setting.

Dodgson's grave marker, too, is exactly what any Victorian would have expected—a design seen in churchyards throughout the land, often marking the graves of the Victorian or Edwardian departed. It seems to have been a favorite among Dodgsons; several other members of the family used the same basic design: a white marble cross in this case surmounting three steps. On Charles Dodgson's cross are the words, "Thy Will Be Done," inspired, no doubt, by the hymn he asked to hear on his deathbed.

Below the cross, the engraving reads:

Where I am there shall
Also my servant be.[10]
Revd. Charles Lutwidge Dodgson,
(Lewis Carroll)
Fell Asleep Jan. 14, 1898
Aged 65 years.
His Servants shall serve him.[11]

"Father in the gracious keeping
Leave we now thy servant sleeping."

The final quote is the refrain from the 1875 hymn "Now the Labourer's Task Is O'er," by John Ellerton.[12] It is a hymn of passing from this life to the next which uses many of the standard Victorian metaphors for Christian passage to the afterlife such as a voyage to another shore and a shepherd bringing home lambs. The final verse reads:

"Earth to earth, and dust to dust,"
Calmly now the words we say,
Leaving him to sleep in trust
Till the Resurrection-day.

The language on Dodgson's gravestone, and especially the use of sleep as a metaphor for death, is no coincidence. While sleep was used as a euphemism for death as early as the New Testament, the Victorians were especially fond of this comparison. Dodgson's friend Frederick Denison Maurice, for instance, wrote:

We say sometimes, "He sleeps in the grave,"—"After life's fitful fever he sleeps well!" . . . You remember the bodily pain, the restlessness of mind, you have seen in one you have known well. The thought that he is in repose is the one you fly to most eagerly. But oh, that dreary, earthly repose! . . . Now compare these expressions with St. Paul's; "He sleeps in Jesus." There is the rest which you were longing to claim for him, the termination of uneasy struggles, of doubts, of sufferings.[13]

Maurice's words might almost have served as a guide in choosing texts for Dodgson's grave; for while the quote from Ellerton's and the phrase "fell asleep" conform to that Victorian comfortable comparison between sleep and death, the quote from John's Gospel makes it clear that Dodgson's sleep is in Christ.

While Dodgson may have lived much of his later life as "practically a layman," he was buried as a clergyman. Not only did his marker identify him as Revd. Charles Lutwidge Dodgson, but the three-tier plinth holding up the cross was a standard sign that the deceased was ordained in the Church of England.

There are two other things worth noting about Dodgson's gravesite. First is that a man who carefully guarded his identity as Lewis Carroll from the general public throughout his adult life allowed his pseudonym on the sacred monument marking his grave. But Dodgson made it clear, in a letter to Falconer Madan of 8 December 1880, that he had no desire to protect his secret beyond the grave: "Your question 'how soon after death may the change [that is making public an author's pseudonym] be allowed?' must be answered, I think, with 'at once: a pseudonym is maintained for the personal comfort of the writer, and is only needed during his life" (*Letters* 397). Surely Dodgson made known his willingness, if not his desire, to be identified as Lewis Carroll on his grave marker.

Dodgson's burial was also traditional in another way—a body was buried, not an urn of ashes. To be sure, this was the norm at the time, but by 1898, Dodgson could have been legally cremated. The first crematorium in the United Kingdom had begun operations in Woking, just a few miles from Guildford, in 1885. It is no surprise that Dodgson chose a traditional burial, for cremation was still used only in a small number of cases, but the proximity of the crematorium suggests that opting for traditional burial of the body may have been a conscious choice by Dodgson and his family.

Theologically, Dodgson would have had no trouble with cremation, as we can tell from his writing on the resurrection of the body in an 1885 letter to Edith Rix:

> "the Resurrection of the Body"—is very interesting to me, and I have given it much thought.
>
> *My* conclusion was to give up the *literal* meaning of the *material* body altogether. *Identity*, in some mysterious way, there evidently is; but there is no resisting the scientific fact that the actual material usable for *physical* bodies has been used over and over again so that each atom would have several owners. . . . all the other insuperable difficulties (such as people born with bodily defects) are swept away at once if we accept St. Paul's "spiritual body," and his simile of the grain of corn.[14] . . . I accept the idea of the material body being the "dress" of the spiritual—a dress needed for material life. (*Letters* 603–4)

Charles Dodgson didn't only think about death on his own deathbed or when attending funerals. The *Alice* books have many death jokes and allusions; Dodgson's longest poem (other than the *Snark*), *Phantasmagoria*, is about a ghost; the *Snark* itself ends in a symbolic death as the Baker "softly and suddenly vanishes away"; and there are many other discussions of and allusions to death in Dodgson's poetry and prose, especially in the *Sylvie and Bruno* books. Though Dodgson's diaries tend to be factual records of what he did rather than theological ponderings, his letters include many discourses on death and the life to come.

Dodgson saw death as both an ever-present reality and a litmus test for moral living—we should not live in any scene where we would not wish to die, he wrote in the preface to *Sylvie and Bruno*. He also viewed death as a trial to be borne, and looked back upon with relief. "In that 'strange region,'" Dodgson wrote of the afterlife in an 1891 letter to an invalid, "there will be one very happy thought to dwell on, 'death is over!'" (*Letters* 853). And in an 1896 letter to his sister Louisa, he wrote, "I sometimes think what a grand thing it will be to be able to say to oneself 'Death is *over,* now: there is not *that* experience to be faced, again!'" (*Letters* 1100).

Throughout his writings on death, and especially in letters of condolence to friends who have lost loved ones, Dodgson used familiar metaphors to refer to the afterlife—the most common being "the other shore" or the "other side of the river." In an 1876 letter of condolence, he wrote, "these partings will not seem so long when we look back on them from the other side of the river" (*Letters* 254); in an 1882 letter, he said, "I find that as life slips away (I am over fifty now), and the life on the other side of the great river becomes more and more the reality" (*Life* 340); again in 1885 he wrote, "You have my sympathy in the sorrowful time you are spending—such a time as we all go through, again and again, as our loved ones pass over to the other shore" (*Letters* 571).

Most of Dodgson's descriptions of the afterlife in his letters and other writings are even less concrete than "the other shore." They include, from the letters, "the happier land," "that strange region," and "that brighter world." In *Easter Greeting* he writes of "a brighter dawn."

What did Dodgson believe happened immediately after death? Dodgson did not come to his ideas about the afterlife lightly. They were formed through a careful reading and study of scripture, the acceptance of certain axioms about God, logical reasoning, and wide reading of contemporary theological thought. In short, Dodgson's beliefs about life everlasting were formed in the intersection of faith, logic, and scholarship.

The Thirty-Nine Articles, to which Dodgson had subscribed both on entering Oxford University in 1850 and on his ordination in 1861, have this to say about life after death:

The Old Testament is not contrary to the New; for both in the Old and New Testament everlasting life is offered to mankind by Christ.

Predestination to life is the everlasting purpose of God, whereby, before the foundations of the world were laid, He hath constantly decreed by His counsel secret to us, to deliver from curse and damnation those whom He hath chosen in Christ out of mankind, and to bring them by Christ to everlasting salvation as vessels made to honour.

The Romish Doctrine concerning Purgatory . . . is a fond thing, vainly invented, and grounded upon no warranty of Scripture, but rather repugnant to the Word of God.[15]

These statements from the articles form the foundation of Dodgson's beliefs about the afterlife, a belief he restated nearly every morning during his decades at Oxford in morning chapel when he recited the creed, saying, "I believe in . . . the Resurrection of the body, And the life everlasting." But, as is clear from his disquisition on the resurrection of the body, Dodgson developed beliefs far more detailed than these statements of faith in the formularies of the church.

Dodgson's clearest and most detailed account of what he believed happens immediately after death came in an 1889 letter to Mary Brown. It shows not only the depths of Dodgson's thought on the subject but how his beliefs were formed first and foremost by scripture:

As to the words "today shalt thou be with me in paradise,"[16] and the words in the Apostles' Creed "he descended into hell," the usual interpretation is that *both* words refer to the "place of departed spirits," where, as we believe, the disembodied spirits await the time of the resurrection, when they shall be clothed in their "spiritual body" and shall appear before the judgment-seat of Christ, and so shall pass to heaven or to hell.

The parable of the rich man and Lazarus seems to teach that even among the disembodied spirits a *distinction* is made, some being in happiness and others in sorrow. The two separate portions of this world of spirits are called, in the Greek, "paradise" (or "Abraham's bosom") and "hades."

In I Cor. 15.55 it is translated "grave": in 10 other places, "hell," which I think a misleading translation, being liable to be confused with the Greek word *gehenna* (which is also translated hell), the name of the place to which the wicked shall be sent *after* the resurrection. The word *gehenna* occurs in

12 places. That it refers to a place not reached till *after* the resurrection is clear from Matt. 10. 28.

So, in answer to your question "Do you think because a man may drink, he will be sent straight to hell?" I say, in the first place, that it is *not* the teaching of the Bible (though no doubt it *is* taught in many *human* writings, such as sermons and hymns) that *any* one is sent, either to heaven or to hell, *immediately* after death. (*Letters* 745–46)

The doctrine of "the intermediate state" between death and final judgment occurred not only in Dodgson's writing but in his library, especially in two books by the Tractarian Herbert Mortimer Luckock, *After Death* and its sequel, *The Intermediate State.* Luckock argues that the intermediate state is not simply a place of waiting, but that progress toward perfection is possible. "If it be admitted that the soul exists after death," writes Luckock, "and is conscious, it seems almost impossible to believe that it remains altogether unchanged."[17] Dodgson touched on this possibility in his discussion of eternal punishment, where he writes;

There are *two* conceivable conditions in which men may find themselves after death. These are:

(1) having been deprived of "free-will";

(2) retaining it. (*Letters* 1041)

Dodgson mentioned this possibility of free will after death—a belief that fits in well with Luckock's notion of progression in the intermediate state—in both his essay "Eternal Punishment" and in letters to his sister Elizabeth and to Mary Brown. In his 28 June 1889 letter to Mary Brown, he wrote: "If any one says 'it is certain that the Bible teaches that, when once a man is in *Hell,* no matter how much he repents, there he will stay for ever,' I reply '*if* I were certain the Bible taught that, I would give up the Bible.' . . . And if any one urges 'then, to be consistent, you ought to grant the *possibility* that the Devil himself might repent and be forgiven,' I reply 'and I *do* grant it!'" (*Letters* 747).

Dodgson believed not only in free will after death but in a connection between hell and heaven available to all who repent and turn from their sins—a connection not recognized in Anglican Church dogma of the time.

The possibility that the state of the soul is not fixed at death gives rise to another question—that of the efficacy of prayers for the dead. In his book

The Spirits in Prison, a copy of which Dodgson had in his library, Edward Hayes Plumptre argued that the state of the soul is not fixed and that the teachings of the early church (upon which the Tractarians leaned so heavily) indicated that the voice of that church "went up without a doubt or misgiving, in prayers for the souls of the departed."[18]

Dodgson's own opinion on this subject he stated briefly in a letter to his sister Elizabeth: " 'Prayers for the dead' . . . *I* think . . . a good practice, quite consistent with the will of God" (*Letters* 1042). Would Dodgson have seen any use in prayers for the dead if he did not entertain the idea of progression of souls after death?

This gives rise to the question of whether Dodgson saw any possibility of interaction between the living and the dead. The Victorian era was a great age for ghost stories and interest in spirituality and the supernatural. Dodgson's library contained no fewer than forty-six books on the supernatural—including books on ghosts, magic, werewolves, mesmerism, witches, and vampires. Adding ghost stories and poems of the supernatural, the total is much higher. Dodgson was an early member of the Society for Psychical Research[19]— clearly he gave thought to issues of the supernatural. What, exactly, Dodgson believed about the broad field of supernaturalism is difficult to pin down, for he did not write about this in the detail that he wrote about Christian spirituality. However, he was clearly a seeker and a thinker, and while it is dangerous to conclude from the presence of a book in Dodgson's library his belief in a particular tenet (he owned, for instance, two books defending slavery), several of his books suggest that he hoped to incorporate belief in the supernatural into his Christian worldview. Horace Bushnell's *Nature and the Supernatural as Together Constituting One System of God* (1862), William Howitt's *The History of the Supernatural . . . Demonstrating a Universal Faith* (1863), and Asa Mahan's *Modern Mysteries* (1855) all attempt to reconcile supernaturalism with Christianity, and all sat on Dodgson's shelves.

Other volumes in Dodgson's library explained supernatural phenomena in scientific terms, such as Catherine Crowe's *The Night Side of Nature* and Henry Drummond's *Natural Law in the Spiritual World.* (Dodgson also owned two responses to Drummond's controversial book, which claimed that "there is reason to believe that many of the Laws of the Spiritual World, hitherto regarded as occupying an entirely separate province, are simply the Laws of the Natural World.")[20]

Dodgson mentioned the Victorian craze for séances and related supernatural phenomena in a letter to James Langton Clarke in 1882: "Trickery will not do as a complete explanation of all the phenomena of table-rapping, thought-reading, etc. I am more and more convinced. At the same time, I see no need as yet for believing that disembodied spirits have anything to do with it" (*Letters* 471). Dodgson went on to describe the possible existence of a natural force (about which he had read in a Society for Psychical Research pamphlet) that could explain these phenomena.

Dodgson wrote in his fiction and poetry about phenomena included under the umbrella of Victorian spiritualism, from the mysterious vanishing of the Baker at the end of *The Hunting of the Snark* to the eerie state and fairy world of *Sylvie and Bruno*. Most notably, one of his longest poems, *Phantasmagoria*, was about a ghost—though not the soul of a dead human but rather the resident of an entirely unseen world with its own hierarchy and rules.

Dodgson's interest in ghosts extended beyond the fictional, as can be seen by his association with Thomas Heaphy. On 5 October 1861, there appeared in Charles Dickens's weekly periodical *All the Year Round* an account by Heaphy of an encounter with a ghost. Dodgson, having admired Heaphy's artwork in a recent exhibition, called on him in London on 23 April 1867. "We had some talk about 'Mr. H's Story,'" wrote Dodgson in his diary, "and he told me that the dinner party really consisted of five, as the governess came down and sat on the same side of the table as the ghost-lady."

As to whether Dodgson saw the possibility of interaction between the living and the dead, he best answers this question in an 1879 letter to Ethel Barclay:

> You say you don't see "how [children] can be guided aright by their dead mother, or how light can come from her." Many people believe that our friends in the other world can and do influence us in some way, and perhaps even "guide" us and give us light to show us our duty. My own feeling is, it *may* be so: but nothing has been revealed about it. That the angels do so is revealed, and we may feel sure of *that;* and there is a beautiful fancy (for I don't think one can call it more) that a mother who has died leaving a child behind her in this world, is allowed to be a sort of guardian angel to that child. (*Life* 208–9)

This same hope, that the dead might watch over the living, is reflected in the last stanza of Dodgson's 1868 poem "The Valley of the Shadow of Death." The narrator here refers to his late wife as he says:

But if there be—O if there be
   A truth in what they say,
That angel-forms we cannot see
   Go with us on our way;
Then surely she is with me here,
   I dimly feel her spirit near—
The morning mists grow thin and clear,
   And death brings in the day.[21]

Dodgson believed that, following the last judgment, the soul, clothed in the "spiritual body," will go either to heaven or hell, but what were his views on paradise and damnation? The one doctrine of the Victorian Anglican Church on which Dodgson spent the most ink was that which stated that those sent to hell would suffer eternal punishment. This doctrine came under widespread fire during the Victorian era.

The controversial *Essays and Reviews,* published in 1860 (see p. 155 in this volume), included an essay by Henry Bristow Wilson in which Wilson questioned, by implication, the doctrine of eternal punishment. Wilson, as a result of his essay, was found guilty of heresy in the Court of Arches, but the Privy Council overturned his conviction in 1864. This decision resulted in a meeting of clergy at Oxford on 29 February 1864, who drafted a declaration on the subject, subsequently signed by eleven thousand clergymen of the Church of England. The declaration stated that "the 'punishment' of the 'cursed,' equally with the 'life' of the 'righteous,' is 'everlasting.'"[22]

Dodgson would have been aware of all of this as he began to form his own view of eternal punishment. That view would ultimately go against not just the eleven thousand signatories to the Oxford Declaration, but against his friend Henry Parry Liddon and his own sponsor at Christ Church, Edward Bouverie Pusey, who had spoken passionately in Convocation on 3 March 1864 in condemnation of the Privy Council decision to exonerate Wilson.

In a letter to an unnamed recipient dated 30 November 1874, Liddon wrote:

> Certainly I believe that the "usual interpretation" of those passages of Scripture which speak of "Eternal" Punishment is the true one. Mr. Maurice's treatment of that word, as descriptive of a quality having no relation to time, always struck me as more ingenious than true. . . .

Nor can I think that your proposals for getting over the difficulties which you feel about the doctrine will really hold water.

As to the first, we cannot think that God frightens us with threatenings which He really does not mean to carry out, without doing Himself an obvious dishonor.

As to the second, although we may rightly shrink from saying that any given individual is certainly so unfaithful to light and grace as to incur the eternal loss of God, we do know that many are so. God knows who they are.

It is impossible—for me at least—to doubt that this awful doctrine is a part of Divine Revelation.[23]

Liddon here refers to Frederick Denison Maurice's *Theological Essays,* published in 1853, nine years before Dodgson began his acquaintance with Maurice. His stance on eternal punishment presented in these essays ultimately led to Maurice's dismissal from King's College, London, and strongly influenced Dodgson's thinking. Liberal churchmen like Maurice found eternal punishment a key doctrine they struggled to reconcile with their notion of an all-loving God. In rejecting the doctrine, Maurice argued the word "eternity" must have the same meaning throughout the New Testament, and since this word often refers to God, it cannot be simply a collection of negatives—without beginning and end. "If it is right, if it is a duty to say that eternity in relation to God has nothing to do with time or duration," Maurice wrote, "are we not bound to say also that in reference to life or to punishment it has nothing to do with time or duration?"[24]

Dodgson owned Maurice's *Theological Essays,* along with a copy of the 1878 book *Eternal Hope,* by Maurice's former student Frederic W. Farrar. Farrar, too, argued against the doctrine of eternal punishment, claiming, as many others did, that the doctrine was based on faulty translations in English Bibles of the three words, "hell," "everlasting," and "damnation."

Dodgson clearly followed the debate on this issue. He owned a copy of Edward Bouverie Pusey's 1864 sermon *Everlasting Punishment,* as well as *What Is of Faith as to Everlasting Punishment?,* Pusey's response to Farrar's book. In his repudiation of Farrar's stance, Pusey wrote, "Dr. Farrar did not observe that in his eagerness against everlasting punishment, he, while rejecting the Roman Purgatory, assumed the most terrible teaching about Purgatory, held of old and now in the Roman Church, which depicts it simply as a hell not eternal."[25] Pusey's book against Farrar brought its own reaction found in Dodgson's library, Frank Oxenham's *What Is the Truth as to Everlasting Punishment?* Oxenham agreed with Farrar's point about translation and asked whether the word αἰώνιος always means "endless." Oxenham argued that the doctrine of eternal punishment implied, "The charge against God of amazing cruelty and injustice, such cruelty and injustice as would cover their perpetrator, were he a human being, with ineffaceable infamy, and secure for him the abhorrence of mankind."[26]

Dodgson would ultimately incorporate Maurice's ideas about the meaning of language, Farrar's on translation, and Oxenham's on the incompatibility of the doctrine with the love of God into his writing on eternal punishment. His first major attempt to explain his thinking came in an 1889 letter to Mary Brown:

> Now put side by side with [the idea that God is perfectly good] the theory "God will punish two persons *equally,* who commit the same sin, though the temptation may have been, owing to difference of circumstances, irresistible by one, and easily resisted by the other." I say "this contradicts the *perfect* goodness of God. One of the two must be false. I hold to the *first* theory, namely, that God is perfectly good: and I deny the *second.*" That is, I say "God will *not* act thus." If you urge "but such-and-such a text asserts it. Hence, if the Bible is inspired by a God of truth, and if this text be genuine, and rightly translated, then God *will* act so," I reply "then I deny one or other of these conditions: and I say that either the Bible is not inspired, or the text is not genuine, or it is mistranslated."
>
> From the belief that God is perfectly good, I conclude, as *necessary* sequences, that He will take account of *all* circumstances in judging of any action of man—that he will not punish, except for *wilful* sin, where the sinner was free to choose good or evil—that he will not punish *for ever* any one who *desires* to repent, and to turn *from* sin. (*Letters* 746–47)

This letter came several years before Dodgson began work his book on religious difficulties, but clearly he was already working out his ideas for possible publication. He wrote the letter using his Electric Pen, a duplicating device that allowed him to make copies of the original from a stencil. "I am writing this, in order to keep a copy," he said (*Letters* 745). Having taken some effort to get his thoughts down in the form of a logical argument, he wished to have a record for himself.

The other letter in which he wrote at length about eternal punishment was to his sister Elizabeth in November 1894. He would first send the manuscript of his article on the subject to the printers in June 1895, so this letter may have been a working draft for that article:

There are *two* conceivable conditions in which men may find themselves after death. These are:

    (1) having been deprived of "free-will";

    (2) retaining it.

In the first case, the man is incapable of doing either right, or wrong, in the future: so that all the *guilt,* that can possibly attach to him, is that of sins committed in *this* life.

In the second case, he is able to do right, or to do wrong, according to the way in which he uses his "free-will."

Hence this second case may be subdivided into *two.* (I shall take the two *extreme* cases.)

    (2) (a) he *always* chooses *right:* so that he sins no more, through all eternity: and in *his* case (as in No. (1)) all the *guilt,* that can possibly attach to him, is that of sins committed in *this* life.

    (2) (b) he *always* chooses *wrong:* so that he is for ever adding to his sins, and incurring fresh guilt.

Now, when we are considering whether the infliction of "eternal punishment" is, or is not, consistent with the perfect justice that we ascribe to God; i.e. whether it is, or is not, *credible,* to one who believes in God's perfect goodness, just think what a totally different thing it is to *believe* in it, in each of these 3 cases.

In the first case, God would be inflicting pain, for all eternity, on a being whose sins had all been committed during a few years . . . and who had long ceased to have *any* power to repent, or amend.

In the second case, He would be inflicting it on a being who had sinned during a few years, and who had been doing his very best, for *millions* of years, to repent of, and to hate, sin, and to love goodness.

In the third case, He would be constantly punishing for constant *sin,* and would be banishing from His presence one who, by his own free choice, was *keeping* himself unfit for that presence, and unable to be happy; but who *could,* at any moment, repent, and so change his condition, and his relation to God. . . .

My own view is, that, if I were forced to believe that the God of Christians was capable of inflicting "eternal punishment" in the first, or the second, of these three cases, I should give up Christianity. In the *third* case, punishment seems to me *quite* consistent with perfect justice. (*Letters* 1041–42)

All of this reading and writing on eternal punishment ultimately led to Dodgson's composing the first of his planned essays on "religious difficulties." On 20 July 1895, he wrote in his diary, "Today I have made a beginning of the work of getting 'Solvent Principles' into type, by sending to Clay the MS on 'Eternal Punishment.'" This is the only place in which Dodgson refers to the proposed book on religious difficulties as *Solvent Principles*. Dodgson did further work on the piece in 1897, preparing for his sermon on the topic preached at St. Mary's, Oxford, on 24 October. A surviving set of galley sheets of the essay is dated by the printers 28 October 1897, just after that sermon. But the essay was not destined for publication during Dodgson's lifetime.[27] Dodgson began the final version of this essay, titled "Eternal Punishment," by setting out three incompatible propositions:

I.   God is perfectly good.
II. To inflict Eternal Punishment on certain human beings, and in certain circumstances, would be wrong.
III. God is capable of acting thus.

In order to settle which of the three must be abandoned, he first states what is meant by the first two propositions:

I.
God is perfectly good.

As to the meaning of this word "good," I assume that the Reader accepts, as an Axiom antecedent to any of these three Propositions, the Proposition that the ideas of Right and Wrong rest on eternal and self-existent principles. . . .

I assume, then, that this Proposition means that God always acts in accordance with the eternal principle of Right, and that He is, therefore, perfectly good.

II.

To inflict "Eternal Punishment" on certain human beings and in certain circumstances, would be wrong.

The word "Punishment" I assume to mean, here, "suffering inflicted on a human being who has sinned, and *because* he has sinned." . . .

The word "Eternal" I assume to mean "without end."

As to the human beings who are here contemplated as the subjects of Eternal Punishment, there are three conceivable cases, viz.:—

(A) The case of one who has ceased to possess Free-Will, and who therefore has no further power either to sin or to repent. In such a case, Eternal Punishment would be suffering inflicted through infinite time, and therefore itself infinite in amount as punishment for sins committed during a finite time.

(B) The case of one who retains Free-Will, and who has ceased to sin, has repented of all past sins, and is choosing good *as good*. In this case also Eternal Punishment would be infinite suffering, inflicted as punishment for sins committed during a finite time.

(C) The case of one who does not come under either of these descriptions, that is, one who retains Free-Will and continues for ever to choose *evil*. In such a case Eternal Punishment would be infinite suffering, inflicted as punishment for infinite sin.

I assume that the reader would *not* feel any difficulty in recognising the justice of inflicting continuous suffering as punishment for continuous sin.

Hence we may set aside case (C) altogether.

Also we may combine cases (A) and (B) into one, and interpret Proposition II. as asserting that it would be wrong to inflict infinite suffering, on human beings who have ceased to sin, as punishment for sins committed during a finite time.

Dodgson then considers each of the propositions in turn, so that, "the Reader will then be able to see for himself *which* two of the three have the *strongest* claims on his assent, and *which* he must, therefore, abandon."

First, then, let us consider the Proposition.

I. *"God is perfectly good."*

The grounds on which this claims our assent, seem to be, first, certain *intuitions* (for which, of course, no *proofs* can be offered), such as "I believe that I have Free-Will, and am capable of choosing right or wrong; that I am responsible for my conduct; that I am not the outcome of blind material forces, but the creature of a being who has given me Free-Will and the sense of right and wrong, and to whom I am responsible, and who is therefore perfectly good. And this being I call 'God.'"

And these *intuitions* are confirmed for us in a thousand ways by all the facts of revelation, by the facts of our own spiritual history, by the answers we have had to our prayers, by the irresistible conviction that this being whom we call "God" *loves* us, with a love so wonderful, so beautiful, so immeasurable, so wholly undeserved, so unaccountable on any ground save His own perfect goodness, that we can but abase ourselves to the dust before Him, and dimly hope that we may be able some day to love Him with a love more like His great love for us.

The abandonment of this Proposition would mean practically, for most of us, the abandonment of the belief in a God, and the acceptance of Atheism.

Secondly, let us consider the Proposition.

II. *To inflict infinite suffering, on human beings who have ceased to sin, as punishment for sins committed during a finite time, would be wrong.*

. . . There is . . . *one* principle which clearly applies equally to both [punishment by man and punishment by God]: we recognise that some *proportion* should be observed, between the amount of crime and the amount of punishment inflicted. . . .

In the sight of *God,* our guilt consists in the sinful *choice,* and we rightly hold that two men, who had resolved, in similar circumstances, on committing the same crime, would be equally guilty in His sight, even though only *one* had actually committed the crime, while the *other* had been accidentally prevented from carrying out his intention.

Hence we may assume that God's purpose, in the enactment of punishment, is the prevention of the sinful *choice,* with all the evils consequent upon it. When once the punishment has been *enacted,* it must necessarily, unless some change takes place in the circumstances contemplated in the enactment, be *inflicted.* . . . We cannot believe [God] to be ignorant of any of the circumstances, or capable of announcing that He will do what He does not really intend to do.

We must trust His perfect knowledge of the thoughts of men, for judging who is guilty and who is not, and the only principle of right and wrong that seems reasonably applicable, is the sense that some *proportion* should be observed between the amount of sin and the amount of the punishment awarded to it.

And here comes in the one consideration which, as I believe, causes all the difficulty and distress felt on this subject. We feel intuitively that sins committed by a human being during a finite period must necessarily be *finite* in amount; while punishment continued during an infinite period must necessarily be *infinite* in amount. And we feel that such a proportion is unjust.

... There is another intuition, felt, I believe, by most of us, of which no account has yet been taken. It is that there is some eternal *necessity*, wholly beyond our comprehension, that *sin* must result in suffering. This principle is, I believe, enshrouded in, and may to some extent make more credible to us, the unfathomable mystery of the Atonement. And this principle must be allowed for, I think, in considering the present subject.

... When all this has been considered, its outcome seems to me to be the irresistible intuition that infinite punishment for finite sin would be unjust, and therefore wrong. ...

To set aside this intuition, and to accept, as a just and righteous act, the infliction on human beings of infinite punishment for finite sin, is virtually the abandonment of *Conscience* as a guide in questions of Right and Wrong, and the embarking, without compass or rudder, on a boundless ocean of perplexity.

... Such are the difficulties that meet us, if we propose to take the *second* possible course, and to reject Proposition II.

The *third* possible course is to accept Propositions I. and II., and to reject III. We should thus take the following position. "I believe that God will *not* act thus. Yet I also believe that, whatever He has declared He will do, He *will* do. Hence I believe that He has *not* declared that He will act thus."

The difficulties, entailed by choosing this *third* course, may be well exhibited in another set of incompatible Propositions, as follows:—

1. *God has not declared that He will act thus.*

2. *All that the Bible tells us, as to the relations between God and man, are true.*

3. *The Bible tells us that God has declared that He will act thus.*

As these three Propositions cannot possibly be *all* of them true, the acceptance of (1) necessarily entails the rejection of either (2) or (3).

If we reject (2), we are at once involved in all the perplexities that surround the question of Biblical Inspiration. The theory of *Plenary*

Inspiration—which asserts that *every* statement in the Bible is absolute and infallibly true—has been largely modified in these days, and most Christians are now, I think, content to admit the existence of a *human* element in the Bible, and the possibility of *human* error in such of its statements as do not involve the relations between God and Man. But, as to *those* statements, there appears to be a general belief that the Bible has been providentially protected from error: in fact, on any other theory, it would be hard to say what value there would be in the Bible or for what purpose it could have been written.

The more likely course would seem to be to reject (3). Let us consider what difficulties *this* would entail.

We are now supposed to have taken up the following position: "I do not believe that the Bible tells us that God has declared He will inflict Eternal Punishment on human beings, who are either incapable of sinning, or who, being capable of sinning, have ceased to sin."

. . . The interpretation of the passages, which are believed to teach the doctrine of "Eternal Punishment," depends largely, if not entirely, on the meaning given to one single word αἰώνιος. This is rendered, in our English Bibles, by the word "eternal" or "everlasting": but there are many critics who believe that it does not necessarily mean "endless." If this be so, then the punishment, which we are considering, is finite punishment for finite sin, and the original difficulty no longer exists.

In conclusion, I will put together in one view the various modes of escape, from the original difficulty, which may be adopted without violating the inexorable laws of logical reasoning. They are as follows:—

(1) "I believe that the infliction, on human beings, of endless punishment, for sins committed during a finite time, would be unjust, and therefore wrong. Yet I cannot resist the evidence that God has declared His intention of acting thus. Consequently I hold Him to be capable of sinning."

This would practically mean the abandonment of Christianity.

(2) "I believe that God is perfectly good, and therefore that such infliction of punishment would be right, though my conscience declares it to be wrong."

This would practically mean the abandonment of conscience as a guide to distinguish right from wrong, and would leave the phrase "I believe that God is perfectly *good*" without any intelligible meaning.

(3) "I believe that God is perfectly good. Also I believe that such infliction of punishment would be wrong. Consequently I believe that God is not capable of acting thus. I find that the Bible tells us that He *is* capable of acting

thus. Consequently I believe that what the Bible tells us of the relations between God and Man cannot be relied on as true."

This would practically mean the abandonment of the Bible as a trustworthy book.

(4) "I believe that God is perfectly good. Also I believe that such infliction of punishment would be wrong. Consequently I believe that God is not capable of acting thus. I find that the Bible, in the English Version, seems to tell us that He *is* capable of acting thus. Yet I believe that it is a book inspired by God, and protected by Him from error in what it tells us of the relations between God and Man, and therefore that what it says, according to the real meaning of the words, may be relied on as true. Consequently I hold that the word, rendered in English as 'eternal' or 'everlasting,' has been mistranslated, and that the Bible does not really assert more than that God will inflict suffering, of unknown duration but *not* necessarily eternal, punishment for sin."

Any one of these four views may be held, without violating the laws of logical reasoning.

Here ends my present task; since my object has been, throughout, *not* to indicate one course rather than another, but to help the Reader to see clearly *what* the possible courses are, and *what* he is virtually accepting, or denying, in choosing any *one* of them.

Though Dodgson says it has not been his object "to indicate one course rather than another," it is clear that he points the reader toward his own conclusion—that the entire doctrine of eternal punishment rests on nothing more substantial than a mistranslation. He makes this clear in a letter to his sister Elizabeth, in which he also says that his high church brother Edwin *did* believe in eternal punishment:

Now I will write down 3 incompatible Propositions: and you will see that *each* of the three courses is adopted by a large number of people.

(1) "The God, whom we worship, is perfectly good."

(2) "It would be wrong to inflict eternal punishment on a being, except in the case of that being *continuing to sin.*"

(3) "The God, whom we worship, is capable of doing this, even in the case of that being *having ceased to sin.*"

No sane person can believe all three of these. But it is quite possible to believe any *two.*

Those who believe (1) and (2), and deny (3) (which is *my* case) are usually called *Broad Church.*

Those who believe (1) and (3), and deny (2) (which is the case with Edwin) are mostly *High Church.*

Those who believe (2) and (3), and deny (1) are mostly *Atheists:* for I imagine nobody *now* would go on worshipping a God whom he believed capable of doing wrong. (*Letters* 1044–45)

Dodgson was largely mute on what, exactly, one might expect in heaven and hell, but a passage in *Sylvie and Bruno Concluded* gives a glimpse of his view on eternal life:

"The one idea," the Earl resumed, "that has seemed to me to overshadow all the rest, is that of *Eternity*—involving, as it seems to do, the necessary *exhaustion* of all subjects of human interest . . . [W]hen I transport myself, in thought, through some thousands or millions of years, and fancy myself possessed of as much Science as one created reason can carry, I ask myself 'What then? . . . It has been a very wearying thought to me." . . .

"Let me tell you how I have put it to myself. I have imagined a little child, playing with toys on his nursery-floor, and yet able to *reason,* and to look on, thirty years ahead. Might he not say to himself 'By that time I shall have had enough of bricks and ninepins. How weary Life will be!' Yet, if we look forward through those thirty years, we find him a great statesman, full of interests and joys far more intense than his baby-life could give—joys wholly inconceivable to his baby-mind—joys such as no baby-language could in the faintest degree describe. Now, may not our life, a million years hence, have the same relation, to our life now, that the man's life has to the child's? And, just as one might try, all in vain, to express to that child, in the language of bricks and ninepins, the meaning of 'politics,' so perhaps all those descriptions of Heaven, with its music, and its feasts, and its streets of gold, may be only attempts to describe, in *our* words, things for which we *really* have no words at all. Don't you think that in *your* picture of another life, you are in fact transplanting that child into political life, without making any allowance for his growing up?"[28]

It was the hope of the group standing on the winding hilltop in Surrey that January day, a group that included a few family and a few friends, that the late Charles Lutwidge Dodgson, known to them all as a man of deep faith, was now resting in the bosom of his Savior Jesus Christ. And so it was with sadness but also with the light of hope, that they listened to the choir boys sing:

Peace, perfect peace, death shadowing us and ours?
Jesus has vanquish'd death and all its powers.

It is enough: earth's struggles soon shall cease,
And Jesus call us to heav'n's perfect peace.
Amen.

Acknowledgments

I am deeply indebted to scores of Lewis Carroll scholars who have come before me, in particular Morton N. Cohen, Edward Wakeling, Selwyn Goodacre, Falconer Madan, Sidney Herbert Williams, Anne Clark, Fran Abeles, Jenny Woolf, Jeffrey Stern, and Roger Lancelyn Green. Other Carrollian friends have provided encouragement and advice throughout the decade-plus this book was in the making, especially Mark and Catherine Richards and August Imholtz. The support, encouragement, and assistance of Stephanie Lovett has been invaluable. Anna Worrall has been a champion for this book. Scores of institutions have provided materials, and I am especially thankful to the British Library, the Bodleian, Worcester Public Library, Rugby Public Library, Rugby School Archives, Oxford Diocesan Archives, Cheshire County Archives, North Yorkshire County Archives, Christ Church (Oxford) Library, Lambeth Palace Library, Princeton University Library, Harvard University Library, and New York University Library. Many thanks to Caroline Luke and Elisabeth Mead of the C. L. Dodgson Estate. For the background in Anglicanism that is necessary for such a study, I thank especially Rev. Faulton Hodge and Rev. Steve Rice. For her love, support, and patience, my deepest thanks go to Janice Lovett.

Notes

The frequently cited sources below are cited parenthetically in the text.

Diaries   Carroll, Lewis, *Lewis Carroll's Diaries: The Private Journals of Charles Lutwidge Dodgson.* Edited by Edward Wakeling. Vols. 1–10. London: Lewis Carroll Society, 1993–2007.

Letters   Cohen, Morton N., ed. *The Letters of Lewis Carroll.* New York: Oxford University Press, 1979.

Life   Collingwood, Stuart Dodgson. *The Life and Letters of Lewis Carroll.* London: T. Fisher Unwin, 1898.

1. This Child Is Regenerate

1. Lucy Lutwidge identifies herself as C. L. Dodgson's godmother in an inscription in a copy of the Book of Common Prayer which she gave him in 1839.

2. Charles Lutwidge Dodgson attended the Westminster play at least twice, in 1852 and 1857.

3. See James Mure, Henry Bull, and Charles Scott, *Lusus alteri Westmonasterienses: Sive prologi et epilogi. Pars secunda, 1820–1865* (Oxford: J. Parker, 1867), 189–95. Dodgson contributed the epilogue in a year when the play was not, as usual, a comedy of Terence (some of which had been criticized for their portrayal of immorality) but rather one of Plautus, of which the *Morning Post* said, "pure is it in purpose, and . . . sound in moral" ("The Westminster Play," 20 December 1865, 5).

4. See James Mure, Henry Bull, and Charles Scott, *Lusus alteri Westmonasterienses:, Sive prologi et epilogi* (Oxford: J. Parker, 1863), 249–304.

5. A "First" is the highest academic distinction in a subject at Oxford.

6. Christ Church is, uniquely at Oxbridge, a dual foundation of college and cathedral. When the Diocese of Oxford was created in 1541, the collegiate chapel became the diocesan cathedral. The dean of the college also serves as dean of the cathedral.

7. See [Maria Marcia Fanny Trench], *The Story of Dr. Pusey's Life,* 2nd ed. (London: Longmans, Green, 1900), 22.

8. W. R. Stephens, *A Memoir of Richard Durnford, D.D. Sometime Bishop of Chichester* (London: John Murray, 1899), 327.

9. Though the population of Daresbury village in 1831 was only 143, the chapelry included nine townships: Daresbury, Keckwick, Moor, Preston, Acton Grange, Over Walton, Lower Walton, Hatton, and Newton.

10. The *Morning Chronicle* ("Ecclesiastical Promotions," 3) reported on 26 February 1827 that Dodgson had been presented the Daresbury living; Joseph Foster's *Index ecclesiasticus* (Oxford: Parker, 1890), 53, gives the official date as 27 March 1827.

11. The first record of Dodgson at Daresbury is a burial he performed on 16 September 1827.

12. "Testimonial of Respect to a Clergyman," *Manchester Courier and Lancashire General Advertiser*, 12 August 1843, 6.

13. "The Late Rev. Thos. Vere Bayne, Incumbent of Broughton," *Manchester Courier and Lancashire General Advertiser*, 30 December 1848, 6.

14. "Funeral of the Late Rev. Thomas Vere Bayne, Incumbent of Broughton," *Manchester Courier and Lancashire General Advertiser*, 6 January 1849, 5.

15. "The Sabbath and the Watermen of Our Inland Rivers and Canals," *Manchester Courier and Lancashire General Advertiser*, 27 July 1839, 6.

16. *Report from the Select Committee of the House of Lords Appointed to Inquire into the Expediency of Restraining the Practice of Carrying Goods and Merchandize on Canals, Navigable Rivers, and Railways on Sundays*, 4 May 1841, 62.

17. See "Whit-Monday," *Manchester Courier and Lancashire General Advertiser*, 13 June 1829, 3.

18. See "The Bishop," *Chester Chronicle*, 9 October 1829, 2.

19. The opposing forces of the high church Oxford Movement, the low church evangelical revival, and the broad church movement (which hoped to unify the opposing high and low parties) would threaten the unity of the Church of England during the ensuing decades. In 1854, Harvey Newcomb would write, in his *Cyclopedia of Missions* (New York: Scribner, 1855): "After passing through various phases, the Church of England is now divided into three parties. They are familiarly denominated as the Low, High, and Broad Church. The Low Church takes the Calvinistic view of the [39] articles; and is earnest in moral reforms, in promoting spiritual religion, and missions to the heathen. . . . The High Church has for its watchwords Judgment by works; Baptismal regeneration; Church authority; and Apostolical succession. . . . The Broad Church is well represented by the lamented [Dr.] Arnold [late headmaster of Rugby School]. It makes much of the visible church; of symbols; of the unity of the church under different names." While this is a simplification, it gives an idea of the forces at work in the Church of England during Charles Dodgson's career.

20. Rev. Charles Dodgson, untitled remarks made on 29 November 1841, in "Chester Diocesan Board of Education," *Manchester Courier and Lancashire General Adviser*, 4 December 1841, 2.

21. Untitled notice in *Leeds Intelligencer*, 3 December 1836, 5.

22. "Ordination at Ripon," *Leeds Mercury*, 21 January 1837, 5. It must have been a quick trip, as Dodgson performed baptisms at Daresbury on the Sundays before and after.

23. Ibid.

24. Rev. Charles Dodgson, *A Sermon Preached in the Minster at Ripon, on Sunday Jan. 15, 1837, at the First Ordination Held by the Right Rev. Chas. Thomas Longley, D.D. Lord Bishop of Ripon* (Oxford: J. H. Parker, 1837); hereafter cited parenthetically in the chapter text.

25. See, for instance, his letter of 21 August 1894 to Mary Brown: "My life is so strangely free from all trials and troubles, that I cannot doubt my own happiness is one of the 'talents' entrusted to me to 'occupy' with, till the Master shall return, by doing something to make *other* lives happy" (*Letters* 1032).

26. "University & Clerical Intelligence," *Newcastle Journal*, 5 July 1845, 3.

27. Rev. Charles Dodgson, "The Rev. C. Dodgson on the Ripon Ordination Questions; With Remarks in Reply," *Christian Observer*, August 1838, 486; hereafter cited parenthetically in the chapter text.

28. Clergyman of the Diocese, *The Lord Bishop of Ripon's Cobwebs to Catch Calvinists* (London: Simpkin, Marshall, 1838), 5; hereafter cited parenthetically in the chapter text.

29. The theology of the Dutch reformer Jacobus Arminius (1560–1609).

30. "The Bishop of Ripon's Questions for Ordination, &c." *Christian Observer*, June 1838, 395–97.

31. See, for instance, [E. B. Pusey], *Scriptural Views of Holy Baptism—Continued [Tract 69]* in *Tracts for Our Times*, vol. 2 for 1834–35 (London: Rivington, 1856), 198.

32. Joseph Birch, *The Rev. C. Dodgson's New Tests of Orthodoxy: A Letter Addressed to the Right Honourable The Earl of Shaftsbury*, 2nd ed. (London: J. H. Jackson, 1853), 33; hereafter cited parenthetically in the chapter text.

33. Rev. Charles Dodgson, *The Controversy of Faith: Advice to Candidates for Holy Orders on the Case of Gorham v. The Bishop of Exeter* (London: John Murray, 1850), 3; hereafter cited parenthetically in the chapter text.

34. This very requirement of a clergyman caused Charles Lutwidge Dodgson great anxiety as he considered his possible future in the church (see p. 135 in this volume).

35. William Goode, *The Doctrine of the Church of England as to the Effects of Baptism in the Case of Infants*, 2nd ed. (London: J. Hatchard and Son, 1850).

36. Dodgson here refers to, among other statements in the Formularies, the prayer in the baptismal service following the actual baptism, which begins: "Seeing now, dearly beloved brethren, that this Child is regenerate."

37. *Testimonial to the Rev. C. Dodgson, M.A., Rector of Croft, Examining Chaplain to the Lord Bishop of Ripon, from 185 Clergymen Who Have Received Ordination from the Bishop* (N.p., 1852), [1].

38. Ibid.

39. Ibid., [2].

40. The *Record* was a mouthpiece of the extreme end of the low church, or evangelical movement.

41. Book of Common Prayer.

42. "Churching" refers to a service in the Book of Common Prayer called "The Thanksgiving of Women after Child-Birth, Commonly Called the Churching of Women."

43. The date fell between the end of the fourth volume of his diary (6 September 1864) and the beginning of the fifth volume (13 September 1864).

44. On the first page of his "Journal Number 10," before the entry for 2 April 1868, he recorded his godchildren: Charles Hassard Wilcox (b. 1852, cousin); Louis Henry Dodgson (b. 1850, cousin,); "Southey" (possibly Ronald Southey b. 1865, son of his friend Reginald); Clement Francis Rogers (b. 1866, son of Oxford professor James Rogers); William Melville Wilcox (b. 1866, first cousin once removed); Stuart Dodgson Collingwood (b. 1870, nephew); and Edith Alice Dodgson (b. 1872, niece).

45. Lewis Carroll, "'Alice' on the Stage," *The Theatre,* April 1887, 181.

46. C. L. Dodgson to S. D. Collingwood, MS, Lovett Collection.

47. "Nephew of the Creator of 'Alice,'" *Irish Press,* 1 April 1937, 3.

2. An Instruction to Be Learned

1. Rev. Charles Dodgson, "The Sabbath a Delight (A Village Sermon)," in *Sermons by XXXIX Living Divines of the Church of England,* 233–48 (London: J. Hatchard and Son, 1840), 242; hereafter cited parenthetically in the chapter text. The title of the sermon is from Matthew 6:30. Because the sermon was described as "a village sermon," it seems likely Dodgson preached it at Daresbury.

2. Rev. Charles Dodgson, *Confirmation: A Plain Catechism, Intended Chiefly for the Instruction of Young Persons before Confirmation,* 12th ed. (Warrington: J. Haddock; London: Rivington, n.d.), 10.

3. Lewis Carroll, *Sylvie and Bruno* (London: Macmillan, 1896), 384–88.

4. Ibid., [ix].

5. James Augustus Hessey, *Sunday: Its Origin, History, and Present Obligation, Considered in Eight Lectures Preached before the University of Oxford in the Year MDCCCXL,* 2nd ed. (London: John Murray, 1861), 305. C. L. Dodgson owned this edition.

6. Ibid., ix.

7. Advertisement, *Morning Post,* 9 July 1828, 2.

8. "University Education," *Jackson's Oxford Journal,* 12 February 1870, 5.

9. *Accounts and Papers Relating to Education,* vol. 41, Session 19 (February 1835–10 September 1835), 85. In 1833 Daresbury had "One Daily School, containing 66 children of both sexes," and "One Boarding School, in which 33 females are educated at the expense of their parents."

10. Ibid.

11. "Great Meeting at Warrington," *Morning Post,* 28 January 1839, 3.

12. "National Education," *Manchester Courier and Lancashire General Advertiser,* 12 January 1839, 5.

13. "National Society," *Church of England Magazine*, 31 December 1852, 21.

14. "The Chester Diocesan Board of Education, in Union with the National Society," *Manchester Courier and Lancashire General Advertiser*, 20 November 1841, 1.

15. Rev. Charles Dodgson, untitled remarks made on 29 November 1841, in "Chester Diocesan Board of Education," *Manchester Courier and Lancashire General Adviser*, 4 December 1841, 2.

16. Rev. Charles Dodgson, *The Controversy of Faith: Advice to Candidates for Holy Orders on the Case of Gorham v. The Bishop of Exeter* (London: John Murray, 1850), 89.

17. Rev. Charles Dodgson, untitled speech delivered on 4 December 1860, in "Laying of the Foundation Stone of the Female Training Institution," *Leeds Intelligencer*, 8 December 1860, 6.

18. Rev. Charles Dodgson, *The Providence of God Manifested in the Temporal Condition of the Poorer Clergy: A Sermon Preached in the Collegiate Church of Manchester, On Thursday, July 18th, 1839. At the Meeting of the Society for the Relief of The Widows and Orphans of the Clergy of the Archdeaconry of Chester* (London: J. G. & F. Rivington; Warrington: Haddock, 1839), 9.

19. "University Intelligence," *Lincolnshire Chronicle*, 1 May 1849, 2.

20. Rev. C. Dodgson, untitled remarks made on 29 November 1841.

21. Rev. Charles Dodgson, untitled speech delivered on 13 April 1849, in "Ripon Diocesan Church Building Society and Board of Education Public Meeting at Leeds," *Leeds Intelligencer*, 28 April 1849, 6.

22. Ibid.

23. Dodgson Family, devotional cards, Dodgson Family Collection, Surrey History Center. DFC A/1/2/4–18.

24. In an 1894 letter to his sister Elizabeth, he wrote: "*I* constantly pray to God to have mercy on all who are in rebellion against him. . . . It is almost inconceivable to me that *any* being, capable of free will, can rebel *for ever. Some* day he *must* realise, one would think, the love of God, and the hatefulness of sin" (*Letters* 1045).

25. In the preface to *Sylvie and Bruno*, he wrote of the ever-present threat of death: "The possibility of death—if calmly realised, and steadily faced—would be one of the best possible tests as to our going to any scene of amusement being right or wrong. If the thought of sudden death acquires, for *you,* a special horror when imagined as happening in a *theatre,* then be very sure the theatre is harmful for *you,* however harmless it may be for others; and that *you* are incurring a deadly peril in going. Be sure the safest rule is that we should not dare to *live* in any scene in which we dare not *die*" (xix–xx).

26. Rev. C. Dodgson, *The Providence of God*, 19.

27. Rev. Charles Dodgson, *A Sermon Preached in the Minster at Ripon, on Sunday Jan. 15, 1837, at the First Ordination Held by the Right Rev. Chas. Thomas Longley, D.D. Lord Bishop of Ripon* (Oxford: J. H. Parker, 1837), 5.

28. Ibid., 7–8.

29. In a letter of 18 August 1884, he wrote: "I've had a lot [of *Alice* books] printed on cheaper paper, in plain bindings, and given them to hospitals and Convalescent

Homes—for poor, sick children: and it's ever so much pleasanter to think of one child being saved some weary hours, than if all the town followed at my heels crying, 'How clever he is!'" (*Letters* 547–48).

30. Rev. Charles Dodgson, *A Sermon Preached in Ripon Minster, at the Ordination Held by the Lord Bishop of Ripon, on Sunday, July 29th, 1838* (Warrington: Haddock, 1838), 6–7.

31. Ibid., 7.

32. Lewis Carroll, *Symbolic Logic Part I: Elementary* (London: Macmillan, 1896), xiii.

33. Rev. Charles Dodgson, *"Preach the Gospel": A Sermon, Preached in Ripon Minster at the Ordination Held by the Lord Bishop of Ripon, on Sunday, January 13, 1839* (London: Rivington, 1839), 13.

34. Ibid.

35. Rev. C. Dodgson, *The Providence of God*, 8.

36. Ibid., 6.

37. For more on Dodgson's writings on vivisection, see *The Pamphlets of Lewis Carroll*, ed. Charlie Lovett, vol. 6: *A Miscellany of Works on Alice, Theatre, Religion, Science, and More* (New York: Lewis Carroll Society of North America, 2020).

38. Advertisement in the rear of various volumes of *The Library of the Fathers* (Oxford: John Henry Parker, 1838–85).

39. Ibid.

40. Dodgson Family, MS prayer book, Dodgson Family Collection, Surrey History Center, DFC A/1/3.

41. Dodgson Family, Charles L. Dodgson Reading Log, Dodgson Family Collection, Surrey History Center. DFC A/1/1.

42. Rev. C. Dodgson, *A Sermon Preached in Ripon Minster* (1838), 10.

43. Lewis Carroll, *Alice's Adventures Under Ground* (London: Macmillan, 1886), [v]. For more on Dodgson's views on children and religion, see chapter 7.

44. Lewis Carroll, *Alice's Adventures in Wonderland* (London: Macmillan, 1866), 10.

45. Mrs. Sherwood, *The History of the Fairchild Family*, 6th ed. (London: J. Hatchard, 1822), 96.

46. In 1862, Lewis Carroll may have written "Sequel to 'The Shepherd of Salisbury Plain,'" in response to a poem which borrowed Hannah More's title (see p. 156 in this volume).

47. Rev. C. Dodgson, *The Providence of God*, 14–15.

48. Sherwood, *The History of the Fairchild Family*, 55.

49. Lewis Carroll, *Useful and Instructive Poetry* (New York: Macmillan, 1954), 15.

50. Henry, Selby T., comp., *Good Stories from Oxford and Cambridge and the Dioceses* (London: Simpkin, Marshall, 1922), 86n.

51. In E. G. Wilcox, *The Lost Plum-Cake: A Tale for Tiny Boys* (London: Macmillan, 1897), ix–xi.

52. Parley, *Tales about Europe, Asia, Africa, and America*, 4th ed. (London: Thomas Tegg, 1839), 15; hereafter cited parenthetically in the chapter text.

53. The quotes are from Edgeworth, *Early Lessons, In Four Volumes* (London: Printed for R. Hunter, Baldwin and Cradock, etc., 1829); hereafter cited parenthetically in the chapter text.

54. Rev. C. Dodgson was a talented mathematician and taught his son at an advanced level, even after Charles was grown. In a letter to the magazine *Knowledge* in 1884, C. L. Dodgson writes about a "proof for ascertaining the divisibility of a number by 7. . . . Probably many have discovered it: my father did, for one, and taught it to me some thirty years ago [i.e., when CLD was 22]" (*Knowledge* 6 [4 July 1884]: 15).

55. [Lewis Carroll], "Faces in the Fire," *All the Year Round*, no. 42 (11 February 1860): 369–70. In *Phantasmagoria* the poem appears in slightly altered form:

> An island-farm—broad seas of corn
> Stirred by the wandering breath of morn—
> The happy spot where I was born.

3. For the Good Education

1. This chapter's title is from the Elizabethan Charter of Richmond Grammar School.

2. Rev. C. Dodgson was a supporter of Hook, a high churchman who made great improvements in the church in Leeds. Dodgson preached several sermons at Leeds during Hook's tenure, including Hook's farewell service in 1859. C. L. Dodgson heard Hook preach at St. Mary's, Oxford on 4 March 1857.

3. Memorial from Bishop Longley to Sir Robert Peel, 18 September 1841, B.L. Ms. 40489, f. 187, as cited in Anne Clark, *Lewis Carroll: A Biography* (New York: Schocken, 1979), 28.

4. Sir Robert Peel to Bishop Longley, 22 September 1841, BL Ms. 40489, f. 193, as cited in Clark, *Lewis Carroll: A Biography,* 28.

5. Bishop Longley to Sir Robert Peel, 6 January [1843], BL Ms. 40522, as cited in Clark, *Lewis Carroll: A Biography,* 20–29.

6. BL Ms. 40522, f. 205, as cited in Clark, *Lewis Carroll: A Biography,* 29.

7. Ibid.

8. Ibid., 30.

9. Robert Peel to Bishop Longley, 13 January 1843, BL Ms. 40522, f. 371, as cited in Clark, *Lewis Carroll: A Biography,* 30.

10. Ibid., f. 373, as cited in Clark, *Lewis Carroll: A Biography,* 30.

11. Untitled story in *Chester Chronicle and Cheshire and North Wales Advertiser,* 18 August 1843, 1.

12. "Address to the Bishop of Ripon," *Leeds Intelligencer,* 22 June 1850, 5.

13. "The Recent Address to the Bishop of Ripon," *Leeds Intelligencer,* 29 June 1850, 8.

14. "Deanery of Richmond East," *Leeds Intelligencer,* 23 November 1850, 5.

15. At the time of its creation in 1836, the Diocese of Ripon was divided into two archdeaconries, Richmond and Craven.

16. A. B., "Unequal Appropriation of Church Preferment: Another Proof of the Want of Church Reform," *York Herald*, 6 November 1852, 1.

17. Rev. Charles Dodgson, *A Short Account of the First Establishment of the Croft National School, in the Year 1845* (Darlington: Coates and Farmer, 1846), [3].

18. (London: Rivingtons, 1844). No copy traced. Advertised in Dodgson's *Charges* (1859, 1863, and 1865).

19. Rev. C. Dodgson, *A Short Account of the First Establishment of the Croft National School*, [3]–4.

20. Dodgson was involved in the foundation of similar training institutes in Chester and Ripon and spoke strongly in favor of such institutions.

21. "Croft," *Yorkshire Gazette*, 26 October 1844, 6.

22. Rev. C. Dodgson, *The Controversy of Faith: Advice to Candidates for Holy Orders on the Case of Gorham v. the Bishop of Exeter* (London: John Murray, 1850), 94–95.

23. A magic lantern projected images from glass slides. C. L. Dodgson may have first encountered the magic lantern in *The Boy's Own Book*, a gift from his aunt Lucy Lutwidge on his ninth birthday. The book includes a description of magic lanterns and of a particular sort of magic lantern show called a "Phantasmagoria." Dodgson would later use this term for his first collection of poetry (1869) and its title poem about a ghost.

24. Leslie Wenham, *The History of Richmond School, Yorkshire* (Arbroath: Herald Press, 1958), 167; hereafter cited parenthetically in the chapter text.

25. "The Rev. Jas. Tate, A.M.," *York Herald*, 16 September 1843, 3.

26. James Tate II, MS notebooks, Lovett Collection. Tate knew of theological and doctrinal controversies of the day, though it is unlikely that he discussed these with his students. His notes reference Puseyism, baptismal regeneration, and contain a page with the headings "High say," and "Low say." One passage reads: "We cannot always be engaged in the investigation of doctrine or striving for Truth. Let us [?] in the comfort of an established creed, in natural and happy reflections which arise from a consideration of the Prayer."

27. [Robert Bell], "Vanity Fair," *Fraser's Magazine for Town and Country* 38 (September 1848): 320.

28. E[dward] Bickersteth, *The Christian Student* (Boston: Perkins and Marvin, 1830), 31.

29. Ibid., 110–11.

30. Ibid., 116.

31. This advice was echoed by Dodgson's Rugby headmaster Archibald Campbell Tait, who told his charges on 6 March 1847: "Books thus read for amusement may have a very bad effect in the mind from some great fault in them: of that amusement in our leisure hours we can have no right to seek by means which will become injurious to us in our more serious hours" (Tait MS 350, Lambeth Palace Library).

32. William Pratt, *A Physician's Sermon to Young Men* (London: Balliere, Tindall, and Cox [1872]), 14–15.

33. Ibid., 15.

34. J. B. Birtwhistle, *"We Preach Christ Crucified": A Farewell Sermon, Preached in the Parish Church of Richmond, Yorkshire, on Sunday Evening, August 4, 1844* (Richmond: Matthew Bell, [1844]), 3; hereafter cited parenthetically in the chapter text.

35. F. Scott Surtees, *Education for the People: A Letter Addressed to the Lord Bishop of Ripon* (London: George Bell, 1846), 6–7; hereafter cited parenthetically in the chapter text.

36. "Sermons for the People," *Leeds Intelligencer,* 1 November 1845, 5.

37. F. Scott Surtees, *Sermons for the People, No. I* (London: George Bell, [1845]), 8; hereafter cited parenthetically in the chapter text.

4. Brought Up to Godliness

1. The chapter's title is from "The Collect for the Founder," in *The Book of Rugby School* (N.p., 1856), [90].

2. Founded in 1567 through the will of Lawrence Sheriff, Rugby was one of nine original public schools (boys' boarding schools at which admission is not limited to a geographic region).

3. Randall Thomas Davidson and William Benham, *Life of Archibald Campbell Tait* (London: Macmillan, 1891), 112.

4. Arthur Penrhyn Stanley, *The Life and Correspondence of Thomas Arnold, D.D.* (London: B. Fellowes, 1844), 97.

5. Ibid., 84.

6. Leslie Stephen, ed., *Dictionary of National Biography* (New York: Macmillan, 1885), vol. 2, 114.

7. The broad church movement, of which Arnold was a leading proponent, was not so much a middle ground between evangelicals and the Oxford Movement as it was a liberal approach that made room for both under the umbrella of the church. Broad churchmen thought that many matters of doctrine should be left to the individual to decide rather than imposed by church authority.

8. Davidson and Benham, *Life of Archibald Campbell Tait,* 83.

9. Ibid., 121.

10. Ibid., 6.

11. Butler matriculated on 22 March 1850; Dodgson, on 23 May 1850.

12. Dodgson was the recipient of Tait's forgiveness in April 1849 when he returned late from an excursion. "Dr. Tait was satisfied with our reason," he wrote his sister (*Letters* 9).

13. One peculiar idea of justice at Rugby was echoed in *Wonderland.* In his book *The Three Friends* (London: Henry Froude, 1900), Butler, writing of how, at Rugby, a punishment was inflicted before an appeal could be carried out, stated "that 'punishment first, appeal afterwards,' was the ancient rule and order of the School" (73). In *Wonderland* this rule becomes the Queen of Hearts' cry of "Sentence first—verdict afterwards."

14. Davidson and Benham, *Life of Archibald Campbell Tait,* 140–43.

15. Henry (b. 28 November 1845) was nearly two years younger than C. L. Dodgson and entered Rugby in the Fourth Form. Like Dodgson, he lived in School House and had G. E. L. Cotton as his tutor.

16. Stanley, *The Life and Correspondence of Thomas Arnold,* vol. 1, 145.

17. [Mrs. Charlotte Bickersteth Wheeler], *Memoir of John Lang Bickersteth, late of Rugby School* (London: Religious Tract Society, 1850), 30. C. L. Dodgson had a copy of this book in his library.

18. Dodgson detested the practice of assigning "lines," that is, the copying out of lines of Latin, as punishment: "I spent an incalculable time in writing out impositions—this last I consider one of the chief faults of Rugby School" (*Life* 30).

19. Butler, *The Three Friends,* 17.

20. A. C. Tait, *Lessons for School Life: Being a Selection from Sermons Preached in the Chapel of Rugby School during His Head Mastership* (London: Hamilton, Adams, 1850), 228–29; hereafter cited parenthetically in the chapter text.

21. Davidson and Benham, *Life of Archibald Campbell Tait,* 143.

22. "Robberies at Rugby School," *Northampton Mercury,* 23 December 1847, 2.

23. [Wheeler], *Memoir of John Lang Bickersteth,* 30.

24. Dodgson Family Collection, Surrey History Center (DFC A/2).

25. Information about class rank and masters comes from the Rugby School Lists of 1846–49.

26. George Edward Lynch Cotton, *Short Prayers and Helps to Devotion for the Boys of a Public School* (London: Longmans, Green, 1872), [1]. No copy has been traced of the original edition. The preface to the new edition states, "in this edition there is no fresh matter added."

27. "Rugby School," *Leamington Spa Courier,* 9 December 1848, 4.

28. Tait MS 346, Lambeth Palace Library.

29. Tait MS 352, Lambeth Palace Library.

30. Tait MS 350, Lambeth Palace Library.

31. Tait MS 356, Lambeth Palace Library.

32. Tait MS 351. Lambeth Palace Library.

33. Tait MS 356. Lambeth Palace Library.

34. Tait MS 350, Lambeth Palace Library.

35. [Wheeler], *Memoir of John Lang Bickersteth,* 31.

36. Ibid., 41.

37. Ibid., 46.

38. Psalm 39:6 as worded in The Order for the Burial of the Dead, Book of Common Prayer.

39. Another possible link between the *Alice* books and Dodgson's Rugby years came in the 1 May 1847 issue of the local newspaper, the *Rugby Monthly Advertiser.* The poem "Speak Gently," later attributed to the American poet David Bates, appears on page 1. Dodgson parodied this poem ("Speak roughly to your little boy . . .") in *Wonderland.* The poem has a hazy history but was apparently first included in a collection by Bates in 1849, so this may be a very early printing.

40. Dodgson had his first brush with royalty at Rugby. In October 1847, an article in the *Rugby Monthly Advertiser* (transcribed in the Warwickshire County Library) titled "The Queen at Rugby" reported: "The Queen was expected at Rugby on Monday and for the space of three hours the whole School, amounting to about 500 boys, were awaiting the arrival . . . at the station. However they were doomed to disappointment. The next day, nothing disheartened, although there was a dismal rain falling all the time, they again took their post to greet their Sovereign. Her Majesty arrived about three o'clock, and the shouts of the boys were prolonged with enthusiasm. . . . The special train stopped seven or eight minutes, during which time Her Majesty graciously acknowledged the cheering and applause bestowed upon her."

41. Peter Gray, "National Humiliation and the Great Hunger: Fast and Famine in 1847," *Irish Historical Studies* 32, no. 126 (November 2000): 193.

42. "The General Fast," *Yorkshire Gazette*, 20 March 1847, 2.

43. "Rugby School," *Reading Mercury*, 22 August 1846, 4.

44. Tait MS 356, Lambeth Palace Library.

45. Typed excerpts of letters from Frances Jane Dodgson to Lucy Lutwidge in Dodgson Family Collection, Surrey History Center (DFC/E/1/1–3).

46. William Benham, *Catharine and Crauford Tait, Wife and Son of Archbishop Archibald Campbell Tait of Canterbury: A Memoir* (London: Macmillan, 1879), 17; hereafter cited parenthetically in the chapter text.

47. Davidson and Benham, *Life of Archibald Campbell Tait*, 144.

48. In an interview about Lewis Carroll in the *Westminster Budget* (9 December 1898, 23), Collingwood stated that "Rugby almost crushed him; his shy and sensitive nature could not stand the ways of public school, and he said afterwards that he did not think he could endure the horrors of his school life again."

49. Dodgson Family Collection, Surrey History Center (DFC A/2).

50. Tait MS 359, Lambeth Palace Library.

51. George Edward Lynch Cotton, *Short Prayers and Helps to Devotion for the Boys of a Public School* (London: Longmans, Green, 1872), 3–4.

5. Come to Years of Discretion

1. See *Manchester Courier and General Advertiser*, 17 May 1856, 1. The pamphlet was priced, in many of the advertisements, not just individually but also by the hundred.

2. Untitled review, *Literary Churchman*, 29 November 1856, 469.

3. Rev. Charles Dodgson, *The Controversy of Faith: Advice to Candidates for Holy Orders on the Case of Gorham v. the Bishop of Exeter* (London: John Murray, 1850), 89–91.

4. Rev. Charles Dodgson, untitled remarks made on 29 November 1841, in "Chester Diocesan Board of Education," *Manchester Courier and Lancashire General Adviser*, 4 December 1841, 2.

5. Rev. Charles Dodgson, *Confirmation: A Plain Catechism, Intended Chiefly for the Instruction of Young Persons before Confirmation*, 12th ed. (Warrington:

J. Haddock; London: Rivington, n.d.), 9; hereafter cited parenthetically in the chapter text.

6. The wording here is from the catechism in the Book of Common Prayer.

7. "Note to the Article on 'The Anglican System,'" *Dublin Review* 12 (May 1842): 558.

8. All Saints Daresbury Churchwardens' minutes.

9. Arthur Penrhyn Stanley, *The Life and Correspondence of Thomas Arnold, D.D.* (London: B. Fellowes, 1844), vol. 1, 145.

10. Thomas Arnold, *Sermons Preached in the Chapel of Rugby School with An Address before Confirmation* (London: B. Fellowes, 1845), 280–81.

11. Untitled note in *Royal Leamington Spa Courier and Warwickshire Standard,* 24 May 1845, 2.

12. Tait MS 352, Lambeth Palace Library.

13. Ibid.

14. A. C. Tait, *Four Sermons Connected with Confirmation, Preached in the Chapel of Rugby School* (Rugby: Printed by Crossley and Billington, 1847), [1]; hereafter cited parenthetically in the chapter text.

15. Highton's book (*Religious Teachings: Being Sermons Preached on Various Occasions, and Short Addresses to Boys at a Public School* [London: John W. Parker, 1849]) was attacked in *The Guardian* by an anonymous reviewer who wrote that Rugby had become "a refuge for heresy and latitudinarianism" (quoted in Davidson and Benham, *Life of Archibald Campbell Tait* [London: Macmillan, 1891], 153).

16. Davidson and Benham, *Life of Archibald Campbell Tait,* 152–53.

17. Lewis Carroll Scrapbook (Library of Congress), image 30. The image and obituary were published in the *Illustrated London News,* 10 November 1866, 461. Cotton had gone on to become bishop of Calcutta and was killed when he fell into the Ganges River.

18. Mrs. [Sophia Anne] Cotton, ed., *Memoir of George Edward Lynch Cotton* (London: Longmans, Green, 1871), 11.

19. Ibid., 14.

20. [Thomas Hughes], *Tom Brown's School Days* (Cambridge: Macmillan, 1857), 404–5.

21. George Edward Lynch Cotton, *Instructions in the Doctrine and Practice of Christianity Intended Chiefly as an Introduction to Confirmation,* 3rd ed. (London: Longmans, 1853), vii; hereafter cited parenthetically in the chapter text. Dodgson owned the 1845 first edition, of which no copy has been traced.

22. Tait's *Four Sermons,* [1] states: "My object will have been gained, if any are enabled . . . better to understand or arrange what has, during the last six or seven weeks, been explained to them privately." This preparation started in early April, as Tait wrote, in a sermon preached on 16 May "five weeks have past of our preparing for Confirmation" (42).

23. The Tractarians disapproved of extemporaneous prayer in *worship,* believing it introduced the possibility of heresy to veer from the proscribed liturgy; evangelicals tended to support extemporaneous prayer.

24. Rev. Charles Dodgson, *The Sacraments of the Gospel: Two Sermons, Preached in Ripon Cathedral, on Jan. 3, and Jan. 17, 1864,* 2nd ed. (London: Rivington, 1864), 12.

25. Luke 12:20.

26. Lewis Carroll, *Sylvie and Bruno* (London: Macmillan, 1889), xiii.

27. See, for instance, Rev. C. Dodgson's writing on the subject (see pp. 9–18 in this volume) and Edward Parker's *The Doctrine of Baptismal Regeneration as Explained by the Tractarians, Refuted and Exposed,* published just before this sermon. A review in *Western Times,* 24 April 1847, 8, wrote of Parker's "exposure of Tractarian duplicity, and equivocation, and falsehood."

6. This Thy Table

1. Tait MS 352/3, Lambeth Palace Library.

2. Rev. Charles Dodgson, untitled remarks made on 29 November 1841.

3. The Catechism, Book of Common Prayer.

4. Article 28.

5. Rev. C. Dodgson, *What Do the Wicked Eat and Drink in the Lord's Supper? A Sermon* (Leeds: T. Harrison, 1853), 8–9; hereafter cited parenthetically in the chapter text.

6. Rev. Charles Dodgson, *A Charge Delivered to the Clergy and Churchwardens of the Archdeaconry of Richmond at the Visitation, in May 1868* (London: F. & J. Rivington, 1868), 28.

7. Rev. Charles Dodgson, *What Do the Wicked Eat and Drink in the Lord's Supper?,* 19.

8. Rev. Charles Dodgson, *Sacraments of the Gospel,* 52; hereafter cited parenthetically in the chapter text.

9. The quotes in this section are from the Communion service in the Book of Common Prayer.

10. The sermons caused an uproar in Ripon. The dean of the cathedral, William Goode, a leading evangelical, on 31 January delivered a sermon that Dodgson called "a direct and most pointed attack on the two I had preached." C. L. Dodgson owned a copy of Goode's 1856 work *The Nature of Christ's Presence in the Eucharist,* in which he argued the low church position. On 2 February, Rev. Charles Dodgson made a formal complaint to the bishop, and on 4 February Goode made a formal charge against Dodgson for preaching false doctrine. The disagreement was splashed in the papers, and there ensued a lengthy correspondence among Dodgson, Goode, and Longley (published by Dodgson in the second edition of his sermons). The bishop eventually transferred the case from his jurisdiction to that of the archbishop of York, but Goode refused to bring the matter to the archbishop, concluding it, as Dodgson noted, by "writing a Pamphlet."

11. F. Scott Surtees, *Sermons for the People, No. I* (London: George Bell, [1845]), 72.

12. Ibid., 72–73.

13. A. C. Tait, Manuscript of Reading in School Hall September 1848 and 30 September 1849, Lambeth Palace Library.

14. A. C. Tait, Manuscript of Reading in School Hall, 25 November 1849, Lambeth Palace Library.

15. A. C. Tait, Manuscript of Reading in School Hall, 8 April 1849, Lambeth Palace Library.

16. Paraphrased from the Book of Common Prayer.

17. Morton Cohen has covered Dodgson's relationship with Maurice and the latter's influence on Dodgson in his *Lewis Carroll: A Biography* ([New York: Knopf, 1995], 252–56). Dodgson attended the Vere Street Chapel somewhat regularly, though not exclusively, when in London during the years from 1862 to 1868, though the fact that the George MacDonald family attended as well may have been as much of a draw as Maurice. Dodgson's gradual conversion to a broad churchman may have begun with Maurice's preaching and writing. Dodgson's later writings are in sympathy with Maurice's key assertions about God. As Cohen writes (citing Maurice's own *The Life of Frederick Denison Maurice*), "Maurice's principal teaching is that 'the starting point of the Gospel . . . is the absolute Love of God.'"

18. John 15:5: "I am the vine, ye are the branches: He that abideth in me, and I in him, the same bringeth forth much fruit: for without me ye can do nothing." Charles Lutwidge Dodgson invariably quoted from the Authorized Version of the Bible (aka the King James Version). Though the Revised Version was published in 1881 (New Testament) and 1885 (Old Testament), Dodgson preferred the language of the 1611 Authorized Version. In an 1892 letter to Robert William Dale, he wrote, "There must be hundreds, if not thousands, of probable readers of your book, who love the Authorised Version as familiar to them from childhood, and who simply *hate* (as I do) the New Version, with its wanton defacement of some of the loveliest passages in our dear old Bible" (*Letters* 895).

19. Colossians 1:18: "And he is the head of the body, the church: who is the beginning, the firstborn from the dead; that in all *things* he might have the preeminence."

20. Charles T. Bateman, "'Lewis Carroll' as Preacher," *The Puritan*, July 1900, 533–34.

21. Ibid., 524.

22. Rev. Charles Dodgson, *"Do the First Works": A Sermon Addressed to the Newly-Ordained Clergy at Ripon, on Trinity Sunday, 1851* (London: Geo. Bell, 1851), 18.

23. Ibid., 19.

24. Rev. Charles Dodgson, *Ritual Worship: A Sermon Preached at the Consecration of the Church of St. Thomas, in Leeds, on the Feast of the Purification of St. Mary, 1852* (Leeds: T. Harrison, 1852), 9, 22–23. This sermon elicited a harsh response from Rev. William Randall, who accused Dodgson of unsound doctrine with respect to Absolution and Eucharistic sacrifice in *An Examination of a Sermon, "Ritual Worship"* (London: Thos. Hatchard; Leeds: John Cross, 1852).

25. Rev. Charles Dodgson, *A Charge Delivered to the Clergy and Churchwardens of the Archdeaconry of Richmond, at the Visitation, in May, 1866* (Leeds: Thomas Harrison, 1866), 21.

26. Samuel Wilberforce, *Addresses to the Candidates for Ordination on the Questions in the Ordination Service*, 2nd ed. (Oxford and London: Parker, 1860), 248.

27. Charles T. Bateman, "'Lewis Carroll' as Preacher," *The Puritan*, July 1900, 532.

28. The 1874 Public Worship Regulation Act, introduced by Dodgson's old Rugby headmaster and then archbishop of Canterbury Archibald Campbell Tait, prohibited a wide variety of ornaments and actions. Between 1877 and 1882, four priests were imprisoned under the act (it was not repealed until 1963). Dodgson referred to the case of Sidney Faithorn Green, imprisoned for twenty months.

29. Lewis Carroll, "Traitors in the Camp," *St. James's Gazette,* 24 December 1881, 11.

30. Ibid., 12.

31. Lewis Carroll, *Sylvie and Bruno Concluded* (London: Macmillan, 1893), xix.

32. "Lewis Carroll: An Interview with His Biographer," *Westminster Budget,* 12 (9 December 1898), 23.

33. Edwin Hatch, *The Organization of the Early Christian Churches,* 4th ed. (London: Longman's Green, 1892), 118–19. Dodgson owned a copy of this book in which Hatch stands up against the high church party. Hatch at the time was vice principal of St. Mary Hall, Oxford. Dodgson was close friends with the entire Hatch family and counted the daughters among his closest "child-friends."

7. Diligent Attendance

1. James Heywood, *Oxford University Statutes* (London: William Pickering, 1851), vol. 2, 279.

2. "The Magazines," *Morning Post,* 3 June 1850, 3.

3. This copy of the statutes (dated 1849) was still in Dodgson's library at the time of his death. He also owned copies of the statues from 1856, 1872, and 1882, the later issues reflecting many reforms.

4. R. W. Church, *The Oxford Movement: Twelve Years, 1833–1845* (London: Macmillan, 1892), 133.

5. The Latin form of prayers, for which Christ Church had a special dispensation, was replaced by the English service.

6. Henry L. Thompson, *Henry George Liddell D.D. Dean of Christ Church, Oxford: A Memoir* (New York: Henry Holt, 1899), 152–53.

7. The cathedral served as the college chapel.

8. "Notes on Religious Education at Christ Church," in *Appendix to the First Report of the Cathedral Commissioners, Appointed November 10, 1852* (London: Lyre and Spottiswoode, 1854), 773; hereafter cited parenthetically in the chapter text.

9. Morton Cohen, *Lewis Carroll: A Biography* (New York: Knopf, 1995), 535–36; hereafter cited parenthetically in the chapter text.

10. The equivalent of a Fellow at other colleges. Collingwood writes, "The only conditions on which these old Studentships were held were that the Student should remain unmarried and should proceed to Holy Orders. No statute precisely defined what work was expected of them" (*Life* 52).

11. In the year that Dodgson arrived at Oxford, the academic calendar included four terms (Hilary or Lent Term from 14 January to 23 March; Easter and Act Term

from 10 April to 18 May; Trinity Term from 23 May to 6 July; and Michaelmas Term from 10 October to 17 December).

12. Rev. Charles Dodgson, *"Do the First Works": A Sermon Addressed to the Newly-Ordained Clergy at Ripon, on Trinity Sunday, 1851* (London: Geo. Bell, 1851), 9–13.

13. Ibid., 20.

14. Rev. Charles Dodgson, untitled speech, 11 February 1854, [reported in the third person], in "The Society for the Employment of Additional Curates in Populous Places: Meeting in Ripon," *Leeds Intelligencer*, 11 February 1854, 7.

15. Rev. Charles Dodgson, *A Charge Delivered to the Clergy and Churchwardens of the Archdeaconry of Richmond, at His Primary Visitation, in May 1855* (London: F. and J. Rivington, 1855), 37.

16. Claude Martin Blagden, in *Lewis Carroll Interviews and Recollections*, ed. Morton N. Cohen (Iowa City: University of Iowa Press, 1989), 65.

8. Learning and Godly Conversation

1. Samuel Wilberforce, *Addresses to the Candidates for Ordination on the Questions in the Ordination Service*, 2nd ed. (Oxford and London: Parker, 1860), 16; hereafter cited parenthetically. Dodgson almost certainly heard Wilberforce give these addresses and had a copy of one of the 1860 editions in his library (probably the second).

2. Rev. Charles Dodgson, *A Sermon Preached in the Minster at Ripon, on Sunday Jan. 15, 1837, at the First Ordination Held by the Right Rev. Chas. Thomas Longley, D.D. Lord Bishop of Ripon* (Oxford: J. H. Parker, 1837), 10–13.

3. Rev. Charles Dodgson, *A Sermon Preached in Ripon Minster, at the Ordination Held by the Lord Bishop of Ripon, on Sunday, July 29th, 1838* (Warrington: Haddock, 1838), 4.

4. Rev. Charles Dodgson, *A Charge Delivered to the Clergy and Churchwardens of the Archdeaconry of Richmond, at the Visitation, in May, 1859* (London: F. and J. Rivington, 1859), 30.

5. Rev. C. Dodgson, *A Sermon Preached at Ripon* (1837), 23.

6. Edward Burton, *Lectures upon the Ecclesiastical History of the First Three Centuries: From the Crucifixion of Jesus Christ to the Year 313*, 4th ed. (Oxford: John Henry Parker, 1855). Dodgson had a copy of this edition in his library. Burton was a canon of Christ Church, Oxford, who died in 1836.

7. "Death of Canon Heurtley," *Oxford Journal*, 4 May 1895, 8.

8. John Pearson, *An Exposition of the Creed*, 3rd ed., rev. and corrected by Rev. E. Burton (Oxford: At the University Press, 1847), xi–xii; hereafter cited parenthetically in the chapter text. Dodgson owned a copy of this edition.

9. Untitled review of *The Exposition of The Creed by John Pearson Abridged for the Use of Young Persons,* by the Rev. C. Burney, *Monthly Review*, May 1810, 88–91.

10. These include *A Short Exposition on the Creed* and a series of thirty-three sermons. Isaac Barrow (1579–1640) was a mathematician as well as a theologian. His work on the Creed was similar in scope to that of Pearson. Barrow was one of the

theologians recommended by the bishop of Oxford, Samuel Wilberforce, in his *Addresses to the Candidates for Ordination.*

11. Thomas Jackson (1579–1640) was an Oxford theologian who wrote twelve volumes of commentaries on the Creed, published from 1613 to 1657. Late in life he became an Arminian, a theological group that can be seen as the precursors to the high churchmen of Dodgson's era.

12. William Ince, in the introductory "Memoir," in Charles Abel Heurtley, *Wholesome Words Sermons on Some Important Points of Christian Doctrine* (London, Longmans, Green, 1896), xxxviii.

13. John William Burgon, *Lives of Twelve Good Men,* 4th ed. (London: John Murray, 1889), vol. 2, 263.

14. Ibid., vol. 2, 263–64.

15. Ibid., vol. 2, 265–66.

16. Ibid., vol. 2, 265.

17. Martin Joseph Routh (1755–1854).

18. Burgon, *Lives of Twelve Good Men,* vol. 2, 265.

19. "Diocese of Oxford," *Berkshire Chronicle,* 3 August 1861, 4.

20. Canon 34, Canons Ecclesiastical of the Church of England.

21. MS: Oxford Diocesan Archives. This was a standard form of testimonial letter. The one for Charles's father's ordination as priest (dated 28 April 1825) differs only in two phrases. Charles Waldegrave Sandford was senior censor of Christ Church, and Francis Hayward Joyce was junior censor. The censors act as assistants to the dean, especially in matters of discipline. Both Sandford and Joyce became Students of Christ Church in 1848, two years before Dodgson's arrival, so he had known both for more than a decade.

22. MS: Oxford Diocesan Archives.

23. "Ecclesiastical Notices," *Ecclesiastical Gazette,* 12 November 1861, 117.

24. James Russell Woodford, *Ordination Lectures Delivered in the Chapel of Cuddesdon College* (Oxford and London: J. H. and Jas. Parker, 1861), states on the title page that the ordination lectures were delivered on "May 20, 21, 22, 1861 being the First Three Days of Ember Week." These dates were Monday, Tuesday, and Wednesday.

25. George William Daniell, *Bishop Wilberforce* (London: Methuen, 1891), 49–51.

26. Burgon, *Lives of Twelve Good Men,* vol. 2, 23–24.

27. A. R. Ashwell, *Life of the Right Reverend Samuel Wilberforce, D.D.* (New York: Dutton, 1883), 339. Wilberforce wrote the day after the ordination, "As Woodford beautifully said in his sermon yesterday, there was not a house where there was not, as it were, 'one dead'" (Reginald G. Wilberforce, *Life of the Right Reverend Samuel Wilberforce* [London: John Murray, 1882], vol. 3, 43).

28. Articles of Religion, VI.

29. Wilberforce, *Addresses to the Candidates for Ordination,* 201–2.

30. Rev. Charles Dodgson, *Controversy of Faith: Advice to Candidates for Holy Orders on the Case of Gorham v. the Bishop of Exeter* (London: John Murray, 1850), 21.

31. Bulkeley, MS Deacon's examination.

32. John Walton Murray, *Church Order: The Fifth Book of Hooker's Ecclesiastical Polity Arranged in the Way of Question and Answer* (George Herbert: Dublin, 1869), 23.

33. See *Wilts and Gloucestershire Standard*, 5 March 1859, 5.

34. The second edition, published in 1860, and including a thirteenth address, is consistently cited herein. If Dodgson purchased his copy in 1861, he would have owned this edition.

35. Book of Common Prayer, The Ordering of Deacons.

36. In addition to works on his list to be studied for ordination, Wilberforce's reading list consisted of works by Augustine, St. Anselm, and:

Bengel, Johann Albrecht (1687–1752). *Gnomon Novi Testamenti*, or *Exegetical Annotations on the New Testament*. First published in 1742, it was a landmark study of the New Testament.

Trench, Richard Chenevix (1807–1886). *Notes on the Parables of Our Lord* (1847) and *Notes on the Miracles of Our Lord* (1850). Trench had served as curate for Samuel Wilberforce in 1841 and became Wilberforce's examining chaplain in 1845, a position he still held in 1861. Dodgson had at least two books by Trench in his library, though there is no evidence he owned either of those recommended by Wilberforce.

Wordsworth, Chr[istopher], ed. *The New Testament in the Original Greek with Notes and Introduction* (1856–60). Dodgson owned a copy of this work by the nephew of William Wordsworth and a conservative high churchman.

Works of Isaac Barrow (1630–1677), best known as an English mathematician who contributed to the early development of calculus. His theological writings include expositions on the Apostles' Creed, the Lord's Prayer, the Decalogue, and the sacraments.

Works of Robert Sanderson (1587–1663), an English theologian and casuist. His best-known work was *Nine Cases of Conscience Resolved* (1678).

Works of Joseph Butler (1692–1752), an English theologian, philosopher, moralist, and bishop of Durham. Wilberforce specifically referred to his *Analogy of Religion, Natural and Revealed* (1736), an attack on deism and unbelief. Dodgson owned a two-volume edition of *The Works of Joseph Butler* (Oxford: Oxford University Press, 1844).

Works of Jeremy Taylor (1661–1667), English divine, chaplain to Charles I, and bishop of Down and Connor. Dodgson owned a copy of Taylor's *Ductor dubitantium: or, The Rule of Conscience in All her General Measures; Serving as a Great Instrument for the Determination of Cases of Conscience.*

Works of Lancelot Andrewes (1555–1626), an English divine and bishop who oversaw the translation of the Bible under King James.

Johann Karl Ludwig Gieseler (1792–1854). *Church History* published in five volumes from 1824 to 1855.

Joseph Bingham. *Origines ecclesiasticae, or Antiquities of the Christian Church*, published in ten volumes from 1708 to 1722.

37. Woodford, *Ordination Lectures*, 9–10 (quoting from the Book of Common Prayer); hereafter cited parenthetically in the chapter text.

38. Years after his ordination as a deacon, Dodgson would dispute this obligation with Henry Liddon (see p. 188 in this volume).

39. At the ordination service on Sunday, 22 December, twenty-two men were ordained priests and twenty-five, deacons.

40. Charles Lutwidge Dodgson certificate of Ordination, Dodgson Family Collection, Surrey History Center, DFC/A/4/1.

41. Canon 36, Canons Ecclesiastical of the Church of England.

9. Fresh from God's Hands

1. Lewis Carroll, *Alice's Adventures Under Ground* (London: Macmillan, 1886), [v].

2. Morton N. Cohen, *Lewis Carroll's Photographs of Nude Children* (Philadelphia: Rosenbach Foundation, 1978), 18.

3. According to Collingwood, the first day on which the new English service was read was Dodgson's twentieth birthday, 27 January 1862 (*Life* 92).

4. In his squib *The New Method of Evaluation as Applied to* π (1865), Dodgson related the entire history of the Jowett controversy as a pseudomathematical paper. He called *Essays and Reviews* "a locus possessing length and breadth, but no depth." Of Jowett's religious unorthodoxy, Dodgson wrote "in an earlier age of mathematics J would probably have been referred to rectangular axes, and divided into two unequal parts."

5. He also owned a copy of the offprint of E. B. Pusey's condemnation of *Essays and Reviews*, reprinted from *The Guardian* of 6 March 1861.

6. W[illiam] Thomson, ed., *Aids to Faith: A Series of Theological Essays by Several Writers Being a Reply to "Essays and Reviews"* (London: John Murray, 1861), [iii].

7. The German scholar and diplomat Christian Charles Josias, Baron von Bunsen (1791–1860), spent much of his later life in England and wrote extensively on biblical and other ancient history.

8. Josef L. Altholz, "The Mind of Victorian Orthodoxy: Responses to 'Essays and Reviews,' 1860–1864," *Church History* 51, no. 2 (June 1982): 186–97.

9. "The Bishop of Salisbury vs. Dr. Rowland Williams," *London Daily News*, 10 August 1861, 2.

10. The title was taken from the work by Hannah More, which Dodgson probably read as a child (see p. 44 in this volume).

11. "The Shepherd of Salisbury Plain," *Punch* 42 (1 February 1862): 47.

12. "Sequel to the Shepherd of Salisbury Plain," found in 1952 by Duncan Black in a scrapbook assembled by Dodgson's friend and colleague Thomas Vere Bayne, Christ Church, Oxford.

13. "The Commemoration," *Jackson's Oxford Journal*, 5 July 1862, 5.

14. E. B. Pusey, *Sermons Preached before the University of Oxford between A.D. 1859 and 1872* (Oxford: James Parker, 1872), 35; hereafter cited parenthetically in the chapter text.

15. Lewis Carroll, "Alice on the Stage," *The Theatre*, April 1887, 180.

16. Ibid.

17. Samuel Wilberforce, *Addresses to the Candidates for Ordination on the Questions in the Ordination Service,* 2nd ed. (Oxford and London: Parker, 1860), 9.

18. Rev. C. Dodgson, *The Sacraments of the Gospel: Two Sermons, Preached in Ripon Cathedral, on Jan. 3, and Jan. 17, 1864,* 2nd ed. (London: Rivington, 1864), 52.

19. Probably near the seaside—at the time her husband, Henry Arbuthnot Feilden, was chaplain of St. Raphael's Convalescent Home, Torquay.

20. C. L. Dodgson to Mrs. Fielden, 21 August 1885, MS, Lovett Collection.

21. Lewis Carroll, *To All Child-readers of "Alice's Adventures in Wonderland"* (N.p., 1871), 2–3.

22. Hebrews 12:2.

23. Morton N. Cohen, *Lewis Carroll: A Biography* (New York: Knopf, 1995), 542.

24. "A Letter from Wonderland," *Critic* 29 (5 March 1898): 166–67.

25. Malachi 4:2.

26. Lewis Carroll, *An Easter Greeting to Every Child Who Loves "Alice"* (N.p., 1876), [2–3].

27. Lewis Carroll, *Sylvie and Bruno* (London: Macmillan, 1889), xiii; hereafter cited parenthetically in the chapter text.

28. The poem is a clever acrostic on the dedicatee, the child actress Isa Bowman. Not only does Carroll spell out Isa's name with the first letter of each line, but also with the first three letters of each stanza.

29. See pp. 224–25 in this volume for more information on the latter two.

30. Lewis Carroll, *Sylvie and Bruno Concluded* (London: Macmillan, 1893), x; hereafter cited parenthetically in the chapter text.

31. W[illiam] H[enry] H[ewett], "The Late Lewis Carroll: A Great Humorist and a Devout Churchman," *Eastbourne Gazette,* 19 January 1898, 3.

32. Allen had been rector of Christ Church, Eastbourne, from 1877 to 1890, and so already knew Dodgson, who began his annual visits to Eastbourne in 1877 and for whom Christ Church was his usual place of worship.

33. This first story is a retelling of the poem "Little Christel," by William Brighty Rands. Dodgson owned a copy of Rands's anonymous book *Lilliput Levee,* in which the poem appeared in 1864, after the dream narrative of Alice had been told, but before it was published. The poem also appeared (attributed to "Anon") in Cecil Frances Alexander's collection *The Sunday Book of Poetry,* of which Dodgson owned a copy.

34. Dodgson heard Jenny Lind sing on 18 March 1856 and had a conversation with the famous Swedish Nightingale at a fête on 25 June 1864.

35. Versions of this anecdote appeared at least as early as 1848. It was widely copied (and broadly adapted) in many of her biographies and in the periodical press.

36. According to Dodgson's diary, he encountered the Florence Nightingale anecdote in *Home Words for Heart and Hearth,* the parish magazine for Christ Church, Eastbourne. This magazine was published nationally and included local information bound in.

37. The ante-penultimate stanza of Coleridge's *The Rime of the Ancient Mariner.*

38. Charles Lutwidge Dodgson, "Address by the Rev. C. L. Dodgson at St. Mary Magdalen Church," *S. Mary Magdalen, St. Leonards,* November 1897, [1–2].

10. Preach the Gospel

1. Rev. Charles Dodgson, *Sermon Preached in the Minster at Ripon, on Sunday Jan. 15, 1837, at the First Ordination Held by the Right Rev. Chas. Thomas Longley, D.D. Lord Bishop of Ripon* (Oxford: J. H. Parker, 1837), 7.

2. Charles Lutwidge Dodgson, "Life of Richard Hakluyt," in *Pamphlets of Lewis Carroll*, ed. Charlie Lovett, vol. 6: *A Miscellany of Works on Alice, Theatre, Religion, Science, and More* (New York: Lewis Carroll Society of North America, 2020), 505–6.

3. "University Intelligence," in *Oxford University and City Herald* (19 November 1859), 8. The manuscripts of these speeches are preserved in the archive of the Ashmolean Natural History Society at the Bodleian Library, Oxford. They were first published in *Pamphlets of Lewis Carroll*, ed. Lovett, vol. 6: *Miscellany*.

4. "University Intelligence," *Oxford University and City Herald*, 14 November 1860, 8.

5. First published as "Feeding the Mind" in *Oxford Magazine and Church Advocate* 2, no. 14 (December 1861): 51–54. Quotes are from this version. In 1884, Dodgson delivered a slightly different version of this talk at the vicarage in Alfreton, Derbyshire, at the request of his friend Rev. W. H. Draper. He gave Draper a fair copy of the talk, which was published posthumously.

6. "Prefatory Address," *Oxford Magazine and Church Advocate* 2 (December 1861): [vii].

7. "Ore Working Men's Institute," *Surrey Gazette*, 16 April 1861, 4.

8. The Additional Curates' Aid Society raised funds to hire curates to assist overworked parish priests. Archdeacon Dodgson addressed a meeting of the society in March 1868.

9. L. F. Salzman, *A History of the County of Oxford: Volume 4* (London: Victoria County History, 1939), British History Online, 26 March 2021, www.british-history .ac.uk/vch/oxon/vol1.

10. Ibid.

11. Ibid.

12. Dodgson had hoped to publish *Alice* on 4 July 1865, but, finding that the illustrator John Tenniel was dissatisfied with the quality of the printing of the first edition and agreeing, Dodgson insisted on the book's being reprinted. He received his first copy of the new impression on 9 November, and on 18 November 1865 an advertisement appeared in *The Examiner* (16) stating that *Alice's Adventures in Wonderland* was "published this day."

13. Henry Parry Liddon, *The Russian Journal—II: A Record Kept by Henry Parry Liddon of a Tour Taken with C. L. Dodgson in the Summer of 1867*, ed. Morton N. Cohen (New York: Lewis Carroll Society of North America, 1979), 7; hereafter cited parenthetically in the chapter text.

14. Book of Common Prayer, Concerning the Service of the Church.

15. Samuel Wilberforce, *Addresses to the Candidates for Ordination on the Questions in the Ordination Service*, 2nd ed. (Oxford and London: Parker, 1860), 194.

16. Psalm 107:30.

17. Anne Clark Amor, *Lewis Carroll, Child of the North* (Croft: Lewis Carroll Society, 1995), 84. This contains a description of the days of grieving and of Archdeacon Dodgson's funeral and burial.

18. This is on evidence of the published letters only.

19. Thomas Prout was a Student of Christ Church, a friend of Dodgson, and vicar of Binsey, a small parish just outside Oxford.

20. Herbert Salway was a Student of Christ Church.

21. William Warner, Student of Christ Church.

22. In a letter of 1890, Dodgson calls his brother Edwin an "extreme 'Ritualist'" (*Letters* 815).

23. Morton N. Cohen, *Interviews and Recollections* (Iowa City: University of Iowa Press, 1989), 53.

24. An Undergraduate, "'Lewis Carroll' at Christ Church," *Eastbourne Gazette*, 19 January 1898.

25. Rev. Charles Dodgson, *"Preach the Gospel": A Sermon, Preached in Ripon Minster at the Ordination Held by the Lord Bishop of Ripon, on Sunday, January 13, 1839* (London: Rivington, 1839), 7–8, 14.

26. Paraphrase of Ps. 51:10 "Create in me a clean heart, O God; and renew a right spirit within me."

27. MS notebook of James Tate II.

28. Wilberforce, *Addresses to the Candidates for Ordination*, 13–14, 53.

29. Lewis Carroll, *Sylvie and Bruno Concluded* (London: Macmillan, 1893), xix.

30. Charles T. Bateman, "'Lewis Carroll' as Preacher," *The Puritan*, July 1900, 532.

31. Cohen, *Interviews and Recollections*, 41; hereafter cited parenthetically in the chapter text.

32. Bateman, "'Lewis Carroll' as Preacher," 529.

33. John 15:5: I am the vine, ye are the branches: He that abideth in me, and I in him, the same bringeth forth much fruit: for without me ye can do nothing.

34. Colossians 1:18: And he is the head of the body, the church: who is the beginning, the firstborn from the dead; that in all *things* he might have the preeminence.

35. These words and those above ("By His blood to cleanse, by His Spirit to sanctify") echo words near the end of the Prayer of Humble Access in the Communion Service in the Book of Common Prayer: "that our sinful bodies may be made clean by his body, and our souls washed through his most precious blood."

36. Ephesians 3:20: Now unto him that is able to do exceeding abundantly above all that we ask or think, according to the power that worketh in us.

11. Diligence in Prayer

1. Rev. Charles Dodgson, *Confirmation: A Plain Catechism, Intended Chiefly for the Instruction of Young Persons before Confirmation*, 12th ed. (Warrington: J Haddock; London: Rivington, n.d.), 14; hereafter cited parenthetically in the chapter text.

2. Tait MS 350, Lambeth Palace Library.

3. Ibid.

4. George Edward Lynch Cotton, *Instructions in the Doctrine and Practice of Christianity Intended Chiefly as an Introduction to Confirmation,* 3rd ed. (London: Longmans, 1853), 78–79; hereafter cited parenthetically in the chapter text.

5. George Edward Lynch Cotton, *Short Prayers and Helps to Devotion for the Boys of a Public School* (London: Longmans, Green, 1872), 1–3.

6. Samuel Wilberforce, *Addresses to the Candidates for Ordination on the Questions in the Ordination Service,* 2nd ed. (Oxford and London: Parker, 1860), 144; hereafter cited parenthetically in the chapter text.

7. Morton N. Cohen, *Interviews and Recollections* (Iowa City: University of Iowa Press, 1989), 164.

8. The Prayer of Richard of Chichester reads, in part, "O most merciful Redeemer, friend and brother, May I know Thee more clearly, Love Thee more dearly, Follow Thee more nearly, day by day."

9. Tait MS 26, Lambeth Palace Library.

10. Tait MS 19, Lambeth Palace Library.

11. John Octavius Johnston, *Life and Letters of Henry Parry Liddon* (London: Longmans, Green, 1904), 55.

12. Ibid., 83.

13. Arthur Hugh Clough, *The Oxford Diaries of Arthur Hugh Clough,* ed. Anthony Kenny (Oxford: Clarendon, 1990), 77; hereafter cited parenthetically in the chapter text.

14. Cohen, *Interviews and Recollections,* 65.

15. Liddon's argument was based on the fact that the Book of Common Prayer includes a prayer for "all sorts and conditions of men," and presumably death was merely a condition. Praying for the dead implies that the condition of the soul after death is not fixed, but capable of improvement, a doctrine to which Dodgson subscribed (see p. 260 in this volume).

16. Dodgson's friend Henry Parry Liddon deals with the "scientific objection to prayer" in his Lent Lectures of 1870, published in 1872 as *Some Elements of Religion* (London: Longmans Green). Dodgson had a copy of this book in his library.

17. Job 40:2.

18. Thomas Gray, "The Curse upon Edward."

19. Matthew 7:7.

20. Lewis Carroll, *Sylvie and Bruno* (London: Macmillan, 1896), 389–92.

12. In His Holy Ways

1. Morton N. Cohen, *Lewis Carroll Interviews and Recollections* (Iowa City: University of Iowa Press, 1989), 39; hereafter cited parenthetically in the chapter text.

2. Isa Bowman, *The Story of Lewis Carroll Told for Young People by the Real Alice in Wonderland* (London: J. M. Dent, 1999), 78.

3. Acts 16:31.

4. Stuart Dodgson Collingwood, *The Lewis Carroll Picture Book* (London: T. Fisher Unwin, 1899), 348.

5. Lewis Caroll, *To All Child-readers of "Alice's Adventures in Wonderland"* (N.p., 1871), 2–3.

6. Rev. Charles Dodgson, *Sermon Preached in the Minster at Ripon, On Sunday Jan. 15, 1837, at the First Ordination Held by the Right Rev. Chas. Thomas Longley, D.D. Lord Bishop of Ripon* (Oxford: J. H. Parker, 1837), 7.

7. Lewis Carroll, *Symbolic Logic Part I: Elementary* (London: Macmillan, 1896), xiii.

8. Lewis Carroll, *A Fascinating Mental Recreation for the Young: Symbolic Logic* [London: Macmillan, 1895], 3.

9. Charles Lutwidge Dodgson, *Curiosa Mathematica: Part II, Pillow-Problems Thought out during Wakeful Hours,* 4th ed. (London: Macmillan, 1895), xv. Dodgson changed "Sleepless Nights" to "Wakeful Hours" in this edition to, he said, avoid the misconception that he suffered from insomnia. The last lines are a reference to Luke 11:24–26.

10. Lewis Carroll, *Sylvie and Bruno* (London: Macmillan, 1889), xiv–xv; hereafter cited parenthetically in the chapter text.

11. Bowman, *The Story of Lewis Carroll,* 68.

12. MS, Dodgson family, Surrey History Center, DFC A/29/5.

13. *The Charities Register and Digest* (London: Longmans Green, 1890), 529.

14. Lewis Carroll, "Education for the Stage," *St. James's Gazette,* 27 February 1882, 5.

15. Charles Lutwidge Dodgson, untitled circular accompanying the prospectus for the School of Dramatic Art (Oxford, 1882). The school opened in October 1882 and closed in 1885. In February 1884, Dodgson made a substantial contribution of £22 to the venture.

16. John Octavius Johnston, *Life and Letters of Henry Parry Liddon* (London: Longmans, Green, 1904), 282.

17. Charles Lutwidge Dodgson, "On Dress," MS: Harvard, published in *The Pamphlets of Lewis Carroll,* vol. 6: *A Miscellany of Works on Alice, Theatre, Religion, Science, and More,* ed. Charlie Lovett, 45–47 (Charlottesville: LCSNA and University of Virginia Press, 2020).

18. Lewis Carroll, "Stage Children," *Sunday Times,* 4 August 1889, 7.

19. Lewis Carroll, "The Stage and the Spirit of Reverence," *The Theatre,* 1 June 1875, 287; hereafter cited parenthetically in the chapter text.

20. Dodgson probably saw this at the Royal Strand Theatre, London, where the play ran from at least 5–22 July 1858 (his diaries for this period are missing).

21. Ezekiel 18:16.

22. John 17:15.

23. Edwin Leonard Naylor, *The Irrepressible Victorian: The Story of Thomas Gibson Bowles* (London: Macdonald, 1965), 56.

24. Charles Lutwidge Dodgson, "An Oxford Scandal," *St. James's Gazette,* 16 December 1890, 12.

25. From *The Sorcerer* by Gilbert and Sullivan. Dodgson saw the original production at the Opera Comique on 14 January 1878 and pronounced it "poor" in his diary.

26. Dodgson saw Gilbert and Sullivan's operetta *H.M.S. Pinafore* performed by the children's company of the Opera Comique on 14 January 1881.

27. Lewis Carroll, *Sylvie and Bruno Concluded* (London: Macmillan 1893), xxii; hereafter cited parenthetically in the chapter text. The phrase "darkness that may be felt" is from Exodus 10:21.

28. Matthew 18:6.

29. Genesis 3:5.

30. Ephesians 5:12.

31. Lewis Carroll, "Whoso Shall Offend One of These Little Ones—," *St. James's Gazette,* 22 July 1885, 6.

32. Edward Monro, *Sermons Principally on the Responsibilities of the Ministerial Office* (Oxford and London: John Henry Parker, 1850), 136–37.

33. Marie Corelli, *A Romance of Two Worlds* (Chicago: Geo. M. Hill, 1898), 279–85.

34. "Two Unimpressive Pamphlets," *Pall Mall Gazette,* 23 July 1888, 2–3.

35. For full transcriptions of all Dodgson's writings on vivisection and an essay discussing their place in the ongoing debate, see *Pamphlets of Lewis Carroll*, ed. Charlie Lovett, vol. 6: *A Miscellany of Works on Alice, Theatre, Religion, Science, and More* (New York: Lewis Carroll Society of America, 2020).

36. Joseph Butler (1692–1752), bishop of Durham, who argued for the resurrection of animals in his 1736 work *The Analogy of Religion.* Dodgson received a copy of Butler's works from his headmaster at Rugby as the Second Divinity Prize in October 1849.

37. Lewis Carroll, "Vivisection as a Sign of the Times," *Pall Mall Gazette,* 12 February 1875, 4.

38. Rev. Charles Dodgson, *A Charge Delivered to the Clergy and Churchwardens of the Archdeaconry of Richmond, at his Primary Visitation, in May 1855* (London: F. and J. Rivington, 1855), 32.

39. Carroll, "Vivisection as a Sign of the Times."

40. *Macbeth,* act 3, scene 4.

41. Lewis Carroll, "Some Popular Fallacies about Vivisection," *Fortnightly Review,* 1 June 1875, 850; hereafter cited parenthetically in the chapter text.

42. Lewis Carroll, "Vivisection Vivisected," *St. James's Gazette,* 19 March 1885, 5–6.

43. That is, a clergyman.

44. That is, a woman. The reference is to Deuteronomy 28:56.

45. 2 Samuel 1:26.

46. Stuart Dodgson Collingwood, *The Lewis Carroll Picture Book* (London: T. Fisher Unwin, 1890), 344.

47. Rev. Charles Dodgson, *A Charge Delivered to the Clergy and Churchwardens of the Archdeaconry of Richmond, at the Visitation, in May, 1859* (London: F. and J. Rivington, 1859), 25–26.

48. Charles Lutwidge Dodgson, "Marriage Service," MS: Harvard, published in *The Pamphlets of Lewis Carroll*, ed. Charlie Lovett, vol. 6: *A Miscellany of Works on Alice, Theatre, Religion, Science, and More* (Charlottesville: LCSNA and University Press of Virginia, 2020), 146–47.

13. Thy Will Be Done

1. The text of Hymn 264 in *Hymns Ancient and Modern,* rev. and enlarged ed. (London: William Clowes and Sons, n.d.), is as follows:

My God, my Father, while I stray,
Far from my home on life's rough way,
O teach me from my heart to say, "Thy Will be done."

Though dark my path, and sad my lot,
Let me be still and murmur not,
Or breathe the prayer divinely taught, "Thy Will be done."

What though in lonely grief I sigh
For friends beloved no longer nigh,
Submissive would I still reply, "Thy Will be done."

If thou shouldst call me to resign
What most I prize, it ne'er was mine;
I only yield Thee what is Thine; "Thy Will be done."

Let but my fainting heart be blest
With thy sweet SPIRIT for its guest,
My God, to Thee I leave the rest; "Thy Will be done."

Renew my will from day to day,
Blend it with Thine, and take away
All that now makes it hard to say, "Thy Will be done."

2. John Julian, ed., *A Dictionary of Hymnology* (New York: Charles Scribners, 1892), 778.

3. The pall was a cloth covering the coffin.

4. Harcourt Amory Collection, Houghton Library, Harvard University, MS Eng 781.11 (4–6).

5. Charles T. Bateman, "'Lewis Carroll' as a Preacher," *The Puritan,* July 1900, 532.

6. "Lewis Carroll's Funeral," *London Daily News,* 20 January 1898, 8.

7. 1 Tim. 6:7, Job 1:21 as quoted in The Order for the Burial of the Dead, Book of Common Prayer.

8. Words: William D. MacLagan (1869); Tune: *Rest,* John Stainer (1875); Hymn #428 in *Hymns Ancient and Modern.*

9. Words: Edward H. Bickersteth, Jr. (1875); Tune: *Pax Tecum,* George T. Caldbeck and Charles John Vincent, Jr. (1876); Hymn 280 in *Hymnal Companion to the Book of Common Prayer,* 3rd ed.

10. John 12:26.

11. Revelation 22:3.

12. Hymn 401 in *Hymns Ancient and Modern,* in the section of hymns for "Burial of the Dead." The tune is *Requiescat* by Rev. J. B. Dykes.

13. Frederick Denison Maurice, *Christmas Day and Other Sermons* (London: Macmillan, 1892), 396–97.

14. 1 Corinthians 15:37, 44.

15. Articles IV (Of the Resurrection of Christ); VII (Of the Old Testament); XVII (Of Predestination and Election); and XXII (Of Purgatory).

16. Luke 23:43.

17. Herbert Mortimer Luckock, *After Death,* 9th ed. (London: Longmans, Green, 1892), 36.

18. E. H. Plumptre, *The Spirits in Prison and Other Studies on the Life after Death* (London: Wm. Isbister, 1884), 25.

19. The society was founded on 20 February 1882 "to investigate that large group of debatable phenomena designated by such terms as mesmeric, psychical, and Spiritualistic" (*Proceedings of the Society for Psychical Research,* vol. 1 [London: Trubner and Co, 1884], 3). The *Journal for the Society for Psychical Research* for March 1898, 200, noted that "The Council recorded with regret the death of Charles L. Dodgson, who had been a Member of the Society almost from its commencement."

20. Henry Drummond, *Natural Law in the Spiritual World* (New York: Hurst, n.d.), 5.

21. Lewis Carroll, *Phantasmagoria* (London: Macmillan, 1869), 153.

22. John B. McClellan, *Everlasting Punishment and the Oxford Declaration of February 25 1864: A Brief Act of Protestation* (London: Macmillan, 1864), [3].

23. John Octavius Johnston, *Life and Letters of Henry Parry Liddon* (London: Longmans, Green, 1904), 197–98.

24. Frederick Denison Maurice, *Theological Essays* (London: Macmillan, 1852), 450. Dodgson had a copy of this book in his library.

25. E. B. Pusey, *What Is of Faith as to Everlasting Punishment? In Reply to Dr. Farrar's Challenge in His "Eternal Hope," 1879* (Oxford: James Parker, 1880), 120.

26. F. Nutcombe Oxenham, *What Is the Truth as to Everlasting Punishment? In Reply to Dr. Pusey's Late Treatise "What Is of Faith as to Everlasting Punishment?"* (New York: Dutton, 1881), 136.

27. The complete text is published in *Pamphlets of Lewis Carroll,* ed. Charlie Lovett, vol. 6: *A Miscellany of Works on Alice, Theatre, Religion, Science, and More* (New York: Lewis Carroll Society of North America, 2020), 174–83; and also in Stuart Dodgson Collingwood, *The Lewis Carroll Picture Book* (London: T. Fisher Unwin, 1899), 345–55.

28. Lewis Carroll, *Sylvie and Bruno Concluded* (London: Macmillan, 1893), 258–61.

Selected Bibliography

All Saints Church, Daresbury. MS Parish registers and churchwardens' minutes.

Amor, Anne Clark. *Lewis Carroll, Child of the North.* Croft: Lewis Carroll Society, 1995.

Arnold, Thomas. *Sermons Preached in the Chapel of Rugby School with an Address before Confirmation.* London: B. Fellowes, 1845.

Ashwell, A. R. *Life of the Right Reverend Samuel Wilberforce, D.D.* New York: Dutton, 1883.

B., A. "Unequal Appropriation of Church Preferment: Another Proof of the Want of Church Reform." *York Herald,* 6 November 1852, 1.

Barker, G. F. Russell, and Alan Stenning, eds. *The Westminster School Register from 1764 to 1883.* London: Macmillan, 1892.

Bateman, Charles T. "'Lewis Carroll' as Preacher." *The Puritan,* July 1900, 529–34.

Benham, Wm., ed. *Catharine and Crauford Tait, Wife and Son of Archbishop Archibald Campbell Tait of Canterbury: A Memoir.* London: Macmillan, 1879.

Bickersteth, E[dward]. *The Christian Student.* Boston: Perkins and Marvin, 1830.

Birch, Joseph. *The Rev. C. Dodgson's New Tests of Orthodoxy: A Letter Addressed to the Right Honourable The Earl of Shaftsbury.* 2nd ed. London: J. H. Jackson, 1853.

Birtwhistle, J. B. *"We Preach Christ Crucified": A Farewell Sermon, Preached in the Parish Church of Richmond, Yorkshire, on Sunday Evening, August 4, 1844.* Richmond: Matthew Bell, [1844].

"The Bishop of Ripon's Questions for Ordination, &c." *Christian Observer,* June 1838, 388–403.

Bowman, Isa. *The Story of Lewis Carroll Told for Young People by the Real Alice in Wonderland.* London: J. M. Dent, 1899.

Bulkeley, Henry John. MS Deacon's Examination. Oxford Diocesan Archives.

Burgon, John William. *Lives of Twelve Good Men.* 4th ed. London: John Murray, 1889.

Burton, Edward. *Lectures upon the Ecclesiastical History of the First Three Centuries: From the Crucifixion of Jesus Christ to the Year 313.* 4th ed. Oxford: John Henry Parker, 1855.

Butler, A. G. *The Three Friends.* London: Henry Froude, 1900.

Carroll, Lewis. "Alice on the Stage." *The Theatre,* April 1887, 179–84.

———. *Alice's Adventures in Wonderland.* London: Macmillan, 1866.

———. *Alice's Adventures Under Ground.* London: Macmillan, 1886.

———. *An Easter Greeting to Every Child Who Loves "Alice."* N.p., 1876.

———. "Education for the Stage." *St. James's Gazette,* 27 February 1882, 5.

———. *A Fascinating Mental Recreation for the Young: Symbolic Logic.* [London: Macmillan, 1895].

———. *The Letters of Lewis Carroll.* Edited by Morton N. Cohen. New York: Oxford University Press, 1979.

———. *Lewis Carroll's Diaries: The Private Journals of Charles Lutwidge Dodgson.* Vols. 1–10. Edited by Edward Wakeling. London: Lewis Carroll Society, 1993–2007.

———. *Phantasmagoria.* London: Macmillan, 1869.

———. "Some Popular Fallacies about Vivisection." *Fortnightly Review,* 1 June 1875, 850.

———. "The Stage and the Spirit of Reverence." *The Theatre,* June 1888, 285–94.

———. "Stage Children." *Sunday Times,* 4 August 1889, 7.

———. *Sylvie and Bruno.* London: Macmillan, 1889.

———. *Sylvie and Bruno Concluded.* London: Macmillan, 1893.

———. *Symbolic Logic Part I: Elementary.* London: Macmillan, 1896.

———. *Through the Looking-Glass and What Alice Found There.* London: Macmillan, 1872.

———. *To All Child-readers of "Alice's Adventures in Wonderland."* N.p., 1871.

———. "Traitors in the Camp." *St. James's Gazette,* 24 December 1881, 11.

———. Untitled circular accompanying the prospectus for the School of Dramatic Art. Oxford, 1882.

———. *Useful and Instructive Poetry.* New York: Macmillan, 1954.

———. "Vivisection as a Sign of the Times." *Pall Mall Gazette,* 12 February 1875, 4.

———. "Vivisection Vivisected." *St. James's Gazette,* 19 March 1885, 5–6.

———. "Whoso Shall Offend One of These Little Ones—." *St. James's Gazette,* 22 July 1885, 6.

Church, R. W. *The Oxford Movement: Twelve Years, 1833–1845.* London: Macmillan, 1892.

Church of England. Book of Common Prayer; Canons of the Church.

Clark, Anne. *Lewis Carroll: A Biography.* New York: Schocken, 1979.

Clergyman of the Diocese. *The Lord Bishop of Ripon's Cobwebs to Catch Calvinists.* London: Simpkin, Marshall, 1838.

Clough, Arthur Hugh. *The Oxford Diaries of Arthur Hugh Clough.* Edited by Anthony Kenny. Oxford: Clarendon, 1990.

Cohen, Morton N. *Lewis Carroll: A Biography.* New York: Knopf, 1995.

———, ed. *Lewis Carroll Interviews and Recollections.* Iowa City: University of Iowa Press, 1989.

——. *Lewis Carroll's Photographs of Nude Children.* Philadelphia: Rosenbach Foundation, 1978.

[Collingwood, Stuart Dodgson.] "Lewis Carroll: An Interview with His Biographer." *Westminster Budget* 12 (9 December 1898).

———. *The Life and Letters of Lewis Carroll*. London: T. Fisher Unwin, 1898.

———, ed. *The Lewis Carroll Picture Book*. London: T. Fisher Unwin, 1899.

Cotton, George Edward Lynch. *Instructions in the Doctrine and Practice of Christianity Intended Chiefly as an Introduction to Confirmation*. 3rd ed. London: Longmans, 1853.

———. *Short Prayers and Helps to Devotion for the Boys of a Public School*. London: Longmans, Green, 1872.

Cotton, Mrs. [Sophia Anne], ed. *Memoir of George Edward Lynch Cotton*. London: Longmans, Green, 1871.

Daniell, George William. *Bishop Wilberforce*. London: Methuen, 1891.

Davidson, Randall Thomas, and William Benham. *Life of Archibald Campbell Tait*. London: Macmillan, 1891.

Dodgson, Rev. Charles. *A Charge Delivered to the Clergy and Churchwardens of the Archdeaconry of Richmond, at His Primary Visitation, in May 1855*. London: F. and J. Rivington, 1855.

———. *A Charge Delivered to the Clergy and Churchwardens of the Archdeaconry of Richmond, at the Visitation, in May, 1859*. London: F. and J. Rivington, 1859.

———. *A Charged Delivered to the Clergy and Churchwardens of the Archdeaconry of Richmond, at the Visitation, in May, 1866*. Leeds: Thomas Harrison, 1866.

———. *A Charge Delivered to the Clergy and Churchwardens of the Archdeaconry of Richmond at the Visitation, in May 1868*. London: F. & J. Rivington, 1868.

———. *Confirmation: A Plain Catechism, Intended Chiefly for the Instruction of Young Persons before Confirmation*. 12th ed. Warrington: J. Haddock; London: Rivington, n.d.

———. *The Controversy of Faith: Advice to Candidates for Holy Orders on the Case of Gorham v. The Bishop of Exeter*. London: John Murray, 1850.

———. *"Do the First Works": A Sermon Addressed to the Newly-Ordained Clergy at Ripon, on Trinity Sunday, 1851*. London: Geo. Bell, 1851.

———. *"Preach the Gospel": A Sermon, Preached in Ripon Minster at the Ordination Held by the Lord Bishop of Ripon, on Sunday, January 13, 1839*. London: Rivington, 1839.

———. *The Providence of God Manifested in the Temporal Condition of the Poorer Clergy: A Sermon Preached in the Collegiate Church of Manchester, On Thursday, July 18th, 1839. At the Meeting of the Society for the Relief of the Widows and Orphans of the Clergy of the Archdeaconry of Chester*. London: J. G. & F. Rivington; Warrington: Haddock, 1839.

———. "The Rev. C. Dodgson on the Ripon Ordination Questions; With Remarks in Reply." *Christian Observer*, August 1838, 485–507.

———. *Ritual Worship: A Sermon Preached at the Consecration of the Church of St. Thomas, in Leeds, on the Feast of the Purification of St. Mary, 1852*. Leeds: T. Harrison, 1852.

———. "The Sabbath a Delight (A Village Sermon)." In *Sermons by XXXIX Living Divines of the Church of England*, 233–48. London: J. Hatchard and Son, 1840.

———. *The Sacraments of the Gospel: Two Sermons, Preached in Ripon Cathedral, on Jan. 3, and Jan. 17, 1864.* 2nd ed. London: Rivington, 1864.

———. *A Sermon Preached in the Minster at Ripon, on Sunday Jan. 15, 1837, at the First Ordination Held by the Right Rev. Chas. Thomas Longley, D.D. Lord Bishop of Ripon.* Oxford: J. H. Parker, 1837.

———. *A Sermon Preached in Ripon Minster, at the Ordination Held by the Lord Bishop of Ripon, on Sunday, July 29th, 1838.* Warrington: Haddock, 1838.

———. *A Short Account of the First Establishment of the Croft National School, in the Year 1845.* Darlington: Coates and Farmer, 1846.

———. Untitled remarks made on 29 November 1841. In "Chester Diocesan Board of Education," *Manchester Courier and Lancashire General Adviser,* 4 December 1841, 2.

———. Untitled speech delivered on 13 April 1849. In "Ripon Diocesan Church Building Society and Board of Education Public Meeting at Leeds," *Leeds Intelligencer,* 28 April 1849, 6.

———. Untitled speech [reported in the third person]. In "The Society for the Employment of Additional Curates in Populous Places: Meeting in Ripon," *Leeds Intelligencer,* 11 February 1854, 7.

———. Untitled speech delivered on 4 December 1860. In "Laying of the Foundation Stone of the Female Training Institution," *Leeds Intelligencer,* 8 December 1860, 6.

———. *What Do the Wicked Eat and Drink in the Lord's Supper? A Sermon.* Leeds: T. Harrison, 1853.

Dodgson, Charles Lutwidge. "Address by the Rev. C. L. Dodgson at St. Mary Magdalen Church." *S. Mary Magdalen, St. Leonards,* November 1897, [1–2].

———. Circular accompanying the prospectus for the School of Dramatic Art. Oxford, 1882.

———. *Curiosa Mathematica: Part II, Pillow-Problems Thought out during Wakeful Hours.* 4th ed. London: Macmillan, 1895.

———. "Directions Regarding My Funeral." Harcourt Amory Collection, Houghton Library, Harvard University. MS Eng 781.11.

[———]. "On Dress." MS: Harvard. Published in *The Pamphlets of Lewis Carroll,* vol. 6: *A Miscellany of Works on Alice, Theatre, Religion, Science, and More,* edited by Charlie Lovett, 45–47. Charlottesville: LCSNA and University of Virginia Press, 2020.

[———]. "Feeding the Mind." *Oxford Magazine and Church Advocate,* December 1861, 51–54.

[———]. "Marriage Service." MS: Harvard. Published in *The Pamphlets of Lewis Carroll,* vol. 6: *A Miscellany of Works on Alice, Theatre, Religion, Science, and More,* edited by Charlie Lovett, 146–47. Charlottesville: LCSNA and University of Virginia Press, 2020.

[———]. Ordination papers, Oxford Diocesan Archive.

———. "An Oxford Scandal," *St. James's Gazette,* 16 December 1890, 12.

Dodgson Family. MS devotional cards. Dodgson Family Collection, Surrey History Center. DFC A/1/2/4–18.

———. Prayer book. MS: Dodgson Family Collection, Surrey History Center, DFC A/1/3.

———. Reading Log, Charles L. Dodgson. MS: Charles L. Dodgson. Dodgson Family Collection, Surrey History Center. DFC A/1/1.

Draper, Bourne Hall. *Bible Illustrations; or, A Description of Manners and Customs Peculiar to the East, Especially Explanatory of the Holy Scriptures.* London: John Harris, 1833.

Edgeworth, Maria. *Early Lessons, In Four Volumes.* London: Printed for R. Hunter, Baldwin and Cradock, etc., 1829.

Hatch, Edwin. *The Organization of the Early Christian Churches.* 4th ed. London: Longmans Green, 1892.

Hessey, James Augustus. *Sunday: Its Origin, History, and Present Obligation, Considered in Eight Lectures Preached before the University of Oxford in the Year MDCCCXL.* 2nd ed. London: John Murray, 1861.

H[ewett], W[illiam] H[enry]. "The Late Lewis Carroll: A Great Humorist and a Devout Churchman." *Eastbourne Gazette,* 19 January 1898, 3.

Heywood, James, ed. *Oxford University Statutes.* London: William Pickering, 1851.

[Hughes, Thomas]. *Tom Brown's School Days.* Cambridge: Macmillan, 1857.

Johnston, John Octavius. *Life and Letters of Henry Parry Liddon.* London: Longmans, Green, 1904.

"Lewis Carroll's Funeral." *London Daily News,* 20 January 1898, 8.

Liddon, Henry Parry. *The Russian Journal—II: A Record Kept by Henry Parry Liddon of a Tour Taken with C. L. Dodgson in the Summer of 1867.* Edited by Morton N. Cohen. New York: Lewis Carroll Society of North America, 1979.

The Lord Bishop of Ripon's Cobwebs to Catch Calvinists: Being a Few Remarks on His Lordship's Questions to Candidates at His Late Ordination at Ripon. London: Simpkin, Marshall; Leeds: John Heaton, 1838.

Lovett, Charlie, ed. *The Pamphlets of Lewis Carroll.* Vol. 6: *A Miscellany of Works on Alice, Theatre, Religion, Science, and More.* New York: Lewis Carroll Society of North America, 2020.

Luckock, Herbert Mortimer. *After Death.* 9th ed. London: Longmans, Green, 1892.

Maurice, Frederick Denison. *Theological Essays.* London: Macmillan, 1852.

McClellan, John B. *Everlasting Punishment and the Oxford Declaration of February 25 1864: A Brief Act of Protestation.* London: Macmillan, 1864.

Mure, James, Henry Bull, and Charles Scott, eds. *Lusus alteri Westmonasterienses: Sive prologi et epilogi.* Oxford: J. Parker, 1863.

———, eds. *Lusus alteri Westmonasterienses: Sive prologi et epilogi: Pars secunda, 1820–1865.* Oxford: J. Parker, 1867.

"Notes on Religious Education at Christ Church." In *Appendix to the First Report of the Cathedral Commissioners, Appointed November 10, 1852.* London: Lyre and Spottiswoode, 1854.

Oxenham, F. Nutcombe. *What Is the Truth as to Everlasting Punishment? In Reply to Dr. Pusey's Late Treatise "What Is of Faith as to Everlasting Punishment?"* New York: Dutton, 1881.

Parley, Peter. *Tales about Europe, Asia, Africa, and America.* 4th ed. London: Thomas Tegg, 1839.

Pearson, John. *An Exposition of the Creed.* 3rd ed. Rev. and corrected by Rev. E. Burton. Oxford: At the University Press, 1847.

Plumptre, E. H. *The Spirits in Prison and Other Studies on the Life after Death.* London: Wm. Isbister, 1884.

Pratt, William. *A Physician's Sermon to Young Men.* London: Balliere, Tindall, and Cox, [1872].

Pusey, E. B. *Sermons Preached before the University of Oxford between A.D. 1859 and 1872.* Oxford: James Parker, 1872.

———. *What Is of Faith as to Everlasting Punishment? In Reply to Dr. Farrar's Challenge in His "Eternal Hope," 1879.* Oxford: James Parker, 1880.

Report from the Select Committee of the House of Lords Appointed to Inquire into the Expediency of Restraining the Practice of Carrying Goods and Merchandize on Canals, Navigable Rivers, and Railways on Sundays. 4 May 1841.

"The Rev. Jas. Tate, A.M., Late Master of Richmond School, Yorkshire," *York Herald,* 16 September 1843, 3.

Rugby School Lists. Rugby: Crossley and Billington, 1846–49.

Salzman, L. F., ed. *A History of the County of Oxford: Volume 4.* London, Victoria County History, 1939. British History Online. 26 March 2021. www.british-history.ac.uk/vch/oxon/vol1.

"Sequel to 'The Shepherd of Salisbury Plain.'" Lewis Carroll Circular, May 1973, [20].

Sherwood, Mrs. *The History of the Fairchild Family.* 6th ed. London: J. Hatchard, 1822.

Stanley, Arthur Penrhyn. *The Life and Correspondence of Thomas Arnold, D.D.* London: B. Fellowes, 1844.

Stephens, W. R. W., ed. *A Memoir of Richard Durnford, D.D. Sometime Bishop of Chichester.* London: John Murray, 1899.

St. Peter's Church, Croft-on-Tees. Parish registers.

Surtees, F. Scott. *Education for the People: A Letter Addressed to the Lord Bishop of Ripon.* London: George Bell, 1846.

———. *Sermons for the People, No. I.* London: George Bell, [1845].

Tait, A. C. *Four Sermons Connected with Confirmation, Preached in the Chapel of Rugby School.* Rugby: Printed by Crossley and Billington, 1847.

———. *Lessons for School Life being a Selection from Sermons Preached in the Chapel of Rugby School during His Head Mastership.* London: Hamilton, Adams, 1850.

———. Manuscript notebooks containing sermons, readings, prayers, and journals including Tait MS 19–26 and 350–59. Lambeth Palace Library.

Tate, James II. *First Classical Maps.* 2nd ed. London: George Bell, 1847.

———. Manuscript notebooks. Lovett Collection.

Tertullian. *Apologetic and Practical Treatises.* Translated by Rev. C. Dodgson. Oxford: John Henry Parker, 1842.

"Testimonial of Respect to a Clergyman." *Manchester Courier and Lancashire General Advertiser,* 12 August 1843, 6.

Testimonial to the Rev. C. Dodgson, M.A., Rector of Croft, Examining Chaplain to the Lord Bishop of Ripon, from 185 Clergymen Who Have Received Ordination from the Bishop. N.p., 1852.

Thompson, Henry L. *Henry George Liddell D.D. Dean of Christ Church, Oxford: A Memoir.* New York: Henry Holt, 1899.

Wenham, Leslie P. *The History of Richmond School, Yorkshire.* Arbroath: Herald Press, 1958.

[Wheeler, Mrs. Charlotte Bickersteth]. *Memoir of John Lang Bickersteth, Late of Rugby School.* London: Religious Tract Society, 1850.

Wheeler, Michael. *Death and the Future Life in Victorian Literature and Theology.* New York: Cambridge University Press, 1990.

Wilberforce, Samuel. *Addresses to the Candidates for Ordination on the Questions in the Ordination Service.* 2nd ed. Oxford and London: Parker, 1860.

Wilcox, E. G., *The Lost Plum-Cake: A Tale for Tiny Boys.* London: Macmillan, 1897.

Woodford, James Russell. *Ordination Lectures Delivered in the Chapel of Cuddesdon College.* Oxford and London: J. H. and Jas. Parker, 1861.

Index

Bell, Robert, 59

Beloe, Mr., 117

Bengel, Johann Albrecht, 294n36

Benson, Richard Meux

Bible, the, 3, 9, 10, 13, 25–27, 32, 33, 34, 35, 38, 42, 43, 44, 58, 59, 61, 62, 63, 64, 65, 75, 76, 84, 86, 87, 89, 90, 91, 97, 99, 101, 104, 106, 119–20, 125, 126, 137, 144, 145, 146, 147, 148, 150, 153, 155, 156, 159, 160, 169, 170, 186, 196, 197, 202, 209, 211, 213, 217, 219, 222, 223, 224, 225–26, 233–34, 236–37, 246, 248, 249, 250, 256, 258, 259, 260, 263, 264, 265, 270–72; children's, 170, 224; proposed book of excerpts, 224–25; translations, 225, 290n18

Bible Illustrations (Draper), 42–43

Bickersteth, Edward, 59

Bickersteth, John Lang, 71, 72, 78, 79

Bingham, Joseph, 294n36

Binsey, 190

Birch, Joseph, 15–16

Birtwhistle, J. B., 62

Blagden, Claude Martin, 198, 216, 219

Blakemore, Edith, 198

Blunt, John J., 145, 147, 186

Book of Common Prayer, 1, 3, 16–17, 32, 34, 41–42, 88, 89, 90, 91, 97, 106, 108, 114, 115, 118, 134, 140–41, 145, 146, 148, 151, 155, 181, 188, 204–5, 209–10, 211, 213, 277n1, 288n6

Boteler's Free Grammar School, 6

Bowles, Thomas Gibson, 236

Bowman, Empsie, 19

Bowman, Isa, 19, 113, 165, 220, 225, 296n28

Boy's Own Book, The, 284n23

Brasnose College, Oxford, 5, 18

Bridgewater, Duke of, 5

Bridgewater Canal, 5, 7

broad church, 67, 119, 190, 192–93, 273, 278n19, 285n7

Brown, Mary, 217, 221, 227, 228, 259, 260, 265, 279n25

"Bruno's Picnic" (Carroll), 174

Buckoll, Henry James, 74

Bulkeley, Henry John, 146–47

Bunsen, Baron. *See* Josias, Christian Charles

Bunyan, John, 182; *Pilgrim's Progress,* 42, 182

Burgon, John William, 113, 144

Burton, Edward, 137, 138, 147; *Lectures on Church History,* 137

Bushnell, Horace, 261

Butler, Arthur Gray, 68, 71, 72, 84, 285n13; *The Three Friends,* 71–72, 285n13

Butler, Joseph, 85, 294n36

Calvinism, 9, 10, 13, 35, 226, 278n19

Cambridge University, 5, 29, 123. *See also individual colleges*

canons of the church, 142, 143, 151

Carpenter, William Boyd, 196

Carroll, Lewis. *See* Dodgson, Charles Lutwidge

Cary, Offley Henry, 151

catechism, 9, 13, 14, 27, 29, 30, 34, 64, 89, 91, 96, 104, 106, 108, 209, 288n6. See also *Plain Catechism, A*

Chamberlain, Thomas, 183

charity, 36, 170, 228–30

Charity Organisation Society, 228

Charlotte, Princess, 2

Charterhouse School, 57

Chase, Drummond, 155

Chataway, Gertrude, 154, 164, 216

Cheap Repository Tracts, 44

Cheshire, Diocese of, 4

Chester Cathedral, 7

Chester Diocesan Board of Education, 29, 32

choral services, 56, 114, 120–21, 124, 125, 170, 239

Christ Church, Eastbourne, 173, 174, 192

Christ Church College, Oxford, 2, 3, 4, 6, 7, 20, 21, 22, 54, 86, 113, 122, 123–27, 131–32, 135, 140, 151, 154, 179, 180, 184, 193, 198, 199, 212, 219–20, 250, 254, 263, 277n6, 293n21; servants' service, 190–91

Christ Church Cathedral, Oxford, 123, 125, 131, 137, 140, 142, 155, 158, 190, 216, 218, 219

Dodgson, Charles (archdeacon): baptism, views on, 9–14, 17–18, 91, 160; boards of education, 29, 32, 52; clergy charges, 107, 115, 129–30, 136, 247; Communion, views on, 98, 105–9, 110–11, 160; confirmation, views on, 88–92, 96; Croft National School, 55–56; Croft-on-Tees, becomes rector at, 51–52; Croft-on-Tees, ministry at, 52, 53–54; Daresbury, ministry at, 4–7; death, 2, 54, 188–89; educates his children, 33, 36, 48; education, 1–3; —, views on, 28–33, 36–37, 55–56, 244; floating chapel, 7; Gorham controversy, views on, 12–13, 15; marriage, 4; mathematics, 283n54; ministry, views on, 135–36; ordination, 3, 293n21; prayer, views on, 41, 42; preaching, 7, 9, 25, 31, 36, 55, 194; predestination, views on, 9–10; Richmond, archdeacon of, 53; Ripon, chancellor of, 53; Ripon, examining chaplain, 6, 8–9, 11–12, 14–15, 16–17, 32, 52, 91, 95, 137, 159; Ripon Cathedral, canon of, 53, 54; ritualism, views on, 114–16; rural dean, 52–53; Sabbath, views on, 25; sermons, 9, 31, 36–38, 44, 55, 79, 128–29, 135, 180, 223; Tertullian translation, 32, 39–40; testimonials to, 14–15, 52; universal redemption, views on, 9–10; Westminster School, writing for, 2. Works: *Controversy of Faith*, 12, 14, 15, 18, 30, 89, 91, 93; *"Do the First Works,"* 128; *A Plain Catechism*, 25, 88, 89–91, 94, 96, 107–8, 205–6, 209; *The Position and Duties of the Clergy with Respect to the Religious Education of the People*, 55; *"Preach the Gospel,"* 27–38, 194; *The Providence of God Manifested in the Temporal Condition of the Poorer Clergy*, 38; *Ritual Worship*, 115; *"The Sabbath a Delight,"* 25; *Sacraments of the Gospel*, 108; *What Do the Wicked Eat and Drink in the Lord's Supper?*, 108
Dodgson, Charles Lutwidge: *Alice*, creates stories of, 153–54, 157, 158, 162; arguments, 23, 134–35, 227; baptism, 1, 16–17, 18; —, performs, 20; —, views on, 18–20; Bible reading, 225–26, 249; charitable

donations, 22, 228–30; childhood reading, 42–48, 170; childhood writings, 45; children, speaks to, 173–77; —, views of, 43, 46, 153–54; Christ Church, Oxford, studies at, 124–27; —, chapel attendance, 124–25; —, undergraduate essays, 126–27, 179; churches, serves in, 157, 184–86, 189, 190, 191, 213; Communion, 105, 113–14; confirmation, 88, 90, 93, 104; death, 250–53; divorce, views on, 136, 219, 247–48; education, at home, 29, 33–36, 48, 56, 109; —, views on, 28–29; funeral, 253–55; gives away books, 36, 167, 281n29; godchildren, 20–24; grave, 253, 255–57; illness, 82–83, 251; logic, 37, 197, 223, 228, 247; mathematics, 223, 224, 229, 283n54; nom de plume, 158, 257; ordination, 20, 131, 142, 151–52, 155, 211, 212; —, decisions regarding, 80, 132–37, 185–89; —, examination for, 143–47, 186; —, studies for, 131, 137–41, 147, 186, 214; Oxford University, matriculation, 122; photography, 16, 133, 154; prayer life, 35, 40–42, 71, 75–76, 83–84, 86–87, 98, 219, 233; preaching, 23, 118, 130, 134, 155, 157, 158, 179, 181–84, 185–87, 189, 190–94, 197–203, 212, 213, 214, 223; public speaking, 179–81; religious difficulties, planned book on, 245–47, 265, 267; reverence, xii, 19–20, 82, 219, 226–27, 236–39; Richmond School, 50, 56–65; ritualism, views on, 116–21; Rugby School, 66–70, 73, 75, 85; Sabbath, views on, 26–28; speech hesitation, 71, 136, 179, 198; teacher, 56; theatre, 133, 227, 230–36, 277n2, 281n25; travels abroad, 117, 128, 187–88. Works: "Alice on the Stage," 157; *Alice's Adventures in Wonderland*, xiii, 43–44, 48, 56, 129, 154, 157, 158–62, 163, 166, 167, 177, 187, 189, 257; *Alice's Adventures Under Ground*, 153, 154, 159–62, 163, 166, 167, 168, 172; "Bruno's Picnic," 174; "Christmas Greetings," 163; *An Easter Greeting to Every Child Who Loves "Alice,"* 79, 159, 166–67; *The Endowment of the Greek Professorship*, 155; "Faces in the Fire,"

Mayor, Charles, 73, 77–78
Mayor, Robert Bickersteth, 75
Melbourne, Lord, 50
Merchant of Venice, The (Shakespeare), 226, 234
Miller, Edith, 164, 216, 242
miracles, 60, 147, 217, 218, 220, 246
Modern Mysteries (Mahan), 261
Monro, Edward, 240
More, Hannah, 44, 45
Morning Prayer. *See* daily offices
Moxon, Lilian, 114
"My Fairy" (C. L. Dodgson), 45
"My God, My Father While I Stray," 252, 254, 255, 302n1

Napier, Charles Donald, 79
National Society for the Promotion of the Education of the Poor in the Principles of the Established Church, 29, 55, 229, 244
Natural Law in the Spiritual World (Drummond), 261
Nature and the Supernatural (Bushnell), 261
Newman, John Henry, 3, 8, 68, 123, 203; *Tract XC*, 68
New Method of Evaluation as Applied to π, The (C. L. Dodgson), 295n4
Nightingale, Florence, 176–77
Night Side of Nature, The (Crowe), 261
"Now the Labourer's Task Is O'er" (Ellerton), 256
Nursery Alice, The (Carroll), 166

Oberammergau passion play, 233
Ocklynge Mission-Room, 191
Okell, Mr., 52
On Christian Doctrine (Augustine), 145, 146, 147
ordination, 9, 36, 37, 118, 125, 128, 130, 131–32, 134, 137, 142–45, 148, 150, 151, 156. *See also* Dodgson, Charles; Dodgson, Charles Lutwidge
Ore Working Men's Institute, 180
Oriel College, Oxford, 3

Osney, 183
Oxenham, Frank, 265
Oxford, 8, 20, 22, 24, 113, 116, 120, 143, 154, 155, 157, 179, 183–85, 188, 190, 192, 193, 250, 263
Oxford, Diocese of, 151, 186, 277n6
Oxford Cathedral. *See* Christ Church Cathedral
Oxford High School, 190, 191
Oxford Magazine and Church Advocate, 181
Oxford Movement, 3, 8, 9, 10, 11, 14, 17, 22, 32–33, 38, 39, 40, 65, 67, 83, 120, 123, 128, 183–84, 203, 261, 278n19, 285n7, 288n23
Oxford University, 2–3, 7, 18, 20, 21, 22, 29, 34, 56, 57, 67, 68, 69, 74, 86, 122–23, 124, 125, 127, 133, 142, 198, 203, 215, 236, 244, 250, 258, 259; matriculation, 122; and religious education, 123–24; statutes, 122–23; University Sermon, 122, 124, 125, 215. *See also individual colleges*

Paget, Francis, 191, 254–55
Paley, William, 60
Pall Mall Gazette, 239, 241, 244
Patten, John Wilson, 51
"Peace, Perfect Peace" (Bickersteth), 255, 274
Pearson, John, 137–40, 145, 147, 186; *An Exposition of the Creed,* 137–40, 145
Peel, Robert, 50–51, 53
Pember, Frederick, 151
Pepys, Henry, 92, 93
Peter Parley's Tales about Europe, Asia, Africa, and America (Parley), 46–47
Phantasmagoria (Carroll), 163, 187, 257, 262
Philpotts, Henry, 12
Physician's Sermon to Young Men, A (Pratt) 61
Picture Testament, The, 42
Pilgrim's Progress (Bunyan), 42, 182
Pillow Problems (C. L. Dodgson), 224
Plain Catechism, A (C. Dodgson), 25, 88, 89–91, 94, 96, 107–8, 205–6, 209
Plautus, 2, 40, 277n3
Plumptre, Edward Hays, 261

Rugby School, 24, 66–88, 92–94, 96, 100, 102–4, 105, 110, 111, 112, 159, 206, 207, 209, 215; bullying, 70–71, 72; burglaries, 72; chapel, 84, 88, 92, 93–94, 95, 104, 105, 159; daily life, 73; deaths, 77–79, 101; illness, 72, 77, 82–84, 85; prayers, 75–76

Russian Orthodox Church, 117, 188

"Sabbath a Delight, The" (C. Dodgson), 25

Sabbath day, 25-28, 34, 86, 100, 170, 226

"Sacraments of the Gospel" (C. Dodgson), 108

Sadler, Michael, 198

"Saints of God, The" (MacLagan), 254

Salisbury, Lord, 239

Salmon, Gordon, 54

Salvation Army, 237

Salwey, Herbert, 190

Sanderson, Robert, 294n36

Sandford, Charles W., 143, 293n21

Sandford-on-Thames, 179, 181

Satan, 34, 35, 64, 77, 90, 91, 96, 104, 205, 214, 236, 238, 240, 241, 260

School of Dramatic Art, 231

Scriptorum ecclesiasticorum opuscula (Routh), 141

Scriptural Views of Holy Baptism (Pusey), 12

Scripture. *See* Bible, the

Sedger, Horace, 19

self-examination, 60, 75, 76–77, 81, 86, 97, 100, 101, 112–13, 206, 208

Sermons for the People (Surtees), 63–65, 109–10

Seymour, Isabel, 191

Seymour, Mary, 191

Shadows of the Clouds (Froude), 60

Shepherd of Salisbury Plain, The (More), 44

"Shepherd of Salisbury Plain, The" (poem), 156

Sherwood, Mary Martha, 43, 45; *The Fairchild Family*, 43–45, 48

Short Prayers and Other Helps to Devotion (Cotton), 75, 94, 207–8

sin, 11–12, 19, 34–35, 39, 41–42, 43, 44, 61, 62, 64, 71, 76, 80–81, 84, 87, 90, 96–97, 99, 102, 103, 104, 105, 107, 108, 109, 111,

113, 127, 135, 139, 147, 159, 167, 170, 171, 182, 193, 194, 200–201, 202, 203, 204–8, 210, 211, 212, 213, 214, 215, 216–17, 218, 220, 221, 222, 226, 229, 231–32, 233, 236, 242–44, 248, 249, 260, 265–66, 268–72, 281n25

Sinclair, Henry, 252

Sketches of Church History (Robertson), 145, 146, 147

Sketch of the Reformation in England (Blunt), 145

Small-Pox Fund, 229

Smedley, Frank, 236

Society for Psychical Research, 261–62

Society for the Employment of Additional Curates in Populous Places, 129

Society for the Relief of the Widows and Orphans of the Clergy of the Archdeaconry of Chester, 31

Society for the Rescue of Young Women and Children, 230

Society for the Suppression of Mendacity, 228

"Some Popular Fallacies about Vivisection" (Carroll), 244–45

Southey, Reginald, 280n44

Southey, Ronald, 280n44

"Speak Gently" (Bates), 286n39

Spencer, Herbert, 243

Spirits in Prison, The (Plumptre), 261

spiritualism, 261–62

Spooner, Catherine. *See* Tait, Catherine née Spooner

sport. *See* hunting

"Stage and the Spirit of Reverence, The" (Carroll), 231, 233, 237–38

St. Aldate's Church, Oxford, 184

St. Andrew's Church, Sandford-on-Thames, 157, 179, 181

Stanley, Arthur Penrhyn, 67, 94

Stead, William Thomas, 239–40

St. Edmund's College and Seminary, 24

Stevens, Enid, 226

Stevens, Winifred, 226, 235

St. Gerard's School, 24

St. Giles's Church, Oxford, 184, 185

St. James's Gazette, 118, 234, 240

St. Mary Magdalene Church, Oxford, 113, 184

St. Mary Magdalene Church, St. Leonards-on-Sea, 173

St. Mary's Church, Eastbourne, 191

St. Mary's Church, Guildford, 117, 129, 190, 191, 199, 251, 253, 254

St. Mary's Church, Oxford. *See* University Church of St. Mary's

St. Mary's Church, Richmond, 50, 58, 62, 63, 64, 92, 110

Stories from the Scriptures, 42

St. Paul's Cathedral, London, 57, 128, 215

St. Paul's Church, Oxford, 183–84, 185

St. Peter's Church, Croft, 52, 92, 128, 159

St. Philip and St. James' Church, Oxford, 184

Strong, Thomas Banks, 199, 219

St. Saviour's Church, Eastbourne, 113

St. Thomas Becket Church, Osney, 183

suffering, 200, 219, 248–49

Sullivan, Arthur Seymour, 238, 300n25

Sumner, John, 29

Sunday. *See* Sabbath day

Sunday, Its Origin, History and Present Obligation (Hessey), 28

Sunday School, 4, 26, 27, 29, 33, 44

Sunday Times, 232

Surtees, Scott, 63–65, 77, 92, 109–10, 114. Works: *Education for the People,* 63; *Sermons for the People,* 63–65, 109–10

Sylvie and Bruno (Carroll), 26–27, 48, 79, 101, 117, 119, 168–70, 172, 174, 187, 195, 217–18, 224, 227, 229, 250, 257, 262, 281n25

Sylvie and Bruno Concluded (Carroll), 81, 117, 119, 120, 168, 170–72, 187, 195, 238, 242–44, 245, 257, 273

Symbolic Logic (Carroll), 223, 250

Tait, Archibald Campbell, 66, 67–69, 72, 73, 74, 75, 76–82, 84–86, 93, 105, 106, 110, 114, 159, 160, 162, 167, 215, 284n31, 291n28; illness, 84–85; preaches on confirmation, 93–96, 100–104; sermons and addresses,

76–82, 84–85, 86, 105, 111–13, 206. Works: *Four Sermons Connected with Confirmation,* 96; *Lessons for School Life,* 112

Tait, Catherine née Spooner, 68, 83–84

Tate, James, I, 57–58

Tate, James, II, 50–51, 57–62, 65, 194–95, 206; *First Classical Maps,* 61

Taylor, Jeremy, 294n36

teetotalism, 170–71

temptation, 170, 171, 173, 205, 240–43

Ten Commandments, 26, 61, 64, 89, 91, 96, 97, 294n36

Tenniel, John, 297n12

Tennyson, Alfred, Lord, 63

Terence, 277n3

Terry, Ellen, 165, 226, 234, 247–48

Tertullian, 32, 39–40

Thackeray, William Makepeace, 59

theatre, 19, 133, 227, 230–36, 281n25; children acting in, 231, 232–33, 238; dress in, 231–32

Theatre, The, 235–36, 237

Theological Essays (Maurice), 264

Thirty-Nine Articles, 12, 13, 34, 68, 106, 107, 108, 122–23, 138, 145, 151, 244, 258–59

Thompson, Henry Lewis, 193, 219

Thomson, William, 155–56

Three Friends, The (Butler), 71–72

Through the Looking-Glass (Carroll), 79, 154, 157, 159, 161–62, 163, 166, 167, 177, 187, 257

To All Child-readers of "Alice's Adventures in Wonderland" (Carroll), 163

Tom Brown's School Days (Hughes), 67, 92–93, 95

Tractarianism. *See* Oxford Movement

Tracts for the Times, 8, 12, 68

Tract XC (Newman), 68

Train, The, 158

Transubstantiation, 106

Treatise on Faith and the Creed (Augustine), 139

Trench, Richard Chenevix, 151, 294n36

Trinity Church, Darlington, 52

Trinity College, Cambridge, 2, 57, 94

Trinity College, Oxford, 3